From Puella to Plautus

From Puella to Plautus

An Introduction to Latin Language and Thought

VOLUME 1

Tamara Trykar-Lu

The Catholic Education Press
Washington, D.C.

The paper used in this publication meets the minimum requirements of American National Standards for Information Science—Permanence of Paper for Printed Library Materials, ANSI Z39.48-1984.

∞

ISBN 9781949822007

The publisher thanks the author for preparing the camera-ready copy from which this book was produced.

To my father, Josef Trykar,
who with perseverance and patience
prevented my Latin career from ending prematurely in eighth grade,
and who got me to share his lifelong enthusiasm for language.

Contents

ACKNOWLEDGMENTS

This book would not have been written if it had not been for the generous help and support of many people. My thanks go to (in chronological order):

My husband Nobu, who has never questioned either my need or my ability to undertake such a big project and who has been there at crucial moments.

The monks, teachers, and students at St. Anselm's Abbey School: Abbot Aidan and Father Peter for their trust in my ability and their willingness to let me try my methods; Dr. Herb Wood for instilling in me the belief that I could do anything I really tried, even calculus; Delora Pelosi for showing me the importance of culture studies to complement the linguistic endeavors; my students for being so fascinated by grammar and etymology, and for taxing my ability to come up with ever-new explanations and exercises.

Professor Nelson Minnich, neighbor, friend, and colleague, who from the first day we met treated me as an intellectual equal and serious scholar; not only did he immeasurably bolster my self-esteem, but he set a high level of expectation and gave me some good advice. Charles Safford, long-time buddy, who proofread the English part of this book not once, but many times, forever trying to keep up with my revisions; if there are any errors it is not his fault.

Matthias Andrews, colleague and confidant, who took entire days out of his busy schedule to help me sort through pictures, make lists of things still to be done, and arrange hundreds of pages, and who kept me from losing my bearings.

Willi Heuschneider, my friend, who with gentle questions and a little prodding got me to take up the book again after a one-year hiatus, and whose loving and faithful presence has carried me through many late-night and weekend working hours.

Hsiao Yu "Little Fish" Kuo, who with great patience helped me through the times when my computer and I did not see eye to eye.

My reader Anne Needham: I am very grateful for her suggestions and advice.

All my friends, family, and neighbors, who have given me continuous moral support, open ears for my elaborations on some point of Latin grammar, interesting and interested questions about all the aspects of the book, and countless cups of tea and coffee. To all of you I offer my sincere gratitude.

Tamara Trykar-Lu

PREFACE

There are many reasons to learn Latin, but for speakers of English those reasons are especially cogent: in a way it is their ancestral language, as much as is the English of Beowulf . A knowledge of Latin opens windows onto English, not only in the areas of grammar and vocabulary, but also in culture and tradition: art, mythology, political and legal structures, and plain human nature.

This book was written with the goal of teaching Latin to a variety of people with different backgrounds, on the college or high school level, with or without the aid of a teacher and classroom. Grammatical forms and terminology, as well as syntactical structures are explained in general terms for students who need to become familiar with them befor delving into a foreign tongue. Declension and conjugation patterns in frames should be memorized. The exercises are designed to be done in the book, and in the order in which they occur; this way difficult concepts or structures can be practiced—occasionally in English—before one goes on to the next point (and, I trust, before one looks up the answers).

A short historical and comparative survey of Indo-European, Latin, Germanic, and English, as well as other Romance laguages, puts English into a larger context. At the end of each of thirty-three chapters a particular point of Roman culture is illuminated, such as "Housing in Rome," "Chidren's lives," "Games and Pastimes" (with Roman board games), "Clothing" (with toga and shoe patterns), "Food" (including some recipes from Apicius's cook book), "Law," "Religion," "Medicine," and "Technology." The reading sections and excerpts are arranged in a sort of reverse chronology: since medieval Latin is less complex than classical Latin, the early reading passages are taken from medieval authors. There is gradual progress to readings by Cicero, Ovid, Caesar, Catullus and so on. To understand and enjoy these readings a good dictionary is indispensable; invariably some words have been learned long ago and forgotten, or they were not glossed at all (my oversight, and that of my readers.) A good dictionary is Cassell's Latin-English and English-Latin dictionary; it also gives examples of how Latin authors used a particular word.

A teaching method can most assuredly be both rigorous and entertaining, and I have found many Latin books lacking in one of the two aspects, some in both. On the one hand, I am convinced that speakers of English with a sound vocabulary foundation can handle the 50-odd words per chapter,simply because thay will know an English derivative for most of the Latin words (and perhaps learn a number of English words to boot.) Latin morphology and syntax can surely be mastered with thorough explanations and a sufficient number of exercises. In opposition to H. L. Mencken, I see no reason to underestimate the intelligence of the American Public. On the other hand, there is no need to be always "grave as an ice-bear": I believe strongly in the motivating force of entertaining tidbits, riddles, puzzles, jokes, and, of course, pictures. In my years of teaching I have found that students are always intrigued by the human factor—after all these Romans were people, too—and by how similar their thinking was to ours, and how little some things change.

I hope this book will provide an enjoyable learning experience

Tamara Trykar-Lu

INTRODUCTION

Congratulations! You have decided to learn one of the major languages of the world.

Oh, all right, people say "Latin is a dead language, as dead as it can be, first it killed the Romans and now it's killing me, and why do you want to study Latin anyway, what use is it, do you want to become a priest?" Since the utilitarian argument seems to loom large, let's address it.

True, Latin is seldom spoken nowadays, at least in its original form: it does survive, however, as Italian, Spanish, French, Portuguese. Romanian, and a number of lesser-known languages. Most importantly, though, it survives in the English language. Which first of all has received, or taken, a large part of its vocabulary from Latin. Consider, e.g. (e.g. is, of course, Latin: it stands for *exempli gratia*, for the sake of an example, consider that of 400,000 words in the big Oxford English Dictionary no less than 80 % are of Latin origin, taken either directly from Latin, or by way of French. Even among the 10,000 most frequently used words of English, more than half are from Latin or Greek. In addition, English is the language with the largest number of words, quotations, and abbreviations taken from Latin, without any change, into everyday language. A few examples have to suffice for the moment: forum, agenda, integer, pauper, auditorium, senior, junior, alter ego, Homo sapiens, e.g., i.e. (*id est.* that is), a.m, p.m. (*ante meridiem, post meridiem*), etc. (*et cetera*, and the rest).

If anything, the influence of Latin on English has grown over the centuries; Latin was thought especially useful for coining new words to describe new realities or inventions, such as "elementary education," "malnutrition," "airplane," "percussion." This predilection for Latin is by no means universal, if you consider the German words for airplane and percussion (*Flugzeug, Schlagzeug*) which mean "the stuff that flies," and "the stuff you beat on," or the Icelandic word for airplane, which translates as "the silver bird flying in the sky." In these languages the Germanic stock of words is used and combined in novel ways.

Of course there are instances of overkill, as seen in a report of the London County Council: when a member complained about the proliferation of Latin phrases, another answered "that he would examine the matter *de nuovo*, that it was a *conditio sine qua non* that reports should be intelligible, but that every Latin expression was not *ipso facto* unintelligible, since many such expressions could be used *pari passu* with English equivalents." Whereupon the honorable complainant asked meekly: "Will you form *inter alia* an *ad hoc* committee, or would this be *ultra vires*?" Similarly dubious are some latter-day Latinate—and therefore presumably more genteel—occupational titles: "refuse collector," "mortician," "exterminating engineer," to which the satirical magazine Punch added "aquatic engineer" for dishwasher (the human kind).

English has also borrowed from Latin morphology. It is true that case suffixes, verb endings, and the like mostly diappeared during the years in which English was primarily a spoken language (after 1066, when the educated class was speaking and writing Latin and French); but when English merged with Old French, Chaucer being instrumental in the process, a number of Latin and French denotational prefixes and suffixes (carrying meaning) were introduced, which contributed immeasurably to the expressiveness of English. Among them are dis-, de-, ex-, con-, re-, trans-, in-, sub-, extra, and the adjective suffix -able (as in "movable," "doable,") which was derived from the Latin word *habilis*, easy to handle.

xiv

Even at the syntactical level English has borrowed from Latin, though it remains basically a Germanic language. Examples are: the accusativus cum infinitivo construction ("We considered him to be a total loss," "It is impossible (for) me to understand him." In Wycliffe's translation of the Bible there is even: "It is good us to be here"); the absolute participle ("This said, they lapsed into silence"); the gerund ("the art of speaking much and saying nothing"); the gerundive ("I am to go home, you are to stay here"); the periphrastic passive using the auxiliary verb "to be," in contrast to Germanic languages, such as German, which use "werden," to become.

However, there is more to classical heritage than words: there are thought patterns, ideas, traditions of civilization. Many of them were especially well receiced in America. American founding fathers, like Jefferson, Franklin, and Adams, knew Latin and Greek and incorporated their knowledge into their thoughts and witings. Even now one can find Latin sayings and mottos in many places: *Annuit Coeptis* (he approved of our undertaking), *Novus Ordo Seclorum* (a new order of centuries), *E Pluribus Unum* (out of many grows one), on money, coins, and the Great Seal of the United States; *Excelsior* (higher) is the motto of the state of New York, and *Sic Semper Tyrannis* (thus always to tyrants) that of Virginia; *Labor Omnia Vincit* (work conquers all) seems to be more prevalent than *Amor Omnia Vincit* (love conquers all), presumably testifying to the Calvinist-Puritan heritage of America. Every capital has its Capitol (on the Roman Capitol, or Capitoline Hill, the temple of the head God, Jupiter, was located, as well as the citadel, and the senatorial palace). People call and called their children Gloria, Diana, Laetitia, Virgil, and Horace. Many professions use largely Latin terminology (medicine, pharmacy, botany, zoology, law). Goverment and public buildings in the classical style abound, as does art with classical or mythological subjects. Choral societies sing music with Latin text.

Perhaps most importantly, classical antiquity is considered the ideological basis of modern civilization, of democracy and legality in America, fostering a kind of idealism that can counteract materialism (whether crass or dialectic).

So you see, Latin is not dead at all; it is still used by everyone in this country. Enjoy learning it, and about it!

THE PRONUNCIATION OF LATIN

The alphabet used in classical Latin has the same letters as the English (Roman) alphabet, except that there is no **j** or **w**, and **y** occurs only in foreign (i.e., Greek) words.

Vowels: A vowel can be long or short. A length mark (macron) above a long vowel is used in many textbooks. In this book length marks are limited to the beginning pages to show the pattern. The vowels are pronounced as follows:

LONG	SHORT
a as in *father*	**a** as in *but*
e as in *portray*	**e** as in *get*
i as in *machine*	**i** as in *bit*
o as in *bought*	**o** as in *omit*
u as in *school (never as in cute)*	**u** as in *put*

y is pronounced like French **u** or German **ü**.
When **i** occurs between two vowels, or before a vowel at the beginning of a word, it is a consonant, as in *year*.

Diphthongs: Diphthongs are two vowels together that are pronounced as a single sound. In Latin they are

ae as in *eye*	**au** as in *cow*	**ei** as in *weight*
oe as in *boy*	**ui** as in *queen*	**eu** as in *may you*

Other combinations of vowels like **ea, iu, ie, ue,** etc. don't make diphthongs, but are pronounced as two vowels.

Consonants: The consonants are pronounced as they are in English, except:

c is always pronounced /k/ as in *corn*, never /s/ as in *city*.
ch is pronounced as in *character*.
g is pronounced as in *gold*, not as in *genuine*.

1

VERBS:

1ST AND 2ND CONJUGATIONS

TYPES OF LANGUAGES (1)

There are several ways to classify languages. One, putting them into language families, is introduced in Chapters 4 and 5. Another way is to group them according to the order in which subject, object, and verb of the sentence occur, for instance SVO in English, French, Thai; VSO in Arabic, Hebrew, Irish; SOV in Japanese and Persian. This order is also used quite often in Latin, but only as a matter of style.

One traditional distinction is by **Morphology**, meaning the method by which words in a language are constructed. A morphological typology classifies the degree to which a language is **synthetic**, that is to say, combines concepts and information into one single word. Synthetic languages are also called **inflecting** because they change the structure of words by adding inflectional suffixes (endings), prefixes, or infixes. Latin, Greek, and Arabic are examples of synthetic languages. The opposite of synthetic is called **analytic**. A third type to which Japanese, Turkish, and Finnish belong, but no Indo-European languages, is called **agglutinating**.

An example of a clearly **analytic** language is Chinese. The words are never changed themselves, but more words are added to change the meaning, e.g.:

我 (wo) - *I*,   我 们 (wo men) - (I + Plural sign, for people) = *we*.

The relationship between the parts of the sentence is shown by the order in which the words occur. Latin, on the other hand, is considered a **synthetic** language, where much semantic and morphological information is joined into one word, for instance: amabitur, *he (she, it) will be loved*; this one word, or verb form, expresses 3rd Person Singular (he, she, it), Future (will), Passive (be -ed), Indicative (statement form), and the semantic component 'love'. In the form amo, *I love*, the ending -o means that the form is 1st Person Singular, Present Tense, Indicative, and Active.

In an **agglutinating** language there would be a separate unit for each of these grammatical meanings, making for rather lengthy words, comparable to saying :

'Ipresenttenseyouobjectloveforalongtime'.

English falls somewhere between these extremes, but is actually more similar to Chinese than to Latin: there are few inflectional endings left (not only in comparison to Latin, but also to the Old English of Beowulf), and grammatical relationships are expressed through word order.

Chapter 1   VERBS : FIRST AND SECOND CONJUGATION

A: VERBS IN GENERAL
Saying that verb forms in Latin are mostly **synthetic** means that **morphemes** (prefixes, infixes, or suffixes) are added to a **verb stem**. **Prefixes** usually change the meaning of the verb, as they often do in English, e.g.: note - *de*note; *af*firm - *con*firm - *reaf*firm. **Infixes** (placed in the middle of the word) and **suffixes** express **number**, **person**, **tense**, **mood**, and **voice** of the verb, as they do, to a degree, in English, e.g. we ask**ed**, it rain**s**, we were eat**ing**, he was cuddl**ed**. **Number, person, tense, mood,** and **voice** are **categories** for verbs (there are somewhat different categories for nouns). If you make changes within these categories, you are **conjugating** a verb.

The Verb Categories

   1.   **Number**: As in English, there are two number options for verbs: **Singular (Sg)** and **Plural (Pl)** - one, and more than one. (This two-way distinction is by no means universal; in many languages, Greek for instance, there are verb forms for two persons, called Dual.) In order to avoid confusion with capitalisation in this much used pair, the wods **Singular** and **Plural** will always be captalisd in this text.

   2.   **Person**: There are six person distinctions in Latin as compared to five in English: three in the **Singular** and three in the **Plural**. They correspond to the English ..
          (**Sg**): **I, you** (one person), **he (she, it);**
          (**Pl**): **we, you** (more than one), **they**.   ..

They are also called:
          First Person: Singular = **I**
                     and   Plural = I and other people = **we**;
          Second Person:Singular = **you** (one person)
                     and   Plural = you and other people = **you** (more than one);
          Third Person: Singular = neither I nor you, but a third person = **he, she**, or **it**
                     and   Plural = neither we nor you = **they**.
In cotrast to English, German, or French the Personal Pronouns, I, you, etc. Latin generally does not use personal pronouns, although they may be added for emphasis. In the languages mentioned they are often redundant anyway, e.g.: *he* goe*s*, *du* geh*st*, *nous* mange*ons*. Italian, for instance, usually omits them: parl*iamo*.

   3. **Tense**: There are six tenses in Latin. Although there is some overlapping, these tenses correspond largely to those in English:
          Present: I go
          Future: I will go
          Imperfect (Simple Past, Preterite): I went
          Perfect (Compound Past): I have gone
          Pluperfect (Past Perfect): I had gone
          Future Perfect::I will have gone
"Pluperfect" is actually short for "Plusquamperfect", "more than Perfect". The specific uses of the tenses will be explained later. We will start with the **present** tense.

4. Mood: In Latin there are three moods: **indicative, subjunctive**, and **imperative**.
Their English counterparts are

> **Statement** (I ran; she is eating) = **indicative**
> **Condition** or **irreality** (If I had money, I would eat) = **subjunctive**
> **Command** (Go! Don't dawdle!) = **imperative**
> Latin commands can be given in the Singular and the Plural.

We will begin with the **indicative** and **imperative** forms.

5. Voice: As in English, there are **active** and **passive** voice:

> The dog bit the man. (Active)
> The man was bitten by the dog. (Passive)

We will start with the **active** forms.

To analyze a **conjugated** Latin verb form one must therefore list five categories. (There are also verb forms that are considered unconjugated, such as **participles** and **infinitives**. They are lacking some of the categories, usually person or number.)

Examples:	1 - Person	2 - Number	3 - Tense	4 - Mood	5 - Voice
tenebat:	3rd Person	Singular	Imperfect	Indicative	Active
	of **tenere**, *to hold*: he/she/it held				
portabuntur:	3rd person	Plural	Future	Indicative	Passive
	of **portare**, *to carry*: they will be carried				
tacuisses:	2nd Person	Singular	Pluperfect	Subjunctive	Active
	of **tacere**, *to be silent*: you would have been silent				

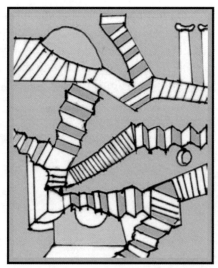

TTL

No reason for panic!
We will proceed step by step.

GRADUS AD PARNASSUM
Steps to Parnassus

Mount Parnassus in Greece
was considered the seat of the gods,
especially Apollo and the Muses.
The ascent was thought to be somewhat
difficult and confusing.

B : LATIN VERBS

Writers of Latin grammar books have over the years found it convenient to group Latin verbs in four classes, or **conjugations**, according to the vowels in which their stems end. To find the **present stem** of a verb in the first, second (and fourth) Conjugation, you need only remove the final letters **-re** from the **infinitive** form. (This is the form listed in first place in the vocabulary section of this book and in some dictionaries.)
You are then left with the **stem**, which ends in a characteristic **vowel**:

    -a- in the **1st**, or a- conjugation;
    -e- in the **2nd**, or e- conjugation;
    (-i- in the 4th, or i- conjugation).
    (In the 3rd conjugation most stems end in consonants.)

Remember the other use of the term **conjugation**, namely making changes to person, number, tense, mood, and voice of a verb!

Examples of verb stems and Conjugations:

Infinitive	Meaning	Present stem	Conjugation
portare	*to carry*	porta-	1
laudare	*to praise*	lauda-	1
debere	*to owe*	debe-	2
monere	*to warn*	mone-	2
laborare	*to work*	labora-	1

The stem vowel -e- of the second conjugation is always long. In many textbooks a length mark or **macron** is sometimes placed above the -e- to avoid confusion with the 3rd conjugation, which uses a dummy vowel to avoid collision of too many consonants. In this book, as in original texts, no length marks are used; in vocabularies and patterns any syllable to be stressed will have an accent on it, which generally falls on the next to last syllable.

EXERCISE A: Give the **present stems** of the following verbs and write conjugation **1** or **2**:

1. rogáre	*to ask*	roga-	1
2. navigáre	*to sail*	_____	____
3. dare	*to give*	_____	____
4. docére	*to teach*	_____	____
5. flére	*to cry*	_____	____

.

6. spectáre	*to look at*	_____	____
7. timére	*to fear*	_____	____
8. vidére	*to see*	_____	____
9. habére	*to have*	_____	____
10. laboráre	*to work*	_____	____

With this **present stem** we can form three tenses: the **present, imperfect,** and **future**. First we add these suffixes, or endings, to form the **present indicative active**, all persons, Singular (Sg) and Plural (Pl):

	Sg	
1. Pers.	**-o (-m)**	
2. Pers.	**-s**	
3. Pers.	**-t**	
	Pl	
1. Pers.	**-mus**	
2. Pers.	**-tis**	
3. Pers.	**-nt**	

Memorize all patterns in these frames, perhaps by writing them down several times.

The ending **-m** will be used later for irregular verbs, imperfect or subjunctive forms.

Since these endings are consonants, or begin with consonants, they can easily be added to the vowel stems. The one exception is the 1st person Singular, where the vowel ending **-o** is used for the present tense, not the consonant ending **-m**. Consequently two vowels collide there. This problem is treated differently in each conjugation: in the first conjugation the original **-ao** (*portao) had been contracted into **-o** already in early Latin, whereas in the second conjugation the two vowels were left intact, resulting in **-eo** (doc**eo**).

Now we can conjugate the **present tense** of
  portare, *to carry*, (first conjugation) and
  docere, *to teach*, (second conjugation):

Sg

1. pórt**o**   I carry, I am carrying, I do carry

2. pórta**s**   you carry, you are carrying

3. pórta**t**   he/she/it carries, is carrying

Pl

1. portá**mus**   we carry, we are carrying

2. portá**tis**   you carry, you are carrying (Plural!)

3. pórta**nt**   they carry, they are carrying

Notice that there is no progressive form in Latin; all possible English translations of the Latin forms are listed here to impress this fact on your mind. "I do carry" is used for emphasis in English, but more importantly in its negative form, "I don't carry", and for questions, "Do you carry?". When reciting these forms aloud, stress the accented syllable and avoid the beginner's mistake of stressing the ending. (* am**o**, am**as**, am**at**)
Stress is usually put on the next to last syllable.

Sg

1. docé**o**   I teach, I am teaching, I do teach

2. dóce**s**   you teach, you are teaching, you do teach

3. dóce**t**   he/she/it teaches, is teaching, does teach

Pl

1. docé**mus**   we teach, are teaching, do teach

2. docé**tis**   you teach, are teaching, do teach

3. dóce**nt**   they teach, are teaching, do teach

The 1st and 2nd Persons, **porto, portas, portamus, portatis** usually include the pronoun (subject) in the verb form. Only occasionally are they expressed separately as personal pronouns or nouns, mostly for emphasis:

> **Ego** cogito, ergo sum.   *I think, therefore I am.*

For the third person, however, the opposite holds: there is usually a noun or pronoun subject:

> Caesar urbem visitat.   *Caesar is visiting the city.*
> Illa haec dixit.   *She said the following.*

The form **portat** can therefore mean:

> he carries, he is carrying, he does carry
> she carries, she is carrying, she does carry
> it carries, it is carrying, it does carry
> ...carries, ...is carrying, ...does carry (supply subject - man, woman, beast)

and **portant** can mean:

> they carry, they are carrying, they do carry
> ...carry, ...are carrying,....do carry (supply subject)

If there is no noun or pronoun subject, he, she, it can be distinguished only by the context. Likewise **portant** can have a masculine, feminine (or neuter) subject, just like English "they".

 **EXERCISE B:**   Conjugate the verbs and give the English meaning of each form:
(a few forms are given already to help you along)

	debere *to owe*	**laudare** *to praise*
1.	**debeo** *I owe*	**laudo** *I praise*
Sg 2.		
3.		**laudat** *he (she, it) praises*
1.		
Pl 2.	**debetis** *you owe* (Pl)	
3.		

amare *to love*   **habitare** *to dwell*

		amare	habitare
	1.	_amo_____I_love_____	_____
Sg	2.	_____	_____
	3.	_____	_____
	1.	_____	_____
Pl	2.	_____	_____
	3.	_____	_____

habere *to have*   **dare** *to give*

		habere	dare
	1.	_____	_____
Sg	2.	_____	_____
	3.	_____	_____
	1.	_____	_____
Pl	2.	_____	_____
	3.	_____	_____

EXERCISE C: From their English derivatives, try to guess the meaning of the following 1st and 2nd conjugation verbs; usually the basic meaning applies:

Infinitive		English Derivative
1. amare	_____	amiable
2. ambulare	_____	ambulatory
3. cantare	_____	cantor
4. captare	_____	captive
5. clamare	_____	clamor
6. cogitare	_____	cogitate
7. dare	(to give)	Dative
8. donare	_____	donation
9. exspectare	_____	expect

.

10. festinare	(to hurry)	---
11. habitare	_____	habitat
12. imperare	_____	imperative
13. intrare	_____	entrance
14. invitare	_____	invitation
15. laborare	_____	labor
16. laudare	_____	laudable
17. monstrare	_____	demonstrate
18. narrare	_____	narrative
19. navigare	_____	navigation
20. occupare	_____	occupy
21. oppugnare	(to attack)	---
22. orare	(to ask, pray, beg)	oratory
23. parare	_____	prepare
24. portare	_____	portable
25. potare	_____	potable
26. properare	(to hurry)	---
27. pugnare	_____	pugnacious
28. rogare	_____	interrogate
29. salutare	_____	salute
30. servare	(to save, guard)	preserve
31. spectare	_____	spectator
32. stare	_____	static
33. visitare	_____	visit
34. vocare	_____	vocal
35. volare	_____	volatile

1. debere	_____	debit, debt
2. docere	_____	docile
3. flere	(to cry)	---
4. gaudere	(to be happy)	---
5. habere	_____	have
6. iacere	_____	adjacent
7. monere	_____	monitor
8. movere	_____	move
9. parere	(to obey)	---
10. placere	_____	please
11. respondere	_____	response
12. ridere	_____	ridiculous
13. sedere	_____	sedentary
14. tacere	_____	taciturn
15. tenere	_____	tenacious
16. timere	_____	timid
17. valere	_____	valid

Now compare with the Vocabulary list below: see, how easy Latin is!

1.	**amáre**	to like, love
2.	**ambuláre**	to walk
3.	**cantáre**	to sing
4.	**captáre**	to take, capture
5.	**clamáre**	to exclaim, shout, make noise
6.	**cogitáre**	to think
7.	**dáre**	to give
8.	**donáre**	to give (as a present)
9.	**exspectáre**	to await, expect
10.	**festináre**	to hurry, hasten
11.	**habitáre**	to live
12.	**imperáre**	to order, command
13.	**intráre**	to enter
14.	**invitáre**	to invite
15.	**laboráre**	to work, suffer
16.	**laudáre**	to praise
17.	**monstráre**	to show
18.	**narráre**	to tell, recount
19.	**navigáre**	to sail
20.	**occupáre**	to occupy, lay siege to
21.	**oppugnáre**	to attack
22.	**oráre**	to ask, pray, beg
23.	**paráre**	to prepare
24.	**portáre**	to carry
25.	**potáre**	to drink
26.	**properáre**	to run, hurry
27.	**pugnáre**	to fight
28.	**rogáre**	to ask
29.	**salutáre**	to greet
30.	**serváre**	to guard, save
31.	**spectáre**	to look at
32.	**stáre**	to stand
33.	**visitáre**	to visit
34.	**vocáre**	to call
35.	**voláre**	to fly
1.	**debére**	to owe; ought to, should, must
2.	**docére**	to teach
3.	**flére**	to cry
4.	**gaudére**	to be happy, rejoice
5.	**habére**	to have
6.	**iacére**	to lie (down**)**
7.	**monére**	to warn
8.	**movére**	to move
9.	**parére**	to obey
10.	**placére**	to please

11. respondere	to answer	
12. ridere	to laugh	
13. sedere	to sit	
14. tacere	to be silent	
15. tenere	to hold	
16. timére	to be afraid, fear	
17. valére	to be well, strong	
18. vidére	to see	

For many verbs in this list only one possible meaning is given, in order to make it easier to remember. Some verbs can have many different uses and meanings, like **habere**, just like its English counterpart, *to have*. When looking up verbs in a dictionary, often the 1st Person Singular present is listed: **porto, timeo**.

EXERCISE D: In a large dictionary (The Oxford Latin Dictionary, or the like) look up the verbs **laborare** and **tenere** and write down all the English translations listed. In an English-to-Latin dictionary find all the Latin verbs listed for *to carry*.

EXERCISE E   Form the 1st person Singular of all verbs in the list. Remember that in the 1st person Singular all first conjugation verbs lose their stem vowel -a- (voco, porto, laudo), but all second conjugation verbs keep their stem vowel -e- (debeo, doceo, respondeo, gaudeo. etc.)

EXERCISE F   Translate:

1. portatis	6. salutamus	11. ambulamus	16. narrant
2. canto	7. Videt	12. navigare	17. occupamus
3. tenet	8. spectant	13. gaudet	18. timemus
4. movemus	9. laborat	14. valetis	19. dat
5. fleo	10. rides	15. doces	20. paras

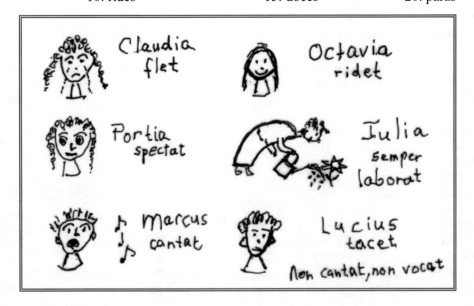

Negative Statements and Questions

By simply putting the word **non** before the verb, you can make statements negative. The use of helping verbs (to do, to be) for negative statements and for questions is required only in English, not in Latin:

Ridemus.	*We laugh.*	**Non ridemus.**	*We don't laugh.*
	We are laughing.		*We are not laughing.*
		(Literally:	*We not laugh.*)
Laborat.	*She works.*	**Non laborat.**	*She doesn't work.*
	She is working.		*She is not working.*

If you add the suffix **-ne** to the first word of the sentence (it need not be the verb), you have a yes-or-no question. If you add **-ne** to **non**, producing **nonne**, the question is expected to have the answer *yes*. To say "yes" or "no" you must repeat the verb.

Laboratne Iulia? *Is Julia working?* **Laborat.** *Yes.* **Non laborat.** *No.*
Nonne Iulia laborat? *Does Julia not work? Doesn't Julia work?* **Laborat.** *Yes, she does.*

EXERCISE G: Pick the appropriate form:
portas - non portas - portasne? - nonne portas?

1. do you carry?
2. you are carrying
3. you don't carry
4. aren't you carrying?
5. you carry

6. you are not carrying
7. don't you carry?
8. you do carry
9. are you carrying?

EXERCISE H: Say in Latin:

1. she is crying
2. he is not looking
3. she does not look
4. you (Pl) see
5. we sing
6. aren't you (Sg) working

7. they sail
8. I am not laughing
9. we don't show
10. does he teach?
11. you (Sg) owe
12. it pleases

Watch phrases (2) and (3) !

Now we can talk about some people:

Tullius, Marcus, Marius, Rufus, and **Lucius** are boys or men.
Claudia, Iulia, Portia, Tullia, and **Octavia** are girls or women.

Some other useful words to be memorized:

Interrogative Pronouns (or question words):

quis?	*Who?*	**quid?**	*what?*
ubi?	*where?*	**quo?**	*whereto? to where?*
cur?	*why?*	**quomodo?**	*how?*
quando?	*when?*	**unde?**	*from where?*

Coordinating Conjunctions: **Subordinating Conjunctions:**

et	*and*	**sed**	*but*	**quod**	*because*			
aut	*or*			**si**	*if, when*	**nisi**	*if not; except*	

Adverbs:

saepe	*often*	**semper**	*always*		**numquam**	*never*
hic	*here*	**ibi**	*there*		**satis**	*enough*
diu	*for a long time*	**multum**	*much*		**Nouns:**	

nemo *no one, nobody*
nihil *nothing*

EXERCISE I: Translate:

1. Marcus cantat. Quid cantat? _____

2. Quis ridet? Octavia ridet. _____

3. Cur non laboras, Portia? Iulia semper laborat. _____

4. Ubi habitant Marcus et Lucius? _____

5. Quid spectatis? Quid videtis? _____

6. Spectamus, sed nihil videmus. _____

7. Marius amat navigare; Claudia amat ambulare._____

8. Intramus. Valemus. Gaudemus. Non flemus. _____

9. Tullius vocat, sed Lucius tacet. Cur tacet et non gaudet? _____

_____

10. Claudia flet, sed non flet Octavia. _____

11. Quando ridet Claudia? Numquam ridet._____

The Imperative Mood (Command Form)

The word **imperative** is derived from **imperare**, *to order* or *command*. Since there are two forms for *you*, Singular and Plural, there must also be two command forms, one each for Singular and Plural, depending on whether the speaker addresses one person or more than one. For first, second, (and fourth) conjugation verbs the Singular imperative is the stem alone, without endings:

       specta! *look!*   **move!** *move!*   **labora!** *work!*

For the Plural, we add the ending **-te** (not to be confused with the regular 2nd person Plural ending **-tis**):
     spectate! *look!*   **movete!** *move!*   **laborate!** *work!*   But: labora**tis** you work

In a later, or a more colloquial and simple form of Latin the **negative** command uses the word **ne**, instead of **non**. Otherwise it works just like the statement form:
     ne specta! *don't look!*   **ne cantate!** *don't sing!*

In classical Latin, two forms of negative commands are commonly used. One is rather simple to learn: it consists of the forms **noli!** (Sg) or **nolite!** (Pl) *don't*, followed by the infinitive of the verb in question. Examples: **noli flere!** *don't cry*   **nolite ridere!** *don't laugh*   **nolite cantare!** *Don't sing*
The other form is a little more complicated and will be introduced in a later chapter.

There are several ways of making a distinction between Singular and Plural commands in English sentences, by addressing people, for instance:

     Stop complaining, all of you! (Pl)   Give it to me, stupid!
       Sit down, Claudia! (Sg)   Guys, please don't sing!
       Walk slowly, girls!

EXERCISE J: Give the **Singular** and **Plural** imperatives of:

1. tacere   _____tace_____   _____tacete_____

2. monstrare   _____   _____

3. respondere   _____   _____

4. habere   _____   _____

5. narrare   _____   _____

6. intrare   _____   _____

7. parare   _____   _____

    8. parere   _____   _____

    9. dare   _____   _____

    10. valere   _____   _____

    Now translate these forms!   How would you make them negative in Latin? (2 ways)

To Be - or not to be

A most essential verb in many languages, the verb **to be** is often quite irregular. In English its conjugation uses at least four different verb stems: "be/been", "am/are", "is", and "was". In Latin two stems are used for the present tense of the verb **esse**, *to be*:

1. **sum**	I am
2. **es**	you are
3. **est**	he/she/it is; ...is; **there is**
1. **sumus**	we are
2. **estis**	you are
3. **sunt**	they are; ...are; **there are**

    The **infinitive** of this verb is **esse**, *to be.*
    The **imperatives** are: **es!** *be!* (Sg) and **este!** *be!* (Pl)
    Negative command forms of **esse** will be expressed with subjunctive forms (chapter 15).

    Examples: The verbs **esse** and some others use the **predicate nominative** after them. (see chapter 2)

Claudia est puella.	Claudia is a girl.
Marcus est puer.	Marcus is a boy
Ubi estis?	Where are you all?
Sunt puellae hic?	Are there any girls here? (or: Are the girls here?)
Marcus est piger.	Marcus is lazy.
Iulia est sedula.	Julia is hard-working.
Est sedula.	She is hard-working.
Este contenti!	Be content!

EXERCISE K: Say in Latin:

1. Where is Claudia? _____
2. Who are you? (Sg) _____
3. Marcus is here. _____
4. Where are you all? _____
5. I am Tullius. He is Lucius. _____
6. Where are we? We are in a town. [in oppido] _____
7. There is nobody here. _____
8. He likes to be in the house [in casa]. _____
9. To be or not to be... _____
10. Be calm [tranquilli], (all of you)! Don't shout! Be silent!

_____

EXERCISE L: Analyze and translate the following verb forms like the examples given (they are of course all in the present tense and active voice):

Ind. = Indicative; Imp. = Imperative

Form	Person	Number	(Tense)	Mood	(Voice)	of :	Translation
portatis	2	Pl	Present	Ind.	Active	portare	you carry
gaude!	2	Sg	"	Imp.	"	gaudere	be happy!
1. damus	1	Pl	"	Ind.	"	dare	we give
2. rideo							
3. vale!							
4. date!							
5. habent							
6. flet							
7. vocatis							
8. paro							
9. laudas							
10. ora!							

Quomodo Vales? - How Are You Doing?   (Greetings and Visits)

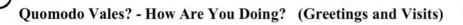

Salutare, *to greet*, lives on in Romance languages: **saluti** (*greetings*) in Italian;
salut (*Hi! Bye!*) in French; **saudades** (*greetings*) in Portuguese.

Salve! Salvete! is the Latin greeting (**salve** is still used in Italy)
Vale! Valete! means "good-bye" or "stay well".

Hospes is a *guest*, *stranger*, but also the *host*.

Expressions:

Quomodo vales?	How are you doing?
Bene.	Well.
Satis bene.	Well enough.
Non ita bene.	Not so well.
Non male.	Not bad.
Male.	Bad.
Optime.	Great.
Pessime.	Terrible.

EXERCISE M: Translate the following sentences into Latin. Hints are given following the exercise. Look at them beforehand! Words in parentheses need not be translated:

1. Lucius is crying. Why is he crying?   _____

2. Claudia and Portia are laughing.   _____

3. Marius is singing, but we are working.   _____

4. Where does Octavia walk?   _____

5. What are you looking at, Claudia? What do you see? _____

6. Why are you (people) not working? Work! _____

7. Portia loves to sing. She is happy.   _____

8. Who is singing? I am singing. I like to sing Don't sing! (Sg)

    _____

9. Who lives here? We do.   _____

10. Julia must walk, but Tullius does not like to walk he sails.

    _____

(2) Is the verb Singular or Plural?

(3) You can use **nos**, *we*, for emphasis in addition to the correct verb ending, but you don't have to.

(5) Remember that **spectare** means "to look **at**"!

(6) (People) just tells you the verb number.

(7) To "sing" is infinitive; so is "walk" in sentence (10).

(8) **Ego**, *I,* can be used for "I am singing." (Compare sentence (3))
Remember to use **ne** or **noli (nolite)** for the Imperative!

(9) In Latin you must repeat the verb in order to express either "we do, I do", etc., or "yes". Non + verb means "no", or "we don't, he doesn't" and so forth.

+++

From the syllables below make seven verb forms! Clues are given, but they are not literal.
(Hint: first pick out syllables which contain or are verb endings.)

a - bent - de - es - ga - gat - ha - ma - mus - na - o - pon - por - res - ro - tas - tis - vi

1. 1st Pl _____
           (sweet love)

5. 1st Sg _____
           (no answer?)

2. 2nd Sg _____
           (heavy to carry)

6. 3rd Sg _____
           (What's the question?)

3. 2nd Pl _____
           (to be or not)

7. Imp.Sg _____
           (in the water with a ship)

4. 3rd Pl _____
           (to have or not)

+++

Lectio I: **Colloquium**: Marcus et Iulia.   (Reading I: A Conversation: Marcus and Julia)

        Marcus: Salve, Iulia!

        Iulia: Salve!

        Marcus: Quo ambulas, Iulia?

        Iulia: Cur rogas?

5   Marcus: Amo navigare, sed Lucius non est hic.

        Iulia: Ubi est Lucius?

        Marcus: Lucius est domi. Non amat navigare.
              Est aegrotus si navigat.
              Sed tu? Amas navigare mecum?

10   Iulia: Hodie non navigo. Debeo laborare.

        Marcus: Laborare, laborare! Semper laboras.
               Debes cantare et gaudere.

        Iulia: Canto et gaudeo et quoque laboro.

        Marcus: Es optima. Es ornamentum puellarum.
15   Vale, sedula!

        Iulia: Vale, piger!

---

(7) domi - at home; (8) aegrotus - sick; (9) tu - you (Sg); mecum - with me; (10) hodie - today; (13) quoque - also;   (14) optima - the best (girl); ornamentum puellarum - (lit: ornament of girls) credit to all girls; (15) sedula - industrious (girl); (16) piger - lazy (boy).

And here a few sentences of original Latin, for you to get used to!

Sententiae:

1. Ora et labora!   2. Festina lente!   * lente - slowly
3. Qui laborat orat.   *qui - (he) who

4. Nemo timendo ad summum pervenit locum.
*summus locus - the highest place; pervenire - to come

5. Homo homini deus est (si suum officium sciat)
   *if he knows his duty
6. Saepe est etiam super palliolo sordido sapientia.
   *super palliolo sordido - with,above a dirty coat.

BENE LABORAS! OPTIME!

Lectio II: Salve!

sum mortuus - I am dead

A: **Fill in the blanks and answer the questions:**

1. To **conjugate** a verb in the present tense, you must add different _____

   to the _____ of a verb.

2. How many **verb conjugations** are there in Latin? _____

3. **Singular** and **Plural** are called _____.

4. **Indicative, subjunctive,** and **imperative** are called _____.

5. Which two English forms are the same in Latin:

   (a) he carries   (b) does he carry?   (c) he doesn't carry
   (d) is he carrying?   (e) isn't he carrying?

6. Is there a progressive form in Latin ("she is carrying") ?   Y / N

7. A dash, or length mark, placed over a vowel is called a _____.

8. **Amare, docere, esse** are _____ forms.

9. **Est** can be translated as _____, _____,

   _____, _____, _____.

10. Do Latin **imperative**, or command, forms distinguish between Singular and Plural? Y / N

11. To make a Latin **statement** negative, one uses the word _____.

12. To make a Latin **command** negative, one uses the word _____.

B: Review the following words:

   quoque - si - vale! - valere - debere - properare - cur - quando - servare - iacere - nihil -
   satis - hic - saepe - semper - ridere - placere - dare - numquam - quomodo - unde.

C: Do not confuse:

   habere - habitare;   parare - parere;   volare - valere.

Greetings - Salutatio

Salutatio (*greetings, salutation*) was the obligation of the Cliens (*client*) toward his Patronus (*patron*). Clients were poor people or freed slaves who were "adopted" by their patrons and supported with money, or with food, and also with legal advice. This was called the patron's Gratia (*benevolence*) toward his clients. The clients in turn also showed their Gratia (*thanks*), either by supporting their patrons in their quest for public offices, or by simply showing goodwill, speaking well of their patrons, and displaying a thankful attitude. Having a great number of clients raised the reputation of the patron. During the daily morning Salutatio the client could voice his requests or needs, or he received instructions for tasks.

Salutatio

Look at all the clients of Antonius! -
Yes, he wants to run for public office next month:
Director of Street Cleaning and Public Facilities.

Travels, Visits, Guest houses

Since Roman roads were well constructed and extensive, traveling was comfortable. People traveled by horse or donkey, in carts, on foot, or by boat. They were itinerant merchants, soldiers, officials, as well as tourists and explorers, or people who wanted to see relatives or friends, visit famous places, or study with a famous person. In a cart or carriage one could cover about seventy kilometers a day. There were maps and travel guides; milestones told travelers how far they had progressed. In all cities of the Roman Empire there were inns, in which guests could eat and drink, and sometimes sleep in simply furnished rooms above the tavern. An extraordinarily large number of guest houses was found in Pompeii.

Sign posted in a guest house in Pompeii:

> **Assibus hic bibitur: dipundium si dederis, meliora bibes;**
>
> **quattus si dederis, vina Falernia bibes.**

With (single) pennies one can drink here: if you give twopence, you will drink better wines;
if you give four pence, you will drink Falernian wine.
(Falernian was one of the best and most famous wines.)

Sign in front of a tavern:

> **VIATOR AUDI SI LIBET INTVS VENI**
>
> **TABVLA EST AENA QVAE TE CVNCTA PERDOCET**

Wayfarer, listen, come inside, if you please!
There is an iron table there, which teaches you everything.

And in Pompeii, where there is much graffiti this sentiment was found scratched on the wall
in a decidedly humble inn:

> **Miximus in lecto; fateor, peccavimus, hospes.**
> **Si dices: Quare? Nulla matella fuit.**

We have pissed in the bed; I confess, we have sinned, dear host.
If you will ask: "Why?" There was no chamber pot .
(Incidentally: this is a distich; see Metrics, Vol.2)

Chapter 1 : Answers and Translations

Exercise A:

roga- 1; naviga- 1; da- 1; doce- 2; fle- 2; specta- 1; time- 2; vide- 2; habe- 2; labora- 1.

Exercise B:

debeo, debes, debet, debemus, debetis, debent - I owe, you owe,...
laudo, laudas, laudat, laudamus, laudatis, laudant - I praise, you praise
amo, amas, amat, amamus, amatis, amant - I love, you love,...
habito, habitas, habitat, habitamus, habitatis, habitant - I live,...
habeo, habes, habet, habemus, habetis, habent - I have,...
do, das, dat, damus, datis, dant - I give,...

Exercise F: (Not all translations given)

1. you (Pl) carry, (you are carrying, etc.) 2. I am singing 3. he/she/it holds 4. we move 5. I am crying 6. we greet 7. she sees 8. they are looking 9. he is working 10. you (Sg) are laughing 11. we walk 12. to sail 13. he is happy 14. you all are well 15. you (Sg) are teaching 16. they tell 17. we occupy 18. we fear 19. she gives 20. you (Sg) are preparing

Exercise G:

1. portasne? 2. portas 3. non portas 4. nonne portas? 5. portas 6. non portas 7. nonne portas? 8. portas 9. portasne?

Exercise H:

1. flet 2. non spectat 3. non spectat 4. videtis 5. cantamus 6. nonne laboras? 7. navigant 8. non rideo 9. non monstramus 10. docetne? 11. debes 12. placet

Exercise I:

1. Marcus is singing. What is he singing?
2. Who is laughing? Octavia is.
3. Why are you not working, Portia? Iulia always works.
4. Where do Marcus and Lucius live?
5. What are you looking at? What do you see?
6. We are looking, but we see nothing. (we don't see anything)
7. Marius loves to sail, Claudia loves to walk.
8. We enter. We are well. We are happy. We don't cry.
9. Tullius calls, but Lucius is silent. Why is he silent and not happy?
10. Claudia is crying, but Octavia isn't.
11. When does Claudia laugh? She never laughs.

Exercise J:

1. tace! tacete! (be quiet!) 2. monstra! monstrate! (show!) 3. responde! respondete! (answer!) 4. habe! habete! (have!) 5. narra! narrate! (tell!) 6. intra! intrate! (enter!) 7. para! parate! (prepare!) 8. pare! parete! (obey!) 9. da! date! (give!) 10. vale! valete! (be well! farewell!)

.

Exercise K:
1. Ubi est Claudia? 2. Quis es? 3. Marcus hic est. 4. Ubi estis? 5. Sum Tullius. Est Lucius.
6. Ubi sumus? Sumus in oppido. 7. Nemo est hic. (Est nemo hic, etc.) 8. Amat esse in casa. 9.
Esse aut non esse... 10. Este tranquilli! Ne clamate! Tacete!

Exercise L:
1. 1 Pl Ind. of dare 2. 1 Sg Ind. of ridere 3. 2 Sg Imp. of valere 4. 2 Pl Imp. of dare
5. 3 Pl Ind. of habere 6. 3 Sg Ind. of flere 7. 2 Pl Ind. of vocare 8. 1 Sg Ind. of parare
9. 2 Sg Ind. of laudare 10. 2 Sg Imp. of orare

Translations:
1. we give 2. I am laughing 3. farewell! 4. give! 5. they have 6. he is crying 7. you are calling 8. I
prepare 9. you praise 10. pray!

Exercise M:
1. Lucius flet. Cur flet? 2. Claudia et Portia rident. 3. Marius cantat, sed (nos) laboramus.
4. Ubi Octavia ambulat? 5. Quid spectas, Claudia? Quid vides? 6. Cur non laboratis? Laborate! 7.
Portia amat cantare. Gaudet. 8. Quis cantat? (Ego) canto. Amo cantare. Ne canta! 9. Quis habitat
ibi? (Nos) habitamus. 10. Iulia ambulare debet, sed Tullius ambulare non amat; navigat.

Riddle:
1. amamus 2. portas 3. estis 4. habent 5. respondeo 6. rogat 7. naviga!

Lectio I: Reading 1
M: Hi, Julia! J: Greetings! M: Where are you walking to? J: Why are you asking? M: I like to sail,
but Lucius is not here. J: Where is Lucius? M: Lucius is at home. He doesn't like sailing. He gets
(is) sick when he sails. But you? Do you like to sail with me? J: Today I don't sail. I have to work.
M: Work, work! You are always working. You ought to sing and be happy. J: I sing and am happy
and also work. M: You are the best. You are a credit to all girls. Good bye, industrious one!
J: Good bye, lazy one!

Lectio II: Reading 2
Good day! How are you? - Great! I am happy. - Good bye.
Hello, how are you doing? - Fine! I am satisfied (content) - See you.
Greetings, Julia, how is it going? - Good enough. Not bad - Stay well! (Bye)
Hi, kids, how are things? - Not so good! - Take care, you two!
Hey (little one)! How are you getting along? - Badly! Lousy! I am dead! - Cheer up! Bye, bye!

Sententiae: Sentences
1. Pray and work! (Motto of the Benedictine Order)
2. Hurry slowly! (sort of 'Haste makes waste.')
3. He who works is praying.
4. Nobody comes through fear(ing) to the highest place.
5. Man is a god to man (if he knows his duty).
6. Often there is wisdom even with a dirty coat.

Summarium: Summary
1. endings, stem 2. four 3. number 4. mood 5.(b) and (d) 6.No 7. macron 8. Infintive
9. he is, she is, it is, there is, ...is 10.Yes 11. non 12. ne

2

NOUNS:

1ST OR A - DECLENSION

TYPES OF LANGUAGES (2)

For a comparison of analytic and synthetic features consider this sentence:

First in **English**:
Yesterday we went into a store and bought a little red pencil.　　　(* 12 words *)

Here is a Mandarin **Chinese** version of this sentence, with a literal translation:

昨天　我们　去　店裡　買

past time	day	me + others	go	past	store	to inside	buy	past
(yesterday)		(we)		(went)		(into)		(bought)

一支　　小紅　色鉛筆

one　stick-like object　little　red　colour mineral graphite　pencil.
　　　　　　　　　　　　　　　　　　　　　(graphite, lead)

　　　　　　　　　　　　　　　　　　　　　(* 15 - 18 words *)

And now the same sentence in **Latin**:

Heri　　in　tablinam　inivimus　　et　stylum　rubrum　emimus.

Yesterday　into a store　we went in　and　a pencil　red　we bought.

　　　　　　　　　　　　　　　　　　(* 8 words *)

If you look at a bilingual Latin-English (prose) text, you will see that the
Latin text is often considerably shorter than the English!
Now you know why.

Chapter 2:   **Nouns: The First Declension**

     A: About Nouns

Just as verb forms change to show Person and Number, so nouns change to show **case** and **number**. The word **case** is derived from the Latin word **cadere**, *to fall*; that is to say that the cases have 'fallen off' a supposed norm, namely the **nominative** or subject case. For this reason cases other than the Nominative are sometimes called **oblique cases**; they express anything beyond the mere naming of the subject. Cases show the **function** of a noun within a sentence, such as **direct object, indirect object, possessive.**
In English, **pronouns** still express cases by changing their forms:

     He is here. - I saw **him**.   (Subject - Direct Object)
     She has a cat. - I like **her**. (Subject - Direct Object)
     Whose cat is it? (Possessive)
     I didn't tell **them** the story. (Indirect Object)

Noun cases in English, on the other hand, are usually shown by means of prepositional phrases:
of the house (possessive), **to my friends** (indirect object); or else, cases are expressed by the word order of the sentence:

     The dog (subject) bit the man (direct object).
     The man (subject) bit the dog (direct object).

One type of possessive case is formed with a suffix: my father**'s** house; the parent**s'** obligations.

Aqua, herba, statuae, feminae, columnae; homo habet librum.

B: Latin Nouns

In Latin no prepositions are used to show noun cases: in true synthetic fashion one must form them by adding different **suffixes**, or **endings**, to the (noun-) **stem**. There are six cases in Latin; all have Singular and Plural forms. Here they are listed in one of the arrangements customarily used in grammar books:

Abbreviations	*Name*	*Use*
Nom., N	Nominative	Subject; Predicate Subject
Gen., G	Genitive	Possessive: **of** or **'s, s'**
Dat., D	Dative	Indirect Object: **to** or **for** (a person); In Latin the Dative also must follow some Verbs.
Acc., A	Accusative	Direct Object; also must follow certain Latin prepositions, e.g. those showing motion to a place
Voc., V	Vocative	Address: "Oh Marcus!" Often not listed, since it is usually identical to the Nominative
Abl., Ab	Ablative	expresses separation or origin: **from;** means by which, or manner in which something is done: **by;** position in which: **on, in;** must follow certain prepositions. The English translations of the Ablative must always use a Preposition, such as **by, with, through, from,** etc.

Besides showing **case** Latin nouns also have **number** (Singular and Plural) and **gender: masculine, feminine,** or **neuter.** The concept of gender is easily understood when dealing with **natural gender:** male persons or male animals are **masculine (m.)**, female ones are **feminine (f.)**, some animals are **neuter (n.)**, (a word meaning "neither of both", masculine or feminine, that is). A little more difficult to grasp is the concept of **grammatical gender**, since it is entirely arbitrary and bears no relation to the noun or its meaning (as, indeed, the very names of objects bear no relation to their meaning, shape, or the like).

Examples:
fenestra (window) **f.**	tempus (time) **n.**..	os (mouth) **n.**
labor (work) **m.**	manus (hand) **f.** .	legio (legion) **f.**
portus (harbor) **m.**	porta (gate) **f.** .	donum (gift) **n.**

Adding different endings to a noun stem is called **declining** the noun; we speak of noun **declension**. As was the case with the word **conjugation**, the word **declension** can also have a second meaning, namely "a group of nouns which are declined after a like pattern." There are five noun-declensions in Latin, which are either numbered one through five or named after their characteristic stem-vowels:

1st = **a** - Declension;	4th = **u** - Declension;
2nd = **o** - Declension;	5th = **e** - Declension.
3rd = **consonant** - Declension;	

This classification in declensions offers considerable aid in learning the genders of nouns. The nouns in each declension, with the exception of the 3rd, have a characteristic ending in the nominative, and they have mostly the same gender. To analyze a Latin noun one must therefore list case and number; the gender must be known if one wants to use qualifying adjectives, personal pronouns, or relative and demonstrative pronouns.

 **EXERCISE A:** In the following sentences underline every noun and pronoun, then indicate above each underlined word in what case it would be, if you translated the sentence into Latin. Give reasons for your answers. (source: Isaac Borosz)

Examples:

    NOM   DAT   ACC   ABL   GEN
The <u>student</u> gave   to the <u>teacher</u>   many <u>presents</u>   from the <u>home</u>   of the <u>mayor</u>.

  GEN   NOM   GEN   ACC
The <u>boy's</u>   <u>dog</u>   attacked   the <u>girl's</u>   <u>kitten</u>.

1. Can this boy find a home for the priceless green gorilla?

2. I killed the fly quickly and efficiently with a very heavy hammer.

3. Ben-Him is the cousin of Ben-Hur.

4. Harold's job is too difficult for him.

5. The queen kicked the servant of the king, because she hated the servant's nose.

6. The servant shouted nasty things to the queen.

7. Will the owner of this wonderful woolly mammoth please come forward?

8. He ate the fish with his fork.

9. The Romans carried many things from the captured city into Rome.

10. The city of the king is the largest on this side of the ocean.

11. He gives the dog supper from his own plate.

12. The magic moose marched with graceful steps from the comic book and went swimming in

    the balmy lake.

The First Declension

Nouns of the **1st declension** end in **-a**, like **puella**. With few exceptions (natural gender for male persons) these nouns are **feminine**. Latin nouns use neither definite nor indefinite articles (the, a); their meaning is incorporated into the noun. Since the following paradigm (= declined example) denotes a person, the ablative is used with a preposition (**ab** or **a,** *by, from*). More on the ablative see in "More about Latin cases."
The **stem** of these nouns is found by removing the **-a** from the word as it is listed.

Singular

N	puell **a**	the girl, a girl, girl
G	puell **ae**	of the girl, of a girl, the girl's, a girl's, girl's
D	puell **ae**	to the girl, to a girl, to girl
A	puell **am**	the girl (Dir. Obj), a girl (D.O.), girl (D.O.)
Ab	a puell **a**	by, from the girl, a girl, girl

Plural

N	puell **ae**	(the) girls
G	puell **arum**	of (the) girls, (the) girls'
D	puell **is**	to (the) girls
A	puell **as**	(the) girls (D.O.)
Ab	a puell **is**	by, from (the) girls

More about Latin Cases

The **nominative** is the case to use for the **subject** and **predicate subject**. Only nouns in the Nominative can be the subject of a sentence; they need not stand at the beginning of the sentence or before the Verb. Their form will almost always show that they are nominative. Just as in English, the subject and the verb must agree in **number** (Sg or Pl)

Puella cantat.	The girl is singing. (sings, does sing)
Cantat puella.	"
Agricolae laborant.	The farmers work. (are working, do work)
Intrat femina.	The woman enters, etc.
Femina est poeta.	The woman is a poet. (Predicate subject with linking verb *to be*)

The **accusative** denotes the **direct object**, but only if it is used without a preposition. In the sentence **spectamus casam**, *We look at the house,* **casam** is a direct object; in the sentence **Navigamus ad insulam,** *We sail to the island,* **insulam** is part of a prepositional phrase. Since direct objects in English are recognizable only by their position in the sentence, not by their form, you must be careful when translating sentences into Latin, not to forget the direct object, and wind up with two subjects instead. The words
Puella spectat casa.# makes no sense in Latin; since both nouns are in the Nominative, there is no functional relationship between the nouns. The sentence should read: **Puella spectat casam.** Verbs which use direct objects are called **transitive;** these include **spectare** - *to look at;* **timere** - *to be afraid of;* **exspectare** - *to wait for;* **intransitive** verbs include **ambulare, properare, navigare** - *to walk, run, sail;* **iacere** - *to lie down;* **tacere** - *to be silent.* They have no direct object, but use prepositional phrases instead: ambulare **ad casam**; navigare **in insulam.**

The only verbs which do not require direct or indirect objects after them (or in Latin occasionally the Ablative) are linking verbs, mainly *to be.* (See above: **Femina est poeta**) Remember though, that there need not be a separate word for the subject of a sentence: the subject can be contained in the verb. A Latin sentence can therefore consist of one word.

Amat.	He loves. (He is in love.) She loves.
Amat puellam.	He loves the girl.
Puellam amat.	"
Puella amat.	The girl loves.

NB! Note the difference: Amat **puella.** Amat **puellam.**   **NB!**

Since in Latin nominative and accusative are distinguishable by form, strict adherence to word order is unnecessary (a characteristic difference between synthetic and analytic languages! You can read about it in the *Language* page of chapter 3).

The **vocative** Sg and Pl is usually like the Nominative in form: **puella!** *girl!* **puellae!** *girls!* In classical Latin the vocative is placed, between commas, in second position in the sentence, after the imperative: Spectate**, puellae,** lunam et stellas! Girls, look at the moon and the stars!

The **ablative**, which in textbooks often has a length-mark (yes: macron) placed over the ending, to distinguish it from the nominative, presents a new concept, which is complicated slightly by the fact that in Latin sometimes prepositions are used with it, at other times not. The ablative of means (for instance in: He came **by ship**, or: They hoisted the stone **with a pulley)** uses no preposition in Latin. The Ablative of accompaniment (He came **with a friend**) must use a preposition. (See details in Chapter 18.) However, all Latin ablatives, with or without prepositions, must be translated by a prepositional phrase in English; some of the prepositions used are *from, with, by, through, by means of'*. *By, from or with* will be used in the example-declensions in this book.

The **dative** is used for the **indirect object**, often a person, to or for whom one does, gives, or tells something (The "something" would be the direct object.) In English there are two ways to mark an indirect object, and two possible positions in the sentence for it:

We gave the money **to my brother**.   or   We gave **my brother** the money.

In the second sentence, even though no preposition is used, the position of the noun in the sentence shows **my brother** to be the indirect object, still meaning "to my brother".

The **genitive** denotes **possession**. Though it is true that words can occur in almost any order in a Latin sentence, one usually avoids placing a Genitive between two nouns, since it would be difficult to tell where it belongs in meaning.

Since there are fewer than the ten different endings (twelve with the vocative) that would be needed to form five cases in the Singular and Plural, some of the endings have to do double or triple duty. This occurrence is called **syncretism**, and frequently it requires some detective work when reading Latin. In the 1st Declension, for example, there is syncretism between genitive Singular, dative Singular, and nominative Plural: they all use the ending **-ae.** Often the verb number or the meaning of the verb give a clue; or the cases of the other nouns in the sentence:

> **Puellae** *sunt* in casa. (**Nom. Pl.**)   The girls are in the house.
> **Puellae** casa *est* ibi. (**Gen. Sg.**)   The girl's house is there.
> **Puellae** cas*am damus* (**Dat. Sg.**)   We give the house to the girl.

Some general rules for syncretism:

1. All nouns in all Declensions have Syncretism of **Dative** and **Ablative** Plural.

2. All **Neuter** nouns, (you will learn some in the next chapter), regardless of Declension, have Syncretism of Nominative and Accusative, Singular and Plural. Moreover, their ending in the Nominative and Accusative Plural is always **-a.**

EXERCISE B: Say in Latin, naming the case and number (Sg/Pl) you are using:

1. the girls _____   2. the girls (Direct Object) _____   3. the girl's _____

4. the girls' _____   5. a girl's _____   6. to girls _____

7. by the girl _____   8. the girl (Direct Object) _____   9. for the girls_____

10. to a girl _____   11. girls! _____

EXERCISE C: Fill in the blanks:

1. The **direct object** is in the _____ case.

2. The endings for **ablative Sg and Pl** of the 1st Declension are _____ and _____.

3. In the sentence: *He tickled the mouse with a pitchfork*, "with

   a pitchfork" is in the _____ case.

4. The endings for **accusative Sg** and **Pl** of the first declension are _____ and _____.

5. In the sentence: *He is a farmer* the word "farmer" is in the

_____ case.

EXERCISE D: Supply the missing information (use **puella**):

Latin Form	Case	Number	Function	English meaning
Example:				
puella	Nom.	Sg	Subject	(the, a) girl
1. _____	____	____	_____	to the girl
2. _____	____	Sg	Direct Object	_____
3. _____	Acc	Pl	_____	_____
4. _____	____	Pl	Possession	_____
5. puellae	____	Pl	_____	_____
6. _____	____	____	Origin	from the girl
7. puellis	Dat	____	_____	_____
8. _____	Gen	Sg	_____	_____

Videte puellas !
Sunt Tullia et Octavia.
Puellae spectant villam.
Tullia Octaviae villam monstrat.
Villa puellarum non est.
Puellae villam non habent.
Villa placet puellis.

Quid nunc?
What now?

Vocabulary: The Nominative Singular is followed by the Genitive Singular ending.

1. agrícola,ae (m.)	farmer
2. ancilla,ae	maid
3. aqua,ae	water
4. casa,ae	house, hut
5. causa,ae	cause, reason
6. cena,ae	meal, dinner
7. cópia,ae	supply, mass, a lot
8. dómina,ae	mistress (of the house)
9. fábula,ae	story
10. família,ae	family
11. fémina,ae	woman
12. fília,ae	daughter
13. fortúna,ae	fortune, luck
14. gallína,ae	hen
15. herba,ae	grass
16. íncola,ae (m.)	inhabitant
17. ínsula,ae	island
18. lingua,ae	language, tongue
19. líttera,ae	letter (of the alphabet)
20. litterae,arum (Pl.)	letters; epistle
21. luna,ae	moon
22. memória,ae	memory
23. mensa,ae	table
24. natúra,ae	nature
25. nauta,ae (m.)	sailor
26. pátria,ae	fatherland
27. pecúnia,ae	money
28. poéta,ae (m.)	poet
29. puélla,ae	girl
30. pugna,ae	fight
31. serva,ae	slave, servant
32. silva,ae	forest
33. stella,ae	star
34. terra,ae	land, earth
35. tuba,ae	trumpet, tuba
36. uva,ae	grape
37. vacca,ae	cow
38. via,ae	way, road
39. villa,ae	farmhouse
40. vita,ae	life

Geographical names:

Británnia,ae	Britain
Itália,ae	Italy
Gallia,ae	Gaul (today's Switzerland and part of France)
Germánia,ae	Germany; home of the German tribes

Which of the above nouns have **natural gender** (i.e. they are male or female persons or animals) **?**

   1. Feminine:_**(Exercise E)**_____

   2. masculine:_____

The gender of masculine a-declension nouns does not show in the declension pattern. However it must be known when using adjectives or pronouns (personal, demonstrative, relative, etc.)

EXERCISE E: Find an English derivative for as many of the vocabulary words as possible,
            for instance: **aqua** --> aquatic, aquarium, aquifer, aqueous;
            but not **aquiline;** that comes from **aquila** = eagle.
            (If in doubt, look in a big dictionary, where etymologies are given.)

Here are some answers that may surprise you:
lunatic: crazy people were supposed to be influenced by the **moon.**
vaccinate: serum, at first for **cow-pox**, was gained from **cows**
insulin: its name refers to parts of the pancreas called **islands** of Langerhans
Pennsylvania is the **forest of Penn** (William)
Villanova: well, somebody must have built a **new farmhouse** there
trivial is the gossip which you can hear at the place where **three roads** meet

EXERCISE F: (nominative and accusative) Translate:

   1. Poeta cantat.
   2. Femina invitat poetam.
   3. Agricolam puella vocat.
   4. Navigat nauta.
   5. Agricolae amant terram.
   6. Lunam spectat poeta.
   7. Femina et serva laborant.
   8. Femina portat aquam.
   9. Puellae spectant stellas.
10. Non amant cenam filiae.
11. Gallina clamat.
12. Insulas nautae occupant.
13. Videmus lunam.
14. Nautae non ambulant, sed navigant.
15. Agricola et femina et nauta et poeta patriam amant.
16. Britannia est insula.
17. Ne timete vaccas! Nolite timere vaccas !
18. Estne aqua? Non est.
19. Occupantne nautae etiam [also] silvas et terram?
20. Poetae linguam Italiae amant. Quis est poeta Italiae?
21. Sum poeta et non pugno.
22. Quo navigatis? Navigamus ad Britanniam.

23. Litterae non sunt lingua.
24. Salvete, puellae!
25. Domina monet servas: "Laborate, servae, et tacete!"

EXERCISE G: Translate, watching for direct objects (underline them first!):

1. The farmer carries <u>water.</u>
2. The girl does not like the farmhouse.
3. The poet tells stories.
4. Cows do not carry water.
5. The water does not carry the cows.
6. The woman is looking at the road.
7. The girls are singing.
8. Poets praise the fatherland.
9. We praise the poets.
10. The cows do not see the house.
11. The mistress saves the cows.
12. Do you see the cow?
13. Are you afraid of a chicken?
14. Occupy the island, sailors, but don't drink the water!
15. The maid prepares the meal.
16. The woman asks the farmer: "Do you like the food?"

EXERCISE H: Translate these sentences which use all cases:

1. Agricola feminae pecuniam dat.
2. Femina vaccae aquam dat. (Aquam femina dat vaccae. Etc.)
3. Puellae monstrant poetae stellas. [ambiguous!]
4. Nautae insulam puellis monstrant.   5. Agricolae nautis uvas dant.
6. Est copia aquae in insula.   7. Vaccae agricolarum sunt in via.
8. Agricolae vaccae sunt in via. [Common sense does help sometimes!]
9. Agricolae habitant in villis, in silvis habitant poetae.
10. Domina ambulat in villam; ancilla laborat in villa.
11. Narramus puellis fabulas.   12. Monstrate, puellae, poetis stellas!
13. Aqua est fortuna nautarum.
14. Laudamus memoriam et linguam poetarum.
15. Vita agricolae non est vita poetae.   16. Insulae sunt in aqua.
17. Vaccis herbas puellae dant.   18. Quis habet agricolae pecuniam? Non habeo.
19. Agricola non tenet gallinam in villa, quod semper clamat.
20. Monet ancillas agricola, si non laborant.
21. Ne pugnate, puellae! Non habetis causam pugnae.
22. Intramus in villam et exspectamus cenam.
23. Natura memoriam et linguam poetis dat.   24. Ubi estis? Sumus in feminae villa.
25. In agricolae familia sunt agricola, femina, et filiae.
26. Incolae Italiae sunt feminae, agricolae, ancillae, dominae, puellae, servae, poetae.
27. Poetae puellas litteras docere debent.
28. Agricolae cogitant de [about] vaccis; nauta cogitat de aqua; puellae cogitant de vita; ancilla
    cogitat de cena; gallinae etiam cogitant de cena; vaccae numquam cogitare debent.

Vaccae numquam cogitare debent

EXERCISE I: Translate into Latin, using all cases.

1. We live on an island; you, girls, live in a farmhouse.
2. Often we walk into the forest and look at the grass.
3. The girls show (their) cows to the farmers.
9. There is a lot of grapes in the house, but there is no water.
10. Do you fear the water, Tullia? I like to sail in the water.
11. The farmer's daughter teaches the cows.
12. The cows don't walk into the house, but lie on the road.
13. Ask the farmer: "Where is the money? Answer, farmer!"
14. Often the mistress does not give the servants (their) money.
15. Aren't there any gates in farmhouses?
16. The farmer is a poet, the sailor is a poet, but the poet is silent.

(1) we, you: use **nos, vos** for emphasis and contrast; on = in (here: put **insula** into the **ablative**)   (3) and (4) Remember the difference between *to a person* (dative) and *to a place* (in or ad + accusative)
(6) Which is the direct object, which the indirect object?
(9) say: nothing of water, or: water is not.
(12) and (15) into = in + accusative; on, in = in + ablative.
(16) Remember: to be silent is a verb.

All nouns are in the nominative.

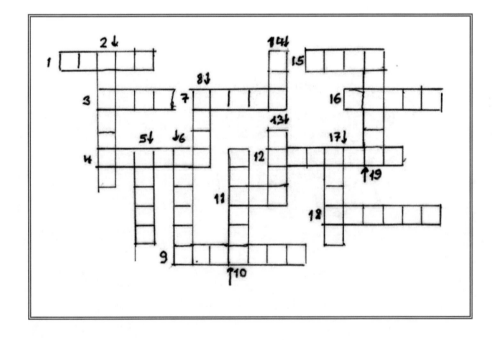

1. supply	11. grape
2. money	12. how?
3. meal	13. water
4. inhabitant	14. road
5. reason	15. moon
6. speech	16. daughter
7. land	17. table
8. trumpet	18. star
9. servant	19. mistress
10. island	

Lectio I: Nauta et Agricola

Est nauta in via. Spectat agricolam et rogat:

Nauta: Estne villa hic? Debeo habere aquam et cenam.
Agricola: Fortasse. Ubi habitas?
Nauta: Sum nauta. Patria mea est Gallia.
5 **Agricola:** Visitasne Italiam?
 Nauta: Non visito, sed laboro.
Agricola: Habitasne in aqua?
Nauta: Minime. Navigo in aqua, sed habito in terra.
Agricola: Habesne pecuniam?
10 **Nauta:**   Habeo.
Agricola: Optime. Agricola nautae cenam dat, agricolae nauta
              pecuniam dat.
Nauta: Ita est.

Lectio II: Tumultus In Casa Agricolae (Part I of Soap Opera)

Agricola clamat: Ubi est cena? Exspecto cenam. Subito! Quis debet parare
15 cenam? Cur exspectare debeo? Cur ancilla non laborat? Festinate, puellae!
Cur sedetis hic? Cur cena non est in mensa? Ubi est gallina?
Cur non est cocta (cooked) ? Ubi sunt uvae? Ridetisne? Respondete!
Nonne habete linguas? Ego laboro et vos gaudete. Date agricolae cenam!
Tandem. Cur debemus potare aquam? Aquam non amo...
20   Mala casa, malae puellae!

---

(3) fortasse - perhaps; (4) mea - my; (8) minime - not at all, hardly;
(13) ita est - yes; (19) tandem - finally; (20) mala, malae - bad.

EXERCISE J: Rewrite the dialogue (Lectio 1) to make the **sailor** Plural!
Mea, *my*, in line 4 becomes **nostra**, *our*.

S U M M A R I U M

A: Answer these questions about what you have learned in Chapter 2:

1. Noun cases show the _____ of a noun in the sentence.

2. The **Subject** of a sentence is always in the _____ case.

3. The **Accusative** case shows that the noun is the _____ of the sentence.

4. The **Indirect Object**, *to, for a person,* is in the _____ case.

5. The Latin **Ablative** is rendered in English with the prepositions _____,

    _____, _____, _____, etc.

6. Most of the time the **Vocative** looks just like the _____ case.

7. The **Vocative** is put in _____ place in the sentence.

8. The Subject must precede the Objects in a Latin sentence. **Y / N**

9. The **Predicate Subject** must always be in the _____ case.

10. A Latin sentence can consist of **one word. Y / N**

11. The **Subject** and the **Verb** of the sentence must agree in _____.

12. The use of the same ending for different cases is called _____.

13. There are _____ genders in Latin.

14. **Neuter**, *neither,* means 'neither _____ nor _____.'

15. Most nouns in the **1st Declension** have _____ gender.

16. The ending for the **Dative** and **Ablative Plural** is _____.

B: Review these words:

uva - copia - agricola - ancilla - incola - mensa - poeta - pecunia - pugna - patria - nauta

Which of the above nouns are **masculine?**

C: Do not confuse:

via - vita;   casa - causa;   lingua - littera;   filia - femina

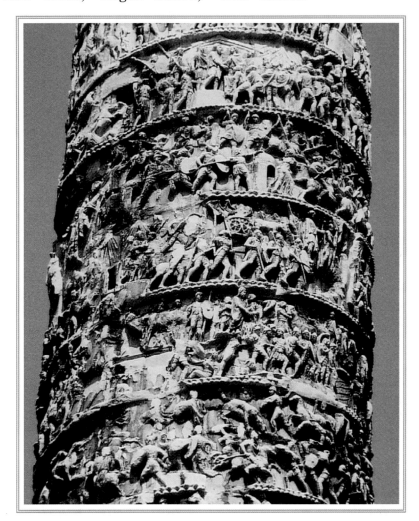

nautae navigant, imperatores imperant, milites (soldiers) pugnant, incolae clamant, familiae orant, poetae rident, filiae spectant, servae properant, patria laborat...

(Trajan's Column, Rome)

LIFE IN THE COUNTRY

Agriculture was the basis of life for Rome. There were small farmers in Italy, who later were replaced by landed owners, who employed some farm workers, but mostly used slaves. At Caesar´s time the law required one third of the labor force to be paid workers, because so many small farmers had lost their farms and had fallen into unemployment and poverty.

The **Villa Rustica** was a large compound of buildings; it resembled a village. Raw materials like olives, wheat, and grapes could be manufactured into oil, bread, and wine on the premises.

The J.P.Getty Museum in Malibu is housed in a reconstruction of the *Villa dei Papiri* in Herculaneum, a typical *Villa Rustica*.

Roman farmers used fertilizers and irrigation, or dehydration, where necessary, as well as crop rotation. Their implements included plows, sickles, scythes, pitchforks, shovels, spades, hoes, boxes, and baskets. Among their farm animals were horses, donkeys, and oxen.

**Hand mills like these were later replaced by larger ones,
in which the pestle was driven by two men, or by a donkey.**

A scene of country life

Casa was originally a hut in which peasants and poor people lived. These houses were constructed of boughs and branches and the spaces were filled in with dirt. Much later, **casa** came to mean `house´ in general, as it still does in Italian and Spanish.

Chapter 2: ANSWERS AND TRANSLATIONS

Exercise A: 1. boy (Nom) home (Acc) (for) gorilla (Dat) 2. I (Nom) fly (Acc) (with) hammer (Abl)
3. Ben-Him (Nom) cousin (Nom) (of) Ben-Hur (Gen) 4. Harold's (Gen) job (Nom) for him (Dat)
5. queen (Nom) servant (Acc) (of the) king (Gen) she (Nom) servant's (Gen) nose (Acc)
6. Servant (Nom) things (Acc) (to the) queen (Dat) 7. owner (Nom) (of) mammoth (Gen) 8. He
(Nom) fish (Acc) (with) fork (Abl) 9. Romans (Nom) things (Acc) (from) city (Abl) (to) Rome (Acc)
10. city (Nom) (of) king (Gen) (on) side (Abl) (of) ocean (Gen) 11. He (Nom) dog (Dat) supper
(Acc) (from) plate (Abl)   12. moose (Nom) (with) steps (Abl) (from) book (Abl) (into) lake (Acc)

Exercise B: 1. puellae (Nom) 2. puellas (Acc) 3. puellae (Gen) 4. puellarum (Gen) 5. puellae
(Gen) 6. puellis (Dat) 7. (a) puella (Abl) 8. puellam (Acc) 9. puellis (Dat) 10. puellae (Dat)

Exercise C: 1. Accusative 2. -a, -is 3. Ablative 4. -am, -as 5. Nominative
Exercise D:

1. puellae	Dat	Sg	Indir. Obj.	(to the girl)
2. puellam	Acc	(Sg)	(Dir. Obj.)	the girl
3. puellas	(Acc)	(Pl)	Dir. Obj.	the girls
4. puellarum	Gen	(Pl)	(Possession)	of the girls
5. (puellae)	Nom	(Pl)	Subject	the girls
6. a puella	Abl	Sg	(Origin)	(from the girl)
7. (puellis)	(Dat)	Pl	Indir. Obj.	to, for the girls
8. puellae	(Gen)	(Sg)	Possession	the girl's

Exercise E: 1. feminine: ancilla, domina, femina, filia, gallina, puella, serva, vacca
  2. masculine: agricola, incola, nauta, poeta

Exercise F:
1. The poet sings. 2. The woman invites the poet. 3. A girl calls the farmer. 4. The sailor is sailing.
5. Farmers love the land. 6. The poet looks at the moon. 7. The woman and the slave are working.
8. The woman is carrying water. 9. The girls look at the stars. 10. The daughters don't like the
meal. 11. The hen is cackling. 12. The sailors occupy islands. 13. We see the moon. 14. Sailors
don't walk, but sail. 15. The farmer and the woman and the sailor and the poet (all) love their
homeland. 16. Britain is an island. 17. Don't be afraid of the cows! 18. Is there any water? No. 19.
Are the sailors invading even the forests and the land? 20. The poets love the language of Italy.
Who is a poet of Italy? (Dante, Boccaccio, Petrarca, to name a few) 21. I am a poet and do not
fight. 22. Where are you sailing (to)? We are sailing to Britain. 23. Letters of the alphabet are not a
language. 24. Greetings, girls! 25. The mistress admonishes the slaves: "Work, slaves, and be
quiet!"

Exercise G:
1. Agricola aquam portat. 2. Puella villam non amat. 3. Poeta narrat fabulas. 4. Aquam non
portant vaccae. 5. Aqua non portat vaccas. 6. Femina viam spectat. 7. Cantant puellae. 8.
Patriam poetae laudant. 9. Poetas laudamus. 10. Vaccae casam non vident. 11. Servat domina
vaccas. 12. Videsne vaccam? 13. Gallinamne times? 14. Occupate insulam, nautae, sed ne
potate aquam! 15. Ancilla cenam parat. 16. Femina agricolam rogat: "Amasne cenam?"

Sad Story:
The sailor loves the water. The farmer loves not the water, but the land. A woman loves the farmer. A girl also loves the farmer. Therefore a girl and a woman love the farmer. But the farmer does not like women and girls. He likes cows and the land and greenery and woods.
The woman and the girl walk with the poet. They look at the moon and the stars. Stupid farmer!

Exercise I:
1. The farmer gives money to the woman. 2. The woman gives water to the cow. 3. The girls show the stars to the poet. (or: The poets show the stars to the girl.) 4. The sailors show the girls the island. 5. Farmers give the sailors grapes. 6. There is a lot of water on the island. 7. The farmers' cows are in the road. 8. The farmer's cows are in the road. (not: the cow's farmers) 9. Farmers live in country houses, poets live in the woods. 10. The mistress is walking into the farmhouse; the maid is working in the farmhouse. 11. We are telling the girls stories. 12. Girls, show the poets the stars! 13. The water is the sailors' fortune. 14. We praise the memory and the language of poets. 15. The life of the farmer is not the life of the poet. 16. Islands are in the water. (There are islands in the water.) 17. The girls are giving the cows grass. 18. Who has the farmer's money? Not me. 19. The farmer does not keep the chicken in the house, because it screeches all the time. 20. The farmer warns the maids, if they don't work. 21. Don't fight, girls! You have no reason to fight. (lit: of fight) 22. We enter the house and wait for dinner. 23. Nature gives memory and language to poets. 24. Where are you? We are in the woman's farmhouse. 25. In the farmer's family there are the farmer, his wife, and the daughters. 26. The inhabitants of Italy are women, farmers, maids, mistresses, girls, slaves, poets. 27. The poets should teach the girls. 28. The farmers think about the cows; the sailor thinks about the water; the girls think about life; the maid thinks about dinner; the chickens also think about dinner; (the) cows never have to think.

Exercise J:
1. Habitamus in insula, habitatis, puellae, in villa.
2. Saepe in silva ambulamus et herbam spectamus.
3. Puellae agricolis vaccas monstrant.
4. Nautae ad insulam navigant et in insula laborant.
5. Ubi sunt puellae? Non sunt puellae!
6. Narra, poeta, puellis fabulam!
7. Intrate, servae! Sedemus in casa et exspectamus feminas.
8. Valete, poetae! Habete viam longam.
9. Est copia uvarum in villa, sed non est aqua.
10. Timesne aquam, Tullia? Amo navigare in aqua.
11. Agricolae filia vaccas docet.
12. Vaccae in villam non ambulant, sed in via iacent.
13. Roga(te) agricolam: "Ubi est pecunia?" Responde, agricola!
14. Domina saepe ancillis pecuniam non dat.
15. Nonne sunt portae in villa?
16. Agricola est poeta, nauta est poeta, sed poeta tacet.

Riddle: 1 copia 2 pecunia 3 cena 4 incola 5 causa 6 lingua 7 terra 8 tuba 9 ancilla 10 insula 11 uva 12 quomodo 13 aqua 14 via 15 luna 16 filia 17 mensa 18 stella 19 domina

LECTIO I : The Farmer and the Sailor

There is a sailor on the road. He looks at the farmer and asks:
S: Is there a farmhouse here? I must have water and dinner.
F: Perhaps. Where do you live?
S: I am a sailor. My home is Gaul.
F: Are you visiting Italy?
S: I am not visiting, but working.
F: Do you live in the water?
S: Hardly. I sail on the water, but I live on land.
F: Do you have money?
S: Yes.
F: Splendid. The farmer gives the sailor dinner, and the sailor gives the farmer money.
S: That's right.

Exercise J: Rewrite the Dialogue in the Plural

Sunt nautae in via. Spectant agricolam et rogant:
N: Estne villa hic? Debemus habere aquam et cenam.
A: Fortasse. Ubi habitatis?
N: Sumus nautae. Patria nostra est Gallia.
A: Visitatisne Italiam?
N: Non visitamus, sed laboramus.
A: Habitatisne in aqua?
N: Minime. Navigamus in aqua, sed habitamus in terra.
A: Habetisne pecuniam?
N: Habemus.
A: Optime. Agricola nautis cenam dat, agricolae pecuniam nautae dant.
N: Ita est.

LECTIO II : Uproar in the Farmer's House

The farmer is yelling: "Where is dinner? I am waiting for dinner. Get a move on! Who is supposed to fix dinner? Why do I have to wait? Why is the maid not working? Hurry, girls! Why are you sitting here? Why is dinner not on the table? Where is the chicken? Why is it not cooked? Where are the grapes? Are you laughing? Answer! Cat's got your tongues? I work and you are making merry. Give the farmer his food! Finally. Why must we drink water? I don't like water...Bad house, bad girls!"

Summarium:

1. function 2. Nominative 3. Direct Object 4. Dative 5. by, with, through, from, by means of
6. Nominative 7. second 8. No 9. Nominative 10. Yes 11. Number   12. Syncretism
13. three 14. masculine, feminine 15. feminine 16. **-is**

3

CAVE CANEM

NOUNS: 2ND OR O - DECLENSION
PREPOSITIONS

THE ORDER OF WORDS

We have seen that in heavily synthetic languages, such as Latin, nouns, verbs, and adjectives are marked with suffixes (and infixes, as you will see in the next chapter), to show case, gender, number, person, tense, and the like. Although the forms sometimes have to do double duty (SYNCRETISM), on the whole they are quite distinct. The order of words in the sentence is therefore of less importance than, say, in English; an Accusative (puellam) is an Accusative, no matter where it stands in the sentence. This can be illustrated with English Personal Pronouns. They are the most extensively marked words; this marking is done with suffixes, or by using what seems to be another word altogether: he - him; they - them; she - her; I - me. (This is also true for Latin Pronouns.) Therefore their case, gender, and number are always known:

He said this. 'My word', said he. Him I don't know. I don't know him. He doesn't know me. This he doesn't know. Ask her!

In these sentences word order can be used for emphasis, but there is no doubt as to subject and object. With nouns, on the other hand, word order is crucial in English, since the cases are mostly unmarked. 'The dog eats a bone' is certainly not the same as 'The bone eats a dog.' In Latin, on the other hand, nouns are as distinctly marked as English or Latin pronouns; word order is therefore not very important. The following six sentences then have the same meaning (with slight variations of emphasis):

Puella silvam spectat.	\	
Puella spectat silvam.	\	
Silvam spectat puella.	___\	The girl is looking
Silvam puella spectat.	/	at the forest.
Spectat puella silvam.	/	
Spectat silvam puella.	/	

When one switches the order of Subjects, Verbs, and Objects in English, one may change the meaning (He can't swim. -> Can't he swim? Dog eats bone. - Bone eats dog.) Or the sentence might become poetic, ungrammatical, or even unintelligible. (The girl is looking at the forest. -> Looking is at the forest the girl. -> *Forest girl the looking at is the.)

There are few rules for word order in Latin; actually they should be considered conventions rather than rules: the adjective stands after its noun, unless it is emphasized (vinum rubrum - wine red; canis fidus - the dog faithful); the verb can often be found at the end of its sentence or phrase, because the beginning and end of the sentence are places of special emphasis. That's the extent of it! Questions can consequently not be formed in Latin, as they can in English and many other languages, by switching the positions of the Verb and the Subject (She is hungry. -> Is she hungry?) Instead a 'question suffix' must be added to the first word of a Latin sentence, whatever that first word may be.

Chapter 3: NOUNS : THE SECOND DECLENSION; PREPOSITIONS

Like the 1st declension the 2nd is restricted in respect to endings and genders. three different endings occur in the nominative Singular: **-us, -um,** and **- -** (that is to say, **no ending**). Nouns ending in **-us** or **--**, such as **amicus**, *friend*, or **puer**, *boy*, are **masculine**; nouns ending in **-um**, like **donum**, *gift*, are **neuter**. There are a very few feminine nouns in the 2nd declension (for example **pinus**, *pine,* and all trees). Aside from the nominative and accusative Singular of neuters (which must be alike), and the nominative and accusative Plural of neuters (which must end in -a) the case endings are alike for all three types of nouns. An exception is the vocative Singular of the nouns ending in **-us**, which ends in **-e.**

	Masculine			**Neuter**	
	friend	*boy*	**Singular**	*gift*	
N	amic **us**	puer	|	don **um**	(the, a friend, boy, gift)
G	amic **i**	puer **i**	|	don **i**	(of the, a, friend 's)
D	amic **o**	puer **o**	|	don **o**	(to the, a friend)
A	amic **um**	puer **um**	|	don **um**	(the, a friend dir.obj)
V	amic **e**	puer	|	don **um**	(Oh friend)
Ab	ab amic **o**	a puer **o**	|	don **o**	(by, with, from the friend)
			Plural		
N	amic **i**	puer **i**	|	don **a**	(friends, boys, gifts)
G	amic **orum**	puer **orum**	|	don **orum**	etc.
D	amic **is**	puer **is**	|	don **is**	
A	amic **os**	puer **os**	|	don **a**	
V	amic **i**	puer **i**	|	don **a**	
Ab	ab amic **is**	a puer **is**	|	don **is**	

Vocabulary: The Nominative is followed by the Genitive ending, except for nouns which have no ending in the Nominative. For these the **entire** Genitive is given, because some of them keep the **-e-** of the stem in all cases (puer, **p**ueri), while others drop it (ag**e**r, agri). The Genitive tells you which is the case.

Latin	English	English Derivative
ager,agri	field	**agriculture**
amicus,i	friend	**amicable**
animus,i	spirit, mind, reason	**animated**
annus,i	year	**annual**
argentum,i	silver	**Argentina**
asinus,i	donkey	**asinine**
aurum,i	gold	**aureole**
avus,i	grandfather	**avuncular**
bellum,i	war	**bellicose**
caelum,i	sky, heaven	**celestial**
carrus,i	cart	**carriage**
castra,castrorum (Pl.only)	camp	**Win*chester*,**
cibus,i	food	**Lan*caster***
consilium,i	plan	**counsel**
Deus,i Voc.Sg:deus, Pl:di	god	**deity**
dominus,i	master, lord	**dominate**
donum,i	gift	**donate**
equus,i	horse	**equine**
ferrum,i	iron; sword	**ferrotype**
Filius,i Voc.Sg: fili	son	**filial**
forum,i	marketplace	**forum**
frumentum,i	grain	
gallus,i	rooster	
gaudium,i	joy	**gaudy**
hortus,i	garden	**horticulture**
imperium,i	realm, power	**imperial**
lectus,i	bed	
liber,libri	book	**library**
liberi,liberorum (Pl. only)	children	
ludus,i	game, school	**ludicrous**
magister,magistri	teacher	**master**
modus,i	way, method	**mode**
mundus,i	world	**mundane**
nuntius,i	messenger, message	**enuntiate**
officium,i	office, duty	**office**
oppidum,i	town, fortress	
periculum,i	danger	**peril**
populus,i	people	**popular**
pratum,i	meadow, pasture	
puer,pueri	boy	**puerile**
servus,i	slave, servant	**servant**
socius,i	comrade, ally	**sociable**

stabulum,i	stable	**stable**
studium,i	zeal	**studious**
templum,i	temple	**Templar**
ventus,i	wind	**vent**
vesper,vesperi	evening, Evening Star	**Vespers**
vicinus,i	neighbour	**vicinity**
vicus,i	village, alley	
vinum,i	wine	**wine**
vir, viri	man	**virile**

EXERCISE A: What they do: Translate the sentences

1. Vicini salutant vicinos.

2. Asini portant frumentum.

3. Amici potant vinum.

4. Magistri docent liberos.

5. Pueri non amant ludum; amant ludos.

6. Galli clamant et volant.

7. Servi semper laborant.

8. Equi ambulant in pratis.

9. Domini iacent in lecto et imperant.

10. Filii vident lunam et stellas.

11. Avi narrrant fabulas.

12. Viri sedent in villa et gaudent.

13. Dei (di) spectant viros et feminas et rident.

Now don't look and answer the questions with nouns and verbs. Watch the verb number!
('Quis' is always Singular):
All right, you can peek a little.

1. Quis ambulat in pratis? __Equi ambulant._   **2. Quis sedet in villa? _____**

3. Quis potat vinum? _____   **4. Quis iacet in lecto? _____**

5. Quis narrat fabulas? _____   **6. Quis docet liberos? _____**

7. Quis salutat vicinos? _____   **8. Quis portat frumentum? _____**

9. Quis semper laborat? _____   **10. Quis non amat ludum? _____**

11. Quis clamat et volat? _____   **12. Quis ridet? _____**

EXERCISE B: Practice your noun cases!

1. the friend _____   2. friends _____

3. a friend's _____   4. the friends' _____

5. in the farmhouse _____   6. the man _____

7. men (Acc.) _____   8. to the girls _____

9. of the woman _____   10. the women's _____

11. of the children _____   12. on the road (in + Abl.) _____

13. to the boy _____   14. in town _____

15. to the woman _____   16. the field _____

17. the field (Acc.) _____   18. with words _____

19. horses (Nom. and Acc.) _____   20. farmers (Nom. and Acc.) _____

21. the gate _____   22. on the island _____

23. to the island _____   24. trumpets _____

25. with trumpets _____   26. words (Nom. and Acc.) _____

27. of the gift _____   28. of the son _____

29. sons (Nom. and Acc.) _____   30. daughters (Nom. and Acc.) _____

31. gods (Nom. and Acc.) _____   32. of gods _____

33. to a god _____   34. from teachers _____

35. of the world _____   36. the word (Nom. and Acc.) _____

37. to the slave _____   38. with danger _____

39. of wars _____   40. in the year of the Lord _____

Quid vides?
See exercise G !

56 Introduction to Latin Language and Thought

EXERCISE C: **Translate** the sentences:

1. Amici amicos amant.
2. In caelo spectamus lunam et stellas.
3. Magister in ludo pueros et puellas docet.
4. Hodie cenam parare non debemus; servi cenam ab amicis portant.
5. Avus liberis libros donat; liberi gaudent.
6. Habemus equos in agris et gallos et gallinas in stabulo.
7. Neque viri neque feminae, neque liberi neque servi pericula belli amant.
8. Pueri amicus equum spectat.
9. Pueros portant equi, sed pueri non portant equos.
10. Habemus cibum, habemus vinum, gaudemus.

EXERCISE D: **Translate** into Latin:

1. Tullia is a girl. Marcus is the girl's friend.

2. Tullia is the daughter of the farmer and (his) wife.

3. They are the neighbors of Marcus.

4. The farmer's family lives in a farmhouse.

5. Tullia's grandfather also lives in the house.

6. The farmer has cows and horses, roosters, and hens in the stables.

7. Marcus visits the family often and works in the fields.

8. He is not a man of words, but he thinks much. (multum)

9. Sometimes he gives gifts to Tullia and the grandfather.

(1) Which nouns are the predicate subjects? In what case is 'girl's' and 'friend'?
(4) **Familia** is Singular! "in a farmhouse" - use **in + ablative.**
(5) Use **in + ablative.**
(6) Don't forget **direct objects !**
(9) "To Tullia" and "(to) the grandfather" are **indirect objects !**

Prepositions

Prepositions are words that help establish a **relationship** between **nouns** and **verbs** in a sentence. In English, prepositional phrases show case (**to** the men; **of** the house) as well as place, time, manner, circumstances, and so forth (behind, toward; after, during; besides; because of). As we have seen, prepositions are **not** used in Latin to form the noun cases. Latin prepositions refer in their basic meaning to **place** or **location**. From there, temporal, causal and circumstantial meaning are derived. Most Latin prepositions are followed by the **accusative** case of the noun, some by the **ablative**; two of the prepositions can have either case after them, depending on the meaning.

Mus, muris - mouse

A: Prepositions with the Accusative

Preposition	Meaning when referring to:		
	place	**time**	**other**
ad	to, towards, at, near	until	approximately
usque ad	up to	up to	
ante	before, in front of	before	
apud	at (someone's), with		
circa / circum	around	around	
contra	against		
extra	outside of	besides	
infra	under		
inter	between, among		
intra	within		
iuxta	next to		
ob	against, across		on account of, because of
per	through	during	by means of, thoroughly
post	after, behind	after	
praeter	past		besides
prope	near	near	
propter			on account of because of
secundum	along		according to
super / supra	above	beyond	beyond
trans	across, to the other side		
ultra	beyond, on the other side		

B: Prepositions with the Ablative

The word ablative is derived from a form of the verb **auferre**, *to carry away*, hence the ablative is also called the case of separation. With one exception, prepositions with the ablative have the meaning "from, away from, without, out of," and the like.

Preposition	Meaning when referring to:		
	place	time	other
ab (a) *	from, away from	since	
cum, una cum	with, together with		
de	(down) from		about, concerning
ex (e) *	out of	since	following
prae	before	before	
pro	before		for, instead of, in relation to, on behalf of
sine	without		

* **a** and **e** are used before nouns and pronouns that begin with consonants, **ab** and **ex** before those beginning with a vowel: **a puella, ab agricola; e templo**

C : Prepositions with Accusative and Ablative

These two prepositions use the **accusative**, whenever **movement** to a place is involved (question: whereto?), and **ablative** when a **location** is given (question: where?); their **temporal** meaning with the ablative is "during".

		Place	time	other
in	Acc:	into, to, onto, against		against
	Abl:	in, on, at	during	
sub	Acc:	under, close to to the foot of		
	Abl:	under, at the foot of	during	

Examples:

in insul**am**:	to the island (we sailed - whereto?) = **Acc.**
in amic**os**:	against friends (we acted hostile) = **Acc.**
in hort**o**:	in the garden (we sat - where?) = **Abl.**
sub mens**a**:	under the table (the dog lies - where?) = **Abl.**
sub mens**am** :	under the table (we throw the food for the dog - whereto?) = **Acc.**

EXERCISE E: Knowing the basic meaning of prepositions often helps in finding out the meaning of compound verbs. What would be most likely the meaning of
the following verbs:

1. transportare
2. circumdare
3. circumsedere
4. adesse
5. abesse
6. superesse
7. adiuvare
8. circumspectare
9. obesse
10. permovere

EXERCISE F: Many of these prepositions have similar meanings in English. Give the meaning of the
prepositional prefix in the following words (L. **ae** -> E. **e**)

1. **preter**natural _____   2. **post**modern _____

3. **ultra**conservative _____   4. **iuxta**position _____

5. **super**fluous _____   6. **circum**vent _____

7. **intra**murals _____   8. **ante**bellum _____

9. **trans**continental _____   10. **ob**stacle _____

11. **contra**dict _____   12. **inter**continental _____

13. **per**mutation _____   14. **ex**pel _____

15. **sub**terranean _____   16. **de**formed _____

17. **ab**sence _____   18. **ad**dress _____

19. **infra**structure _____   20. **pre**recorded _____

EXERCISE G: From the picture on page 55, name as many objects or people in Latin as you can!
Put your answers in the **Accusative** Singular or Plural!

Video: _____

_____

_____

_____

EXERCISE H: Translate:

1. sub terra _____   2. in culinam _____

3. ad (in) insulam _____   4. cum amicis _____

5. ab agro _____   6. trans patriam _____

7. ad silvam _____
8. De Bello Gallico (Gallicus = Gallic, of Gaul)

_____

9. sine vino _____   10. apud Romanos _____

11. praeter hortum _____   12. ante bellum _____

13. Evangelium secundum Matthaeum (Evangelium = Gospel) _____

14. prope villam _____

15. Hannibal ad portas! (sometimes 'ante') _____

16. usque ad vesperum _____   17. intra muros [*walls*]_____

18. propter gratiam tuam _____   19. iuxta avum _____

20. ex oppido _____   21. per aquam _____

22. post cenam _____   23. pro cibo _____

EXERCISE I :   Put the noun into the Plural (same case!) and translate the Singular forms:

1. in oppidum   ___in_oppida_____   _____into the town_____
2. in aquam   _____   _____

3. in aqua   _____   _____
4. ab silva   _____   _____

5. ex villa   _____   _____
6. sub oppidum   _____   _____

7. in bello   _____   _____
8. in periculum   _____   _____

9. cum puella   _____   _____
10. sine puero   _____   _____

| EXERCISE J: | Answer the questions with Latin sentences: |

1. Ubi laborant servi? (in the fields)
2. Quo volant galli? (into the house)
3. Quo navigant nautae? (to the island)
4. Ubi Marcus habitat? (next to (his) friend)
5. Ubi sunt pueri? (in school)
6. Unde volant gallinae? (out of the stable)
7. Unde volant galli? (down from the farmhouse)
8. Ubi est equus? (behind the house)
9. Ubi sedet avus (in front of the house)
10. Ubi est caelum? (above the house)
11. Ubi ambulamus? (in the forests)
12. Quo ambulamus? (into the forests)
13. Ubi habitat puella? (in town)
14. Ubi iacet gallus? (under the table)
15. Quo debemus portare aquam? (from the garden to the kitchen)
16. Ubi stat asinus? (in the road)

Remember: **unde** - from where; **ubi** - where; **quo** - whereto
to a person = dative; **to** a place = ad or in + accusative

Lectio I

Ubi habitat puella? *In villa iuxta castellum. Ambulamus cum asino per vicum ad villam praeter casas et inter agros agricolarum. Portamus donum pro puella, et vinum pro familia. Asinus stat ante villam et exspectat cibum et aquam. Non videt gallos et gallinas: sunt post casam et habent frumentum. Puellae familia nos (us) invitat in villam. Intramus et sedemus circa mensam. Potamus vinum et ridemus et gaudemus.*

EXERCISE K :	Match the descriptions with English words which use Latin Prepositions as prefixes (cf. Exercise F)

1. Rays that are "under" the visible spectrum of colors, lower than red: _____

2. Medical care one gets after an operation: _____

3. A person who keeps to himself, concentrates on his own thoughts and feelings: _____

4. And a person who is gregarious and outgoing: _____

5. Someone who is under you in rank: _____

6. Something which occurred before recorded time: _____

7. Something besides the normal curriculum: _____

8. What you get when you measure around an object: _____

9. Rays "beyond" the spectrum: _____

10. A room where you wait, before seeing the king: _____

EXERCISE L:	What is the opposite? (Careful, sometimes the case changes!)

1. post cenam _____

2. supra aquam _____

3. ab insula _____

4. contra amicum (use: "on behalf of ") _____

5. in casam _____

6. ante portas _____

7. extra muros _____

8. cum femina _____

Lectio II : Tumultus in Casa Agricolae (Part II of Soap Opera)

Cur dominus semper clamat et non gaudet? Ubi est domina?
Non est in casa, est in oppido cum amicis.
Calamitas in casa! Servi et ancillae non laborant.
Nemo est in culina. Liberi clamant et pugnant.
5   Dominus monet liberos:
"Tace, Claudia! Tacete, Quinte, Rufe, Luci! Pare, Iulia!"
Liberi rident. Non amant laborare, sed amant ludos.
Gallus et gallinae volant in casa et sedent in mensa.
Asinus stat iuxta portam et clamat: I-A-I-A, quod frumentum
10   de agris in casam portare non amat.
Nihil cibi; nihil vini; nihil aquae.
Avus iacet in lecto et flet:
"Mala domina, mali liberi, malus servus,
malae feminae, mala casa, malus mundus!
15   Iuvate, di immortales!"

(2) amicis = (Abl.(and Dat.) Pl. both of amicus and of amica, male or female friend)
    deus and dea on the other hand have different Dat. and Abl.: deis (**m**), deabus (**f.**)
(3) calamitas - calamity; culina - kitchen
(6) Luci - (Vocative of Lucius);
    nihil cibi - lit. nothing of food; no food
(13) mala, mali, malus, etc. - bad;   (15) iuvare - to help
    di - vocative Plural of deus, god: gods!

Lectio III   *PICNIC*

Ambulat agricola, *Ambulat cum femina.* *Cur non habent carrum?* *Cur non habent equum?* *Servi, servae, ubi sunt?* *Ambulant post casam.* *Ambulant in silvam.*	*Sedent extra muros.* *Iacent mox in herba.* *Edunt cibum bonum.* *Potant vinum rubrum.* *Vident caelum pulchrum.* *Gaudent...*

murus,i - wall; mox - soon; edunt - they eat; bonum - good; rubrum - red;
pulchrum - beautiful

Lectio IV : Colloquium: Quattuor (*four*) Animalia: Gallus, Gallina, Equus, Asinus

Gallus:	Ego sum optimus. Volo ad caelum. Gaudeo. Canto...	
Gallina:	Non cantas! Clamas, stupide! Sed ego canto et volo et ova produco. Ego sum optima.	
Equus:	Ego etiam canto...	
Gallus et		
Gallina:	Minime! Non cantas. Ne canta! (Noli cantare!) Tace!	**5**
Equus:	Sed ego laboro. Porto filios filiasque domini in forum, ambulo ante carrum, visito avum in oppido, pugno in bello, propero in pratum cum liberis. Sum optimus.	
Asinus:	(tacet)	
Gallus:	Sed tu, asine? Responde! Volasne?	**10**
Asinus:	Non volo...	
Gallina:	Ovane producis?	
Asinus:	Minime.	
Equus:	Nonne in pericula belli festinas?	
Asinus:	Non festino...	**15**
Gallus:	Quid ergo? Ubi habitas?	
Asinus:	In stabulo habito.	
Gallina:	Habesne lectum?	
Asinus:	Lectus meus est herba.	
Equus:	Cibumne habes?	**20**
Asinus:	Habeo frumentum pro cibo.	
Gallus:	Habesne officium?	
Asinus:	Officium meum est laborare in agris et portare frumentum.	
Gallina:	Potasne vinum?	
Asinus:	Es gallina stupida! Vinum est pro domino. Poto aquam.	**25**
	Et sum optimum animal.	
Gallus et Gallina		
et Equus:	Cur es?	
Asinus:	Vos non cantatis, sed ego canto! I-AAAAA. I-AAAAA.	

---

animal (3rd Declension, neuter) - animal (animalia is Nom. or Acc. Pl); (1) optimus,a,um - (the) best; (2) ovum,i - egg; producere (3rd Conjugation) - to produce; (7) pratum - Meadow; (12) producis - you produce; (16) ergo - therefore, then.

A. Answer the questions or fill in the blanks:

1. The characteristic stem-vowel of the 2nd Declension is ____.

2. **Which 3 endings are possible in the Nominative Singular of the 2nd**

   Declension? _____, _____, and _____.

3. Nouns ending in _____ and _____ are masculine, nouns ending in _____ are neuter.

4. In addition to the nominative and vocative Singular, neuter nouns also differ

   from masculine nouns in the _____ and _____ Plural.

5. Of the nouns **amicus, puer, donum**, the one with a separate vocative Singular

   form is _____.

6. Latin prepositions are followed by either the _____ or

   the _____ case, or both.

7. Since the ablative is the case of separation, prepositions with the ablative

   usually have the basic meaning _____.

8. Of the prepositions **prae, per, praeter, pro**, the two meaning *before* are

   _____ and _____.

9. Is the basic meaning of Latin prepositions time, place, or circumstances? _____

10. The prepositions in and sub when expressing direction use the _____

    case, to express location they use the _____ case.

11. The preposition prae appears in English as the prefix _____. (Twice in this sentence!)

12. **The Vocative Singular of Lucius is _____, the Vocative Plural**

    of deus is _____.

B. Review the Words:

animus - annus - caelum - cibus - cena - frumentum - hortus - pratum - periculum - ventus - vesper - vicinus - imperium - gaudium - secundum - propter - usque ad

C. Supply the **male** counterparts:

        Feminine   Masculine
          serva
          domina
          dea
          gallina
          filia
          ava
          anima (´soul ´)
          amica
          femina
          puella

D. Don´t confuse:

  liberi - libri; modus - mundus; carrus - castra; prope - propter; prae - praeter; intra - infra; intra - inter; prae - pro.

E. Who are these people (in English)?

      vir _____; ancilla _____; nuntius _____;

      socius _____; populus _____; magister _____;

      vicinus _____; amicus _____; puer _____.

Housing and Living in the City

Housing conditions were quite varied in Rome and Italy. Well-to-do people lived in private houses (DOMUS) built for one family and their household, including slaves. Sometimes shops (TABERNA) were located in the front part of the house. These houses had their rooms grouped around a central court-yard, the ATRIUM. One entered the atrium from the street, through a small vestibule (VESTIBULUM) and a hallway (OSTIUM). From the atrium the other rooms were reached: the dining-room (TRICLINIUM), bedrooms (CUBICULUM), and kitchen (CULINA). To the rear of the atrium lay a big work-room (TABLINIUM), and behind it there was a small garden, which was often surrounded by a covered walkway (PERISTYLUM). The servants sometimes had living-quarters on a second floor, in small rooms. There were no windows facing the street, only shops open to the street. These shops were sometimes leased to artisans or tradesmen. The kitchen often served also as a toilet-room. The floor of the house was made either of marble, or of mosaics, cement, or brick.

Here is how Mark Twain saw what was left of the 'sumptious private mansions' in Pompeii after the eruption of Vesuvius: [mansions]

> which we could not have entered without a formal invitation in uncomprehensible Latin, in the olden times, when the owners lived there - and we probably wouldn't have got it. These people built their houses a good deal alike. The floors were laid in fanciful figures wrought in mosaics of many-colored marbles. At the threshold your eyes fall upon a Latin sentence of welcome, sometimes, or a picture of a dog, with the legend 'Beware of the Dog', and sometimes a picture of a bear or a faun with no inscription at all. Then you enter a sort of vestibule, where they used to keep the hat-rack, I suppose; next a room with a large marble basin in the midst and the pipes of a fountain; on either side are bedrooms; beyond the fountain is a reception-room, then a little garden dining-room, and so forth and so on. The floors were all mosaic, the walls were stuccoed, or frescoed, or ornamented with bas-reliefs, and here and there were statues, large and small, and little fish-pools, and cascades of sparkling water that sprang from secret places in the colonnade of handsome pillars that surrounded the court, and kept the flower-beds fresh and the air cool.
> (Mark Twain, *The Innocents Abroad,* New York, p.227 f.)

The houses of rich people had an elaborate heating system, the HYPOCAUSTUM (Greek, meaning *heat from below*. A hollow space under the floor and inside the walls was heated from a stove outside the house. The air circulated through openings in the walls.

Less wealthy people used coal-pans, which rested on high or low tripods. In Pompeii heating basins were found which also heated warm water and dispensed it through faucets. The hearth in the kitchen was often used for heating, too.

Hypocaustum in Kos, Greece

Coalpan on tripod from Pompeii

Poor Romans lived in tenements (INSULAE), which were meant to alleviate the housing crunch in Rome. They were often constructed so shoddily that they fell to ruin after a few years; nevertheless rents were very high. The poet Juvenal claimed that for a year's apartment rent in Rome one could buy a whole house in the country. Rent-gouging by hired middlemen was rampant, and many people had to sublet a room to make ends meet.

The tenement buildings were rather narrow and comparatively high, up to sixty feet; usually they comprised three to four stories. The higher levels could be reached by outside stone stairs. The apartments, which consisted of one or several rooms, had large windows or porches facing the street, but they could barely be heated and were not very sanitary. They had neither kitchens nor baths and as a rule no toilets. But not to worry: people bought most of their food already cooked in shops or at street stands, public baths were abundant, public fountains supplied good water, and public toilet facilities could be used - for a fee.

Since many people heated or cooked in open receptacles, house fires were common. At the time of Augustus an effective fire brigade of seven thousand men was formed in Rome (VIGILES). They also served as police. In other cities the fire department consisted of rag-collectors, who suffocated the fires with blankets and rags, or of construction workers with axes and ladders. Many Romans complained that fire departments were located close to rich people's homes, while they never made it to the tenements in time to prevent them from burning to the ground.

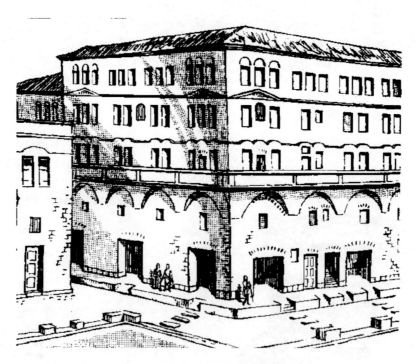

Roman Tenement Housing (Reconstruction)

Chapter 3 : Answers and Translations

Exercise A:

1. Neighbors greet neighbors. 2. Donkeys carry grain. 3. Friends drink wine.
4. Teachers teach children. 5. Boys don't like school; they like games. 6. Roosters scream and fly.
7. Slaves always work. 8. Horses walk in the meadows. 9. Masters lie on the bed and give orders.
10. Sons see the moon and the stars. 11. Grandfathers tell stories. 12. Men sit in the farmhauses
and rejoice. 13. The gods look at men and women and laugh.

Exercise B:

1. amicus 2. amici 3. amici 4. amicorum 5. in villa 6. vir 7. viros 8. puellis 9. feminae
10. feminarum 11. liberorum 12. in via 13. puero 14. in oppido 15. feminae 16. ager 17. agrum
18. verbis 19. equi, equos 20. agricolae, agricolas 21. porta 22. in insula 23. ad insulam
24. tubae 25. tubis 26. verba, verba 27. doni 28. filii 29. filii, filios 30. filiae, filias 31. dei (di),
deos 32 deorum 33. deo 34. a magistris 35. mundi 36. verbum, verbum 37. servo 38. periculo
39. bellorum 40. Anno Domini

Exercise C:

1. Friends love friends. 2. In the sky we look at the moon and stars.   3. The teacher teaches boys
and girls in school. 4. Today we don't have to prepare dinner; the slaves are bringing dinner from
friends. 5. Grandfather gives (some) books to the children; the children are happy.   6. We have
horses in the fields and roosters and hens in the stable.   7. Neither men nor women, neither
children nor slaves like the dangers of war. 8. The boy's friend looks at the horse. 9. Horses carry
boys, but boys don't carry horses. 10. We have food, we have wine, we are happy.

Exercise D:

1. Tullia est puella. Marcus est puellae amicus. 2. Tullia est filia agricolae et feminae.
3. Sunt vicini Marci.   4. Familia agricolae habitat in villa. 5. Avus Tulliae quoque habitat in villa.
6. Agricola vaccas, equos, gallos, et gallinas in stabulis habet. 7. Marcus familiam saepe visitat et
in agris laborat. 8. Non est vir verborum, sed multum cogitat. 9. Aliquando Tulliae et avo dona dat.

Exercise E: 1. to carry across 2. to surround 3. to sit around 4. to be near 5. to be away 6. to be
away 7. to help 8. to look around 9. to be against 10. to move thoroughly

Exercise G: Quid vides: Video feminam, casas, pratum, caelum, elephantum, viros, tubam,
insulam, aquam, lunam, stellam, lectum, gallum, cibum, vinum, mensam, librum, litteras, liberos,
puerum, puellas, viam, carrum, equum.

Exercise H:

1. underground 2. into the kitchen 3. to the island 4. with friends 5. from the field 6. across the
fatherland 7. to the forest 8. About the Gallic War (written by Caesar) 9. without wine 10. at (with)
the Romans' 11. past the garden 12. before the war 13. The Gospel according to Matthew
14. near the farmhouse 15. Hannibal (is) at the gates 16. until evening 17. within the walls
18. because of your thankfulness   19. next to the grandfather 20. from, out of the town
21. through the water 22. after the meal 23. for, instead of food

Exercise I :

1. in oppida (into the town) 2. in aquas (into the water) 3. in aquis (in the water) 4. ab silvis (from
the forest) 5. ex villis (out of the farmhouse) 6. sub oppida (to the foot of the town) 7. in bellis (in
the war) 8. in pericula (into danger) 9. cum puellis (with a girl) 10. sine pueris (without the boy)

Exercise J: 1. Servi laborant in agris. 2. Galli volant in villam. 3. Nautae navigant ad insulam.
4. Marcus habitat iuxta amicum. 5. Pueri sunt in ludo. 6. Gallinae volant ex stabulo. 7. Galli volant
de villa. 8. Equus est post villam. 9. Avus sedet ante villam. 10. Caelum est supra villam.
11. Ambulamus in silvis. 12. Ambulamus in silvas. 13. Puella habitat in oppido. 14. Gallus iacet

sub mensa. 15. Aquam ab horto in culinam portare debemus. 16. Asinus stat in via.
Exercise K:
1. infrared 2. postoperative 3. introvert 4. extrovert 5. subordinate 6. prehistoric
7. extracurricular 8. circumference 9. ultraviolet 10. antechamber
Exercise L:
1. ante cenam 2. sub aqua(m) 3. ad insulam 4. pro amico 5. ex casa 6. post portas 7. intra muros 8. sine femina

Reading 1: Ubi habitat puella.

Where does the girl live? In the farmhouse nect to the castellum. We walk with our donkey through the village past the houses and between the fields of the farmers. We are carrying a gift for the girl and wine for the family. The donkey is standing in front of the farmhouse and expects food and water. He doesn't see the roosters and hens: they are behind the house and have grain. The family of the girl invites us into the house. We step in and sit around the table. We drink wine and laugh and are happy.

Reading 2 : Uproar in the House

Why is the master always yelling and is not happy? Where is the mistress? She is not in the house, she is in town with her friends. Disaster in the house! The slaves and maids are not working. Nobody is in the kitchen. The children scream and fight. The master warns the children: "Be quiet, Claudia! Hush, Quintus, Rufus, Lucius! Obey, Julia!" The children are laughing. They don't like to work, they like games. The rooster and the hens fly around in the house and sit on the table. The donkey stands next to the door and brays: IA - IA, because he does not like to carry the grain from the fields into the house. (There is) no food, no wine, no water. Grandfather is lying in his bed and crying: "Bad mistress, bad children, bad slave, bad women, bad house, bad world! Help, immortal gods!

Reading 3: PICNIC

The farmer walks, he walks with his wife. Why have they no cart? Why have they no horse? Where are the children? The slaves and maids, where are they? They walk behind the house, they walk into the forest. They sit outside the walls, soon they lie in the grass. They eat good food, they drink red wine, they see the beautiful sky. They are having fun...

Reading 4: The Rooster, the Hen, the Horse, the donkey.

Rooster: I am the greatest (best). I fly (up) to the sky. I am happy. I sing...   **Hen:** You don't sing! You scream, stupid! But I sing and fly and produce eggs. I am the greatest.   **Horse:** I sing, too!
Rooster and **Hen:** No way! You don't sing. Don't sing! Be quiet!   **Horse:** But I work. I carry the sons and daughters of the master to the market, I walk before the cart, I visit the grandfather in town, I fight in the war, I run (hurry) into the meadow with the children. I am the best.   **Donkey:** (is quiet)   **Rooster:** But you, donkey? Answer! Do you fly?   **Donkey:** I don't fly...   **Hen:** Do you produce eggs?   **Donkey**: Of course not.   **Horse:** Don't you hurry into the dangers of war?
Donkey: I don't hurry...   **Rooster:** What then? Where do you live?   **Donkey:** I live in a stable.
Hen: Do you have a bed? **Donkey:** My bed is the grass.   **Horse:** Do you have food?   **Donkey:** I have grain as food.   **Rooster:** Do you have a duty?   **Donkey:** My duty is working in the fields and carrying grain.   **Hen:** Do you drink wine?   **Donkey:** You are a stupid hen! The wine is for the master. I drink water. And I am the best animal. **Rooster** and **Hen** and **Horse:** Why is that?
Donkey: You all don't sing, but I sing! I-AAAAAA. I-AAAAAA.
Summary: 1. -o- 2. -us, --, -um 3. us, --; -um; 4. nom., acc.; 5. amicus 6. acc., abl.
7. from 8. prae, pro 9. place 10. acc., abl. 11. pre- 12.Luci; di.

4

IMPERFECT AND FUTURE TENSES
IRE: COMPOUNDS OF ESSE: POSSE

LANGUAGE FAMILIES OF THE WORLD

Most estimates put the number of languages in the world around 4000, a relatively small number considering that there are more than 5 billion people to speak them. Many of these languages are related to each other and are grouped into language famlies by linguists. The **Indo-European** language family, to which Latin belongs, is but one family of many, but its languages are among the most widely spoken: English, Hindi (spoken by ca. 280 million people in India), Spanish, Russian, Bengali (spoken by 170 million in Bangladesh and India), Portuguese, German, and French are some examples. Of the ten most populous languages only Chinese, Japanese, and Arabic are not Indo-European.

There are also a handful of non-Indo-European languages in Europe: Turkish belongs to the Altaic family, which has Japanese, Korean, and Mongolian in it. Hungarian, Finnish, Lap (in Northern Scandinavia), and Estonian (which is not a Baltic language like Latvian and Lithuanian) are Uralic languages. The Basque language, which is spoken in the coastal areas of Northern Spain and Southern France, is a **language isolate**, so called, because it cannot be related to any other language in the world. Etruscan, an ancient language spoken in Italy before Rome and Latin became powerful, is also considered a language isolate. Because of the scarcity of its written material it can not yet be understood properly.

Besides the Indo-European family, some other large language families in the world (with some members given in parentheses) are:

Amerindian, with numerous subfamilies, e.g.

       Algonquian (Blackfoot, Cree, Cheyenne), **Athapascan** (Apache, Navajo),
       Iroquoian (Cherokee), **Uto-Aztecan** (Hopi, Aztec), and **Mayan.**

Afro-Asiatic (Arabic, Hebrew, Amharic, Somali)

Niger-Kordofanian (Swahili, Yoruba, Ibo, Zulu, Ewe)

Sino-Tibetan (Mandarin, Cantonese, Hakka, Wu, Tibetan, Burmese)

Altaic (Japanese, Korean, Mongolian, Tartar, Turkish, Uzbek)

Austro-Tai (Indonesian, Javanese, Thai, Tagalog, Malay, Malagasy, Fijian,
       Hawaiian, Samoan, Maori, Tahitian)

Among these the Chinese languages are used by nearly one billion speakers; the Apache language, on the other hand, is thought to have less than 10 speakers.

Chapter 4: IMPERFECT AND FUTURE TENSES

Using the **present stem** of the verbs you have learned, you can also form the **imperfect** and **future** Tenses, using **infixes** that are characteristic for the tense. The infix for the imperfect is **-ba-**, for the future it is **-bi- (**also has the variations **-b-, be-, bu-)**. These infixes are put between the stem and the endings, like this:

THE IMPERFECT

		portá **ba** m	I carried, I used to carry, I was carrying
Sg.		portá **ba** s	you carried, used to carry, etc.
		portá **ba** t	he/she/it carried
		porta **bá** mus	we carried
Pl.		porta **bá** tis	you carried
		portá **ba** nt	they carried
		docé **ba** m	I taught, used to teach, was teaching
Sg.		docé **ba** s	you taught, etc.
		docé **ba** t	he/she/it taught
		doce **bá** mus	we taught
Pl.		doce **bá** tis	you taught
		docé **ba** nt	they taught

The **imperfect** is used to show actions that are **continuous, habitual, repeated, or attempted** or **started** in the **past** ("imperfect" = not finished).

EXERCISE A: Translate, picking the version you think most appropriate: ("was ...ing", "used to", or simply past tense)

1. amabat
2. videbatis
3. dabas
4. habebant
5. timebamus
6. Nauta semper navigabat in insulam.
7. Portabamus aquam in casam, sed nunc habemus asinum.
8. Laborabam plus, nunc laboro minus. (plus - more; minus - less)
9. Ubi habitabat Claudia? Habitabat in Italia.
10. Pueri et puellae cantabant.

THE FUTURE TENSE

	portá **b** o	I will (shall) carry, I will be carrying
Sg	portá **bi** s	you will carry, etc.
	portá **bi** t	he/she/it will carry
	portá **bi** mus	we will carry
Pl	portá **bi** tis	you will carry
	portá **bu** nt	they will carry
	docé **b** o	I will (shall) teach, I will be teaching
Sg	docé **bi** s	you will teach, etc.
	docé **bi** t	he/she/it will teach
	docé **bi** mus	we will teach
Pl	docé **bi** tis	you will teach
	docé **bu** nt	they will teach

The future tense is translated as "will" (shall), "will be ...ing", or "going to ..."

| EXERCISE B: | Translate: |

1. dabis   2. flebo   3. Spectabitis stellas.   4. Movebit mensam.
5. Potabimus vinum, sed potabamus aquam.   6. Laudabit agricola poetas.
7. Agricolae sedebunt in villa; laborabant.   8. Pecuniam habebimus.
9. Parabisne cenam? Parabo.   10. Gaudebitis et valebitis.

The **Imperfect** and **Future** of esse, *to be*

	éram	I was	**éro**	I will be
Sg	**éras**	you were	**éris**	you will be
	érat	he/she/it was; there was; ...was	**érit**	he/she/it will be; there will be; ...will be
	erámus	we were	**érimus**	we will be
Pl	**erátis**	you were	**éritis**	you will be
	érant	they were; there were; ...were	**érunt**	they will be; there will be; ...will be

Note that the vowel for the **past** is still **-a-** (*was*), and for the **future -i-(-u-)** (*will*)

Here are some more useful **adverbs:**

hodie today   **cras** tomorrow   **heri** yesterday
interea meanwhile, in the meantime   **postea** later, afterward
                                                          (but:**post** - *after* = Preposition)

 **EXERCISE C:**   The Farmhouse. Say in Latin:

1. Where was (your) friend yesterday?
2. He was in town.
3. Where were you (Sg) meanwhile?
4. I was in (my) farmhouse.
5. Will you all (Pl) be there in the evening? [no preposition]
6. We will be there tomorrow.
7. Why are you (Sg) not in the farmhouse now?
8. I am often not there, but I will be there today.
9. Is (your) friend there now?
10. No, he is always in town when I am in the farmhouse.

The verb Ire, *to go*

The verb **ire,** *to go,* has an irregular present tense in Latin; the imperfect and future are regular:

Present

Sg	1.	**eo**	I go, I am going
	2.	**is**	you go, are going
	3.	**it**	he/she/it goes, is going
Pl	1.	**imus**	we go, are going
	2.	**itis**	you go, are going
	3.	**eunt**	they go, are going

The **imperatives** are **i !** and **ite !** - *Go!*

Imperfect			Future		
Sg	1. **ibam**	I went		1. **ibo**	I will go
	2. **ibas**	you went		2. **ibis**	you will go
	3. **ibat**	he/she/it went		3. **ibit**	he/she/it will go
Pl	1. **ibamus**	we went		1. **ibimus**	we will go
	2. **ibatis**	you went		2. **ibitis**	you will go
	3. **ibant**	they went		3. **ibunt**	they will go

Compounds of esse; posse

Just like other verbs, **esse** and **ire** are often combined with prepositions to form new verbs with meanings related to, but different from, the root verb. They are conjugated like **esse** and **ire**. Some common ones are:

> ## Compounds of esse, *to be*
>
> | | | |
> |---|---|---|
> | **abesse** | to be away | (absum, aberam, abero) |
> | **adesse** | to be present | (adsum, aderam; adero) |
> | **deesse** | to be lacking, missing | etc. |
> | **interesse** | to be present, take part | |
> | **obesse** | to harm (*to be against*) | |
> | **posse** | to be able [see below] | |
> | **praeesse** | to be in charge (*to be before*) (+ Dative) | |
> | **prodesse** | to be useful (*to be for*) [drop the -d- before consonants] | |
> | **superesse** | to be left over (*above the number required*) | |

Posse *to be able*

This verb, whose infinitive was contracted from # potesse #, consists of a prefix with the meaning "powerful", and the verb **esse**; this prefix has two alternate forms: **pos-** before **-s-** , and **pot-** before vowels (that is to say, for the entire imperfect and future tenses). The conjugation then is:

> ### Present
>
> | | | | |
> |---|---|---|---|
> | Sg | 1. **pos sum** | I can, I am able | |
> | | 2. **pot es** | you can, you are able | |
> | | 3. **pot est** | he/she/it can, is able | |
> | | | | |
> | Pl | 1. **pos sumus** | we can, we are able | |
> | | 2. **pot estis** | you can, you are able | |
> | | 3. **pos sunt** | they can, they are able | |
>
> | | | Imperfect | | | Future | |
> |---|---|---|---|---|---|---|
> | Sg | 1. | **pot eram** | I could, was able | **pot ero** | I will be able |
> | | 2. | **pot eras** | | **pot eris** | |
> | | 3. | **pot erat** | | **pot erit** | |
> | | | | | | |
> | Pl | 1. | **poteramus** | | **poterimus** | |
> | | 2. | **poteratis** | | **poteritis** | |
> | | 3. | **poterant** | | **poterunt** | |

Compounds of ire, *to go*

abire	to go away
adire	to go toward
exire	to go out of, leave
inire	to go in; to begin
interire	to perish, to go "among" the dead (also **perire**)
obire	to go toward, meet; also: to die (meet death)
perire	to perish
praeterire	to pass over, pass by, omit
redire	to go back, return

Do not confuse:

abesse - **abire**:	to **be** away -	to **go** away
adesse - **adire**:	to **be** present -	to **go** toward
interesse - **interire**:	to **be** present -	to **go** under, perish
obesse - **obire**:	to **be** against -	to **go** toward (meet)
	(= harm)	

Now memorize the others according to their prepositions:

de means **from**; **de**esse means to be (away) ___*from*__, (lacking)

prae means **before**; **prae**esse means to be _____, (in charge)

pro means **for**; **pro**desse means to be _____, (useful)

super means **over**; **super**esse means to be (left) _____

ex means **out**; **ex**ire means to go _____;

in means **in**; **in**ire means to go _____; (also start)

perire just sounds like **perish**

praeter means **past**; **praeter**ire means to go _____, (also omit)

re, not a preposition, means **back, again**; **re**dire = to go _____

EXERCISE D: Translate:

1. absumus _____

2. adest _____

3. adit _____

4. poterat _____

5. redeunt _____

6. oberitis _____

7. prosumus _____

8. praetereo _____

9. interest _____

10. possunt _____

11. abi _____

12. supererunt _____

13. we will be present _____

14. it was lacking _____

15. are you returning? (Sg) _____

16. he used to be here _____

17. we ought to begin _____

18. you are present (Sg) _____

19. you are meeting (Sg) _____

20. perish! (Sg) [2 verbs] _____ _____

21. They can be here [= present] today. _____

22. They were not able to go out of the house [use ex] yesterday.

_____

23. she was calling _____ 24. you will look (Pl) _____

25. You will be able to see the fields.(Sg) _____

26. She used to give the children grapes. _____

27. I shall sail to Italy. _____

28. The boy loved the girl, but the girl did not love the boy.

_____

29. They are not looking at the teacher; look, children, at the teacher!

_____

30. We will go to town tomorrow, and we will visit grandfather.

_____

Lectio I : In Casa Avi

Cras visitabimus avum. Ibimus in silvam, ad casam avi. Intrabimus in casam, salutabimus avum, avo donum dabimus et casam spectabimus. Avus cenam parabit. Post cenam in silva ambulabimus et avus nobis [to us] herbas monstrabit et docebit nos [us] de herbis. Poterimus navigare etiam ad insulam. Vespero redibimus in casam. Potabimus vinum et avus narrabit fabulas de silvis et aquis. Ridebimus et gaudebimus.

Lectio II : Amicus Noster Lucius

Ubi eramus liberi, nos, Rufus et Claudia, habitabamus in insula. Ibi villam habebamus. Amabamus insulam. Saepe ambulabamus in silva aut navigabamus cum avo, qui fabulas de aqua et de silvis narrabat. Interdum amicos et amicas
5 invitabamus et amicis insulam monstrabamus. Ancilla cenam parabat.
Habebamus quoque amicum nomine Lucii. Lucius erat asinus. Vocabamus Lucium: "Luci, Luci!" Lucius respondebat: "I-AAAA". Exspectabamus Lucium, sed Lucius neque parebat neque movebat. Iacebat in herbis aut sedebat in prato.
Debebamus igitur ambulare in pratum et captare Lucium. Tum Lucius portabat
10 nos liberos, Claudiam et Rufum, et amicos amicasque. Ambulabat lente per silvam. Caelum et prata videbamus et gaudebamus. Subito Lucius aquam spectabat, et subito festinabat ad aquam, clamabat et movebat caudam. Aquam valde amabat.
Nos sedebamus in asino, timebamus periculum, orabamus, flebamus et caudam
15 Lucii tenebamus. "Sta, Luci! Sta!" vocabamus. Prope aquam Lucius subito stabat. Nos cadebamus et iacebamus in aqua.
Lucius innocens potabat aquam et - ridebat!

==

Translate the Imperfect as a habitual past: "used to" or "would". (2) ubi - when, where; Nos - we; (4) interdum - in the meantime; (5) nomine - by the name of; (7) neque...neque.. neither...nor... (8) igitur - therefore; tum - then; (9) lente - slowly; (11) cauda,ae - tail; (12) valde - very (much); (15) cadere (3rd Conj.) - to fall; (16) innocens - innocent

---

Prologus (Joannes I : 1-5)

In principio erat Verbum, et Verbum erat apud Deum,	beginning
Et Deus erat Verbum.	
Hoc erat in principio apud Deum.	this
Omnia per ipsum facta sunt:	all things/ him(self)/ were made
Et sine ipso factum est nihil, quod factum est.	nothing
In ipso vita erat, et vita erat lux hominum:	light / of people
Et lux in tenebris lucet,	darkness / lights, shines
Et tenebrae eum non comprehenderunt.	did comprehend

Responde Latine (whole sentences, please): (to Reading II)
If you want to use dependent clauses: **quod** = because

1. Ubi habitabant Rufus et Claudia? _____

2. Habebant casam? _____

3. Eratne Rufus puella? _____

4. Ubi ambulabant liberi? _____

5. Quid erat Lucius, asinus aut puer? _____

6. Quid liberi amicis monstrabant ? _____

7. Quis parabat cenam? _____

8. Quomodo respondebat Lucius, ubi liberi vocabant? _____

9. Quis Lucium captare debebat? _____

10. Ubi Lucius sedere amabat? _____

11. Quid liberi videbant in silva? _____

12. Cur Lucius subito festinabat? _____

13. Quid Lucius amabat? _____

14. Cur liberi flebant? _____

15. Quid liberi vocabant? _____

16. Ubi Lucius subito stabat? _____

17. Ubi liberi iacebant? _____

18. Quid Lucius potabat? _____

19. Ridebantne liberi? _____

20. Cur Lucius ridebat? _____

S U M M A R I U M

A. Questions and blanks:

1. The infix to show future tense is _____, for the imperfect it is _____.

2. Alternate forms of **-bi-** are ____ , _____ , and _____.

3. The Latin Imperfect can be translated into English as _____,
_____, or simply with the _____.

4. The forms eras and eris show that the vowel for the past is ____, for the future _____.

5. Eo, it, imus, ibas are forms of _____, which means _____.

6. Sumus, es, erant, ero are forms of _____, which means _____.

7. Three Latin words consisting of one letter only are **a, e,** and **i.** What do they mean?

_____, _____, _____.

8. The prefix **pos- (pot-)** of possum, potes, means _____.

9. Three verbs meaning **to perish, to die** are _____,
_____, _____.

10. The four prefixes which are used with **esse** <u>and</u> **ire** are _____,

_____,_____, _____.

B. Review these words:
cur? - quomodo? - quoque - quando? - quo? - quod - numquam - saepe - cras - ubi - deesse - obesse - superesse - abesse - inire - obire - perire - praeterire - ridere - monstrare

C. Do not confuse:
eramus - erimus; abesse - abire; ite! - este!; hodie - heri; interea - inter - intra; post - postea.

Children In Rome

Children were part of the family and therefore property of their father, the PATER FAMILIAS, who in old times could expose them in the wilderness if they were deemed too weak or sick to survive. When children were eight days old, they received a BULLA (a golden amulet) and a name.

Children went to school between the ages of seven and fifteen. There was no obligation to go; rather it was considered a privilege. Perhaps for this reason the Latin word for school, LUDUS, also means *game.* It signified that one did not have to work. The children of poor parents could often not afford school, since they needed to work; nevertheless, many slaves learned how to read and write. On the way to school a slave, called "pedagogue" (from Greek = leader of children), accompanied the children and carried their wax tablets and styles. Children learned reading, writing, and arithmetic, mostly by recitation and repetition. Writing was first done on wax tablets, then later on with pen and ink on papyrus rolls. If the children were lazy, the teacher hit them with a switch. Teachers were mostly Greek and were paid by the parents.

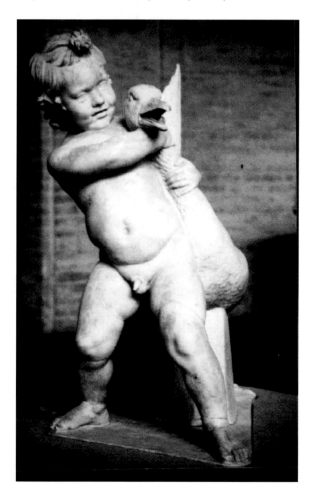

Boy with a pet goose.

Children also played games. They used balls of cloth filled with feathers or hair, dolls, wooden or clay animals, tops, hoops, hobby horses, little carts, swings, and seesaws. Young girls, who were eligible to be married after age twelve (boys fourteen), sacrificed their toys to the god or goddess of marriage on the day before their wedding, thereby taking leave of childhood. When boys reached manhood, they received the TOGA VIRILIS (man´s toga) and put their BULLA into a shrine for safekeeping.

Children also played board games, similar to checkers. One such game is shown on the title leaf of this chapter, another is given here:

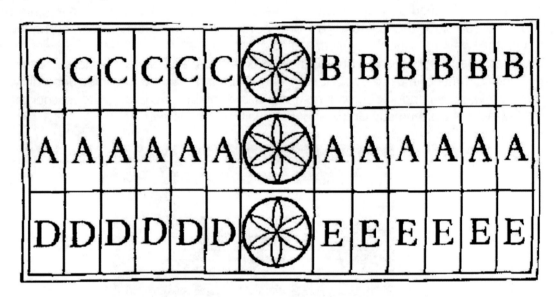

HOW TO PLAY THE   **LUDUS XII SCRIPTORUM**

This game was mentioned many times in old writings and must have been quite popular. There are several versions of this game; this one uses 24 stones, 12 white and 12 black, and 2 dice. At the start of the game the two players choose black or white; all pieces are set on the fields marked A, so that each field has one white and one black stone on it. The players throw the dice alternately; after rolling a double the player gets a second turn. The stones are moved to the end of line A, from there through B, C, D, and to E. The player can decide whether he wants to use the points of each die separately, to move two stones, or add them up, to move one stone. If in fields B, C, and D the player's stone lands on a field that is occupied by one of the opponent's stones, this stone is thrown out and must return to the first free A-field. If there are two opposing stones, the field cannot be used, but must be skipped over. If all fields are blocked in such a way that neither the points of one nor of both dice can be used, the player loses his turn. When all stones of one player have arrived on the fields E, the player can start removing them, again by rolling the dice. The number of points may be greater than the number needed to exit. The player who has removed all his stones first wins the game.

Chapter 4: Answers and Translations

Exercise A:
1. she used to love 2. you (Pl) saw 3. you (Sg) gave 4. they used to have 5. we feared 6. The sailor was always sailing to the island. 7. We used to carry water into the house, but now we have a donkey. 8. I used to work more, now I work less. 9. Where did Claudia live? She lived in Italy. 10. The boys and girls were singing.

Exercise B:
1. you will give 2. I will cry 3. You will look at the stars. 4. He is going to move the table. 5. We will drink wine, but we used to drink water. 6. The farmer will praise the poets. 7. The farmers will sit in the house; they were working. 8. We are going to have money. 9. Are you going to prepare dinner? Yes. 10. You will be happy and strong.

Exercise C:
1. Ubi erat amicus heri? 2. In oppido erat.
3. Ubi eras interim? 4. Eram in villa.
5. Eritisne ibi vespero? 6. Cras ibi erimus.
7. Cur non es in villa? 8. Saepe non sum ibi, sed ibi ero hodie.
9. Amicusne nunc est ibi? 10. Non est, semper est in oppido, si sum in villa.

Exercise D:
1. we are away 2. she is present 3. he goes toward 4. she was able 5. they are returning 6. you will harm 7. we help 8. I pass by 9. he takes part 10. they can 11. go away! 12. they will be left 13. aderimus 14. deerat 15. redisne? 16. aderat, intererat 17. debemus inire 18. ades 19. obis 20. peri! interi! 21. Hodie adesse possunt. 22. Ex casa exire heri non poterant. 23. vocabat 24. spectabitis 25. Agros videre poteris. 26. Liberis uvas dabat. 27. Navigabo in Italiam. 28. Puer puellam amabat, sed puella puerum non amabat. 29. Non spectant magistrum; spectate, liberi, magistrum! 30. Cras ibimus in oppidum et avum visitabimus.

Reading 1 : At Grandfather's House
Tomorrow we will visit grandfather. We will go into the forest, to the house of grandfather. We will enter the house, greet grandfather, give grandfather a gift and look at the house. Grandfather will prepare a meal. After the meal we will walk in the forest and grandfather will show us herbs and teach about the herbs. We will also be able to sail to an island. In the evening we will return to the house. We will drink wine and grandfather will tell stories about the woods and the waters. We will laugh and be happy.

Reading 2 : Our Friend Lucius
When we were children, we, Rufus and Claudia, we used to live on an island. There we had a country house. We loved the island. We often walked in the forest or sailed with our grandfather, who used to tell stories about the water and the woods. Once in a while we used to invite friends, girls and boys, and show them the island. A maid used to prepare dinner.
We also had a friend by the name of Lucius. Lucius was a donkey. We used to call Lucius: "Lucius, Lucius!" Lucius answered: "I-AAAA". We would wait for Lucius, but Lucius neither obeyed nor moved. He used to lie in the grass or sit in the meadow.
So we had to walk into the meadow and capture Lucius. Then Lucius would carry us children, Claudia and Rufus, and the boy and girl friends. He would walk slowly through the forest. We would

see the sky and the meadows and be happy. Suddenly Lucius would catch sight of the water, and suddenly he would race to the water, bray, and move his tail. He loved the water very much.

We would sit on the donkey and fear the danger, we would pray, cry and hang on to Lucius's tail. "Stand, Lucius! Stand still!" we would call. Near the water Lucius would suddenly stand still. We would fall down and lie in the water.

Innocent Lucius would drink the water and - laugh!

Respond in Latin

1. Rufus et Claudia habitabant in insula.
2. Habebant villam.
3. Rufus non erat puella, erat puer.
4. Liberi ambulabant in silva.
5. Lucius erat asinus.
6. Liberi amicis insulam monstrabant.
7. Ancilla parabat cenam.
8. Lucius non respondebat. Non parebat, non movebat.
9. Liberi Lucium captare debebant.
10. In prato sedere amabat.
11. Caelum et prata videbant.
12. Lucius subito festinabat, quod aquam videbat.
13. Lucius aquam amabat.
14. Liberi flebant, quod periculum timebant.
15. Vocabant 'Sta, Luci, sta!'
16. Lucius subito prope aquam stabat.

17. Liberi in aqua iacebant.
18. Lucius aquam potabat.
19. Liberi non ridebant, sed flebant.
20. Lucius ridebat, quod aquam habebat et gaudebat, quod liberos in aqua spectabat, quod asinus est.

Summary:
1. -bi- , -ba- 2. -bo, -bu- 3. used to, would, Past Tense 4. -a-, -i- 5. ire, to go 6. esse, to be 7. from (ab), out of (ex), go! 8. powerful 9. perire, interire, obire 10. ab-, ad-, inter-, ob-

Amicus noster Lucius

5

PERSONAL PRONOUNS
IS, EA, ID
INTERROGATIVE PRONOUNS

THE INDO-EUROPEAN LANGUAGE FAMILY TREE

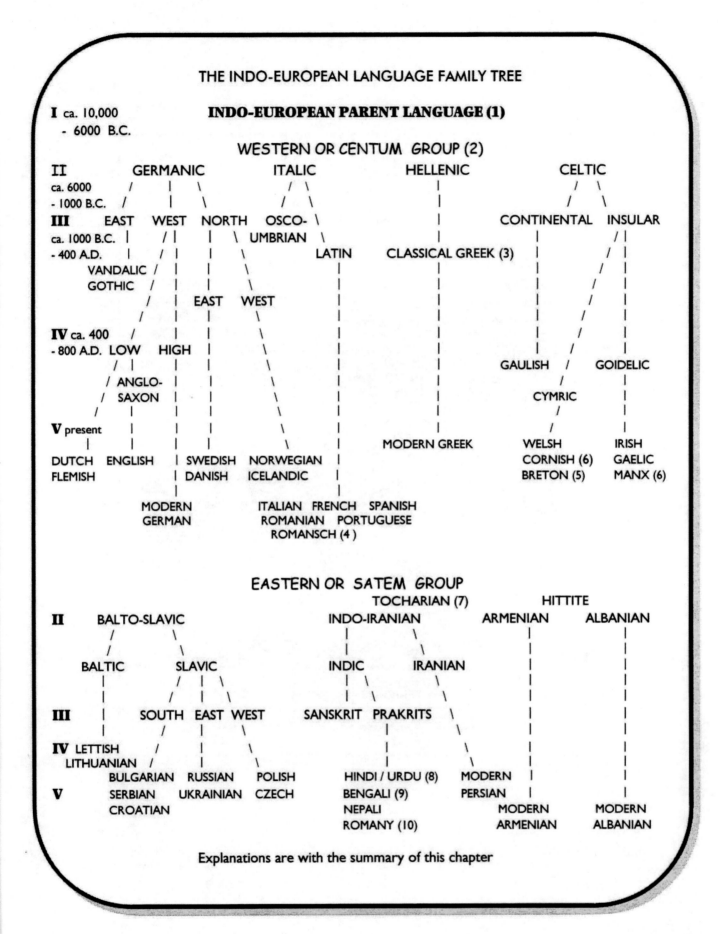

INDO-EUROPEAN PARENT LANGUAGE (1)

I ca. 10,000 - 6000 B.C.

WESTERN OR CENTUM GROUP (2)

II ca. 6000 - 1000 B.C.   GERMANIC   ITALIC   HELLENIC   CELTIC

III ca. 1000 B.C. - 400 A.D.   EAST WEST NORTH OSCO-UMBRIAN   CONTINENTAL INSULAR
LATIN   CLASSICAL GREEK (3)

VANDALIC
GOTHIC

EAST WEST

IV ca. 400 - 800 A.D. LOW HIGH

ANGLO-SAXON   GAULISH GOIDELIC

CYMRIC

V present   MODERN GREEK   WELSH   IRISH

DUTCH ENGLISH SWEDISH NORWEGIAN   CORNISH (6) GAELIC
FLEMISH DANISH ICELANDIC   BRETON (5) MANX (6)

MODERN GERMAN

ITALIAN FRENCH SPANISH
ROMANIAN PORTUGUESE
ROMANSCH (4)

EASTERN OR SATEM GROUP

TOCHARIAN (7)   HITTITE

II   BALTO-SLAVIC   INDO-IRANIAN   ARMENIAN ALBANIAN

BALTIC SLAVIC   INDIC IRANIAN

III   SOUTH EAST WEST   SANSKRIT PRAKRITS

IV LETTISH
LITHUANIAN

BULGARIAN RUSSIAN POLISH   HINDI / URDU (8) MODERN
V   SERBIAN UKRAINIAN CZECH   BENGALI (9)   PERSIAN
CROATIAN   NEPALI   MODERN   MODERN
ROMANY (10)   ARMENIAN   ALBANIAN

Explanations are with the summary of this chapter

Chapter 5:   PRONOUNS (PERSONAL, INTERROGATIVE, REFFLEXIVE); CONJUNCTIONS

A: FIRST AND SECOND PERSON PERSONAL PRONOUNS

As you have seen before, these pronouns (= for, in place of nouns) seldom occur in the nominative, as subjects, because they are already contained in the verb forms: **eramus** : *we were;* **portabo** : *I will carry;* **habebatis** : *you used to have.* Occasionally they will be used for emphasis or contrast: **nos** laboramus, **vos** sedetis in casa. They are, however, indispensable as direct and indirect objects and as objects of prepositions. The genitive of these personal pronouns is rare, and irregular, and is therefore omitted for the time being.

	1st Sg		2nd Sg		1st Pl		2nd Pl	
N	ego	I	tu	you	nos	we	vos	you
D	mihi	to me	tibi	to you	nobis	to us	vobis	to you
A	me	me	te	you	nos	us	vos	you
Ab	a me	by me	a te	by you	a nobis	by us	a vobis	by you

The preposition **cum**, *with,* is placed after the ablative pronoun and the form is written in one word: **mecum, tecum, nobiscum, vobiscum** - with me, you, us, you (Pl)

Examples:

> Gratias **tibi**. - Thanks to you.
> Da **mihi** pecuniam! - Give me the money!
> Dominus **vobiscum.** - The Lord (be) with you.
> Videmus **vos**. Videmus **te**. - We see you.
> **Ego** cogito, ergo sum. - I think therefore I am.
> Habesne amicum **tecum** ? - Do you have (your)
> friend with you?

Via Romana

B: PERSONAL PRONOUNS, THIRD PERSON

The most commonly used third person pronoun is **is, (ea, id),** *he, she, it..*
Others used are the demonstrative pronouns **hic** and **ille** (see chapter 8)

	M		F		N	
			Singular			
N	**is**	he, it	**ea**	she, it	**id**	it
G	**eius**	of him, of it his, its	**eius**	of her, it her, its	**eius**	of it, its
D	**ei**	to him, to it	**ei**	to her, to it	**ei**	to it
A	**eum**	him, it	**eam**	her, it	**id**	it
Ab	**(ab) eo**	by him, by it	**(ab) ea**	by her, by it	**eo**	by it
			Plural			
N	**ei**	they (masc.)	**eae**	(fem.)	**ea**	(neuter)
G	**eorum**	of them, their	**earum**		**eorum**	
D	**eis**	to them	**eis**		**eis**	
A	**eos**	them	**eas**		**ea**	
Ab	**(ab) eis**	by them	**(ab) eis**		**eis**	

The most true and tried method of memorizing this paradigm is horizontally, by case, first Singular, then Plural:

> **is,ea,id; eius,eius,eius; ei,ei,ei; eum,eam,id; eo,ea,eo;**
> **ei,eae,ea; eorum,earum,eorum; eis,eis,eis; eos,eas,ea; eis,eis,eis.**

With the exception of the genitive and dative Singular, which are unique to pronouns and number adjectives, and which are the same for all three genders, the endings for this pronoun follow the first and second declensions.

Very important: The distinction is by **gender**, **not** by persons and objects!
Consequently the English pronoun **it** can be translated by three Latin forms:

    is, for masculine objects: **equus** = **is** (it); **cibus** = **is** (it);

    ea for feminine objects: **mensa** = **ea** (it); **pugna** = **ea** (it);

    id for neuter objects: **vinum** = **id** (it).

Conversely, the pronouns **is** and **ea** can be translated as either **he** and **she**, or **it**, depending on to whom or what they refer. The preposition **ab** is used only with persons: **ab eo**, *by him, from him*.

In English there are three genders in the Singular (he, she, it) but only one in the Plural (they).

In Latin there are three genders in the Plural as well:

    ei - they (viri, equi); eae - they (feminae, mensae); ea - they (officia, oppida).

Note the translations **his**, **her**, **its**, and **their** for the **genitive** of the pronoun. **Eius, eorum, earum** are the only Latin words for these English possessive adjectives, if they are not **reflexive** (meaning not reflecting back to the subject of the sentence).

Examples:

    Reflexive: The farmer lost his horse. (his = the farmer's, the subject's)

    Not reflexive::   The farmer lost her horse. (her = his wife's or daughter's =

                                               someone else's, not the subject's)

 **EXERCISE A:**   Decide whether the possessive adjectives are **R**(eflexive) or **N**(ot):

    1. The woman put the money into <u>her</u> purse. ___
    2. I haven't seen <u>her</u> purse. ___
    3. These people lose <u>their</u> shirts betting on horses. ___
    4. This businessman can never keep track of <u>his</u> belongings. ___
    5. This merchant is so discombobulated. Do you think a secretary
       could sort <u>his</u> stuff? ___
    6. The success has gone to <u>his</u> head. ___
    7. The women left <u>their</u> shoes here. ___
    8. We don't want <u>their</u> shoes. ___
    9. This music is awful; I can't understand <u>its</u> popularity. ___
    10. To every animal <u>its</u> own. ___

In contrast to English, in Latin **his, her, and its** are the same word: **eius;** but **their** has different forms according to gender: **eorum, earum, eorum**

EXERCISE B: Replace each noun with the correct **pronoun** form:
                Examples: feminae (G.Sg): **eius**   servos: **eos**   vinum: **id**

    1. puellae (Nom.Pl.)   2. dona   3. equi (Gen. Sg.)   4. vino (Ab.Sg.)

    5. feminae (Dat.Sg.)   6.viro (Dat.Sg.)   7. liberorum   8. pratum

    9. vicinus   10. carri (Nom.Pl.)   11. pecuniae (Gen.Sg.) 12. periculis

 **EXERCISE C:**   In the following sentences translate only the **underlined pronouns;** watch the gender of "it" and "their"!

1. He gave <u>us</u> all his old books.

2. Have you seen the moon today? No I have not seen <u>it</u>.

3. Did Claudia take <u>his</u> horse? No, I took <u>it</u>.

4. The student needs the book! Give <u>it</u> <u>to him</u> !

5. Here come the girls; have you seen <u>their</u> grandfather?

6. Look at <u>me</u>, when you are speaking <u>with me</u>!

7. You ran so fast that we could not follow <u>you</u>. (Pl.)

8. For heaven's sake, give <u>them</u> the gift; they deserve <u>it</u>.

 **EXERCISE D:**   Translate: Sentences with pronouns. :

1. Date nobis cibum in mensa!

   _____

2. Ambulabisne mecum in silva?

   _____

3. Casa eius est prope silvam.

   _____

4. Pueri habent asinum. Ecce (look there) eorum asinus! Videsne eum?

   _____

5. Tullia semper laborat. Visitabimus eam et spectabimus hortum eius.

   _____

6. Habemus pecuniam nobiscum. Eam vobis dabimus.

   _____

7. Ubi sunt liberi? Eis libros monstrare debemus. Eos eis dabimus.

   _____

8. Oramus te Dominum: Dona nobis pacem! (peace)

   _____

9. Vos laboratis in horto, sed nos non laboramus.

   _____

10. Ambulamus post te, Marce; post nos ambulat servus; post eum ambulat asinus.

   _____

 **EXERCISE E:** Another quick replacement exercise for **is, ea, id** .
Translate the sentences, and then replace the underlined nouns with pronouns:

Example: Spectamus lunam. *We look at the moon.* **Spectamus eam.**

1. <u>Equo</u> frumentum damus.
2. Equo <u>frumentum</u> damus.
3. <u>Puellae</u> spectant stellas.
4. <u>Puellae</u> casa est in oppido.
5. <u>Puellae</u> monstrabimus insulam.
6. Puellae monstrabimus <u>insulam</u>.
7. <u>Pueris</u> non respondetis.
8. Magistri etiam docent <u>puellas</u>.
9. <u>Feminarum</u> hortos visitabamus.
10. Puella ambulat cum <u>amico</u>.
11. Ne movete <u>dona</u>!
12. Claudia amicum <u>magistri</u> amat.

 Got it? No? Go back to the beginning of the chapter!
This stuff is vital!

C : REFFLEXIVE PRONOUNS

Pronouns which refer to ("reflect") the Subject of the sentence are called **reflexive pronouns**. They are **personal pronouns**, not to be confused with the **possessive adjectives** (my, your, his, her, its, their). In English the **reflexive pronouns** are usually rendered as **myself, yourself, yourselves, himself, themselves,** and so on.

> The stepmother looked at **herself** in the mirror.
> We hurt **ourselves** playing ball.
> I sing to **myself** in the shower.
> Do you have the book **with you**?

In Latin the forms of the first and second Person (Singular and Plural) of the **reflexive pronoun** are identical with the dative, accusative, and ablative of the **personal pronoun**. (There is no nominative; I myself, he himself, and the like are expressed with a different Latin word.) All third person reflexive pronoun forms are the same, Singular and Plural, meaning that there is only **one** Latin word for

himself, herself, and **themselves: se**   and for

to himself, to herself, to themselves: sibi

		Reflexive Pronouns				
		Sg			**Pl**	
	1st	2nd	3rd	1st	2nd	3rd
D .	mihi	tibi	sibi	nobis	vobis	sibi
A	me	te	se	nos	vos	se
Ab	a me	a te	a se	a nobis	a vobis	a se

The preposition **cum** is again put **after** the pronoun and both are written as one word :
secum (mecum, tecum, nobiscum, vobiscum).

Examples:

Pueri debent **se** docere.	The boys must teach themselves.
Viri **sibi** cenam parant.	The men are preparing dinner for themselves.
Potesne **te** videre in aqua?	Can you see yourself in the water?
Semper portat pecuniam **secum**.	He always carries money with him.
or:	She always carries money with her.
	(A sentence like this needs clarification or a context.)

EXERCISE F: Translate using Reflexive Pronouns. (Words in parantheses need not be translated.)

1. Look at yourself! _____ 2. Look at yourselves! _____

3. Claudia likes to give herself presents.

_____

4. They often invited themselves.

_____

5. Sometimes (aliquando) I tell stories to myself.

_____

6. He can not hold himself (back): he always laughs.

_____

7. She should ask herself: Am I thinking?

_____

8. We can (give an) answer to us ourselves.

_____

9. Do you have the book with you? (Pl)

_____

10. The poets often praise themselves.

_____

D: INTERROGATIVE PRONOUNS AND ADVERBBS

Interrogative pronouns and **adverbs** are question words. They get their name from the Latin verb **rogare**, *to ask*. You have already learned several of them. Review: Give the meaning of **quis? quid? quo? cur? quomodo? quando? ubi?** The whole paradigm of **quis? quid?** *who? what?* follows. There is of course only one form for masculine and feminine, since one usually does not know for whom one is asking. However, there is a Plural! (See chapter 8)

N	**quis**	who	**quid**	what
G	**cuius**	whose	**cuius**	of what, whose
D	**cui**	to whom	**cui**	to what
A	**quem**	whom	**quid**	what
Ab	**a quo**	by whom	**quo**	by what

Also memorize the expressions **quis nostrum,** *which of us*, and **quis vestrum,** *which of you.*

EXERCISE G: Translate the interrogative pronoun sentences: Note that, as in Latin, as in English, interrogative pronouns are placed at the beginning of the sentence. So you see, even in Latin word order is not entirely arbitrary.

1. Quis es? Sum puer.
2. Quis est? Est poeta.
3. Quis est in villa? Agricola et femina sunt in villa.
4. Cum quo [quocum] ambulabas? Cum amico ambulabam.
5. Cum cuius amico ambulabas? Ambulabam cum amico avi.
6. Quem vides? Video virum cum equo.
7. Quid vides? Video lunam et stellas.
8. Quid est in mensa? Cena est in mensa.
9. Quem puellae amant? Amant pueros.
10. Quid puellae amant? Amant hortum.
11. Quid equi potant? Aquam potant.
12. Cui datis vinum? Avo vinum damus.
13. Cui agricolae cenam dabant? Nautis cenam dabant.
14. Cuius gallus semper clamat? Eius gallus semper clamat.
15. Quis nostrum habet pecuniam? Ego eam habeo.

EXERCISE H: Translate using all the pronouns:

1. What did you see in the house?
2. To whose son did you give the book.
3. Give her the book! Give him the book!
4. I saw you, but I did not walk with you.
5. With whom did you eat dinner?
6. He drank wine, but did not like it; then he drank water and liked it.
7. Who gave you the money? His servant gave it to me.
8. To whom should we give a gift?
9. Who is she? She is the farmer's daughter.
10. Whom will we invite in the evening?
11. Whose house is on the island? The house of the sailor.
12. What did the girls carry to the gardens?

(2) to...son is ? If you said dative, you were right. Whose is always Genitive!
(3) Careful with "her" and "him"!
(5) cenare, *to eat dinner*
(7) Remember "his" (actually: of him)?
(9) If you want to make sure about
(11) "Whose" is ...? Right. "House" is ...?   "she" you can use **ea.**

E : COORDIATING AND SUBORDINATING CONJUNCTIONS; Adverbs

Conjunctions (from **iungere,** *to join*) are words which join or connect parts of sentences. **Coordinating Conjunctions** connect **like** sentences or clauses: either two, or more, main clauses, or subordinate clauses. **Subordinating Conjunctions** connect **different** sentences: a main sentence or clause, and one or more subordinate clauses. (This is a summary; some of the words have been introduced before)

1. Coordinating Conjunctions:		
et; ac; atque; -que and	**ut** - as, like	**etiam, quoque** - also
sed; vero/verum; at, autem but; moreover	**neque** and not	
et...et... both...and...	**aut; vel** or	
neque...neque... neither...nor...	**aut...aut...** either...or...	
tam...quam... as...as...	**non solum...sed etiam...** not only...but also...	
itaque, igitur therefore	**nam** for (because)	
tamen nevertheless	**enim** namely	
	ergo therefore, consequently	

2. Subordinating Conjunctions	(all with the Indicative, because that's all you have learned so far):		
quod, quia, quoniam because	**ut** as	**si** if	**nisi** if not; unless; except
ubi when(ever); as soon as	**quamquam** although		**antequam, priusquam** before
dum while, as long as	**etsi** even if		**postquam** after

3. Here are some more useful and necessary **Adverbs:**

adhuc up to no	**antea** before(hand)	**ceterum** besides	**cras** tomorrow
deinde then, after that	**diu** for a long time	**ecce** see there!	**eo** to there
fere almost	**fortasse** perhaps	**forte** by chance	**frustra** in vain
heri yesterday	**hic** here	**hodie** today	**iam** already
non iam no longer	**ibi** there	**inde** from there	**item** likewise
interdum once in a while	**interea** in the meantime		**ita, sic, tam** so
iterum again	**libenter** gladly	**longe** far, by far	**mox** soon
magis more	**magis...quam** more...than	**magnopere** very (much)	

mane early	**multum** much	**nondum** not yet	**numquam** never
nunc now	**olim** once upon a time	**paene** almost	**paulatim** gradually
paulo (by) a little	**paulo post** a little later	**postea** later, afterwards	**profecto** indeed
postremo lastly, finally	**primo, primum** at first	**praeterea** besides	**quo** where to? By what?
quam how, as, than	**quasi** just as, as if	**raro** seldom	**saepe** often
satis enough	**quondam** once upon a time	**semper** always	**sero** (too) late
solum alone, only	**sicut, velut** just as, like	**simul** at the same time	**subito** suddenly
statim immediately	**tum** then, at that time	**tandem** finally	**tantum** only
ubique everywhere	**undique** from everywhere	**unde** from where	
valde very	**vere, vero** indeed, in truth	**vix** hardly	

EXERCISE I: Translate the sentences:

1. Amicus eius non solum agricola et dominus villae, sed etiam nauta est.
2. Videbamus neque dominum neque servum, sed hodie videbimus et dominum et servum.

3. Non erit cena pro pueris, nisi sedebunt ad mensam.
4. Pueri non respondent, quamquam eos vocamus.

5. Tacere debes, quod, ut video, cantare non potes.
6. Si liberi flent, familia gaudere non potest.

7. Date libros aut pueris aut puellis, sed ne date eos magistris! [Nolite dare]
8. Nisi magister nos volare docet, ambulare debemus.

9. Ancilla liberos monet: "Ne sedete [Nolite sedere] in mensa, ubi cibus est in mensa."
10. Feminae et ancillae semper festinant, quamquam festinare non debent.

**Magister volare
nos docet.**

Lectio I: A Maccaronic Rhyme.
          (Maccaronic poetry is written in a mix of 2 or more languages.)

St. Martin was a saintly man,
But liked to drink **cerevisiam**;   cerevisia / beer
He did not have **pecuniam**
And had to leave his **tunicam**.   tunica / here: coat

Lectio II: Ursus in Taberna - The Bear in the Tavern

Ursus in tabernam intrat et cerevisiam imperat.
Tabernarius stupefactus ad casam domini currit et vocat:
"O domine! O domine! Ursus in taberna sedet et cerevisiam desiderat!"
Dominus respondet: "Redi, stulte, ad tabernam! Ibi habemus magnam
5   copiam cerevisiae. Si ursus desiderat cerevisiam, da ei cerevisiam!
Sed postula ab eo pretium sestertium!"

Tabernarius ad tabernam properat et urso cerevisiam dat.
Tum postulat pretium sestertium.
Ursus non respondet, sed cerevisiam potat.
10   Tabernarius adhuc stupefactus eum rogat:
"Nonne ursi raro tabernam visitant?"
"Vere," respondet ursus, "raro tabernam visitare possumus,
     propter cerevisiae pretium immoderatum."

(2) tabernarius,i - tavern-keeper; stupefactus - dumbfounded; currit - he runs;
(4) stultus,i - stupid person; magnus,a,um - large;
(6) postulare - to demand; pretium,i - price; p.sestertium - ca. $25;
(12) vere - truly;
(13) immoderatus,a,um - outrageous.

Description of a miser   (Lucilius)
...cui neque iumentum neque servus nec comes ullus:
 Bulgam, et quidquid habet nummorum, secum habet ipse,
 cum bulga cenat, dormit, lavit. Omnia in una
 sunt homini bulga: bulga haec devincto lacerto est.

... He has neither beast of burden nor slaves nor any companion:
 His sack and whatever he has of money he has with him,
 with his sack he eats and sleeps and bathes. His one and only
 the sack is for him. This sack is attached to his arm.

Lectio III : Marcus et puellae

(10) certe - surely; (11) stulta - stupid (girl); (12) rana loquax - squawky frog; (21) tres - three; (22) optimae - the best (fem. Plural)

There were many epithets in Latin; some of them occur in the comedies of Plautus, such as: **trivenefica** - arch witch; **stimulorum seges** - bag of bones; **lumbrix** - earthworm.

A. Questions and blanks:

1. The pronouns **ego, tu, nos,** and **vos** are pronouns for the _____ and _____

    person, Singular and Plural.

2. The third person pronoun, masculine, feminine, and neuter Singular is _____, _____, _____.

3. A reflexive pronoun refers to the _____ of the sentence.

4. The reflexive pronoun form for the accusative and ablative, Singular and Plural,

    all genders, is _____.

5. What type of sentences do interrogative pronouns begin? _____

6. Sentences that are alike are connected by _____ conjunctions,

    sentences which are different by _____ conjunctions.

B. Don´t confuse:

quis - quid; quid - quod, tam...quam - quamquam; ubi - ibi; si - nisi - neque; atque - aut.

THE INDO-EUROPEAN LANGUAGE FAMILY (NOTES)

(1) Neither the Indo-European parent language nor the languages of step II have been transmitted in written form. They have, however, been reconstructed according to the findings of comparative and historical linguistics.

(2) The **centum** and **satem** languages were so named after their respective words for the number one hundred.

(3) Of the languages in step III large bodies of written texts have been preserved in **Latin, Classical Greek, Sanskrit, Avestan,** and **Hittite.** Other languages were preserved in more or less numerous inscriptions (e.g. Oscan, Umbrian, West and North Germanic.)

(4) **Romansch** is the fourth national language of Switzerland (besides German, French, and Italian). It is spoken in the Eastern canton of Graubünden (Grischun in Romansch).

(5) **Breton** was originally spoken in Bretagne (France) and died out there around 1750; it was reintroduced from Britain.

(6) **Cornish** was spoken in Cornwall, and **Manx** on the island of Man.

(7) **Tocharian** writings were found in China. Numerous clay tablets (around 10,000) with **Hittite** inscriptions were discovered in Mesopotamia.

(8) **Hindi** is the name of this language in India, **Urdu** in Pakistan.

(9) **Bengali** is spoken in India by approximately thirty million people.

(10) **Romany,** or **Roma,** is the language of the Gypsies,, not to be confused with either **Romanian** or **Romansch.**

VOCABULARY REVIEW, CHAPTERS 1 THROUGH 5

(Answers are in the Answer Section.)

EXERCISE A: Write down as many verbs as you can think of that are **utterances** of one kind or another (**speak, yell, order, sing,** etc.; there should be about fifteen). Now look in the answer section and add those you could not think of! Writing helps you to memorize.

EXERCISE B: This is an exercise in association. Write down the first **verb** that comes to mind, when you hear or read each noun: (You can not use any verb more than once.)

1. nauta - _____

2. vinum - _____

3. villa - _____

4. avus - _____

5. ancilla - _____

6. asinus - _____

7. puer et puella - _____

8. magister - _____

9. fabula - _____

10. gallus - _____

EXERCISE C: Think of (and write) fifteen nouns which designate **people:**

EXERCISE D: Review some prepositions:

prae, praeter, pro, prope, propter, per

prae: think of **pre**face (it stands **before** the actual book); **pre**destined (it is decided **before**hand). Find three more words with **pre-** and explain their meaning in terms of "before" (time or place).

praeter: besides - sorrry: **preter**natural is it.
pro: the **pro** and **contra** (or the **pro** and **con**) of a matter (for and against);

to **procras**tinate means to postpone something toward tomorrow, **cras**.
Can you explain **proclaim, provide, provoke**?

prope: Think of **prop**inquity. **Close to, near.**

propter: You are on your own with this one. **Because of, on account of.**

per: **per**spective means actually that you look "through" a space or object.
More commonly the prefix **per-** means **altogether, thoroughly**, as in **per**tinaceous.

EXERCISE E:	Give the Latin word(s), and their meaning, from which each of the following English words are derived: (I assume you know what the English words mean.) Each Latin word occurs only once! Some words have two roots.

1. pugnacious   _____

2. ambulatory   _____

3. monster   _____

4. monstrance   _____

5. laudatory   _____

6. placebo   _____

7. valedictorian _____

8. mundane   _____

9. vespertine   _____

10. superannuated _____

11. cornucopia   _____

12. preoccupation _____

13. impugn   _____

14. possibility   _____

15. intimidate   _____

Daily Life in The City

Romans of different classes had widely different lifestyles, but there were common points also. The majority of working people were slaves, but there were free workers, too: artisans, tradesmen, vendors, even unskilled laborers. Free workers were entitled to public welfare, including food. Unemployment was a constant problem, especially aggravated by the scores of impoverished farmers who left their farms for the city.

Some of the differences between the well-to-do and the have-nots: rich people lived in beautiful villas, which were well-furnished and secured against thieves. Their food was cooked and served by slaves and other servants, who took care of the house. In the mornings these patrons received their clients and gave them money or a basket with food. Poorer people lived in tenements, in apartments of varying size. They had no kitchens or toilets; hence the apartment dwellers bought their food, already cooked, in stores or at food stands and their bread at the bakers'; they fetched their water from public fountains and used public pay toilets. All Romans frequented public baths, although some villas had private baths. Barbers shaved, combed, and perfumed men. Women fixed their hair at home or had it done for them.

Rome was a magnet for foreigners: merchants, money lenders, artists, philosophers. They all wanted to take part in the life of the capital. The focal point of public life was the **forum,** the market square. There one could find temples, triumphal arches, and buildings containing business establishments, law courts, or government offices. People met at the Forum to discuss politics, give election speeches, or vote for and against laws; eulogies for famous people were delivered here. Men also met frequently in taverns for drinking, discussions, and gambling.

**View of the Forum Romanum with the Basilica Julia
and the Temple of Antoninus and Faustina**

All people wanted to be entertained in grand style. From their leaders they demanded **panem et circenses** (**bread and games**). They got chariot races - up to one hundred a day! - mostly in the Circus Maximus, where admission was free and much money was wagered. In addition there were gladiator fights, animal fights, staged sea battles, and numerous theater performances.

Life in the city was very noisy. Since vehicular traffic was permitted only at night, goods had to be delivered at night, usually by shouting and cursing carriage drivers. During the day the streets were crowded with people, litters, and animals. Even 1800 years later Mark Twain could feel echoes of these times in the streets of Pompeii:

> "It was a quaint and curious pastime, wandering through this old silent city of the dead - lounging through utterly deserted streets where thousands and thousands of human beings once bought and sold, and walked and rode, and made the place resound with the noise and confusion of traffic and pleasure. They were not lazy. They hurried in those days. We had evidence of that. There was a temple on one corner, and it was a shorter cut to go between the columns of that temple from one street to the other than go around - and behold, that pathway had been worn deep into the heavy flagstone floor of the building by generations of time-saving feet! They would not go around when it was quicker to go through. We do that way in our cities." (Mark Twain, <u>The Innocents Abroad</u>, N.Y. 1911, p.228-229)

**Forum Romanum: The Temple of Saturn contained
the Treasury of Rome**

Chapter 5 : Answers and Translations

Exercise A:
1. R   2. N   3. R   4. R   5. N   6. N   7. R   8. N   9. N   10. R

Exercise B:
1. eae 2. ea 3. eius 4. eo 5. ei 6. ei 7. eorum 8. id 9. is 10. ei 11. eius 12. eis

Exercise C:
1. nobis 2. eam 3. eius, eum 4. ei, eum 5. earum 6. me, mecum 7. vos 8. eis, id

Exercise D:
1. Give us the food on the table! 2. Will you walk with me in the forest? 3. His (her) house is near the forest. 4. The boys have a donkey. Look, there is their donkey! Do you see him (it)? 5. Tullia is always working. We will visit her and look at her garden. 6. We have money with us. We will give it to you. 7. Where are the children? We ought to show them the books. We will give them to them. 8. We beg you, Lord: Give us peace! 9. You are working in the garden, but we are not working. 10. We walk behind you, Marcus; behind us walks the slave; behind him walks the donkey.

Exercise E:

1. We give grain to the horse.	Ei frumentum damus.
2. "	Equo id damus.
3. The girls look at the stars.	Eae spectant stellas.
4. The girl's house is in the town.	Eius casa est in oppido.
5. We'll show the girl the island.	Ei insulam monstrabimus
6. "	Puellae eam monstrabimus.
7. You don't answer the boys.	Eis non respondetis.
8. Teachers also teach girls.	Magistri eas etiam docent.
9. We visited the women's gardens.	Earum hortos visitabamus.
10. The girl walks with her friend.	Puella ambulat cum eo.
11. Don't move the gifts!	Ne movete ea.
12. Claudia loves the friend of the teacher.	C. eius amicum amat.

Exercise F:
1. Specta te! 2. Spectate vos! 3. Claudia sibi dona dare amat.
4. Saepe se invitabant. 5. Aliquando narro mihi fabulas.
6. Se retinere (tenere) non potest: semper ridet.
7. Ea se rogare debet: Egone cogito? 8. Respondere nobis possumus.
9. Librumne habete vobiscum? 10. Poetae saepe se laudant.

Exercise G:
1. Who are you? I am a boy. 2. Who is he? He is a poet. 3. Who is in the farmhouse? The farmer and his wife are in the house. 4. With whom did you walk? I walked with a friend. 5. With whose friend did you walk? I walked with a friend of my grandfather. 6. Whom do you
 see? I see a man with a horse. 7. What do you see? I see the moon and the stars. 8. What is on the table? Dinner is on the table. 9. Whom do the girls love? They love the boys. 10. What do the

girls love? They love their garden. 11. What do horses drink? Horses drink water. 12. To whom are you giving the wine? We are giving it to grandfather. 13. To whom did the farmers give a meal? They gave a meal to the sailors. 14. Whose rooster is always screaming? His rooster is. 15. Which of us has the money? I have it.

Exercise H:
1. Quid videbas in casa? 2. Cuius filio librum dabas? 3. Da ei librum! (both are the same) 4. Te videbam, sed non ambulabam tecum. 5. Cum quo cenabas? 6. Vinum potabat, sed id non amabat; tum aquam potabat et eam amabat. 7. Quis tibi pecuniam dabat? Servus eius eam mihi dabat. 8. Cui donum dare debemus? 9. Quis est (ea)? Est filia agricolae. 10. Quem invitabimus vespero? 11. Cuius villa est in insula? Nautae villa est ibi. 12. Quid puellae ad hortos portabant?

Exercise I:
1. His friend is not only a farmer and the master of the house, but also a sailor. 2. We saw neither the master nor the slave, but today we will see both the master and his slave. 3. There will be no dinner for the boys, unless they sit at the table. 4. The boys are not responding, although we are calling them. 5. You ought to be silent, because, as I see, you can not sing. 6. If the children are crying, the family cannot be happy. 7. Give the books either to the boys or the girls, but don't give them to the teachers! 8. Unless our teacher teaches us to fly, we have to walk. 9. The maid warns the children: "Don't sit on the table, when the food is on the table!" 10. The women and the servants are always hurrying, although they don't have to hurry.

Reading 2: The Bear in the Tavern
A bear enters a tavern and orders a beer. The stupefied tavern-keeper runs to his master's house and screams: "O master, o master! There is a bear sitting in the tavern and he desires a beer!" The master answers: "Go back, stupid, to the tavern. We have quite a lot (a great supply) of beer there. If the bear desires a beer, give him a beer! But demand from him a sestertium as payment!"
The tavern-keeper goes back to the tavern and gives the bear a beer. Then he asks for a sestertium. The bear does not answer, but drinks his beer. The tavern-keeper, still amazed, asks him: "Isn't it rare for a bear to visit a tavern?" "Yes, indeed", answers the bear, "it is rare that we can visit a tavern, because of the outrageous price of beer."

Reading 3: Marcus and the Girls
1. Hi, Rufus, how are you? Hi, Tullia! All right.
2. Is Marcus here? No, he is not.
3. Where is he? He is gone.
4. When did he leave? Early.
5. When is he going to return? Maybe in the evening.
6. You are of no use. I don't have to be helpful.
7. Go to hell, you ass! Good-bye to you, too, hen!
8. Greetings, Octavia! Where are you going? To Marcus' house. Why are you asking about Marcus?
9. Marcus is my boyfriend. Hardly! He is mine!
10. He is not! He loves me. For sure he loves me.

11. He can't love you, stupid! Super-stupid (yourself)!
12. Stupid hen! Squawky frog!
13. Get lost! Go to your house!
14. Look, there comes Marcus. Marcus is walking with Claudia.
15. Claudia! That stupid (lady)! That hen! Frog!
16. Good day, girls! How are you? Well! Super! Why are you walking with Claudia?
17. Today Claudia is my girlfriend.
18. And yesterday? Yesterday Octavia was my girlfriend.
19. And tomorrow? I will be your girlfriend? No way! You are a horrible boy!
20. Go away! Animal! Go to hell!
21. Good-bye, donkey! Good-bye, girls! I love all three of you!
22. Boys are so stupid! Girls are the best! We will go home!

Summarium:
1. Firstst, Second 2. is, ea, id 3. subject 4. **se** 5. questions 6. coordinating, subordinating

Review:
Exercise A:
cantare - clamare - imperare - invitare - laudare - narrare - orare - rogare - salutare - vocare - docere - flere - gaudere - monere - respondere - ridere
Exercise B: (suggestions)
1. nauta - navigare; 2. vinum - potare; 3. villa - habitare; 4. avus - visitare; 5. ancilla - laborare;
6. asinus - portare; 7. puer et puella - amare; 8. magister - docere; 9. fabula - narrare;
10. gallus - clamare

Exercise C:
puella - puer - filia - filius - femina -
vir - domina - dominus - serva - servus
amica - amicus - ancilla - agricola -
incola - nauta - poeta - ava - avus -
dea - deus - magister - nuntius -
socius - vicinus - liberi

LABYRINTHUS - HIC HABITAT MINOTAURUS
    (Graffiti in Pompeii)

Public Pay Toilet (Island of Kos). Up to twenty-five people sat companionably next to each other, chatting, gossiping, or conducting business.

6

ADJECTIVES: 1ST AND 2ND DECLENSION
ADVERBS
POSSESSIVE ADJECTIVES

Indo-European Languages I

From the family tree in the previous chapter one can see that English is most closely related by ancestry (or is cognate) to Dutch and German; they are all descendants of the Western branch of Germanic. If this close affinity comes as news to anybody trying to learn German, consider the even more astonishing relationship between English, Greek, Gaelic, Russian, Armeniam, Hindi, and Persian! One of the first scholars to recognize this fact was Sir William Jones, a British orientalist, who studied Sanskrit, the oldest written-down language on the Indian subcontinent. Jones said, in 1786, that the strong affinity between Sanskrit, Latin, and Greek could not have been produced by accident, but only because they came "from some common source, which perhaps no longer exists."
Historical linguists later reconstructed this lost 'parent' language, using comparative methods; they called it **Proto-Indo-European, PIE.**

PIE is thought to have been spoken some 6000 years ago by a nomadic people somewhere in Europe or Eastern Asia. The ancestors of these people are not known, but there is a possibility that **PIE** and the Uralic language family may have had a common ancestor. (There are even theories which postulate a 'Proto-World' language and attempt to fit all languages into a 'world family tree.')

Chapter 6:   Adjectives: First and Second Declension

Adjectives have already occurred in the readings (in chapters. 2, 3): **mala** casa, **malae** puellae, **malus** mundus. As you can see, adjectives are **declined**, just like nouns. They modify nouns and must agree with them in gender, number, and case. Therefore they must have endings for all cases of all genders, Singular and Plural. Not counting the vocative that makes 30 endings - which you already know: for the **masculine** you use the endings of **amicus** or **puer** (2nd Declension masculine.), for the **feminine** those of **puella** (1st Declension), and for the **neuter** those of **donum** (2nd Declension neuter). Here then is the declension of **bonus, bona, bonum**, *good*, as it modifies nouns:

bonus equus, *a good horse*, **bona puella**, *a good girl,* **bonum vinum,** *good wine.*

	Masculine	Feminine	Neuter
		Singular	
N	bonus equus	bona puella	bonum vinum
G	boni equi	bonae puellae	boni vini
D	bono equo	bonae puellae	bono vino
A	bonum equum	bonam puellam	bonum vinum
Voc	(oh) bone eque !	(bona puella)	(bonum vinum)
Ab	bono equo	a bona puella	bono vino
		Plural	
N	boni equi	bonae puellae	bona vina
G	bonorum equorum	bonarum puellarum	bonorum vinorum
D	bonis equis	bonis puellis	bonis vinis
A	bonos equos	bonas puellas	bona vina
Ab	bonis equis	a bonis puellis	bonis vinis

Examples:

villa **magna** - a big house
boni libri - good books
puer **parvus** - the small boy
dona **pulchra** - beautiful gifts
deos **iratos** (Acc.) - angry gods

liberi **mali** - bad children
amicum **carum** - a dear friend (Acc.)
feminarum **fessarum** - of the tired women
puellae **sedulae** - industrious girls
vaccis **fuscis** - to (Dat.), from (Abl.) the brown cows

Adjectives are customarily placed **after** their nouns; exceptions are **bonus**, *good*, and **multus,** *much, many*. For emphasis, all adjectives can also be placed before the noun, or, indeed, anywhere in the sentence, a stylistic device often used by poets (*Hyperbaton*).

Just as some nouns of the 2nd Declension have the ending **-er** in the nominative (puer, ager), so do some adjectives. Among these are adjectives that drop the **-e-**, e.g., **pulcher, pulchra, pulchrum**, *beautiful* and others that keep it, e.g., **liber, libera, liberum**, *free*. All three nominative forms must be given for these adjectives.

VOCABULARY

Here are fifty-some common adjectives, grouped in ascending order of difficulty (that is to say: how difficult they are to remember). If you find some useful adjectives missing here (such as "short", "strong", "fast") it is because they are declined like nouns of the third declension (chapters 11 and 12).

For an alphabetical listing of all adjectives in this chapter, with English glosses, see end of chapter. (pg 127)

A: Cognates, or near-cognates (you can guess them): not alphabetical.

1. **adversus,a,um**	adverse
2. **antiquus,a,um**	old, ancient
3. **certus,a,um**	certain
4. **incertus,a,um**	uncertain
5. **iustus,a,um**	just
6. **iniustus,a,um**	?
7. **validus,a,um**	strong
8. **firmus,a,um**	?
9. **futurus,a,um**	
10. **falsus,a,um**	
11. **timidus,a,um**	etc.
12. **securus,a,um**	
13. **sanus,a,um**	
14. **studiosus,a,um**	
15. **stupidus,a,um**	
16. **severus,a,um**	
17. **longus,a,um**	
18. **iratus,a,um**	

B: Adjectives whose English derivatives give a clue to their meaning. The English words are often abstract nouns ending in -tude or -ty. Try to guess the meaning! Solution on page 118. Not alphabetical

	Meaning	English Derivative
1. **magnus,a,um**		magnitude
2. **latus,a,um**		latitude
3. **altus,a,um**		altitude
4. **multus,a,um**		multitude
5. **pulcher,**		pulchritude
pulchra, pulchrum		
6. **beatus,a,um**		beatitude
7. **plenus,a,um**		plenitude
8. **gratus,a,um**		gratitude
9. **fidus,a,um**		fidelity
10. **dexter,**	right	dexterity
dextra, dextrum		
11. **sinister,**	left	sinister
sinistra, sinistrum		
12. **pius,a,um**		pious

	Meaning	Engl. Der.
13. clarus,a,um		clarity
14. verus,a,um		veracity
15. acerbus,a,um		acerbity
16. malus,a,um		malpractice
17. stultus,a,um		stultify
18. liber, libera, liberum		liberty
19. mirus,a,um		miracle
20. miser, misera, miserum		miserable
21. vacuus,a,um		vacuum
22. notus,a,um		noted
23. ignotus,a,um		ignore
24. bonus,a,um		bonus
25. ferus,a,um		ferocious
26. novus,a,um		novelty
27. pauci,ae,a (Plural only)		paucity

C: A little harder to remember, since there are few English derivatives, but not impossible:

1. parvus,a,um	small	
2. piger, pigra, pigrum	lazy, slow	
3. fessus,a,um	tired	
4. laetus,a,um	happy	
5. foedus,a,um	ugly	
6. angustus,a,um	narrow	
7. secundus,a,um	favorable	(not to be confused
8. iucundus,a,um	pleasant	with the Preposition
9. cupidus,a,um	greedy	"secundum")
10. amarus,a,um	bitter	
11. improbus,a,um	wicked	
12. bellus,a,um	pretty	(no relation to
13. formosus,a,um	well-shapen	bellum - war)
14. sedulus,a,um	industrious	
15. carus,a,um	dear, expensive	
16. ceteri,ae,a (Plural only)	the remaining (ones)	
17. cuncti,ae,a (Plural only)	all	

D: The **Possessive Adjectives**

meus,a,um	my	
tuus,a,um	your (Sg.)	
suus,a,um	his, her, its	(reflexive)
noster, nostra, nostrum	our	
vester, vestra, vestrum	your (Pl.)	
suus.a.um	their	(reflexive)

E: Colors:

	Meaning	Derivative
albus,a,um	white	albino
niger, nigra, nigrum	black	negro
ruber, rubra, rubrum	red	ruby
caeruleus,a,um	blue	cerulean
flavus,a,um	yellow, blond	
canus,a,um	grey	
roseus,a,um	pink	rosy
fuscus.a.um	brown. dark	obfuscate

F: Listing of Adjectives ending in -er

drop -e-	**keep -e-**
piger, pigra, pigrum	liber, libera, liberum
pulcher, pulchra, pulchrum	(liberi, *children,* were free
dexter, dextra, dextrum	members of the household)
sinister, sinistra, sinistrum	miser, misera, miserum
acer, acra, acrum	
ruber, rubra, rubrum	
niger, nigra, nigrum	
noster, nostra, nostrum	
vester, vestra, vestrum	

Solution to **B**:

magnus - big; **latus** - wide; **altus** - high, deep; **multus** - much; **pulcher** - beautiful; **beatus** - happy; **plenus** - full; **gratus** - thankful; **fidus** - faithful; **clarus** - clear, famous; **verus** - true; **acerbus** - bitter; **malus** - bad; **stultus** - stupid; **liber** - free; **mirus** - wonderful,strange; **miser** - wretched; **vacuus** - empty; **notus** - well-known; **ignotus** - unknown; **bonus** - good; **ferus** - wild; **novus** - new; **pauci** - few; **pius** - dutiful, devoted.

testudo celeris (fast)

et

lepus piger

Potesne narrare fabulam
de testudine et lepore?

In most cases the adjective and its noun will have the **same ending:**
> bon**us** amic**us**, puell**a** parv**a**, vacc**ae** nostr**ae**, don**a** pulchr**a**.

However, in the following instances they are **not the same**:
> 1) If the nominative Singular of the noun or the adjective ends in **-(e)r** (no ending):
> e.g., vi**r** clar**us**; amic**us** nost**er**; asin**us** pig**er**.
> But occasionally they happen to be the same:
> e.g., pue**r** pig**er**; ag**er** vest**er**; magist**er** nost**er**.

> 2) If the noun has **natural gender**; in this case the adjective has to take the endings of the
> natural gender:
> agricol**a** sedul**us**, naut**a** laet**us**; poet**a** clar**us**; poet**ae** clar**i**;

The possessive adjective **suus,a,um** can be used only, when 'his,her, its, their' is reflexive. (See chapter 4)
Otherwise you must use **eius, eorum, earum.**
> Viri videbant **suos** equos.   The men saw their (own) horses.
> Viri videbant **eorum** equos.   The men saw their (someone else's) horses.

 **EXERCISE A:**   Translate**:**

1. amicus meus   2. boni viri (2 cases)

3. puella bella   4. mala bella

5. mundus parvus   6. magnum periculum

7. puer stultus   8. via angusta

9. vinum rubrum   10. magister fessus

11. ager latus   12. cena cara

13. nauta improbus   14. asinus fidus

                                  15. dominus iustus

 **EXERCISE B:**   **Decline in Singular and Plural !**

vir improbus
donum magnum
femina clara
nauta laetus
equus liber

Latin adjectives agree with their nouns not only in attributive position (which is the position we have used so far - right next to the noun), but also in predicative position (which means it is part of the predicate, i.e. the part of the sentence that makes a statement about the subject - usually the verb, or a linking verb and an adjective or noun,etc.)

Examples:

Vinum est rubrum.	The wine is red. [predicative]
Potamus vinum rubrum.	We drink red wine. [attributive]
Luna clara est in caelo alto.	The bright moon is in the high sky. [attr.]
Hodie caelum est caeruleum.	Today the sky is blue. [pred.]
Stellae sunt clarae.	The stars are bright. [pred.]

Adverbs are formed from adjectives by adding the ending **-e** to the stem, for instance, **male,** *badly,* **severe,** *strictly,* **certe,** *certainly.* Irregular is **bene,** *well.* **Optime,** *very well, best,* is also an Adverb.

EXERCISE C: Find **Latin opposites**:

1. pulcher - _____

2. parvus - _____

3. pauca (neuter Plural) - _____

4. bonus - _____

5. angustus - _____

6. verus - _____

7. clarus - _____

8. sedulus -   _____

9. miser -   _____

10. certus -   _____

11. plenus -   _____

12. secundus -   _____

13. dexter -   _____

14. securus -   _____

When the adjective **multus** is used together with another adjective, they are usually connected by **et** in Latin (but not by **and** in English):

Habebat multos **et** pulchros equos.	He had many beautiful horses.
Multae **et** sedulae ancillae laborant in villa.	Many busy servants are working in the house.

Adjectives can denote people or things **without the use of nouns**.
    Common examples are:

multi (nom. masc. Pl.)	many people, many men
multae (nom. fem. Pl)	many women
multa (nom./acc. neuter Pl)	many things
multum (nom./acc. neuter Sg)	much
vera	true things, the truth
noti	well-known men or people
pauca	few things
pauci	few men, people
futura	future things; the future

Of course these can be used in **all cases**:

iustorum	of just men	also: **mei,tui -** my, your (people, family)
boni	of a good man; good men	**mea, tua -** my, your (things, possessions)
fidos	the faithful ones (Dir. Obj.)	

 **EXERCISE D:** Translate

1. Habemus bellam casam albam.
2. Eratisne fessi? Eratisne fessae? Erasne fessus? Erasne fessa?
3. Filia agricolae est pulchra; agricolae filius est foedus, sed habet multam pecuniam.
4. Habemus bonum amicum, virum clarum.
5. Magni liberi multum clamant, parvi liberi tacere debent.
6. Puer timidus non amabat cantare; igitur semper timide tacebat.
7. Videtisne equum parvum? Est meus equus parvus.
8. Multi spectant, sed pauci vident. Videbamus multa, si (*when*) spectabamus.
9. Magister multos et novos libros habet; multos liberos exspectat.
10. Multum aurum vir cupidus captabat et laete in hortum suum portabat.
11. Quamquam in insula formosa habitamus, laeti non sumus; nihil deest, sed, quod aqua alta insulam nostram circumdat, exire non possumus.
12. Secundum Tacitum, poetam clarum, Germania multas et foedas silvas nigras habebat. Fortasse tamen multae et beatae puellae erant.
13. Post ludum liberi fessi sunt, quod eorum magister severus est.
14. Vestra aqua amara est. Possumne potare vinum pro aqua?
15. Verba paucorum improborum nobis fabulas de bellis iustis et bonis narrant; boni viri bella foeda non laudant, sed timent ea.
16. Dona magna eis dare non potes; ergo eis dona parva et bella das.
17. Liberine in via dextra aut in via sinistra ambulare debent? Dextra enim lata, sinistra angusta est.
18. Vita avi mei iucunda est; habet enim multa: villam pulchram, servos sedulos, filios et filias validos, agros latos, bonos vicinos, vaccas laetas, asinum fidum, et me.

If genders are **mixed**, the adjective uses **masculine** forms.

EXERCISE E: Rewrite the story about the visit at grandfather's (Chapter 4, Lectio 1) modifying as many nouns as possible with adjectives.
Example: Cras visitabimus **carum** avum [dear] or **nostrum** avum, etc.

EXERCISE F: More practice with adjectives and a review of prepositions:
Say in Latin:

1. under the wide sky (Abl)   _____
2. towards the beautiful islands   _____
3. without the small boy   _____
4. on account of the many words   _____
5. through your (Pl) gate   _____
6. before free men   _____
7. on long grey roads   _____
8. without false friends   _____
9. about great women   _____
10. near a famous town   _____
11. behind the ancient farmhouse   _____
12. among the industrious slaves   _____
13. from the tired farmer   _____
14. beyond the wide fields   _____
15. around the empty house   _____
16. within our town   _____
17. above the yellow house   _____
18. next to the studious girls   _____
19. through the deep water   _____
20. into great dangers   _____
21. according to your (Sg) daughter   _____
22. against her miserable mind   _____
23. besides narrow roads   _____
24. across the ugly black forests   _____
25. for the grateful poet   _____

Since all prepositions take either accusative or ablative, these are the forms you should review:

Acc. Sg.: - um (m.)   - am (f.)   - um (n.)
Acc. Pl.: - os (m.)   - as (f.)   - a (n.)

Abl. Sg.: - o (m.)   - a (f.)   - o (n.)
Abl. Pl.: - is (m.)   - is (f.)   - is (n.)

(6)   Two prepositions possible; use both!
(10) Also two prepositions
(13) Watch gender!
(22) Use **suus,a,um;** watch the gender! It is determined by the word **animus**, which is
     masculine, not by "her". **Suus** could also mean "his" or "their" (just like in French).
(25) Watch natural gender!

EXERCISE G: Now try a few sentences:

1. Be always just and strong, men and women, for God loves the just and strong (people).

   _____

2. The woman showed her shy friends the country-house of the famous poet.

   _____

3. After many years we will visit our grandfather in beautiful Italy.

   _____

4. The farmer was happy, because his children were industrious.

   _____

5. Yesterday your (Pl) teacher was strict, because the boys were lazy and not studious.

   _____

6. The timid women cried and were silent, because they feared their wicked master.

   _____

7. The Romans used to live in big towns, the Germans in small villages.

   _____

8. The wild horses ran [hurried] out of their stable into the angry farmer's new garden.

   _____

(1) Is the imperative Sg or Pl? Which case is "men and women"?
     With which case is it identical? What gender is used for a mix
     of males and females?
(2) In what case is "her shy friends"?
(4), (6), (8) Are "his" and "their" reflexive?
(8) In what case is "into (the) new garden"? And "the angry farmer's"?

Vir bonus et sedulus

Lectio II : Puer et Puella et Equus Augustus

Sunt puer parvus cum tuba magna et puella parva cum equo parvo. Vocat equum Augustum. Puer filius nautae est, et puella est filia agricolae. Boni agricolae agri in provincia sunt. Puer et puella ambulant in via longa ad oppidum altum.

Puer spectat equum et rogat puellam: "Estne tuus equus? Est bonus equus. Cur ambulamus cum equo et ego porto magnam tubam? Nonne equi portant pueros et puellas?"

Puella exclamat: "Naturam tuam laudare non possum. Es puer stultus. Equus meus est parvus. Non portat pueros feros et tubas magnas."

Puer rogat: "Ubi vides puerum ferum? Non sum malus. Puella bona non es. Cum pueris parvis pugnas et in magno periculo sum. Non amo pugnare tecum et simul portare magnam tubam sub oppidum altum et ambulare iuxta equum validum. Quis nostrum est stultus! Ego non sum!"

Puella respondet: "Amas multa verba. Parvi pueri pugnant verbis. Amo parvos pueros multorum verborum. Equus meus Augustus puerum et puellam et tubam portabit."

Lectio III : Nostra Villa Antiqua

Ante multos annos, ubi puer parvus eram, in villa in Italia habitabamus. Nostra villa erat parva, sed parva villa pulchra erat. Villa erat alba cum tecto rubro et habebat multas portas, fenestras claras, et cubicula lata cum lectis commodis. In culina habebamus magnam mensam et multum cibum, et ancillam amicam quae cenam
5   parabat.

Post villam erat hortus amoenus et circum villam videbamus agros plenos frumento et silvas magnas altasque. Viae prope villam nostram angustae erant.

Possidebamus quoque asinum canum fidumque, vaccas fuscas et gallos nigros et rubros. Non habitabant bestiae in villa, sed in stabulo. Asinus sedulus portabat
10   aquam et frumentum de agris in villam. Vaccae ambulabant in pratis. Galli autem semper clamabant volabantque in villam. Tum vocabamus: "Volate, galli stulti, in hortum!"
Eramus beati in parva villa nostra.

----

(2) tectum,i - roof (3) fenestra,ae - window; cubiculum,i - bedroom; commodus,a,um - comfortable; culina,ae - kitchen (4) quae - who (Relative Pronoun) (6) amoenus,a,um - lovely (8) possidere - to own (compound of sedere)

Fill the blanks with adjectives. Watch their endings!

1. Villa est _____.

2. Habemus gallos _____.

3. Videsne mensam _____?

4. Sum puer _____.

5. Noster asinus est _____.

6. Habitamus in oppido _____.

7. De fenestris villae nostrae possumus videre agros _____

    et silvas _____.

8. Tuba pueri _____ est _____.

9. Est puella _____ cum equo _____.

10. Sedemus in hortis _____.

11. Spectate equos agricolae _____!

12. Cantabimus carmina poetarum _____.

    (11) and (12) Watch the gender of agricola and poeta !

Lectio III: Fabula Misera sed Vera (Gellius, after Greek original)

Agricola laetus cum filio suo et asino fido in via it ad oppidum.
Ambulat vir, post eum ambulat asinus, in asino puer sedet.
Obviam est eis vir clarus; salutat eos et rogat: "Cur, quaeso, vir
sedulus et fessus ambulat in via, et puer formosus et piger
5   sedet in asino? Hoc non est iustum." Ergo filius de asino

descendit et ambulat in via. Agricola asinum ascendit et cuncti laeto animo ad oppidum eunt.

Obit eos vir bonus, eos salutat et rogat: "Quomodo vir validus et firmus in asino sedere potest, et puer parvus et infirmus in

10   via longa ambulare debet? Hoc iustum non est." Ergo agricola descendit de asino, et pater et filius ambulant iuxta asinum, pater dextra, filius sinistra asini.

Et eis obviam est vir notus, salutat eos et rogat: "Quid spectare debeo? Verum esse potest? Cur hic stulti ambulant

15   iuxta asinum validum? Cur asinus eos non portat, ut debet? Non iustum est hoc." Ergo agricola et filius eius sedent in asino, ambo, puer ante virum, vir post puerum. Gaudent, quod ambulare non debent.

Obit eos vir severus et iratus, eos salutat et rogat: "Estisne

20   viri improbi? Cur ambo sedetis in asino misero. Asinus valere non potest, si duos viros validos portare debet. Nonne videre potestis asinum esse fessum, quod multum laborat? Non est iustum hoc."

Ergo agricola et puer pedes asini ligant supra baculo et -

25   portant eum in oppidum.

Fabula monstrat haec: cunctis viris iustus, iucundus, gratus esse non potes.

---

(3) obviam esse - to meet; quaeso - I beg you, "pray"; (6) descendere, ascendere (3rd Conjugation) - to descend, to ascend; cuncti - all; (11) pater (3rd declension) - father; (17) ambo - both; (21) duos - two; (24) pedes - the feet; ligare - to tie; baculum,i - stick.

Here are all these adjectives once more, in alphabetical order. Do you know them already?

acerbus,a,um	sharp, acid
adversus,a,um	adverse
albus,a,um	white
altus,a,um	high
amarus,a,um	bitter
angustus,a,um	narrow
antiquus,a,um	old, ancient
beatus,a,um	happy
bellus,a,um	pretty
bonus,a,um	good
caeruleus,a,um	blue
canus,a,um	grey
carus,a,um	dear, expensive
certus,a,um	certain
ceteri,ae,a (Plural only)	the remaining (ones)
clarus,a,um	bright, clear; famous
cuncti,ae,a (Plural only)	all
cupidus,a,um	greedy
dexter,dextra,dextrum	right
ferus,a,um	wild
fessus,a,um	tired
fidus,a,um	faithful
firmus,a,um	firm, strong, healthy
flavus,a,um	yellow
foedus,a,um	ugly
formosus,a,um	well-shapen, beautiful
fuscus,a,um	brown, dark
futurus,a,um	future
falsus,a,um	wrong, false
gratus,a,um	grateful, pleasing
ignotus,a,um	unknown
improbus,a,um	wicked
incertus,a,um	uncertain
iniustus,a,um	unjust
iratus,a,um	irate, angry
iucundus,a,um	pleasant
iustus,a,um	just
laetus,a,um	happy
latus,a,um	wide
liber,libera,liberum	free
longus,a,um	long
magnus,a,um	big, great
malus,a,um	bad, wicked
meus,a,um	my
mirus,a,um	wonderful, strange
miser,misera,miserum	miserable, poor
multus,a,um	much, many

niger,nigra,nigrum	black
noster,nostra,nostrum	our
notus,a,um	known
novus,a,um	new, young
parvus,a,um	small
pauci,ae,a (Plural only)	few
piger,pigra,pigrum	lazy, slow
pius,a,um	dutiful, devoted
plenus,a,um	full
pulcher,pulchra,pulchrum	beautiful
roseus,a,um	pink
ruber, rubra, rubrum	red
sanus,a,um	sane, healthy
secundus,a,um	favorable
securus,a,um	secure
sedulus,a,um	industrious
severus,a,um	severe
sinister,sinistra,sinistrum	left
studiosus,a,um	studious, busy, industrious
stultus,a,um	stupid
stupidus,a,um	stupid
suus,a,um	their
timidus,a,um	timid
tuus,a,um	your (Sg)
vacuus,a,um	empty
validus,a,um	strong
verus,a,um	true
vester,vestra,vestrum	your (Pl)

Puer et equus Augustus

A. Answer the questions and fill in the blanks:

1. Are adjectives declined or conjugated? _____

2. Adjectives modify _____.

3. The endings used for the adjectives in this chapter are those of the _____

    and _____ declension.

4. Do Latin adjectives commonly stand before or after their nouns? _____

5. **Meus, noster, suus** are _____ adjectives.

6. What two endings are possible for the nominative Singular masculine of these adjectives?

    _____ and _____.

7. If the noun has natural gender (like **nauta**), which gender does the modifying adjective follow,

    grammatical or natural? _____

8. The possessive adjective suus is always used _____.

9. If "his", "her", or "their"are not reflexive, one must use the pronouns _____, _____,

    and _____.

10. The adjective "wonderful" in the phrase "a wonderful garden" is used in _____

    position.

11. Do adjectives in predicative position agree with the nouns to which they refer? Y/N _____

12. The meaning of **multi** is _____ _____; the meaning of **multa** is _____

    _____.

B. Review these words:

pulcher - plenus - gratus - dexter - sinister - cuncti - ceteri - malus - notus - pauci - parvus - fessus - foedus - sedulus - angustus - improbus - flavus - canus - iucundus

C. Do not confuse:

ceteri - cuncti; parvus - pauci; canus - carus - clarus; bellus - bellum (noun); improbus - ignotus; magnus - multus; liber,a,um - liberi,liberorum - libri; meus - me; tuus - tu; noster - vester; secundus,a,um - secundum.

D. Name only the Latin conjunction(s) you would use for each sentence:

1. **Neither** rain **nor** snow would stop them. _____

2. He wants to marry her, **because** she is **not only** smart, **but also** wealthy. _____

3. **Although** we have little money, we live like kings. _____

4. Don´t speak, **unless** you are asked. _____

5. She is **either** deaf **or** dense. _____

6. My brother is almost **as** good-looking **as** I am. _____

7. **As** we have seen before, people never learn. _____

8. Question: Which four Latin words have you learned for **and**? _____, _____, _____, _____.

Pedes asini ligant supra baculo et eum in oppidum portant.

Gardens; Fauna and Flora

The Roman garden was found at the rear of the house. It was enclosed by walls, which often had landscapes or seascapes painted on them to convey the impression of distance. A **porticus** (covered walkway with columns) surrounded the garden. In the middle of the garden there was usually a fountain or water basin. Large gardens resembled parks in size and composition. Small gardens were mostly used for growing herbs and vegetables.

Here is a sample of plants and birds that were found in wall frescoes of a garden room in Pompeii. Many of these had symbolic meaning for the Romans:
    snowball
    oleander (a poisonous plant, used against snake bites)
    palm tree
    laurel (dedicated to the god Apollo)
    pine tree (the tree of Jupiter)
    lily
    chamomile
    March violet (symbol of the love goddess Venus)
    ivy
    cypress (sacred to Pluto, used at funerals)
    strawberry tree (an evergreen, which symbolized immortality)

rose
plane tree (symbol of resistance to life´s blows)
chrysanthemum
poppy (dedicated to the earth goddess Demeter, it symbolized the
     power of sleep and oblivion)
morning glory

Birds depicted there were dove, bluejay, thrush, partridge, duck, egret, oriole, magpie,
   sparrow, swallow, crow and nightingale.

**Acanthus leaves inspired ornaments as well as the
capitals of Corinthian columns**

Plants found in Roman gardens:

Useful Plants

ficus carica   fig tree
rubus fructicosus   black raspberry
fragaria   strawberry
verbena officinalis   verbena
thymus   thyme
campanula rapunculus   bluebell
origanum vulgare   oregano
artemisia   mugwort
linum   flax
papaver somniferum   poppy
coriandrum   coriander
foeniculum vulgare   fennel
apium graveolens   celery
physalis   cherry

Culinary Herbs

laurus nobilis   laurel
rosmarinus officinalis   rosemary
salvia officinalis   salvia
mintha piperita   peppermint
ocimum basilicum   basil
allium sativum   garlic

Medicinal Herbs

helleborus niger   hellebore
valeriana officinalis   valerian
paeonia   peony
hyssopus officinalis   hysop
gentiana lutea yellow   gentian
cyclamen purpurascens   cyclamen
mandragora   mandrake
hyoscyamus niger   henbane

Ornamental Plants

cupressus sempervirens   cypress
viola odorata   violet
acanthus spinosus   hogweed
lavandula angustifolia   lavender
iris germanica   iris
rosa gallica   rose
lilium candidum   white lily
daphne   camelia
buxus sempervirens   boxwood
aconitum napellus   monkshood
digitalis purpurea   foxglove
narcissus pseudonarcissus   daffodil
vinca minor   periwinkle

Chapter 6: Answers and Translations

Exercise A:
1. my friend 2. good men, of a good man 3. a beautiful girl 4. bad wars 5. a small world 6. great danger 7. a stupid boy 8. a narrow road 9. red wine 10. a tired teacher 11. the wide field 12. an expensive meal 13. a wicked sailor 14. the faithful donkey 15. a just master

Exercise C:
1. foedus 2. magnus 3. multa 4. malus 5. latus 6. falsus 7. ignotus 8. piger
9. laetus 10. incertus 11. vacuus 12. adversus 13. sinister 14. timidus

Exercise D:
1. We have a pretty white house. 2. Were you tired? (4 ways) 3. The farmer's daughter is beautiful; the farmer's son is ugly, but he has much money. 4. We have a good friend, a famous man. 5. Big children shout a lot, small children ought to be silent. 6. The timid boy did not like to sing; therefore he was always fearfully silent. 7. Do you see the little horse? He is my little horse. 8. Many people look, but few see. We saw much, when we looked. 9. The teacher has many new books; he expects many children. 10. The greedy man grabbed much gold and carried it happily into his garden. 11. Although we live on a beautiful island, we are not happy; nothing is lacking, but, because the deep water surrounds the island, we can not get out. 12. According to Tacitus, a famous poet [writer, actually: historian], Germany had many ugly black forests. Perhaps there were nevertheless many happy girls. 13. After school the children are tired, because their teacher is strict. 14. Your water is bitter; can I drink wine instead of water? 15. The words of a few wicked men tell us stories about just and good wars; good men do not praise ugly wars, but fear them.
16. You can not give them large gifts; therefore you give them small and pretty gifts. 17. Ought the children to walk on the right or the left road? For the right one is wide, the left one narrow. 18. The life of my grandfather is pleasant; for he has many things: a beautiful country house, hard-working slaves, healthy sons and daughters, wide fields, good neighbours, happy cows, a faithful donkey, and me.

Exercise F:
1. sub caelo lato 2. ad insulas formosas 3. sine puero parvo 4. ob multa verba 5. per portam vestram 6. ante viros liberos, prae viris liberis 7. in longis viis canis 8. sine amicis falsis 9. de magnis feminis 10. prope (ad) oppidum clarum (notum) 11. post villam antiquam 12. inter servos sedulos 13. ab agricola fesso 14. ultra agros latos 15. circa (circum) casam vacuam 16. intra oppidum nostrum 17. supra villam flavam 18. iuxta puellas studiosas 19. per aquam altam 20. in magna pericula 21. secundum filiam tuam 22. ob suum animum miserum 23. praeter (extra) vias angustas 24. trans foedas silvas nigras 25. pro poeta grato

Exercise G:
1. Este, viri et feminae, semper iusti et validi (firmi); deus enim iustos et validos amat.
2. Femina amicis timidis villam poetae clari monstrabat.
3. Post multos annos visitabimus avum nostrum in bella Italia.
4. Agricola laetus erat, quod liberi sui seduli erant.
5. Heri magister vester severus erat, quod pueri erant pigri et non studiosi.
6. Feminae timidae flebant et tacebant, quod dominum suum improbum timebant.
7. Romani in magnis oppidis, Germani in vicis parvis habitabant.
8. Equi feri e stabulo suo in hortum agricolae irati novum properabant.

Reading 1 : The Girl and the Boy and the Horse Augustus

There are a small boy with a large trumpet (tuba) and a small girl with a small horse. She calls the horse "Augustus". The boy is a sailor's son, the girl a farmer's daughter. The fields of the good farmer are in the province. The boy and the girl walk on a long road towards a high town. The boy looks at the horse and asks the girl: "Is he your horse? He is a good horse. Why are we walking with a horse and I am carrying a large tuba? Don't horses carry boys and girls?"

The girl exclaims: "I cannot praise your nature. You are a stupid boy. My horse is small. It does not carry wild boys and large tubas." The boy: "Where do you see a wild boy? I am not bad. You are not a good girl. You fight with small boys and I am in great danger. I don't like to fight with you and at the same time carry a large tuba up to the high town and walk next to a strong horse. Which of us is stupid? Not me!"

The girl answers: "You do like many words. Small boys fight with words. I like small boys with (of) many words. My horse Augustus will carry the boy and the girl and the tuba."

Reading 2 : Our Old House

Many years ago, when I was a small boy, we lived in a farmhouse in Italy. Our house was small, but the small house was beautiful. The house was white with a red roof, and it had many doors, clear windows, and wide bedrooms with comfortable beds. In the kitchen we had a large table and much food, and a dear maid who prepared the meal. Behind the house there was a lovely garden and around the house we used to see fields full with grain, and large high forests. The roads near our house were narrow. We also owned a faithful grey donkey, brown cows, and black and red roosters. The animals were not living in the house, but in the stable. The hard-working donkey carried water and grain from the fields into the house. The cows walked in the pastures. But the roosters were always clamoring and flying into the house. Then we used to yell at them: "Fly into the garden, you stupid chickens!"

We were happy in our little house.

Reading 3 : A Pitiful but True Story

A happy farmer walks on the road to the city with his son and his trusted donkey. The man walks, behind him walks the donkey, on the donkey sits the boy. A man meets them, he greets them and asks: "Why, pray, is a hard-working and tired man walking on the road, and a well-shapen and lazy boy is sitting on the donkey? This is not just." Therefore the son climbs down from the donkey and walks on the road. The farmer climbs onto the donkey, and all of them go to town with a happy mind. A good man meets them, greets them and asks: "How come a healthy and strong man can sit on the donkey, and a small and weak boy must walk on the long road? This is not just." Therefore the farmer descends from the donkey, and the father and the son walk next to the donkey, the father on the right, the son on the left. And there comes a well-known man their way, greets them and asks: "What must I see? Can it be true? Why are these stupid men walking next to a strong donkey? Why does the donkey not carry them, as he ought to? This is not just." Therefore the farmer and his son sit on the donkey, both, the boy before the man, the man behind the boy. They are happy, because they don't have to walk. A man meets them, strict and angry, greets them and asks: "Are you rascals? Why are you both sitting on the poor donkey? The donkey cannot be well, if he has to carry two strong men. Can't you see that the donkey is tired, because he works a lot? This is not just." So the farmer and the boy tie the donkey's legs together above a stick and - carry him into town.

The story shows this: you can't be just, agreeable, and pleasing to all men.

Summary: A: 1. declined 2. nouns 3. first (a), second (o) 4. after 5. Possessive 6. -us, -- 7. natural 8. reflexively 9. eius, eorum, earum 10. attributive 11. Yes 12. many people, many things.

D: 1. neque...neque 2. quod; non solum...sed etiam... 3. quamquam 4. nisi 5. aut... Aut... 6. tam...quam 7. ut 8. et, ac, atque, -que.

7

PERFECT TENSE
PLUPERFECT AND FUTURE PERFECT TENSES
NUMBERS

Indo-European Languages II

PIE had words for farm animals, vehicles, body parts, as well as for abstract ideas relating to law, religion and society. To locate the speakers of **PIE** geographically, linguists were helped especially by the words for fauna and flora. There were, for instance, no words for 'palm-tree', and 'grapevine', which excluded southern and Mediterranean areas. There were, however, words for beech and birch trees, although not for oak, locating them perhaps between the Baltic Sea and the Ural mountains. We also know that between 2000 and 1000 BC, **PIE** had split up into three branches (Greek, Anatolian, and Indo-Iranian), because we have written evidence in all three, dating to that time.

Many people think that older languages were more simply constructed than their modern descendants. One look at reconstructed **PIE** shows this to be a misconception: there were three genders (masculine, feminine, neuter), at least six, possibly eight cases (all the Latin ones, plus Locative and Instrumental, of which traces are preserved in Latin); there were inflections used for persons, tense, number, mood, voice, and aspect (like *I am eating* - right now, and *I eat* - in general); adjectives agreed in gender, number, and case with their nouns. Different grammatical forms were often related to each other by **ablaut** or **vowel gradation,** as in English: **s**i**ng, s**a**ng, s**u**ng,** and **s**o**ng;** or **g**oo**se, g**ee**se.**

Chapter 7 :   **THE PERFECT TENSE; NUMERALS**

You have seen that three tenses can be formed from the **present stem** of a verb: the **present, imperfect,** and **future** tenses. To form the other three tenses - **perfect, pluperfect,** and **future perfect** - you need another stem of the verb, the **perfect stem**. For some verbs this stem can be constructed from the present stem (therefore they are sometimes called regular verbs) and for others (the majority, which are then called irregular verbs) it must be memorized, just as in English. You can, for instance, derive "walk**ed**" and "ask**ed**" from "walk" and "ask", but not "gone" and "found" from "go" and "find" (you can, but someone learning English as a foreign language can not).

A : REGULAR VERBS

The perfect stems of 1st Conjugation verbs are, save for a few exceptions, regular. They are formed by **adding -v- to the present stem**, for instance:

Verb	Present Stem	Perfect Stem
portare	porta-	porta**v**-
amare	ama-	ama**v**-
cantare	canta-	canta**v**-

In the 2nd conjugation a number of verbs, but not nearly all, form the perfect stem by **changing the -e- of the present stem to -u-** (which is, after all, only a variant of -v- in Latin):

docere	doce-	doc**u**-
monere	mone-	mon**u**-
tacere	tace-	tac**u**-

To these perfect stems you must now add sets of endings for the tenses. The first set of endings is used **exclusively** for the **perfect tense:**

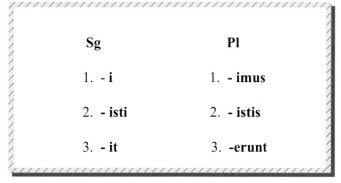

	Sg		Pl
1.	- i	1.	- imus
2.	- isti	2.	- istis
3.	- it	3.	-erunt

Repeat: these endings can be added **only to the perfect stem,** to form the **perfect tense**, like this:

		portare
Sg	1. **portáv i**	I have carried, I carried
	2. **portav ísti**	you have carried, you carried
	3. **portáv it**	he/she/it has carried, he/she/it carried
Pl	1. **portáv imus**	we have carried, we carried
	2. **portav ístis**	you have carried, you carried
	3. **portav érunt**	they have carried, they carried

		docere
Sg	1. **dócu i**	I have taught, I taught
	2. **docu ísti**	etc.
	3. **dócu it**	
Pl	1. **docú imus**	
	2. **docu ístis**	
	3. **docu érunt**	

The **first person Singular** of the perfect tense (**portavi, docui**) is called the **third principal part** of the verb. Now you know three of the four principal parts:

1st Person Singular Present	Infinitive	1st Person Singular Perfect
porto	portare	portávi
doceo	docere	dócui
amo	amare	amávi
taceo	tacere	tácui

You will learn the fourth principal part in chapter 10. The principal parts of a verb are, so to speak, its identification, which is not alike for any other verb. Only by knowing all principal parts can one produce all the forms of a verb.

Irregular verbs must therefore have **all four** principal parts listed in the dictionary, so that you can look them up, if you forget them, or have never learned them..

There is also a **past infinitive** of verbs, which is formed by adding the ending **-isse** to the **perfect stem**: **portav isse, docu isse, tacuisse, amavisse,** etc. It is translated into English as **to have carried, to have taught, to have loved**, as in:

Aeneas is said **to have carried** his father out of burning Troy.

Use of Perfect and Imperfect

The Latin **perfect**, in contrast to the imperfect, denotes a **single, unique, finished action** in the **past**, or a simple statement of a past occurrence. The **perfect** can therefore be given in English as **I have carried** or **I carried**, but **not**, like the **imperfect**, as **I used to carry** or **I was carrying**. The English simple past **I carried** can be either imperfect or perfect tense, depending on the context. **I have carried** can only be perfect.

EXERCISE A: Decide whether you would use **perfect (P)** or **imperfect (I)** for the underlined verbs (no need to translate):

1. We <u>were just eating</u>, when the man <u>barged</u> into the room. ___ ___

2. It <u>rained</u> all day. ___

3. His sister <u>used to work</u> in town. ___

4. <u>Have you eaten</u> already? ___

5. The Romans <u>defeated</u> the Etruscans in 396 B.C. at Veii. ___

6. The Romans <u>defeated</u> the Etruscans in continuous and bloody battles. ___

7. Who <u>called</u> you yesterday? ___

8. When we <u>were</u> children, we <u>obeyed</u> our parents. ___ ___

9. <u>Did</u> your grandmother <u>arrive</u>? <u>Has</u> you grandmother <u>arrived</u>? ___ ___

10. We <u>finished</u> a whole house, while you <u>were lying</u> around all day. ___ ___

EXERCISE B: Form the perfect stem and the 1st and 2nd person Singular perfect of the following verbs (you may assume that the second Conjugation verbs are regular, like **docere**):

Example:

| ambulare | ambulav- | ambulavi, ambulavisti |

1. invitare _____
2. debere _____
3. monstrare _____
4. habere _____
5. iacere _____
6. potare _____
7. spectare _____

8. tacere   _____
9. timere   _____
10. vocare   _____
11. valere   _____
12. rogare   _____
13. parere   _____
14. tenere   _____
15. laborare _____
16. placere _____

EXERCISE C: Form the past infinitive of all verbs above!

EXERCISE D: Translate the following verb forms and write their tense before the question number: present (PR), imperfect (I), future (F), perfect (P):

____ 1. cantavimus   _____   _____
____ 2. cantabimus   _____   _____
____ 3. orabant   _____
____ 4. docuerunt   _____   _____
____ 5. debebunt   _____
____ 6. potamus   _____   _____
____ 7. potavistis   _____
____ 8. tenuit   _____   _____
____ 9. laboravi   _____
____ 10. paruisti   _____   _____
____ 11. paravisti   _____
____ 12. habebam   _____   _____
____ 13. ambulabitis   _____
____ 14. timebant   _____   _____
____ 15. iacuimus   _____
____ 16. tacetis   _____   _____
____ 17. cantate   _____
____ 18. you have invited (Pl)   _____
____ 19. we will live _____
____ 20. he was (Imp)   _____
____ 21. she used to tell _____
____ 22. they are asking   _____
____ 23. we worked [2 tenses] _____
____ 24. call! (Sg)   _____
____ 25. I was looking at _____
____ 26. it is holding   _____
____ 27. they were rejoicing _____
____ 28. he was returning   _____
____ 29. you have shown (Sg) _____
____ 30. obey! (Pl)   _____
____ 31. we will be   _____

___   32. he has invited
___   33. they will go away _____
___   34. I have begged
___   35. they have warned _____

EXERCISE E: Translate the sentences:

1. Asini portaverunt magnam copiam frumenti in villam nostram.
_____

2. Puellae iacuerunt in horto et cantaverunt.
_____

3. Paravi bonam cenam, sed dominus contentus non est.
_____

4. Laborabamus in agris, ubi subito domina nos vocavit.
_____

5. Non ambulavimus in silva, quod timuimus bestias feras.
_____

6. Magister docebat pueros, sed nunc in oppido laborat.
_____

7. Cur pueri tacuerunt? Cibum non amaverunt.
_____

8. Rogavistisne amicum vestrum ob pecuniam? Rogavimus.
_____

9. Ubi habitabant poetae? In oppido. Ubi habitabunt? In villa sua.
_____

   Ubi nunc habitant? In villa nostra.

10. Claudia et Octavia cogitant [believe] pueros malos et stultos esse.
_____

11. Amicus meus non vidit me venire; cogitat me in oppido mansisse.
_____

B : Irregular Verbs

The perfect stem of irregular verbs cannot be formed; it must be memorized. Usually it is given as the 3rd principal part (= 1st person Singular perfect active), e.g. **vidi, mansi, dedi** (of **videre, manere, dare**). Removing the **-i** from these forms produces the perfect stem.
Of the verbs you have learned so far the following are **irregular:**

1. do, dare, **dedi**	to give	(Perf. stem: **ded-**)
2. sto, stare, **steti**	to stand	(**stet-**)
3. fleo, flere, **flevi**	to cry	(**flev-**)
4. maneo, manere, **mansi**	to remain	(**mans-**)

5. moveo, movere, **movi**	to move	**(mov-)**
6. respondeo, respondere, **respondi**	to answer	**(respond-)**
7. rideo, ridere, **risi**	to laugh	**(ris-)**
8. sedeo, sedere, **sedi**	to sit	**(sed-)**
9. video, videre, **vidi**	to see	**(vid-)**

Actually **movi** and **flevi** are not technically irregular, since -v- is just another spelling of -u-, but they are included here anyway.

EXERCISE F: Conjugate the perfect tense of five of the verbs above, and form the past infinitive!

One verb has been done for you as a pattern:

vidi	I saw (have seen)
vidisti	you saw (have seen)
vidit	he, she, it saw (has seen)
vidimus	we saw (have seen)
vidistis	you saw (have seen)
viderunt	they saw (have seen)
vidisse	to have seen, having seen

THE PLUSQUAMPERFECT AND THE FUTURE PERFECT

The remaining two tenses are formed from the same perfect stem. The action of the **plusquamperfect,** or **pluperfect** for short (PP), is **previous** to an action in the **past**, for instance:

When he arrived [past], we **had** already **eaten** [previous to his arrival].

In English the pluperfect always uses the auxiliary verb **had** and a **past participle.**

The action of the **future perfect** (FP) is **previous** to an action or adverb of the future, for instance:
By tomorrow [future] I **will have read** the book [previous to tomorrow].
A storm will come in the afternoon [future]; **will you have finished** the garden work?
[= previous to the storm]. Make a few more English sentences with a future perfect.
In English the auxiliary verbs **will have** and a **past participle** are used for the future perfect.

To form the **pluperfect** in Latin you need only add the imperfect of the verb **esse, to be**, as suffixes to the perfect stem: (**eram, eras, erat, eramus, eratis, erant**)

1. **portáv eram**	I had carried, I had been carrying	
2. **portáv eras**	you had carried,	"
3. **portáv erat**	he/she/it had carried	"
1. **portav erámus**	we had carried	
2. **portav erátis**	you had carried	
3. **portáv erant**	they had carried	

Similarly:

1. **docúeram**	I had taught, I had been teaching
2. **docúeras**	
3. **docúerat**	etc.
1. **docuerámus**	
2. **docuerátis**	
3. **docúerant**	

To form the **future perfect** you need only add the future forms of **esse, (ero, eris, erit, erimus, eritis)** to the Perfect stem. However, you can **not** use the **3rd person plural (erunt)**, because this is already used as an ending for the **perfect** (spectave**runt,** debue**runt,** etc.) Instead use the ending **-erint.**

1. **portáv ero**	I will have carried, I will have been carrying	
2. **portáv eris**	you will have carried	
3. **portáv erit**	he/she/it will have carried	
1. **portav érimus**	we will have carried	
2. **portav éritis**	you will have carried	
3. **portáv erint**	they will have carried	

and:

1. **docúero**	I will have taught, I will have been teaching	
2. **docúeris**		
3. **docúerit**		
1. **docuérimus**	etc.	
2. **docuéritis**		
3. **docúerint**		

Consequently, there are three very similar forms for the 3rd Person Plural:

portavérunt (perfect) ,   portáverant (pluperfect),   portáverint (future perfect)

They are easily distinguished, though, if you remember that **-a-** is the vowel characteristic for the **past** (imperfect, pluperfect), and **-i-** is the vowel characteristic for the **future** (future, future perfect)

EXERCISE G:    Translate these forms: (1 to 15: new tenses; 16 to 28: all tenses)

1. habitaverit
2. ambulaverat
3. vidistis
4. volavimus
5. paravero
6. laudavit
7. navigaverimus
8. monstraveratis
9. manserunt
10. habueratis
11. fleverant
12. amavisti
13. vocaverint
14. tenueras

15. risi
16. visitabas
17. videt
18. vidit
19. potavistis
20. valete
21. debebit
22. festinaverat
23. respondit
24. dederam
25. oppugnaverunt
26. sederunt
27. spectaverant
28. moverint

Also irregular are the perfect stems of **esse** (**fu-**) and **ire** (**i-**), and their compounds:

		esse		ire (ii -> i before s)	
Sg	**fui**	I have been, was	**ii**	I have gone, I went
	fuisti	you have been, were	**isti**	you have gone, you went
	fuit	he, she, it has been, was	**iit**	he/she/it has gone, went
Pl.	**fuimus**	we have been, were	**iimus**	we have gone, we went
	fuistis	you have been, were	**istis**	you have gone, you went
	fuerunt	they have been, were	**ierunt**	they have gone, they went

The Principal Parts of **esse** and its Compounds

1. **sum, esse, fui** — to be (**fu-**)
2. **absum, abesse, afui** — to be away
3. **adsum, adesse, adfui** — to be present
4. **desum, deesse, defui** — to be lacking
5. **intersum, interesse, interfui** — to be present, take part
6. **obsum, obesse, obfui** — to be against, harm
7. **praesum, praeesse, praefui** — to be in charge
8. **supersum, superesse, superfui** — to be left over
9. **prosum, prodesse, profui** — to be for, be of use
10. **possum, posse, potui** — to be able

The Perfect of **ire** and its Compunds:

eo, ire, ii — to go (**i-**)

abii - I have gone away; **adii** - I have gone toward; **exii** - I have gone out; **inii** - I have gone in, begun; **interii, perii** - I have gone down, perished; **praeterii** - I have gone past, omitted; **transii** - I have gone across, crossed.

Lectio I

FABULAE PARVAE

1. Exiit. Rediit.

2. Abiit vir. Rediit cum femina. Abiit vir. Rediit cum asino. Abiit femina. Non rediit. Afuit. Abiit asinus. Neque rediit. Superfuit vir.

3. Nautae navigaverunt. Bestia fera in aqua adfuit. Bestia nautis obfuit et navem [ship] eorum delevit. Nautae in aquam inierunt. Magna copia aquae fuit, sed nautis non profuit: aquam potare non potuerunt, quod salsa [salty] fuit. Etiam cibus defuit. Sed nautae non perierunt: Deus aquae, Neptunus, interfuit et nautas servavit. Nautae ex aqua exire potuerunt. Beati nautae.

NUMERALS

There are four types of number words in Latin:
1. **Cardinal** numbers (one, two, three...)
2. **Ordinal** numbers (first, second, third...)
3. **Distributive** numbers (one each, two each, three each...)
4. **Numerical Adverbs** (once, twice, three times...)

We will begin with **cardinal** and **ordinal** numbers. Of the cardinal numbers, **unus, duo, tres,** and **milia** are declined, as are the **hundreds** from **ducenti** to **nongenti** (200 to 900); **ordinal numbers are all declined.**

Unus, una, unum, *one,* is declined (Singular only, of course!) like an adjective of the first and second declension (**bonus, clarus**), except in the genitive and dative, which are similar to those of **quis,** and of **is, ea, id,** and are shared by many pronouns and numerical adjectives: genitive Singular: **- ius,** dative Singular: **-i.**

	M	F	N
N	unus	una	unum
G	unius	unius	unius
D	uni	uni	uni
A	unum	unam	unum
Ab	uno	una	uno

Duo, duae, duo, *two*: duo is the only remnant of the lost **dual** form (a number besides Singular and Plural for two people or things, which existed in Indo-European and is still preserved in Ancient Greek).

	M	F	N
N	duo	duae	duo
F	duorum	duarum	duorum
D	duobus	duabus	duobus
A	duos	duas	duo
Ab	duobus	duabus	duobus

Tres, tria, *three,* is declined like an adjective of the third Declension (see chapters 11 and 12).
Milia, *thousand(s)* is the Plural of **mille,** *one thousand* (**mille** is not declined).
Milia is a **neuter noun,** declined like a third declension i-stem.

There was no numeral for **zero**; this was introduced at a later time by the Arabs.

	M	F	N
N	tres	tres	tria
G	trium	trium	trium
D	tribus	tribus	tribus
A	tres	tres	tria
Ab	tribus	tribus	tribus

N	milia
G	milium
D	milibus
A	milia
Ab	milibus

Since **milia** is a noun, it must be followed by the **genitive** of a noun, for example:

duo milia virorum, two thousand (of) men
tria milia fabularum, three thousand stories
multa milia stellarum, many thousands of stars
milia verborum, thousands of words   **but: mille verba,** (one) thousand words
vir mille verborum, a man of thousand words

Street number in Roman numerals.

The number 4 is often written "**IV**"

Roman numerals are frequently used for clocks and watches. The Romans themselves had only sundials and water clocks, which were not very accurate. The time between sunrise and sunset was called 'day' and divided into twelve hours. These hours did not have sixty minutes but varied in length between seasons: they were longest in the summer.

Roman Numeral	Cardinals	Ordinals (all decllined)	Arabic Num.
I	unus,a,um	primus (a,um)	1
II	duo,ae,o	secundus (a,um)	2
III	tres,ia	tertius (a,um)	3
IV	quattuor	quartus (a,um	4
V	quinque	quintus (a,um)	5
VI	sex	sextus (a,um)	6
VII	septem	septimus etc.	7
VIII	octo	octavus	8
IX	novem	nonus	9
X	decem	decimus	10
XI	undecim	undecimus	11
XII	duodecim	duodecimus	12
XIII	tredecim	tertius decimus	13
XIV	quattuordecim	quartus decimus	14
XV	quindecim	quintus decimus	15
XVI	sedecim	sextus decimus	16
XVII	septendecim	septimus decimus	17
XVIII	duodeviginti	duodevicesimus	18
XIX	undeviginti	undevicesimus	19
XX	viginti	vicesimus	20
XXI	viginti unus	vicesimus primus	21
	or: unus et viginti	unus et vicesimus	
XXII	viginti duo	vicesimus secundus	22
	or: duo et viginti	duo et vicesimus	
	etc.	etc.	
XXVIII	duodetriginta	duodetricesimus	28
XXIX	undetriginta	undetricesimus	29
XXX	triginta	tricesimus	30
XL	quadraginta	quadragesimus	40
L	quinquaginta	quinquagesimus	50
LX	sexaginta	sexagesimus	60
LXX	septuaginta	septuagesimus	70
LXXX	octoginta	octogesimus	80
XC	nonaginta	nonagesimus	90
C	centum	centesimus	100
CC	ducenti,ae,a	ducentesimus	200
CCC	trecenti (ae,a)	trecentesimus	300
CCCC	quadringenti	quadringentesimus	400
D	quingenti	quingentesimus	500
DC	sescenti	sescentesimus	600
DCC	septingenti	septingentesimus	700
DCCC	octingenti	octingentesimu s	800
CM or DCCCC	nongenti	nongentesimus	900
M	mille	millesimus	1000

In ordinals with two words both are declined, for instance: in the 17th year: **anno decimo septimo**

 **EXERCISE H:**   Write each Roman numeral **in Latin (words)**:

  1. M (mille) 2. IX   3. IV   4. XVIII 5. XXII   6. C   7. LXX   8. XL   9. CCCC   10. XCV

Numerical Adjectives:
  Among these belong:

totus,a,um - *whole, entire*   **nullus,a,um** - *none, no (also used for zero)*
ullus,a,um - *any*   **solus,a,um** - *alone, only*
alter, altera, alterum - *the other (of two)* **alius, alia, aliud** - *another,different (more than two)*
uter, utra, utrum - *which? (of two)*   **neuter, neutra, neutrum** - *neither (of two)*
uterque, utraque, utrumque - *both*

They are declined like **unus**, with their shared **genitives** ending in **-ius,** and their **datives** in **-i** :
**totius, toti; (n)ullius, (n)ulli; solius, soli; alterius, alteri; alius, alii; utrius, utri;
neutrius, neutri; utriusque, utrique.**

 **EXERCISE I :**   Read the phrases and answer the questions:
                                 Habemus in nostra villa rustica:

  unam mensam,   **duas** ancillas,   **tria** stabula,   **quattuor** gallos,   **quinque** servos,
  sex portas,   **septem** equos,   **octo** lectos,   **novem** fenestras,   **decem** vaccas.

  Quot habemus hic: fenestras, portas, viros, feminas, puellas, pueros, asinos, libros?

  1. How can one write six gods in one word?

  2. If one arranges the digits of the word **IVDICIVM** (= **iudicium,** *judgment),* in the
      right order, what **year** does one get, which was thought by people to signify the end
      of the world and the Last Judgment?

  3. How can you show that half of 12 is 7, that 4 minus 1 is 5, and 19 minus 1 is 20?

  4. And how do you read **CID, DVC, DIL, CIX, LID, VI** ?

Lectio II: Nivea

Olim erat parva puella timida, nomine Niveae, quae habitabat in magna regia
cum noverca sua, regina terrae. Noverca autem mala femina erat. Cottidie
ambulabat ad speculum et rogavit: "Speculum, speculum, responde mihi,
quis est pulcherrima in patria nostra?" Speculum semper respondebat: "Vere
5   es tu, regina mea, tu sola es pulcherrima in patria nostra." Post multos
annos autem puella nondum erat parva, sed magna et pulchra. Aliquando
noverca ad speculum adiit et rogavit: "Speculum, speculum, responde mihi,
quis est pulcherrima in patria nostra?" Tum speculum respondit: "Regina
mea, tu es pulchra, sed filia tua est milies pulchrior te." Noverca mala erat
10   irata et puellam necare desideravit. Imperavit amico suo: "I in silvam cum
Nivea et neca eam! Tum da mihi linguam eius pro signo mortis."

Nivea et vir ierunt in silvam, sed vir eam necare non potuit, quod erat pulchra
et cara. Ergo imperavit ei: "Abi in silvam neque redi ad regiam tuam. Noverca
tua femina mala est. Debes cavere eam, quod te necare desiderat." Tum
15   cervum necavit et linguam eius novercae improbae dedit. Noverca falsa
linguam vidit et gaudebat: tandem pulcherrima in patria sua erat.

Nivea erravit in silva usque vidit casam parvam. Ad casam adiit, portam
pulsavit et urbane salutavit: "Salve!" Sed nemo respondit. "Quis hic habitat?"
Nivea rogavit et in casam parvam intravit. Vidit mensam cum septem sellis,
20   septem patellis et septem furcis. Cena in patellis erat. Dextra, prope
portam, cubiculum erat. In cubiculo stabant septem lecti vacui. "Ubi sum?"
Nivea stupefacta se rogavit, quod sellae lectique, patella furcaeque minimi
erant. Nivea autem fumelica erat neque exspectabat incolas casae: sedit ad
mensam et gustavit paulum de quoque patello. Postea in cubiculum
25   ambulavit, et, quod erat fessa, iacuit in lecto et mox in somno erat.

---

(1) nomine - by the name of; quae - who; regia,ae - palace; (2) noverca,ae - stepmother;
regina,ae - queen; cottidie - daily; (3) speculum,i - mirror; (4) pulcherrima - the most
beautiful; (6) aliquando - one day, once; (9) milies pulchrior te - a thousand times more
beautiful than you; (10) necare - to kill; desiderare - to desire; (11) mors, mortis - death;
(14) cavere - to beware of;(15) cervus,i - deer; (errare - to wander around); (18) pulsare -
to knock; urbane - politely; (19) sella,ae - chair; (20) patellum,i - plate; furca,ae - fork;
(22) stupefactus,a,um - amazed, astonished; minimus,a,um - very small; fumelicus,a,um
- hungry; (24) gustare - to taste; quoque (Abl.of quisque) - each; (25) somnus,i - sleep

Erant autem septem nani, qui habitabant in casa parva. Vespero de labore suo in casam redierunt. Niveam non viderunt, sed putabant aliquid esse mirum. Primus nanus rogavit: "Quis potavit de poculo meo?" Secundus: "Quis gustavit cibum meum?" Tertius: "Quis sedit in sella mea?" Quartus: "Quis tenuit furcam meam?"
30   Quintus: "Quis movit mensam nostram?" Sextus: "Quis ambulavit in cubiculum nostrum?" Septimus: "Et quis iacuit in lecto meo?"

Postea Niveam viderunt, quae dormiebat in lecto, et eam circumsteterunt et spectaverunt. Primus nanus monuit: "Ne excitate puellam de somno!" Sed Nivea subito in lecto sedit et nanos spectavit. "Quis es?" eam rogaverunt nani. Tum
35   Nivea narravit historiam suam et septem nani iudicaverunt: "Iuvabimus puellam bellam et servabimus eam. Debet manere in casa nostra." Post cenam sex nani in lectis suis dormiverunt, sed, quod Niveam miseram disturbare non potuerunt, septimus nanus dormivit singulam horam cum quoque amico suo. Postridie Niveam monuerunt: "Mane in casa! Ne exi! Ne responde, si quis portam
40   pulsat!" Tum abierunt, quod laborare debuerunt.

Interea noverca mala adierat ad speculum et rogaverat: "Speculum, speculum, responde mihi, quis est pulcherrima in patria?" Speculum responderat: "Vere tu es pulchra, regina, sed Nivea, quae habitat in parva casa septem nanorum est milies pulchrior te." Noverca erat valde irata et rubra et clamavit: "Puellam stultam
45   necare debebo." Diu cogitavit, tum paravit malum venenatum, mutavit in anum et iit ad casam parvam nanorum. Ibi portam pulsavit et vocavit: "Habeo pulchra mala rubra. Nonne desideras malum rubrum?" Nivea ex fenestra spectavit et vidit anum ignotam et cogitavit per se: "Nonne me monuerunt nani 'Noli exire'? Ego non exibo, sed solum anus mihi malum per fenestram dabit."

50   Feminae respondit: "Pecuniam non habeo." Sed femina: "Donabo tibi", inquit, "malum." Nivea autem, ubi malum gustavit, mox humi iacuit quasi mortua. Noverca mala risit et in regiam suam rediit.

---

(26) nanus,i - dwarf; labor,laboris - work; (27) putare - to think, believe, consider; aliquid - something; (28) poculum,i - cup; (32) quae - who; dormire (4th Conj.) - to sleep; (33) excitare - to arouse, excite; (35) iudicare - to judge, decide; iuvare - to help; (36) servare - to save; (38) singulam horam - for one hour each; (39) postridie - the next day; si quis - if anyone; (45) malum,i - apple; venenatus,a,um - poisoned; mutare - to change; (46) anus,us (f.) - old woman; (50) inquit (inserted into the direct quote) - he/she says, said; (51) humi - on the ground; mortuus,a,um - dead;

Vespero nani redierunt de labore suo. Niveam mortuam viderunt et fleverunt. Tum Niveam intra arcam vitream in hortum suum portaverunt. Ibi arca stabat et

55 nani Niveam cottidie spectare potuerunt; adhuc erat quasi mortua, sed erat pulchra. Aliquando filius regis nomine Artus ambulavit in silva et arcam vitream vidit. Oravit nanos: "Debeo habere arcam cum puella pulchra. Eam amo." Nani cogitaverunt inter se et postea ei dederunt arcam. Servi eius arcam per silvam portare debuerunt. Subito servi ierunt trans radicem arboris: arcam tenere non

60 potuerunt et arca cecidit. Malum exiit e puella et Nivea ad vitam rediit. Cum Arto valido in regiam eius ambulavit. Noverca mala debebat manere in villa sua cum speculo suo. Artus et Nivea autem habebant vitam longam et beatam.

Si mortui non sunt, adhuc hodie vivunt.

---

(54) arca,ae - coffin; vitreus,a,um - glass(y); (56) rex, regis - king; (59) radix, radicis - root; arbor,arboris - tree; (60) cecidit - he/she/it fell; (63) vivunt - they are living.

Nivea et septem nani:
Stultus, Sternuens, Medicus, Morosus, Fortunatus, Pudicus, Somniculosus.
Et gallus pulcher.

A. Questions:

1. Which three tenses can be formed using the **present stem** of a verb? _____,

   _____, _____.

2. From which stem are the Perfect, Pluperfect, and Future Perfect formed? _____

3. In which conjugation do almost all verbs have **regular** perfect stem formation? _____

4. The endings **-i, -isti, -erunt** can be used only to form the _____ tense.

5. **Risi, vidi, amavi** are the _____ principal parts of these verbs.

6. **Ridere, videre, amare** are the _____ principal parts.

7. The **perfect infinitive** of portare is _____.

8. A repeated action in the past is expressed with the Latin _____ tense.

9. A single, unique, finished past action is shown with the _____ tense.

10. Which number or digit did the Romans not have? _____

11. Are all cardinal numbers declined? Y/N _____

12. Are all ordinal numbers declined? Y/N _____

13. What type of word is **milia**? _____

14. The endings for the pluperfect and future perfect are almost identical to the _____

    and _____ tenses of **esse.**

B. Do not confuse:

afui - adfui; profui - potui; afui - abii; abii - adii; abii - abi; mille - milia; quadraginta - quadringenti.

The Etruscans

The history of the Etruscans is so shrouded in mystery that it has a fairytale-like ring to it. Like the Celts, they are thought to have come from Asia Minor, probably around 1000 BC. They settled in central Italy and achieved a high standard of living and culture. Their political organization consisted of a league of cities. Such Etruscan cities were, for instance, Veji, Volterra, Tarquinia, Orvieto, and Perugia. Next to their cities they kept large burial sites, in which many sculptures and tombs have been found during excavations.

Etruscan chariot (Detail)

Bronze wine Jar

Funerary statue

Even though the Etruscans were driven out of Rome or Romanized after 300 BC, their influence on the Romans in many areas was enormous: road construction, temple building, sewage techniques, gladiator games, political and public institutions, and divination from intestines and from birds were all Etruscan contributions.

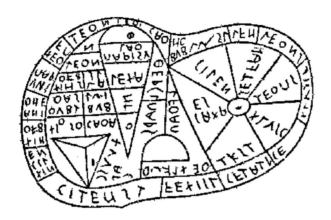

Etruscan drawing of a liver used for divination.

The Etruscan language has remained a mystery to this day. It can be read, since ancient Greek letters were used to write it (from right to left), but little can be understood, since it seems to be a language isolate. Existing inscriptions and bilingual texts are too short and too limited in vocabulary to yield much information. The longest Etruscan text was found on linen pieces wrapped around a mummy. It may be a part of the so-called Etruscan Books, which contained their views on life and fate, and which were often mentioned by Roman authors.

An example of Etruscan:

> **Larth Arnthal Plecus clan Ramthasc Apatrual**
>
> **eslz zilachnthas avils thunem muvalchls lupu.**

(Larth, son of Arnth Plecu and Ramtha Apatrui, died after two times pretorship at age 49.)

Chapter 7: Answers and Translations

Exercise A:
   1. I, P   2. I   3. I   4. P   5. P   6. I   7. P   8. I, I   9. P, P   10. P, I

Exercise B:
1. invitav- 2. debu- 3. monstrav- 4. habu- 5. iacu- 6. potav- 7. spectav- 8. tacu-
9. timu- 10. vocav- 11. valu- 12. rogav- 13. paru- 14. tenu- 15. laborav- 16. placu-

Exercise D:
1. we sang, we have sung (P) 2. we will sing (F) 3. they prayed (I) 4. they (have) taught (P)
5. they will owe (F) 6. we drink (PR) 7. you drank (P) 8. he held (P) 9. I have worked (P)
10. you have obeyed (P) 11. you have prepared (P) 12. I used to have (I) 13. you will walk (F)
14. they feared (I) 15. we lay (P) 16. you are silent (PR) 17. sing! (Imp.) 18. invitavistis (P) 19.
habitabimus (F) 20. erat (I) 21. narrabat (I) 22. rogant (PR) 23. laborabamus, laboravimus (I, P)
24. voca! 25. spectabam (I) 26. tenet (PR) 27. gaudebant (I) 28. redibat (I) 29. monstravisti (P)
30. parete! 31. erimus (F) 32. invitavit (P) 33. abibunt (F) 34. oravi (P) 35. monuerunt (P)

Exercise E:
   1. The donkeys carried a large amount of grain into our farmhouse.
   2. The girls lay in the garden and sang.
   3. I have prepared a good meal, but the master is not satisfied.
   4. We were working in the fields, when suddenly the mistress called us.
   5. We did not walk in the forest, because we feared the wild beasts.
   6. The teacher used to teach the boys, but now he works in town.
   7. Why were the boys silent? They did not like the food.
   8. Have you asked your friend because of the money? Yes.
   9. Where did the poets use to live? In town. Where will they live? In
      their country house. Where are they living now? In our house.
   10. Claudia and Octavia believe the boys to be bad and stupid. (...believe that the boys..)
   11. My friend did not see me come; he thinks I stayed in town. (believes me to have stayed)

Exercise F:
1. He will have lived 2. she had walked 3. you have seen 4. we flew 5. I will have prepared
6. he praised 7. we will have sailed 8. you had shown 9. they remained 10. you had had
11. they had cried 12. you have loved 13. they will have called 14. you had held 15. I laughed 16.
you used to visit 17. she sees 18. he saw 19. you drank 20. farewell! 21. he will owe 22. she
had hurried 23. he answered 24. I had given 25. they have attacked 26. they sat
27. they had looked at 28. they will have moved

Reading 1: Little Stories
1. She left. She came back.
2. The man went away. He came back with a woman. The man left. He came back with a donkey.
The woman went away. She did not come back. She was gone. The donkey went away. He did not
come back either. The man was left over.
3. The sailors sailed. There was a wild beast present in the water. The beast harmed the sailors
and destroyed their ship. The sailors went into the water. There was a great amount of water, but it
was of no use to the sailors: they could not drink the water, because it was salty. Food was lacking

also. But the sailors did not perish: The god of the water, Neptune, was there and saved the sailors. The sailors were able to come out of the water. Happy sailors.

Exercise H:
1. mille (1000) 2. novem (9) 3. quattuor (4) 4. duodeviginti (18) 5. viginti duo (or: duo et viginti) (22) 6. centum (100) 7. septuaginta (70) 8. quadraginta (40) 9. quadringenti (400)
10. nonaginta quinque (95)

RIDDLE:

1. **VIDI (VI** = six; **DI** = gods)
2. **MDCVVIII** = 1613
3. ~~XII~~ = VII   I̶V = V   XI̶X = XX
4. kid, duck, dill, kicks, lid, sex

Reading 2 : Snow-White
Once upon a time there was a small, shy girl by the name of Snow-white, who lived in a large palace with her stepmother, the queen of the land. The stepmother was, however, an evil woman. Every day she would walk up to her mirror and ask: "Mirror, mirror, answer me, who is the most beautiful woman in our homeland?" The mirror would always answer: "Indeed it is you, my queen, you alone are the most beautiful one in our land." After many years, however, the girl was not small any more, but tall and beautiful. One day the stepmother went to her mirror and asked: "Mirror, mirror, answer me, who is the most beautiful woman in our homeland?" Then the mirror answered: "My queen, you are beautiful, but your daughter is a thousand times more beautiful than you." The bad stepmother was livid and wanted to kill the girl. She ordered a friend: "Go into the woods with Snow-white and kill her! Then give me her tongue as a sign of her death."

Snow-white and the man went into the forest, but the man could not kill her, because she was beautiful and dear. Therefore he ordered her: "Walk around in the forest and don't return to your palace. Your stepmother is an evil woman. You must be on your guard from her, because she wants to kill you." Then he killed a deer and gave its tongue to the wicked stepmother. The stepmother saw the substitute tongue and was happy: at last she was the most beautiful woman in the land.

Snow-white wandered around in the forest until she saw a small house. She approached the house, knocked on the door and greeted politely: "A good day to you!" But no-one answered. "Who lives here?" Snow-white asked and entered the little house. She saw a table with seven chairs, seven plates, and seven forks. Dinner was on the plates. On the right, near the door, was a bedroom. In the bedroom stood seven empty beds. "Where am I?" Snow-white asked herself in amazement, because the chairs and beds, the plates and forks were very small. But Snow-white was hungry and did not wait for the inhabitants of the house: she sat at the table and tasted a little from each plate. Afterwards she walked into the bedroom, and, because she was tired, she lay in a bed and soon was asleep [in sleep].

There were, however, seven dwarfs who lived in the small house. In the evening they returned from their work to the house. They did not see Snow-white, but thought that something was strange. The first dwarf asked: "Who drank from my cup?" The second: "Who tasted my food?" The third: "Who sat in my chair?" The fourth: "Who held my fork?" The fifth: "Who moved our table?" The sixth: "Who walked into our bedroom?" The seventh: "And who lay in my bed?"

Then they saw Snow-white, who was sleeping in a bed, and they stood around her and looked at her. The first dwarf warned: "Don't wake the girl up from her sleep!" But Snow-white suddenly sat up in the bed and looked at the dwarfs. "Who are you?" the dwarfs asked her. Then Snow-white told them her story, and the seven dwarfs decided: "We will help the beautifull girl and save her. She must remain in our house." After dinner six dwarfs slept in their beds, but because they could not disturb poor Snow-white, the seventh dwarf slept one hour with each friend. The next day they warned Snow-white: "Stay in the house! Don't go out! Don't answer, if anybody knocks on the door!" Then they went away, because they had to work.

In the meantime the evil stepmother had gone to the mirror and asked: "Mirror, mirror, answer me, who is the most beautiful woman in the land?" The mirror had answered: "Indeed, you are beautiful, Queen, but Snow-white, who lives in the little house of the seven dwarfs, is thousand times more beautiful than you." The stepmother was very angry and red [in her face] and shouted: "I must kill the stupid girl." She pondered for a long time, then she prepared a poisoned apple, changed into an old woman and went to the little house of the dwarfs. There she knocked at the door and called out: "I have beautiful red apples. Don't you want a red apple?" Snow-white looked out of the window and saw the unfamiliar old woman and thought to herself: "Didn't the dwarfs warn me 'Don't go out'? I will not go out, but the old woman will only give me an apple through the window." To the woman she answered: "I do not have any money." But the woman said: "I will give you an apple for a present." When Snow-white tasted the apple, however, she soon lay on the ground as if dead. The evil stepmother laughed and returned to her palace.

In the evening the dwarfs returned from their work. They saw the dead Snow-white and cried. Then they carried Snow-white in a glass coffin into their garden. There the coffin stood, and the dwarfs could look at Snow-white every day; still she was like dead, but beautiful. One day the king's son, named Artus, walked in the forest and saw the glass coffin. He begged the dwarfs: "I must have the coffin with the beautiful girl. I love her." The dwarfs thought among themselves and afterwards they gave him the coffin. His servants had to carry the coffin through the woods. Suddenly the servants went over the root of a tree: they could not hold on to the coffin and the coffin fell. The apple came out of the girl, and Snow-white returned to life. She walked with mighty Artus into his palace. The evil stepmother had to remain in her palace with her mirror. Artus and Snow-white, however, had a long and happy life.
And if they have not died, they are still living today.

The seven dwarfs: **Dopey** (Stultus), **Sneezy** (Sternuens), **Doc** (Medicus), **Grumpy** (Morosus), **Happy** (Fortunatus), **Bashful** (Pudicus), **Sleepy** (Somniculosus)

Summary: 1. Present, Imperfect, Future 2. Perfect stem   3. 1st 4. Perfect 5. 3rd 6. 2nd 7. portavisse 8. Imperfect 9. Perfect 10. zero 11. no 12. yes 13. noun 14. Imperfect, Future.

8

PRONOUNS: DEMONSTRATIVE; RELATIVE;
REFLEXIVE; INDEFINITE
PRONOMINAL ADJECTIVES

A LITTLE QUIZ ABOUT LANGUAGES

True or False:

1. The Indo-European language family is just one of many
   language families in the world.   T   F

2. English *three* and Latin *tres* are cognates.   T   F

3. The similarities among the IE languages are due to
   Borrowing.   T   F

4. Welsh is a Celtic language.   T   F

5. Proto-Indo-European is a reconstructed language.   T   F

6. The Indo-European tribes' homeland was in India.   T   F

7. The Scandinavian languages are Slavic languages.   T   F

8, Provencal, a Romance language, is extinct today.   T   F

9. *Hellenic* is another name for *Armenian*.   T   F

10. Before they were conquered by Caesar, the Gauls spoke
    a Celtic language.   T   F

11. Sanskrit was written down as early as 3000 B.C.   T   F

12. Romanian, spoken in Romania, is a Romance language.   T   F

13. Romany, spoken by Gypsies, is a Romance language.   T   F

14. Catalan is the official language of Andorra.   T   F

15. Older languages, like Proto-Indo-European, were less
    inflected and more simply constructed than their
    descendants spoken today.   T   F

Chapter 8 : PRONOUNS : DEMONSTRATIVE, RELATIVE, INDEFINITE

A: **Demonstrare** or **monstrare** means **to show** or **to point out**. **DEMONSTRATIVE PRONOUNS** are consequently pronouns that point to a noun, such as **this, that, that one there**. The most common Latin demonstrative pronouns are:

1. **hic, haec, hoc** - *this* 2. **ille, illa, illud** - *that*

Their pattern of declension follows **is, ea, id** very closely:

	Sg			Pl		
	M	F	N	M	F	N
N	hic	haec	hoc	hi	hae	haec
G	huius	huius	huius	horum	harum	horum
D	huic	huic	huic	his	his	his
A	hunc	hanc	hoc	hos	has	haec
Ab	hoc	hac	hoc	his	his	his

	M	F	N	M	F	N
N	ille	illa	illud	illi	illae	illa
G	illius	illius	illius	illorum	illarum	illorum
D	illi	illi	illi	illis	illis	illis
A	illum	illam	illud	illos	illas	illa
Ab	illo	illa	illo	illis	illis	illis

When referring to two people who have been previously mentioned, **hic** means **the latter** and **ille, the former**. The demonstrative pronoun does not have to stand before its noun in Latin, as it does in English, but can come after it (pointing backward, so to speak).

Examples:

    hic vir - this man; **hi viri -** these men; **illa puella -** that girl

    illius feminae - of that woman; **illius amici -** of that friend;

    haec dona - these gifts; **huic feminae -** to this woman

These pronouns can also be used by themselves, much like adjectives can; then the noun is implied:

    hic - this man, he; **haec** (Neuter Plural) - these things, or: the following;

    illa - that woman, she; **ille -** that man, he; **illi -** to him.

                  !!! His verbis does not mean **his words**, but...?

There are also three adverbs related to **hic:**

        hic - here; **hinc -** from here; **huc -** to(wards) here

From **ille** and **illa** developed the French and Spanish articles **(le, la, il, las,** etc.).

 **EXERCISE A:**   **Translate:**

1. Amicus huius puellae est poeta.
2. Illa rogavit me: "Vidistine hunc equum bonum?"
3. Hoc anno nostram villam aedificavimus. [*we built*]
4. His verbis nos monuit dominus: "Cavete, liberi, canem!" [cavere, *to beware;* canis, *dog*]
5. Dedimus illi multa et pulchra dona. [Ambiguous]
6. Non amamus hos nautas: (illi) sunt mali.
7. Cur non potavistis illum vinum rubrum?
8. Femina irata huic viro clamavit: "Exi, improbe, ex villa mea!"

Another demonstrative pronoun is **iste**, **ista**, **istud**, *this one, that one*. For its declension see Appendix. In Latin writing, **is, ea, id** is sometimes used as a demonstrative pronoun (**is equus**, *this horse*; **ea dona**, *these gifts*).

B: THE RELATIVE PRONOUN "relates" nouns and their descriptions to each other, for example: The cat who danced on the telephone wire was slightly overweight. The relative clause, starting with "who" tells us more about the cat. In English there are three relative pronouns: **which, who, that.** They distinguish persons (who, that) from objects (which, that). In Latin relative pronouns, like in adjectives, there is no distinction between persons and things, but rather between masculine, feminine, and neuter.
Therefore: The man who walked ...
         The garden, which was blooming...
         The horse that neighed...
all use the same relative pronoun in Latin, namely **qui**, which is the nominative masculine Singular form.

	Sg M	Sg F	Sg N	Pl M	Pl F	Pl N	
N	qui	quae	quod	qui	quae	quae	who, which
G	cuius	cuius	cuius	quorum	quarum	quorum	whose
D	cui	cui	cui	quibus	quibus	quibus	to whom
A	quem	quam	quod	quos	quas	quae	whom
Ab	a quo	a qua	quo	quibus	quibus	quibus	by whom

The appropriate form of the **relative pronoun (RP)** is determined by two considerations:
1. The **gender** and **number** of the **RP** are determined by the preceding noun to which it refers; this noun is called the **antecedent**.
2. The **case** of the **RP** is determined by **its function** in the **dependent clause**.

Examples:

antecedent	dependent clause	(rest of main clause)
1. Equi,	**qui** ambulant in horto,	sunt nostri.
masc., Pl The horses	**RP: Subject = Nominative** **who** are walking in the garden	are ours.

antecedent	dependent clause	(rest of main clause)
2. Equi,	**quos** vidimus in horto, (vidi**mus** = subject, **we**)	sunt pulchri.
masc., Pl The horses,	**RP: Direct Object** (of vidimus) = **accusative** **which** (**whom**) we saw in the garden,	are beautiful.

3. Vidi puellam,	**cui** dederatis pecuniam. (dera**tis** = subject, **you** Pl)	
fem., Sg. I saw the girl	**Indirect Object = Dative** **to whom** you had given the money.	

Because of the special nature of the **genitive** (possessive), the genitive pronoun "whose", **cuius, quorum, quarum,** is always followed by a noun (the "possession") in any one of the cases, for instance:

The man **whose house** is in town... (house = nom.)
  cuius villa
The man **of whose poems** everybody was tired... (of poems = gen.)
  cuius carminum (that's third Declension)
The man **to whose daughter** we gave the chickens... (to...daughter = dat.)
  cuius filiae
The man **whose horses** the thief had stolen... (horses = acc.)
  cuius equos
The man **by whose slaves** the dinner was cooked... (by...slaves = abl.)
  a cuius servis
The men **whose horses** the thief had stolen...
  quorum equos
The women **whose horses** the thief had stolen...
  quarum equos

Prepositions are put **before** the relative pronoun, never at the end of the dependent clause.
The relative pronoun is never implied in Latin; it must alwys be expressed, for instance.:
    This is the man (whom) you saw = Hic est vir, **quem** vidisti.

In Latin one does not differentiate between inclusive and noninclusive relative sentences, as one does in English with a comma:

His wife, who lives in New York, is a painter.   (one wife)

His wife who lives in New York is a painter.   (several wives)

In this book a comma will always be used before and after a <u>Latin</u> relative clause.

EXERCISE B: Translate only the **underlined** parts of the following sentences: the antecedent and the relative pronoun (and the preposition, if necessary):

1. <u>The children to whom</u> the teacher gave the books are brats.
2. We drank <u>the water which</u> was clear.
3. <u>The town in which</u> we live is very old.
4. They are <u>friends with whom</u> one can be happy.
5. <u>The queen, whose house</u> the mob burned down, was sad.
6. <u>Many girls, whose houses</u> were near, had come.
7. Are these <u>the men whom</u> you saw?
8. <u>The boy to whom</u> we owe the money is broke.
9. <u>The farmers whose cows</u> gave the most milk received a prize.
10. I spoke <u>to the lady whom</u> you ran over with your carriage.
11. <u>The gifts which</u> lie on the table are yours.

 Distinguish between the antecedent's function in the main sentence and the relative pronoun's function in the dependent clause!
(2) the water = Dir. Obj.; which = Subject;
(5) (6) two different "whose" (Sg and Pl, and two different cases for "house");
(9) Watch the gender of **agricola**!

EXERCISE C: Now translate the entire sentences and give gender, number, and case for the relative pronoun in each sentence

Gender Case
  Number   of Relative Pronoun

<u>M Nom Pl.</u> 1. Have you seen the horses, which drank the water?

___ ___ ___ 2. The girls, whose friends we greeted, are beautiful.

___ ___ ___ 3. Move the cart that is standing in front of our house!

___ ___ ___ 4. I see a man whose friends are famous.

___ ___ ___ 5. These are the girls to whom we must give the books.

___ ___ ___ 6. The towns, which we visited this year, were old.

___ ___ ___ 7. The island on which we live is small.

___ ___ ___ 8. The gift you gave me is beautiful.

 (1) watch case of "horses" and "which" - they are not the same;
     this is usually the case for antecedent and relative pronoun;
(8) Remember to supply the missing relative pronoun in Latin.

 **EXERCISE D:**   All Pronouns. Translate the sentences:

1. Equus, qui sedet post villam, est miser.
2. Meus filius, cui dedi pecuniam, eam suae amicae dedit.
3. Oppidum, in quo habitamus, habet multos hortos pulchros.
4. Bestiae, quibuscum Hercules pugnare debebat, magnae et ferae erant.
5. Hae sellae sunt magnae, illae sunt parvae.
6. Vidimus solum reliqua illius cenae.
7. Hae puellae non erant foedae, id, quod pueri videre non potuerunt.
8. Quis vestrum portabit frumentum ad oppidum?
9. Dabimus vobis, qui estis amici veri nostri, reliquam pecuniam.
10. Ibi sunt mercatores, quos vidisti, ubi visitavimus oppidum.

C. Interrogative Adjectives, Interrogative Pronouns, and Relative Pronouns

The English words "who", "which", and "what" are often quite troublesome to render in Latin, because of their many varied uses. Compare:

1. Who stole my horse?
2. Do you know who stole my horse?
3. Is this the thief who stole my horse?
4. Which of you stole it?
5. Which man is the thief?
6. What do you think you were doing?
7. What punishment will the thief receive?
8. Where is the horse which he stole?
9. What horse are you talking about?

Which of the above are (in Latin):
   a) interrogative pronouns?
   b) relative pronouns?
   c) neither?

The answer is:
(1), (2), (4), and (6) are **interrogative pronouns**.
   (1) quis
   (2) quis (but you can't translate the verb yet; it must be in the subjunctive,
        because this is an indirect question)

(4) quis vestrum
(6) quid

(3) and (8) are **relative pronouns**.
   (3) qui - Masc. Sg. Nom.
   (8) quem - Masc. Sg. Acc.

  (5), (7), and (9) are neither of the above, but rather **interrogative adjectives**, that is to say, they **modify** nouns, instead of taking their place. The forms used for these interrogative adjectives are identical to the forms of the **relative pronoun**. The whole declension is given here:

	Masculine	Feminine	Neuter
N	**qui vir** which (what) man	**quae fabula**	**quod donum**
G	**cuius viri** of which man	**cuius fabulae**	**cuius doni**
D	**cui viro** to which man	**cui fabulae**	**cui dono**
A	**quem virum** which man	**quam fabulam**	**quod donum**
Ab	**a quo viro** by which man	**qua fabula**	**quo dono**
N	**qui viri** which men	**quae fabulae**	**quae dona**
G	**quorum virorum** of which men	**quarum fabularum**	**quorum donorum**
D	**quibus viris** to which men	**quibus fabulis**	**quibus donis**
A	**quos viros** which men	**quas fabulas**	**quae dona**
Ab	**a quibus viris** by which men	**quibus fabulis**	**quibus donis**

Again, be sure to distinguish between: Who is this? (**quis**) - Whom did you see? (**quem**) - What did you see? (**quid**) - What town did you visit? (**quod oppidum**) - What man did you see? (**quem virum**) - Which girls do you like? (**quas puellas**) The girls you saw are my friends, (**quas vidisti**)

EXERCISE E: The exercise to end all exercises: Translate as many as you can manage in 15 minutes.

1. Who was in the house? _____

2. Which man was in the house?   _____

3. Which of you was present? _____

4. What did you ask?   _____

5. What gift did you give them? _____

6. Why did you walk?   _____

7. Whom did you see? _____

8. Whose book is this?   _____

9. Whose book did you carry? _____

10. What book did you carry? _____

11. What did you carry? _____

12. Which of us took the book? _____

13. Which of us did you see? _____

14. How did you respond to him? _____

15. Into which house did they go? _____

16. To whom did you give the money? _____

17. What did you give to her? _____

18. Which girl did you ask? _____

19. To which men did we give the books? _____

20. To whom did you tell the story? _____

21. Whose horses are these? _____

22. Which horses stood here? _____

23. To whom did you give the books? _____

24. To which friends did you give them? _____

25. To whose friends did you give the books? _____

In Latin the **interrogative pronoun** also has a **Plural**. It is synonymous with the Plural of the relative pronoun and has the same meaning as the Singular interrogative pronoun, except that one knows that more than one person is involved..

Examples:

Qui viderunt te? Who (which people) saw you? = Quis vidit te?

A quibus liberi docti sunt? By whom were the children taught = A quo.

Quas rogavisti? Whom did you ask? (Which ones did you ask?)

(You knew that they were women, though, hence the feminine.)

Vocabulary:

hic,haec,hoc	this
ille,illa,illud	that
iste,ista,istud	that one there
qui,quae,quod	who, which, that
quidam,quaedam,quoddam	a certain (person or thing) (**quiddam** = noun)

    (declined like **qui,quae,quod** + **-dam,** e.g.: cuidam, quendam,quibusdam)

Quisque,quaeque,quodque	each, every (**quidque** = noun)

    (declined like **qui,quae,quod** + **-que,** e.g. : cuiusque, cuique, quoque)

    (do not confuse **quoque,** *with everyone,everything* and **quoque,** *also)*

Quicumque,quaecumque,quodcumque

               whoever, whatever (**quidcumque** = noun)

Lectio I : **Helios et Phaeton** (after Ovid)

Helios erat Deus Solis apud Romanos, qui eum quoque "Sol" et postea "Apollo" appellabant. Eius filius erat Phaeton; ille in terra habitabat. Cottidie Deus Solis equos suos cum quadrigis aureis per caelum agitabat, et Phaeton cum amicis suis equos et quadrigas patris sui spectabat. Quidam ex amicis eum irridere voluit et
5 clamavit: "Cur nobis fabulas falsas narras et Solem patrem tuum vocas?" Phaeton magna cum ira respondit: "Verba mea sunt vera! Deus Solis est pater meus! Tibi illud monstrabo."

Sine mora Phaeton ad regnum patris properavit. Via erat longa, sed celeriter ambulavit et mox ad regiam patris adiit. Numquam antea regiam patris visitaverat,
10 sed equos quadrigasque saepe viderat. Helios puerum longe vidit, quod terram et viros et feminas et liberos in ea de caelo videre potuit.

"Cur huc ad regiam meam isti, mi fili?" rogavit Helios. Phaeton respondit: "Pater, amicus meus me puerum improbum vocat. Dixit: 'Filius Dei Solis tu non es! Sol pater tuus non est!' "
15 "Certe tu es filius meus. Verba tua sunt vera!" Sol respondit. Phaeton oravit: "Tum, bone pater, da mihi signum ! Hoc signo me filium tuum esse monstrabis."

"Hoc donum tibi dabo. Quid desideras, mi fili?"   "Da mihi equos tuos ac quadrigas et hos agitabo."

Helios laetus non erat. "Hoc," inquit, "non est secundum naturam, sed contra
20 consilia deorum. Hic dei laborare debent, non pueri. Equi mei sunt validi ferique. Postremo hoc donum te delebit."

Phaeton stultus et superbus autem quadrigas iterum postulavit. Tandem Helios filio suo quadrigas cum equis feris dedit et eum officium suum et nomina equorum docuit. "Cave equos feros; eos in locos ignotos aut plenos periculis agitare non
25 potes." Prima luce Phaeton in quadrigis superbe stabat. Equis inquietis signum dedit, et illi per portas Aurorae festinaverunt.

---

(1) sol, solis (m.) - sun; (3) quadrigae,arum - chariot; aureus,a,um - golden; agitare - to drive; (4) pater,patris (m.) - father; irridere - to tease, mock; voluit - he wanted; (8) mora,ae - delay; (8) celeriter - quickly; (9) (distinguish: regnum,i - realm; regia,ae - palace); (10) longe - (from) far away; (13) dixit - he said; (16) signum,i - sign; (17) desiderare - to desire; (21) postremo - last, in the end; (22) superbus,a,um - haughty, arrogant; postulare - to demand; (23) suum: - remember that this alwys refers to the subject, in this case Helios: Helios turns his own job over to Phaeton; (24) cave! - beware o!; (25) prima luce - at dawn; inquietus,a,um - restless; (26) Aurora,ae - goddess of dawn.

Mox puer audax per caelum volabat. Equi primum prope terram, tum inter stellas properabant. In horas celerius caelum transibant. Phaeton, puer miser, valde timebat. Nomina equorum memoria non tenebat. Volabat inter spatia, inter lunam et
30 terram, inter stellas atque planetas. Ubique in terra erant ignes, in silvis, in agris, in villis. Flammae frumentum deleverunt. Nihil aquae supererat in terra.

Ceres, dea terrae, magna cum tristitia ad patrem deorum adiit et auxilium rogavit. "O Iuppiter, rex deorum! Tu caeli terraeque imperium tenes. Cunctis viris, feminis, liberis in terra auxilium da! Agri, oppida, caelum ardent. Aqua deest. Necesse est
35 nobis adesse. Serva nos, o Iuppiter!"

Iuppiter, rex deorum, periculum iam viderat. Iratus fulmen contra quadrigas iecit. Phaeton ex quadrigis in terram cecidit et mortuus est. Iuppiter terram inundavit et ignes extinxit et sic terram servavit; filium Solis autem propter superbiam eius delevit.

(27) audax - bold, audacious; (28) in horas - hourly, by the hour; celerius - more quickly; (29) nomen, nominis (n.) - name (nomina = nom. and acc. Pl.); memoria tenere - to hold in memory, to remember; spatium,i - space; (30) ubique - everywhere; ignis, ignis (m.) - fire (ignes = nom. and acc. Pl.; here = ?); (32) tristitia,ae - sadness; auxilium,i - help; (33) rex, regis (m.) - king; imperium,i - reign, power; (34) ardere - to burn; necesse est - it is necessary; (36) fulmen, fulminis (n.) - bolt of lightning; iecit - he hurled; (37) cecidit - he fell; mortuus est - he died; (37) inundare - to flood; (38) extinxit - he extinguished; superbia,ae - arrogance.

Helios agitat quadrigas et equos

Lectio II : Poeta in Foro

(Try to guess the meaning of the words in **bold print**. Don't worry about their Conjugations or Declensions. Look for English derivatives of the more difficult ones at the bottom of this page.)

Tres **monachi** in oppidum ierunt pro copia cibi **annua**. Sedebant laeti in carro suo. Equus amicus ambulabat ante carrum. **Rotae** carri valde **sonabant**, clamabant, **stridebant**. Monachi **clamorem horribilem tolerare** non potuerunt. **Primus** monachus de carro **tumultuoso descendit** et iuxta carrum ambulavit. Tum secundus monachus **saluit** de carro, tum tertius carrum **reliquit**. Tres monachi laeti ambulaverunt iuxta et post carrum.

Spectaverunt liberos in via. Liberi pugnabant. "Estisne **dementes**? Nonne habetis animos, liberi?" monachi **exclamaverunt**.
"Ne pugnate! Este laeti, gaudete, amate!" Pueri monachos spectaverunt et properaverunt in prata magna cum **celeritate**.

Monachi in forum ambulaverunt et multa **acquirere** potuerunt, quod pecuniam **possederunt** : vinum, frumentum, **fructus**, gallinas, vestimenta. Tum poetam clarum spectaverunt et **audiverunt**.
Poeta **declamavit:**

Spectabam **hippopotamum**
amabilem, rotundum;
est **animal immensum,**
sed certe non est **garrulum**;
visitabat **crocodilum,**
amicum **lacrimosum**;
cantabant **carmen** pulchrum,
. **aquosum, dolorosum**;
tum flebant **flumen Nilum,**
natabant in **exsilium.**

(Finis Huius **Historiae)**

Derivatives: rotate (rota,ae) - strident (stridere) - fructose (fructus) - salient (salire) - audio (audire) - amiable (amabile) - garrulous (garrulus,a,um) - lacrimose (lacrimosus,a,um) - aqueous (aquosus,a,um) - dolorous (dolorosus,a,um) - flume (flumen) - natatorium (natare)

A. Questions.

1. Pronouns that "point" to a noun are called _____.

2. Four Latin pronouns which can be used this way are _____, _____,

_____, _____.

3. Latin relative pronouns do not distinguish persons and objects, but rather _____.

4. The noun to which a relative clause refers is called _____.

5. The form of the relative pronoun is determined by its _____ in the

relative clause, and by its _____.

6. Can the Latin relative pronoun be implied (as in English: "the man I saw") ? Y/N ____

7. Are there inclusive and noninclusive Relative clauses in Latin ? Y/N _____

8. The word **quem** can be used as _____ or as _____

pronoun, or as _____ adjective.

9. Does the Latin interrogative pronoun **quis**, *who*, have a Plural? Y/N _____

B. Vocabulary: Mark the correct translation(s):

1. **quis**
(a) what ? (b) whom? (c) who (d) who ?

2. **qui**
(a) who ? (b) which (c) that (d) who

3. **quod**
(a) what ? (b) what (Adjective) (c) whom (d) because

4. **cui**
(a) whose (b) to whom (c) which (d) what

5. **quid**
(a) what ?(Adj.) (b) whom (c) what? (noun) (d) who

Public Games and the Circus

Public games were an integral part of Roman life, a true and tried way to contain the unruly masses. There were circus games **(Ludi Circenses),** gladiator games **(Ludi Gladiatorii),** and theater games **(Ludi Scaenici)**. Originally their purpose was to honor and thank the gods. At the time of the Republic, games were held on 65 days of the year; by the fourthth century AD they were extended to 175 days! Of these there were 101 days of theater, 64 days of circus, and 10 days of gladiator games.

The circus games are said to go back as far as the time of Romulus, the mythical founder of Rome. These games consisted of chariot races, staged naval battles **(Naumachiae),** and sports competitions, especially foot races and wrestling. During Imperial times the circus games were held, with great pomp and circumstance, in the Circus Maximus. Naumachias were held on artificial lakes; the first one under Caesar had 1000 participants, a later one, held by Augustus, even 3000 fighters. Titus and Domitian supposedly had the Colosseum flooded to hold naumachias. The participants, mostly prisoners of war and convicted criminals, fought life-and-death battles.

**Advance advertisement for a stage performance of Ben-Hur
at a Chicago theater, in September 1901.**

The famous film version of the story dates from 1959. Both featured chariot races like the one shown here, reconstructing Roman races at the Circus Maximus in Rome.

Gladiator games, which were also battles to the death, were held in amphitheaters; in Rome they took place in the Colosseum. They may have originated with human sacrifices. Gladiators were professional fighters, usually slaves, who were trained in special schools in the use of swords and other weapons. They were fed a high protein diet for strength. Usually they fought against each other, sometimes they faced wild animals, such as tigers or lions.

Mosaic of Gladiator Fight (Kos) -- The Arena in Trier. Note the exits for men and beasts.

The **Colosseum,** the amphitheater of Rome, was built in AD 72. Begun by Emperor Vespasian, it was called Amphitheatrum Flavium, after his family name. It was dedicated in AD 80 by Emperor Titus, with games that lasted 100 days, and in which 5000 wild animals were killed. The name **Colosseum** was coined during the Middle Ages, from a colossal statue of Nero, almost forty meters high, which stood near the amphitheater.

The Colosseum was built of bricks and faced with marble and travertine (a type of stone with crevices and holes). Its shape is elliptical, with axes of 188 meters and 156 meters length. It held 50,000 to 70,000 spectators in four stories. Admission to the games was free, seating was strictly by rank. The lowest seats, closest to the arena, were reserved for government officials. Woman sat in the top seats, considered the worst.

On the upper storey there were 240 masts for a sun-sail, which could cover all spectators and had to be unfolded by a detachment of sailors from Misenum. Under the arena, animals and equipment were kept in cellars. The building had more than 80 exits and could be vacated within 5 minutes.

The imposing facade is subdivided into three arcades, each one featuring different columns: Doric on the bottom, Ionian in the middle, Corinthian on the top. (The fourth story, with Corinthian columns, was added later.) With its functional design the Colosseum is the predecessor of all modern sports arenas. During the Middle Ages the Colosseum fell into ruin and was further damaged by two earthquakes. Romans plundered the structure for building materials, until it was made a national monument in 1805.

Theate r games consisted of performances of tragedies, comedies, and satyr plays. They were first given in 364 BC to pacify angry gods and to end an epidemic. At first Etruscan actors had to be used, performing in Greek plays, because the Romans did not have their own theater until 240 BC Then Livius Andronicus had a Roman play performed that, however, still was modeled after a Greek original.

Important public games often lasted several days and included both circus and theater games.

Roman Theater in Kos

Chapter 8: Answers and Translations

Exercise A:
1. This girl's friend is a poet. 2. That woman (she) asked me: "Have you seen this good horse?" 3. In this year we built our house. 4. The master warned us with these words: "Beware, children, of the dog!" 5. We have given him (her) many beautiful gifts. 6. We don't like these sailors: they are bad. 7. Why did you not drink that red wine? 8. The angry woman shouted at this man: "You rascal, get out of my house!"

Exercise B:
1. Liberi, quibus... 2. ...aquam, quae... 3. Oppidum, in quo... 4. ...amici, cum quibus (quibuscum)... 5. Regina, cuius villam... 6. Multae puellae, quarum casae... 7. viri, quos... 8. Puer, cui... 9. Agricolae, quorum vaccae... 10. ...feminae, quam... 11. dona, quae

Exercise C:

M	Pl	Nom	1. Vidistine equos, qui potaverunt aquam?
F	Pl	Gen	2. Puellae, quarum amicos salutavimus, pulchrae sunt.
M	Sg	Nom	3. Move carrum, qui stat ante villam nostram!
M	Sg	Gen	4. Video virum, cuius amici clari sunt.
F	Pl	Dat	5. Hae sunt puellae, quibus libros dare debemus.
N	Pl	Acc	6. Oppida, quae hoc anno visitavimus, erant antiqua.
F	Sg	Abl	7. Insula, in qua habitamus, parva est.
N	Sg.	Acc	8. Donum, quod mihi dedisti, pulchrum est.

Exercise D:
1. The horse which is sitting behind the house is miserable.
2. My son, to whom I gave the money, gave it to his girlfriend.
3. The town in which we live has many lovely gardens.
4. The monsters with which Hercules had to fight were large and wild.
5. These chairs are big, those are small.
6. We saw only the leftovers of that dinner.
7. These girls were not ugly, (that) which the boys could not see.
8. Which of you will carry the grain to the town?
9. We will give you, who are our true friends, the rest of the money.
10. There are the merchants whom you saw, when we visited the town.

Exercise E:
1. Quis erat in casa?
2. Qui vir erat in casa?
3. Quis vestrum aderat?
4. Quid rogavisti?
5. Quod donum eis dedistis?
6. Cur ambulavisti?
7. Quem vidistis?
8. Cuius liber est hic?
9. Cuius librum portavisti?
10. Quem librum portavisti?
11. Quid portavisti?
12. Quis nostrum librum captavit?
13. Quem nostrum vidisti?
14. Quomodo ei respondisti?

15. In quam casam inierunt?   16. Cui pecuniam dedisti?
17. Quid ei (illi) dedisti?
18. Quod verbum rogavisti? De quo verbo rogavisti?
19. Quibus viris hos libros dedimus?   20. Cui fabulam narravisti?
21. Cuius equi sunt illi?   22. Qui equi hic steterunt?
23. Cui libros dedisti?   24. Quibus amicis eos dedisti?
25. Cuius amicis libros dedisti?

Reading 1: Helios and Phaeton

Helios was the Sun God [God of the Sun] for the Romans, who also called him "Sol," and later "Apollo." Phaeton was his son, who lived on earth. Every day the Sun God drove his horses with his golden chariot through the sky, and Phaeton looked at his father's horses and carriage with his friends. A certain one of his friends wanted to mock him and exclaimed: "Why do you tell us false stories and call the Sun God your father? Helios is not your father!" Phaeton answered with great anger: "My words are true! The Sun God is my father! I will show it to you." Without delay Phaeton ran to his father's realm. The way was long, but he walked quickly and soon he approached his father's palace. He had never before visited his father's palace, but had often seen the horses and the chariot. Helios saw the boy from far away, because he could see the earth and the men and women and children on it from the sky.

"Why have you come [gone] here to my palace, my son?" Helios asked. Phaeton answered: "Father, my friend called me a wicked boy. He said: 'You are not the son of the Sun God! Helios is not your father!' " - "Certainly you are my son. Your words are true!" Sol answered. - "Good father, then give me a great sign," Phaeton begged. "With this sign you will show me to be your son."

"I will give you this gift. What do you desire, my son?" - "Give me your horses and the chariot and I will drive them."

Helios was not happy. "This," he said, "is not according to nature and to the plans of the gods. Gods must work here, not boys. My horses are strong and wild. In the end this gift will destroy you." Nevertheless the stupid and haughty Phaeton again demanded the chariot. Finally Helios gave his son the chariot with the wild horses and and taught him his new task and the names of the horses. "Beware of the wild horses; you can not [should not] drive them into unknown places or [those] full of dangers."

At dawn Phaeton stood arrogantly in the chariot. He gave the signal to the restless horses and drove them through the gates of Aurora.

Soon the bold boy was flying through the sky. At first the horses were racing close to the earth, then between the stars. By the hour they went across the sky more swiftly. Phaeton, miserable boy, was very much afraid. He did not remember the names of the horses. He flew among the spaces, between the moon and the earth, among the stars and planets. Everywhere on earth there were fires, in the forests, in the fields, in the houses. The flames destroyed the grain. No water was left on earth.

Ceres, the goddess of the earth, went to the father of the gods with great sadness and asked for help. "O Jupiter, king of the gods! You hold the reign of heaven and earth. Give help to all men, women, and children on earth! Fields, towns, and sky are burning. Water is lacking. It is necessary to help us. Save us, o Jupiter!"

But Jupiter, the king of the gods, had already seen the danger. Furious, he threw a bolt of lightning against the chariot. Phaeton fell from the chariot down to the earth and died. Jupiter flooded the earth and extinguished the fires and so destroyed the son of Helios because of his arrogance.

Reading 2 : Three Monks go toTown.
Three monks went to town for their yearly supply of food. They were happy sitting in their cart. The friendly horse walked before the cart. The wheels of the cart made noise, sqealed, screeched. The monks could not bear the horrible noise. The first monk descended from the tumultuous car and walked next to it. Then the second monk jumped from the cart, then the third left the cart. Three happy monks walked next to the cart.
They saw children in the road. The children were fighting. "Are you crazy? Don't you have any sense, children?" exclaimed the monks. "Don't fight! Be happy, enjoy yourselves, like (each other)!"
The boys looked at the monks and ran into the meadows with great speed.
The monks went to the market and were able to buy many things, because they possessed money: wine, grain, fruit, hens, clothes. Then they watched and heard a famous poet.

The poet recited:

I saw a hippopotamus
amiable and round;
he is an immense animal
but certainly not a garrulous one;
he visited the crocodile,
his teary-eyed friend;
they sang a beautiful song,
aqueous, dolorous;
then they cried the river Nile,
and swam into exile.
(The end of this story)

Summary:
A: 1. demonstrative   2. hic, haec, hoc; ille, illa, illud; iste, ista, istud; is, ea, id   3. gender
4. antecedent   5. function, antecedent   6. no   7. no   8. Interrogative Pronoun, Relative
Pronoun, Interrogative Adjective   9. yes   B: 1. (d)   2. (b), (c), (d)   3. (b), (d)   4. (b)   5. (c)

Language Quiz: 1 T;   2 T;   3 F;   4 T;   5 T;   6 F;   7 F;   8 T;   9 F;   10 T;   11 T;   12 T;
13 F;   14 T;   15 F

9

VERBS: 3RD AND 4TH CONJUGATIONS
FERRE, VELLE, MALLE, NOLLE
IRREGULAR PERFECT STEMS

GERMANIC LANGUAGES I

When the Indo-European people started splitting up and migrating, as far as India (Indo-Iranian), Asia (Tocharian), Greece and Asia Minor (Greek, Hittite, and Celtic), and the Baltic, one group went to the area of modern southern Scandinavia, Denmark, and modern North Germany. Their speech developed into what is now called Primitive Germanic or Proto-Germanic. Because it was not recorded, it had to be reconstructed like PIE, using the same comparative principles with the many Germanic languages and dialects. The oldest available text in a Germanic language is a 350 A.D. translation of the Bible into Gothic, a now extinct East Germanic language.

During their migration these emerging Germanic people must have come into close contact with Finnish tribes, because the Finnish language borrowed a number of words from them (which were preserved in Finnish in their original shape - a great help to those who were reconstructing Proto-Germanic). Germanic, on the other hand, probably was influenced by the Finnish tense system: in most Germanic languages 2 tenses, a present and a past, are really all that's needed. Quite a difference from the extensive verb systems of the Romance languages!

When these 'Germans' arrived at their future homeland there were people living there. They were, however, not Indo-European. We know very little of their language other than what has been preserved in names of rivers and the like. The Germans must have incorporated a large amount of the vocabulary of this language into their Germanic language; this would account for the fact that close to one third of the vocabulary of Germanic languages can not be etymologically traced to an Indo-European source.

Chapter 9   VERBS : THE THIRD AND FOURTH CONJUGATIONS

THE THIRD CONJUGATION

Some of the most commonly used verbs are found in the 3rd and 4th conjugations: to do, make, eat, bring, take, fall (3rd), come, hear, sleep (4th). The tense markers and personal endings of the third and fourth conjugations are essentially the same as those of the first and second conjugations, with one difference: the future marker is **-e-** (long), not **-bi-.**

Since the present stems of most verbs in the third Conjugation do not end in a characteristic stem vowel, but in various consonants, the third is also called the **consonant conjugation**. The short vowel **-e-** of the infinitive is only a filler vowel, not part of the stem. To obtain the present stem of third conjugation verbs, the ending **-ere** must therefore be removed from the Infinitive.

> Examples:
> régere   stem: reg-
> dúcere   duc-
> míttere   mitt-

In order to add the endings (which begin with consonants), a vowel must be inserted. This vowel is usually **-e-** (short), or **-i-** ; however, this should not be confused with a **stem vowel,** such as the other conjugations have, or with the future tense marker **-e-**. Therefore it is also called a dummy vowel.

The ending for the 3rd person Plural present is **-unt**. Thus the 1st person Singular and the 3rd person Plural endings can be added directly to the stem. Example: **ducere,** *to lead*

The Present Tense:

	1. **dúc o**		1. **dúc i mus**
Sg	2. **dúc i s**	**Pl**	2. **dúc i tis**
	3. **dúc i t**		3. **dúc unt**

The **infinitive** ends in **-e-re**. This **-e-** is short, and it is **unstressed**. The word stress falls therefore on the "third to last" ("antepenultimate")syllable. This distinguishes infinitives of the second and third Conjugation.

> Examples: (stress marks given only for learning purposes)
>
> | **third** | **second** |
> |-----------|------------|
> | dúcere | docére |
> | míttere | manére |
> | vívere | valére |

There are some verbs that occur in both conjugations; they look identical, but are stressed differently, and have of course different meaning:

> | **third** | **second** |
> |-----------|------------|
> | iácere (throw) | iacére (lie down) |
> | párere (give birth) | parére (obey) |
>
> (Incidentally, the word "parents" comes from the first, not the second.)

EXERCISE A: Conjugate the present tense active of **régere**, *to rule*; **dícere**, *to say;*
                         pónere, *to put*; **míttere**, *to send*; **ágere**, *to do.*

The Imperfect and Future Tenses

The **Imperfect** is formed as it was in the first and second conjugation; the vowel **-e-** is inserted before the
imperfect marker **-ba-** :

	1. **duc é ba m**		1. **duc e bá mus**
Sg	2. **duc é ba s**	**Pl**	2. **duc e bá tis**
	3. **duc é ba t**		3. **duc é ba nt**

The **future** tense for both the third and the fourth conjugation uses the tense marker **-e-** (1st Person Sg. **-a-**),
instead of -bi- like the first and second conjugations.

	1. **dúc a m**		1. **duc é mus**
Sg	2. **dúc e s**	**Pl**	2. **duc é tis**
	3. **dúc e t**		3. **dúc e nt**

There is a danger of confusing tenses, if you don't know in which conjugation a verb belongs: the present of
the second, and the future of the third conjugation look alike (except for the 1st person Sg):

docet = Present - *he, she teaches*   ducet = Future - *he, she **will lead***   (duc**i**t - he leads)
ridemus = Present - *we are laughing*   mittemus = Future - *we **will send***   (mitt**i**mus - we send)
vident = Present - *they see*   ponent = Future - *they **will put***   (pon**u**nt - they put)

EXERCISE B: Give the tense of, and translation for, the following forms:

1. ducent   _____   6. ponit   _____

2. docent   _____   7. mittet   _____

3. vidit   _____   8. docuit   _____

4. videt   _____   9. ponet   _____

5. tacet   _____   10. ridet   _____

THE PERFECT STEM

The perfect stem formation of the third conjugation follows no one pattern, like those of the first or part of the second conjugation. There are groups of similarly formed perfect stems (derived from Indo-European patterns), for insance verbs in which the present stem vowel is lengthened (often into another vowel), such as **ago --> egi**, or verbs which **reduplicate** in the perfect, (a feature also found in Greek), such as **curro --> cucurri.** Verbs will also be listed in groups here; you may prefer to learn them in groups. In any case you must <u>memorize</u> the **principal parts** of these verbs!

Remember that the 1st person perfect is the **third principal part** of a verb. (The **first principal part** is the 1st person Singular present, the **second** is the infinitive. The fourth principal part will be added in chapter 10, with the passive voice.) By removing the ending **-i** from the third principal part, you get the **perfect stem** of the verb. The **endings** used for the perfect are the same as in the other conjugations.

Verbs	Perfect stem	Verbs	Perfect stem
duco, ducere, **duxi** to lead	**dux-**	mitto, mittere, **misi** to send	**mis-**
pono, ponere, **posui** to put	**posu-**	curro, curere, **cucurri** to run	**cucurr-**

The **Perfect** of ducere:

	1. **dúx i**		1. **dúx imus**
Sg	2. **dux ísti**	Pl	2. **dux ístis**
	3. **dúx it**		3. **dux érunt**

The **Pluperfect**

	1. **dúx eram**		1. **dux erámus**
Sg	2. **dúx eras**	Pl	2. **dux erátis**
	3. **dúx erat**		3. **dúx erant**

The **Future Perfect**

	1. **dúx ero**		1. **dux érimus**
Sg	2. **dúx eris**	Pl	2. **dux éritis**
	3. **dúx erit**		3. **dúx erint**

Remember: 3rd person Plural endings: Perf: **-erunt;** Pluperf: **-erant;** Fut: Perf: **-erint**

The past infinitive adds **-isse** to the pefect stem:
duxisse *to have led*; **rexisse** *to have ruled*; **misisse** *to have sent* .

Vocabulary: The first three principal parts are given here; they will be repeated in chapter 10 with their fourth principal part added. Many English derivatives come from the fourth principal parts. (The asterisk * means that the English derivative used here is identical with the English translation of the verb)

ago,agere,egi	to do, drive	agent,action
ascendo,ascendere,ascendi	to ascend	*
bibo,bibere,bibi	to drink	imbibe
cado,cadere,cécidi	to fall	cadence
caedo,caedere,cecídi	to fell, cut down	incision
cedo,cedere,cessi	to go, yield	cede
claudo,claudere,clausi	to shut, close	recluse
cognosco,cognoscere,cognovi	to find out, learn	cognizant
cogo,cogere,coegi	to collect, compel	cogent
colo,colere,colui	to cultivate,venerate	culture
consisto,consistere,constiti	to stand,stop,consist of	*
constituo,constituere,constitui	to set up, decide	constitute
contendo,contendere,contendi	to hurry,strive,contend	*
credo,credere,credidi	to believe	creed,credit
cresco,crescere,crevi	to grow	crescent
curro,currere,cucurri	to run	current
defendo,defendere,defendi	to defend	*
descendo,descendere,descendi	to descend	*
dico,dicere,dixi	to say	diction
disco,discere,didici	to learn	disciple
divido,dividere,divisi	to divide	*
duco,ducere,duxi	to lead, consider	duke
edo,edere,edi	to eat	edible
emo,emere,emi	to buy	
frango,frangere,fregi	to break	fracture
gero,gerere,gessi	to bear, carry, do	gesture
instituo,instituere,institui	to institute, establish	*
iungo,iungere,iunxi	to join	juncture
lego,legere,legi	to read	illegible
ludo,ludere,lusi	to play	ludicrous
mitto,mittere,misi	to send	intermittent
pello,pellere,pepuli	to drive, push	repel
peto,petere,petivi	to ask, beg, attack	petulant
pono,ponere,posui	to put, place	position
posco,poscere,poposci	to demand	
premo,premere,pressi	to press	pressure
quaero,quaerere,quaesivi	to ask, look for	query,inquiry
reddo,reddere,reddidi	to give back	
rego,regere,rexi	to rule	regent
relinquo,relinquere,reliqui	to leave behind	relinquish
rumpo,rumpere,rupi	to tear, break	rupture
scribo,scribere,scripsi	to write	scribe
solvo,solvere,solvi	to loosen (sails), sail	solve
tango,tangere,tetigi	to touch	tangent
tollo,tollere,sustuli	to raise, remove	(sustuli is part of another verb)

trado,tradere,tradidi	to hand over	tradition
traho,trahere,traxi	to drag	tractor
vendo,vendere,vendidi	to sell	vendor
verto,vertere,verti	to turn	avert
vinco,vincere,vici	to defeat	invincible
vivo,vivere,vixi	to live	vivid

 **EXERCISE C:** Give the tense (PR, I, F, P, PQ, FP) and translation for each of the following verb forms. Watch the **-e- :** some of the verbs are second conjugation! Check your translation, then cover the left column and retranslate the forms into Latin!

	Tense	Translation	Retranslation
1. ponit	____		
2. ponet	____		
3. ponunt	____		
4. ducent	____		
5. docent	____		
6. ducebant	____		
7. mittitis	____		
8. misistis	____		
9. agit	____		
10. egit	____		
11. emi	____		
12. legimus	____ ____		
13. vixerant	____		
14. posuerint	____		
15. potuerunt	____		
16. cucurristi	____		
17. valetis	____		
18. vivetis	____		
19. ludebam	____		
20. credidi	____		

For some verbs the **present** and **perfect stems** are **alike.** Since the endings for the 3rd person Sg and the 1st person Pl. are also the same in the present and perfect, these two forms are identical for these verbs.
Example: defendit - he defends (PR), he defended (P); defendimus - we defend (PR), we defended (P)

EXERCISE D: Write these two forms (present / perfect) 3rd person Singular and 1st person Plural for all verbs from the vocabulary list, that have the same present and perfect stem!

· · · · · · · ·
· **Riddle** ·
· · · · · · · ·

! Words - Words !   (A) Similar Words

1	C	.	.	O						D	O			.	.	L	L	.
2	C	.	.	.	O		.	E	.	D	O		.	.	.	L	L	.
3	C	.	.	O			.	.	E	D	O			.	.	.	T	T	.
4	C	.	.	O			.	R	.	D	O			.	.	.	R	R	.
5	C	.	.	O		V	.	.	D	O								
6	C	.	.	.	O										D	.	C	.
7	C	.	.	.	O										D	.	C	.

1. I fall
2. I cut down
3. I yield
4. I collect
5. I cultivate
6. I take (see pg. 190)
7. I wish

1. I give
2. I give back   }
3. I believe   }   compounds
4. I hand over   }   of 'do'
5. I sell   }

I push
I raise
I send
I run
I say
I lead

(B) More Similar Words

	.	.	.	N	G	.	.	.			.	.	.	S	C	.	.	.	
		.	.	N	G	.	.	.			.	.	S	C	.	.	.	
		.	.	N	G	.	.	.			.	.	S	C	.	.	.	

to break, to touch, to join   to grow, to learn, to demand

(C) Change or add one letter at a time:

               AGO

(I)   EGO . | ------>   (I read) . . . .
           v

(I eat)   . . . | ------>   (I buy) . . .
         v

(I yield)   . . . .   ------>   (I fall) . . . .
         v |

(I believe) . . . . .

THIRD CONJUGATION i - STEMS

A small number of third onjugation verbs have **present stems ending in -i**. They can be recognized from their 1st principal part, but **not** from their infinitive, e.g.:

cap**io**, capere, cepi   to take, catch
fug**io**, fugere, fugi   to flee

In the **Present Tense** the endings can be added directly to these i-stems, without inserting a vowel:

	1. **cápi o**		1. **cápi mus**
Sg	2. **cápi s**	Pl	2. **cápi tis**
	3. **cápi t**		3. **cápi unt**

I-stems thus have two present tense forms which are different from those of consonant stems:
the 1st person Singular and the 3rd person Plural: **capio** vs. **duco; capiunt** vs. **ducunt.** The other present forms are alike: **capis - ducis; capimus - ducimus,** and so forth.

In the **imperfect** the endings could be added directly to the stem, but for some reason they are not: these verbs use their -i-, which is part of their stem, and still add an -e-, just like the consonant stems:

	1. **capi é bam**		1. **capi e bámus**
Sg	2. **capi é bas**	Pl	2. **capi e bátis**
	3. **capi é bat**		3. **capi é bant**

The **Future** uses -e- (-a-) as a tense marker:

	1. **cápi a m**		1. **capi é mus**
Sg	2. **cápi e s**	Pl	2. **capi é tis**
	3. **cápi e t**		3. **cápi e nt**

In the **perfect tense** the distinction between i-stems and consonant stems is lost, since the perfect stems are irregular anyway.

Si liberi flent, familia gaudere non potest.

Nolite sedere in mensa, si cibus est in mensa!   .

Principal Parts of i - stems

1.capio,capere,cepi	to take	captive
2.conspicio,conspicere,conspexi	to look (at)	conspicuous
3.cupio, cupere, cupivi	to wish, want	Cupid
4.facio,facere,feci	to make, do	factory
5.fugio,fugere,fugi	to flee	fugitive
6.iacio,iacere,ieci	to throw	projectile
7.incipio,incipere,coepi	to begin	incipient
8.pario,parere,peperi	to bear,bring forth	parents
9.rapio,rapere,rapui	to grasp, snatch	rapture

coepi is actually from another verb; it supplies the missing perfect of **incipere**. (like **sustuli** with **tollere**)

The **imperatives** are **the same** for consonant stems and i-stems. The Singular ends in **-e** (**replacing** the -i of i-stems!), the Plural in **-ite**:
Examples:

Sg.		Pl.
mitte!	send !	**mittite!**
pone!	put !	**ponite!**
cape!	take!	**capite!**
ne lude!	don't play !	**ne ludite!** (noli ludere, nolite ludere, see pg. 201)
fuge!	flee !	**fugite!**

There are four **irregular** Singular Imperatives:

dic!	say!	(Pl **dicite!**)	
duc!	lead!	(Pl **ducite!**)	
fac!	make!	(Pl **facite!**)	
fer!	bring!	(Pl **ferte!**)	(see page 200)

EXERCISE E	Change the following perfect forms to present forms (or third principal parts to first principal parts) and give their meaning: Example: feci - **facio** , I make

1. dixi   _____
2. credidi   _____
3. cepi   _____
4. cucurri   _____
5. lusi   _____
6. legi   _____
7. verti   _____
8. traxi   _____
9. constitui _____
10. cecidi (2!)   _____

11. posui   _____
12. edi   _____
13. pepuli   _____
14. scripsi   _____
15. rupi   _____

EXERCISE F: Give the present infinitives (second principal parts) and the English meaning, of the Latin verbs from which the following English words are derived:

1. impression   _____

2. agenda   _____

3. petition   _____

4. regal   _____

5. cadence   _____

6. intangible   _____

7. illusion   _____

8. victorious   _____

9. currency   _____

10. fugitive   _____

11. aqueduct   _____

12. divert   _____

13. proceed   _____

14. solve   _____

15. trade   _____

EXERCISE G: Give **synopses** (= one form in all 6 tenses) of:

1. 3rd person Plural of **facere**   Example: 3rd person Singular of **pellere**
2. 2nd person Singular of **cadere**   (present stem: **pell-** ; perfect stem **pepul-**)
3. 1st person Plural of **mittere**   Present **pellit** imperfect **pellebat** Future **pellet**
4. 1st person Singular of **ponere**   Perf. **pepulit** Pluperf. **pepulerat** Fut.Perf. **pepulerit**

_____

_____

_____

_____

Here are the verbs one more time, **grouped according to the way in which they form the Perfect**:Write the meaning and as many English derivatives as you can think of (if possible different from those on page 186)!

1. Present **t (d)** --> Perfect **s(s)**		English Derivative(s)
mitto	misi	missive
divido	divisi	
ludo	lusi	
claudo	clausi	
cedo	cessi	antecedent
(other) -->	Perfect **ss**	
premo	pressi	
gero	gessi	

2. Present **c/g/h/v** --> Perfect **x** (= c+s, g+s, etc.)		
dico	dixi	
duco	duxi	
iungo	iunxi	conjunction
rego	rexi	
traho	traxi	
vivo	vixi	
conspicio	conspexi	

3. Present **-a-** --> Perfect **-e-**		
ago	egi	agenda
cogo (=co-ago)	coegi	
capio	cepi	
facio	feci	
iacio	ieci	

4. (**different**) --> Perfect **-vi** or **-ui**		
quaero	quaesivi	
peto	petivi	
cupio	cupivi	
cognosco	cognovi	
cresco	crevi	
solvo	solvi	
colo	colui	
pono	posui	
rapio	rapui	

5. Perfect **Reduplication**

curro	cucurri	
cado	cécidi	
caedo	cecídi	homicide
pello	pepuli	propulsion
tango	tetigi	
posco	poposci	

Note: compounds of these verbs do not reduplicate, for example: impello - impuli; concurro - concurri; occido (cado) / occido (caedo) - occidi

Compounds of **dare**

credo	credidi
trado	tradidi
reddo	reddidi
vendo	vendidi

6. **Drop n/m** from present stem

relinquo	reliqui	relic
vinco	vici	
frango	fregi	
rumpo	rupi	

7. Other Changes

scribo	scripsi
tollo	(sustuli)
incipio	(coepi)

8. **Same Stem** (in some cases lengthened)

defendo	defendi	
ascendo	ascendi	
descendo	descendi	
contendo	contendi	
edo	edi	
verto	verti	incontrovertible
constituo	constitui	
instituo	institui	
bibo	bibi	
lego	legi	
emo	emi	
solvo	solvi	
fugio	fugi	

 **EXERCISE H:**   By now you must know all the verbs! Let's see:

First decide which tense should be used and then which stem is needed !

Tense (PR,I,F, P,PP,FP)   Stem (PR,P)   Latin Verb

   1. I live   _____

   2. you used to make (Sg)   _____

   3. he ruled (Perfect)   _____

   4. we will ask   _____

   5. you had cultivated (Pl)   _____

   6. they will have closed   _____

   7. I used to play   _____

   8. you have given back (Sg)   _____

   9. she will write   _____

10. we had ascended   _____

11. you will have left behind (Pl)   _____

12. they demand   _____

13. I have cut down   _____

14. you will send (Sg)   _____

15. it had grown   _____

16. we will have read   _____

17. you are pushing (Pl)   _____

18. they were finding out   _____

19. I will say   _____

20. you had loosened (Sg)   _____

21. he will have turned   _____

22. we are handing over   _____

23. you used to eat (Pl)   _____

24. they have pressed   _____

25. I had thrown   _____

26. you will have put (Sg)   _____

27. she buys   _____

28. we used to drink   _____

29. you have touched (Pl)   _____

Tense	Stem	Latin Verb
30. they will defeat		_____
31. I will have taken		_____
32. you did (Imperfect) (Sg)		_____
33. it fell (Perfect)		_____
34. we will decide		_____
35. you had yielded		_____
36. they will have run		_____

EXERCISE I: Fill in the blanks:

1. The opposite of **emere** is _____.

2. If you cut down **(caedere)** a tree, it falls (_____).

3. Another word for **rumpere** is _____.

4. If you can't find out **(cognoscere)**, you must believe (_____).

5. The opposite of **iungere** is _____.

6. A **cogent** argument is one which is _____.

7. Another word for **potare** is _____.

8. **Descendere** is the opposite of _____.

9. Two verbs meaning **to do** are _____ and _____.

10. **To carry on a war** in Latin would be _____ _____.

11. So far you have learned at least 5 words meaning **ask, beg, demand:**
    (in all three Conjugations)

_____, _____, _____, _____, _____.

EXERCISE J: Complete the synopses:

Meaning Pers./Nr.	PRESENT	FUTURE	IMPERF.	PERFECT	PLUPERF.	FUT.PERF.
say 3rd sing.						
	agis					
			vincebat			
		monebo				
		regam				
leave 3rd sing.						
				posuimus		
					gesserant	
				duxistis		
	surgo					
collect 3rd plur.						
			tradebas			
		defendent				
						docu-erimus
see 2nd sing.						

THE FOURTH CONJUGATION

The forms of the fourth or i-conjugation are nearly identical to those of the third conjugation i-stems: their **present stem** ends in **-i** (that is to say: **-i** is their **stem vowel**); they add the same endings in the present tense (**-unt** for the 3rd person Plural); they insert an **-e-** in the **imperfect;** and they use **-e-** as a tense marker for the **future**.

    Only two forms are different from third conjugation i-stems:

1. The **infinitive** ends in **-ire**, which is one reason why these verbs are placed in a different conjugation from the third onjugation i-stems.
Examples: **audíre,** *to hear*; **veníre,** *to come* (This is important for the imperfect subjunctive, Ch.15)

2. The **Singular imperative** ends in **-i** instead of -e.
Examples: **audi!** *hear!* **veni!** *come!* (The German car's name 'Audi' is a translation into Latin of the founding family's name, Horch, "listen!")

Looking at the first two principal parts of a verb one can tell to which conjugation a verb belongs, even if the infinitive has no length mark:

deleo, delere	**-eo, -ere**	**2nd**
rego, regere	**-o, -ere**	**3rd**
capio, capere	**-io, -ere**	**3rd i-stem**
audio, audire	**-io, -ire**	**4th**

The conjugation of **audire:**

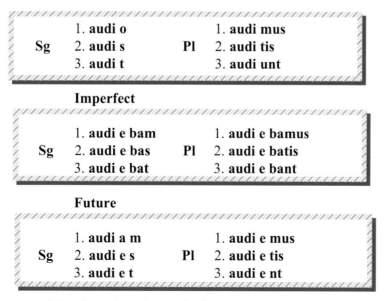

             Present

	Sg		Pl	
	1. audi o		1. audi mus	
	2. audi s		2. audi tis	
	3. audi t		3. audi unt	

             Imperfect

	Sg		Pl	
	1. audi e bam		1. audi e bamus	
	2. audi e bas		2. audi e batis	
	3. audi e bat		3. audi e bant	

             Future

	Sg		Pl	
	1. audi a m		1. audi e mus	
	2. audi e s		2. audi e tis	
	3. audi e t		3. audi e nt	

The **perfect stem** of fourth conjugation verbs frequently ends in **-v-** or **-u-**.

Commmon fourth conjugation Verbs (You can take a few more, can't you?)

audio, audire, <u>audivi</u>	to hear	audio
custodio, custodire, custodivi	to guard	custody
dormio, dormire, dormivi	to sleep	dormant
erudio, erudire, erudivi	to teach, educate	erudite
finio, finire, finivi	to finish	final
impedio, impedire, impedivi	to hinder	impediment
munio, munire, munivi	to build, fortify	ammunition
oboedio, oboedire, oboedivi	to obey	obedient
punio, punire, punivi	to punish	punitive
scio, scire, scivi	to know	prescient
nescio, nescire, <u>nescivi</u>	to not know	
aperio, aperire, aperui	to open	aperture
salio, salire, salui	to jump	salient
comperio, comperire, comperi	to learn	
reperio, reperire, repperi	to find	
sentio, sentire, sensi	to feel	sense
venio, venire, veni	to come	venue

also the following compounds: (same Principal Parts as base verb)

of venire:	advenire	to arrive	advent
	invenire	to find	invention
	convenire	to meet	convention
of aperire:	operire	to close	operation
of sentire:	dissentire	to contradict	dissent
	consentire	to agree	consent

EXERCISE K: Translate the following verb forms, and then give the present infinitive of the verb:

1. audiveratis _____

2. iacui _____

3. ieci _____

4. venisse _____

5. nescio quis _____

6. oboediebat _____

7. veni (2 !) _____

8. erudiemus _____

9. aperuerunt _____

10. finite _____

11. sentitis   _____

12. scivistis _____

13. impediunt   _____

14. muniverimus   _____

Veni   Vidi   Vici

EXERCISE L: Translate:

1. Oppidum non relinquemus. _____

2. Quid dixit bonus puer post cenam? _____

3. Nihil cibi invenire potuimus. _____

4. Dominus haec imperavit, servus solum oboedivit. _____

5. Puella comperit id, quod cupiverat. _____

6. Quando ad villam vestram veniemus? _____

7. Dormivistine bene heri? _____

8. Quis vestrum vinum bibit? _____

9. Debeo reddere librum, quem scripsisti; eum legi. _____

10. Quid facis? Mitto litteras ad puellam amicam. _____

Two Important Verbs: ferre and velle (nolle, malle)

The verbs **ferre** (*to carry, bring*) and **velle** (*to want*) belong among the most basic verbs in Latin, together with **esse, ire,** and **fieri.**

ferre *to carry, bring, report*   principal parts: **fero, ferre, tuli,** (latum = {having been}carried)

Present	Future	Imperfect	Imperative
fero	feram	ferebam	
fers	feres	ferebas	fer!
fert	feret	ferebat	
ferimus	feremus	ferebamus	
fertis	feretis	ferebatis	ferte!
ferunt	ferent	ferebant	

Perfect	Pluperfect	Future Perfect
tuli	tuleram	tulero
tulisti	tuleras	tuleris
tulit	tulerat	tulerit
tulimus	tuleramus	tulerimus
tulistis	tuleratis	tuleritis
tulerunt	tulerant	tulerint

Compounds of **ferre** (with 4th principal part added; see chapter 10):
    Ferre uses three different stems: fer- (present), tul- (perfect), lat- (fourth principal part)

afferre, affero, attuli, allatum	**to bring; to report; to afflict**
auferre, aufero, abstuli, ablatum	**to carry away, rob**
conferre, confero, contuli, collatum	**to bring together; to compare**
deferre, defero, detuli, delatum	**to hand over, report**
differre, differo, distuli, dilatum	**to postpone**
differre, differo - -	**to distinguish, to differ from**
inferre, infero, intuli, illatum	**to carry in, bring on**
offerre, offero, obtuli, oblatum	**to bring towards, offer**
perferre, perfero, pertuli, perlatum	**to tolerate**
proferre, profero, protuli, prolatum	**to produce, show**
referre, refero, rettuli, relatum	**to bring back, report; to refer to**
sufferre, suffero, (sustuli, sublatum)	**to suffer, tolerate**
tollo, tollere, sustuli, sublatum	**to raise, remove**

> **English derivatives:** to confer, conference, collateral, to defer, deferential, to collate, to differ, to infer, inference, to offer, to proffer, oblate, prelate, prolate, to prefer, to refer, to relate, relative, reference, fertile, Ablative, to dilate, to suffer,...

volo, velle, volui
nolo, nolle, nolui
malo, malle, malui

to want
to not want
to prefer

	Present		Imperfect		Future		Perfect
	volo		volebam		volam		volui
Sg	vis	Sg	volebas	Sg	voles		voluisti
	vult		volebat		volet		etc.
	volumus		volebamus		volemus	**Pluperf.**	volueram
Pl	vultis	Pl	volebatis	Pl	voletis		volueras ...
	volunt		volebant		volent	**Fut.Perf.**	voluero
							volueris...
	nolo		nolebam		nolam		nolui
Sg	non vis	Sg	nolebas	Sg	noles		noluisti
	non vult		nolebat		nolet		etc.
	nolumus		nolebamus		nolemus	**Pluperf.**	nolueram
Pl	non vultis	Pl	nolebatis	Pl	noletis		
	nolunt		nolebant		nolent	**Fut.Perf.**	noluero
	malo		malebam		malam		malui
Sg	mavis	Sg	malebas	Sg	males		maluisti
	mavult		malebat		malet		etc.
	malumus		malebamus		malemus	**Pluperf.**	malueram
Pl	mavultis	Pl	malebatis	Pl	maletis		
	malunt		malebant		malent	**Fut.Perf.**	maluero

There are two Imperative forms of **nolle: noli! nolite!** They are used together with the Infinitive of a verb to form a negative command: **Nolite exspectare!** *Don't wait!* **Noli dormire!** *Don't sleep.*

EXERCISE M: Translate the forms:

1. **volo (2)**   2. **ferre**   3. **fere**   4. **vis**   5. **fero (2)**   6. **ferro**
7. **vultis**   8. **tulit**   9. **tollit**   10. **latum (2)**

EXERCISE N: Translate the sentences:

1. Quid vis? Te videre volo.
2. Tullia librum novum legere voluit.
3. Fer, Marce, aquam in casam!
4. Noli me tangere! Nolite clamare!
5. Cur cena, quae erat in mensa, sublata est?
6. Liberi in ludo discere debent; certe ludere malunt.
7. Animalia ab hominibus lingua et animo differunt.
8. Vir improbus pecuniam agricolae abstulit.

Lectio I: De Hercule

Hercules filius erat Alcumenae et Iovis, qui saepe veniebat in terram in formis diversis et stuprum cum feminis fecit. Igitur Iuno, regina deorum, Alcumenae invidebat et Herculem adhuc parvum interficere voluit. Hercules et frater geminus eius Iphicles in cubiculo Alcumenae in magno scuto dormiebant. Media nocte Iuno
5 irata duas serpentes misit, quae in cubiculum intraverunt et ad scutum serpserunt. Scutum paulo moverunt et pueros e somno excitaverunt.

Iphicles, puer timidus, magnopere clamavit. Sed Hercules, puer validus, nihil timebat. Serpentes subito cepit et magna vi compressit. Hoc modo eas interfecit. Alcumena clamorem audivit et Amphitryonem, maritum suum, e somno excitavit.
10 Ille gladium rapuit et ad pueros properavit. Ubi autem ad scutum venit, mira vidit: Hercules ridebat et ei serpentes mortuas monstravit.

Hercules adulescens multa didicit. Corpus suum exercebat et validus erat. Sed eadem diligentia musicae non studebat. Musicus piger erat. Aliquando eius magister musicae, nomine Lini, eum monuit, quod lyram ludere non voluit.
15 Hercules lyram fregit et magistrum interfecit.

Hercules, ubi vir erat, in bello pugnavit et Thebanos in proelium duxit. Post victoriam Hercules copias in patriam reduxit. Thebani maxime gaudebant. Creon, rex Thebanorum, filiam suam Herculi in matrimonium dedit. Vitam beatam cum liberis suis agebant. Subito Hercules in dementiam cecidit. Hanc dementiam Iuno
20 miserat, quod Herculem oderat. Hercules amens liberos suos cecidit.

Postea dementia Herculem reliquit et ille magnum crimen suum valde dolebat. Itaque ad oraculum Delphicum contendit et sibi poenam ab Apolline petivit. Pythia, sacerdos Apollinis, Herculem iussit ad regnum Eurysthei progredi et illi, tyranno malo, decem annos servire. Hic vir ab Hercule poposcit duodecim labores
25 conficere. In multis libris poetarum clarorum de his factis legere possumus.

---

(1) Iovis - (Genitive of Iuppiter); Alcumena,ae - (the wife of Amphitryon, a general; according to mythology she was impregnated both by Jupiter, in the shape of Amphitryon, and by her husband; she gave birth to twin sons: Hercules, the son of Jupiter, and Iphicles, the son of Amphitryon); (2) Iuno - (Jupiter's wife); stuprum cum femina facere - to seduce a woman; invidere (-eo,vidi + Dat.) - to envy, have a grudge; (3) interficere (-io, -feci, -fectum) - to kill; frater,fratris (3rd Decl.) - brother; geminus,a,um - twin; (4) scutum,i - shield; media nocte - in the middle of the night; (5) serpentes (f.) - serpents (this form can be nom. or cc.); serpere,serpo,serpsi,serptum - to slither, how serpents move; (6) paulo - a little; somnus,i - sleep; e somno excitare - to wake from sleep; (7) magnopere - (here: loudly); (8) magna vi - with great force; (9) maritus,i - husband; (10) gladius,i - sword; (11) mortuus,a,um - dead; (12) adulescens - (as a) young man; corpus,corporis (n) - body (here accusative); (13) studere (studui) + Dative - to study, practice; (14) Linus,i - (this musician was the brother of Orpheus); lyra,ae - lyre (an instrument); (16) proelium,i - battle; (17) rex, regis - king; Herculi - to Hercules; (19) dementia,ae - madness; cecidit - (remember that this is the perfect of 2 verbs, see also line 20!); (20) amens,amentis (or demens,dementis) - demented; odi, odisse - to hate; oderat: she hated; (21) crimen,criminis (neuter) (3rd Decl.) - crime; (22) dolere,doleo,dolui - to feel pain, to suffer; poena,ae - punishment; (23) sacerdos (3rd Decl.) - priestess; (25) conficere,-io,-feci - to carry out, perform, execute; factum,i - deed.

Lectio II: Fabulae Pro Domino

Servus domini antiqui cottidie quinque fabulas domino narrabat. Sine fabulis dominus dormire non poterat. Una nocte magnae curae dominum moverunt; etiam post octo fabulas dormire non potuit. Itaque petivit iterum octo fabulas, et servus non gaudebat, quod fessus erat. "Quod cupivisti, domine, iam factum est," dixit domino.

5   Respondit dominus: "Fabulae, quas mihi narravisti, erant multae, sed parvae. Longam volo audire fabulam, quae in multis verbis consistit."

Servus tum coepit: "Fuit olim agricola, cui magna pecunia erat. In oppido pecunia sua emit multas oves. Reduxit illas oves et venit ad flumen magnum, quod eo die habebat magnam aquae copiam. Non vidit agricola pontes aut naves; itaque oves trans flumen
10   traducere non potuit. Tandem invenit naviculam, quae duas oves tenere et transportare potuit."

Ubi haec verba dixit, servus tacuit. Dominus finem fabulae audire voluit et servum petivit: "Dic mihi reliquam fabulam tuam!"
Ille respondit: "Flumen est altum et latum, navicula est parva, atque oves sunt multae .
15   Si duxerit hic agricola cunctas oves suas trans flumen, fabulam, quam coepi, finiam."

---

(4) factum est - (it) has been done; (8) ovis, ovis (f.) - sheep; flumen, fluminis (n.) - river;
(9) pons, pontis (m.) - bridge; navis, navis (f.) - ship; (10) navicula,ae - little boat.

"...ducentae septuaginta tres oves, ducentae septuaginta quattuor, ducentae...."

Lectio III: Daedalus et Icarus (secundum Ovidium)

Daedalus architectus clarus Graecus erat. Cum filio suo Icaro in insulam Cretam iit, ubi Minos, rex notus, vixit. Minos tenuit animal ferum in regia sua, nomine Minotauri; ille erat semi-vir et semi-taurus. Huic animali Daedalus magnum labyrinthum fecit, in quo Minotaurus habitavit. Ubi Daedalus labyrinthum finivit,
5 Minos eum in Creta manere coegit, quod alii de labyrintho secreto nescire debuerunt.

Daedalus et Icarus miseri erant, quod in patriam suam redire voluerunt. Sed insulam Cretam undique aqua circumvenit et sine nave excedere non potuerunt. Daedalus, architectus clarus, dixit: "Minos possidet insulam et aquam et naves,
10 sed non possidet aerem: excedemus per aerem."

Pennas cepit parvas, medias et magnas et eas iunxit cera; hoc modo alas fecit sibi et filio Icaro. Alas in dorsum filii posuit et eum in alis libravit. Deinde alas suas sibi instituit et filio suo haec verba dixit: "Vola post me, ego te ducam. Noli ascendere in superiorem aerem, prope solem; nam sol calidus tanget alas tuas et eas solvet
15 et rumpet. Neque descende in inferiorem aerem, prope aquam, quod aqua alas tuas tanget et gravabit et tu in aquam cades.

Vola in media via et specta me!"

Insulam mane reliquerunt et Daedalus Icarum duxit. Supra aquam volaverunt, viderunt insulas et silvas, agricolas et servos, equos et asinos. Viri et feminae in
20 insulis eos conspexerunt, ut volabant, et crediderunt eos esse deos. Pater et filius alas pepulerunt et intervallum inter eos et insulam iniucundam crevit. Icarus autem bene volare didicerat et altum caelum cupivit. "Age,veni, pater!" clamavit, et currere et ascendere coepit. "Mediam, Icare, viam tene!" Daedalus petivit, "periculum magnum est!" Sed Icarus patrem non audivit. Volare potuit, aerem
25 vincere voluit et mox in altum caelum ascendit, liber velut avis, iuxta solem et prope deos. Sol autem Icarum tetigit et ceram solvit et alas fregit. Subito Icarus miser in aquam cecidit et mortuus est. Daedalus tristis filium quaesivit, sed eum invenire non potuit.

De Icaro misero haec aqua nomen cepit: MARE ICARIUM.

---

(2) rex,regis - king; regia,ae - palace; nomine - by the name of (+ Gen.); animali (dative of animal); taurus,i - bull; (5) alii - others; (8) undique - from all sides; navis,is - ship; (9) possidere - to own; (10) aer,aeris - air (aerem is Acc.); (11) penna,ae - feather; cera,ae - wax; ala,ae - wing; (12) dorsum,i - back; librare - to balance; (13) instituere - to adjust; (14) superior - higher; sol,solis - sun (solem, here and in line 25, is acc.); calidus,a,um - hot; (15) inferior - lower; (16) gravare - to make heavy; (17) medius,a,um - middle; (20) conspicere, conspexi - to see, catch sight of; pater,patris - father; (22) age! - let's go!; (25) velut - as, like; avis,is - bird; (27) mortuus est - he died; tristis - sad..

A. Answer the questions:

1. The third conjugation is also called _____ conjugation.

2. Does the third conjugation have a characteristic stem vowel? Y/N _____

3. The characteristic stem vowel of the fourth conjugation is ____ .

4. The future tense marker for the third and fourth conjugations is _____ .

5. The future tense marker for the first and second conjugations is _____ .

6. The perfect forms **cecidi, pepuli, cucurri, tetigi,** are formed by _____ .

B: Review the vocabulary:

frangere - gerere - emere - poscere - legere - ponere - crescere - colere - incipere - scire - munire

C: Do not confuse:

**cadere - caedere - cedere; dicere - ducere; dicere - discere; relinquere - cedere;
constiti (<-- consistere) - constitui (<-- constituere); edere - emere;
posui (<-- ponere) - potui (<-- posse); vici - vixi; rapere - rumpere.**

**eunt, veniunt,
currunt,
audiunt,
dicunt,
edunt, bibunt,
trahunt,
emunt,
vendunt,
agunt causas.
ludunt -**

vivunt !

THE WATER SUPPLY IN ROME

Cities like Rome and Pompeii were extraordinarily well supplied with fresh water. At the time, the daily use ran about 200 to 250 liters (55 to 65 gallons) per person. (By comparison the average use in Europe today is about 42 gallons a day.) The water was collected from mountain springs, rivers, and lakes and flowed to the cities' distribution centers in mostly underground water supply lines, called **aquae ductus** (aqueducts). Above ground, valleys, plains, and other water lines had to be bridged by these aqueducts; this was done with arched constructions, of which a number are preserved to this day in Italy, France, Spain, and North Africa. When we speak of aqueducts today, we refer mainly to these bridges. Their pillars were built with bricks or stone cubes; the arches, made of stones cut in conical shapes, did not exceed 21 meters in height. If the aqueduct needed to be higher, it was built in several storys. The highest story carried a water canal, approximately 1.5 meters wide and deep, which was protected against sun and pollution by stone plates.

Aqueduct in Nîmes, France

Sextus Iulius Frontinus, the Curator Aquarum of Rome in the first century A.D., lists 11 water supply lines for Rome by name, year of construction, length, diameter, and water quality. The oldest supply lines, the Appia and the Marcia, carried spring water from the Arno Valley, whose quality was judged excellent. The water from the springs in the Albanese mountains was also considered outstanding. The water from the river Arno, on the other hand, was described as muddy and of inferior consistency. The water from Lake Alsietinus was deemed undrinkable, at best usable for street-cleaning, irrigation, and naumachias.

The Roman architect and inventor Pollio Vitruvius (*De Architectura*, 25 BC) describes the **castellum aquae** (water tower), where the water was cleaned with filters of stones and gravel, and distributed in unequal amounts into three pipes:

 1. public water fountains;
 2. public places (baths, theaters)
 3. private customers, who had to pay for the water according to the diameter of their pipes.
Cheating was widespread, though, and could be done, for instance, by tapping public pipelines or by manipulating the pipe diameter.

In cases of water shortage the pipe for public fountains was automatically supplied the longest, because it lay lower in the tower than the other two. Not only is such a water tower with a distributor preserved in Pompeii, but water pipes made of lead were also found there during excavations. These pipes ran under the sidewalks, into private houses, where they could be turned on and off with faucets.

Drawing of a faucet found in Pompeii.

In the fourth century the list of public Roman buildings supplied with drinking or other-use water included eleven large **thermes** (public baths), fifteen **nympheae** (water-fountain buildings), five **naumachias**, about 850 smaller public baths and 1,350 public fountains. The Etruscans and Romans also built an extensive sewage system consisting of underground canals. Its initial purpose was to drain the lower lying swamp districts into the Tiber River. Later on, left over water was used to wash away the city's sewage. The largest of these drainage canals, the Cloaca Maxima, was already entirely cemented, vaulted, and put underground by the year 500 BC. It was constantly improved and repaired, and its opening into the Tiber River can still be seen near the Ponte Rotto.

The Roman water and sewage system was far advanced in matters of efficiency and hygiene over anything known in the Middle Ages or indeed until the nineteenth century. There is, however, a theory that blames the high lead content of the water pipes for large scale lead poisoning, which eventually may have contributed to the downfall of the Roman Empire.

Nymphaea - public water fountain

Chapter 9: Answers and Translations

Exercise B:
1. (F) he will lead 2. (PR) she teaches 3. (P) she saw 4. (PR) he sees 5. (P) he laughed
6. (PR) it puts 7. (F) he will send 8. (P) he taught 9. (F) she will put 10. (PR) she is laughing

Exercise C:
1. (PR) she puts 2. (F) she will put 3. (PR) they put 4. (F) they will lead 5. (PR) they teach
6. (I) they used to lead 7. (PR) you are sending 8. (P) you have sent 9. (PR) he does
10. (P) he did 11. (P) I have bought 12. (PR, P) we read, we have read 13. (PQ) they had lived
14. (P) they will have placed 15. (P) they were able, could 16. (P) you ran 17. (PR) you are well
18. (F) you will live 19. (I) I used to play 20. (P) I believed

Exercise D: (See verb list in groups, page 192, Nr. 8: same stem)
Riddle : Words, Words: cado, caedo, cedo, cogo, colo, capio, cupio; do, reddo, credo, trado, vendo; tollo, pello, mitto, curro; frangere, tangere, iungere; crescere, discere, poscere. **Change letter: down**: AGO, EGO, EDO, CEDO, CREDO; **across**: EGO - LEGO; EDO - EMO; CEDO - CADO.

Exercise E:
1. dico - I say 2. credo - I believe 3. capio - I take 4. curro - I run 5. ludo - I play 6. lego - I read
7. verto - I turn 8. traho - I pull 9. constituo - I decide 10. cado - I fall; caedo - I cut down 11. pono - I put 12. edo - I eat 13. pello - I push 14. scribo - I write 15. rumpo - I break

Exercise F:
1. premere - to press 2. agere - to do 3. petere - to seek 4. regere - to rule 5. cadere - to fall 6. tangere - to touch 7. ludere - to play 8. vincere - to defeat 9. currere - to run 10. fugere - to flee
11. ducere - to lead 12. vertere - to turn 13. cedere - to go, yield 14. solvere - to loosen 15. tradere - to hand over

Exercise G:

1.	PR faciunt	I faciebant	F	facient	P	fecerunt	PQ	fecerant	FP fecerint
2.	PR cadis	I cadebas	F	cades	P	cecidisti	PQ	cecideras	FP cecideris
3.	PR mittimus	I mittebamus	F	mittemus	P	misimus	PQ	miseramus	FP miserimus
4.	PR pono	I ponebam	F	ponam	P	posui	PQ	posueram	FP posuero

Exercise H:
1. vivo 2. faciebas 3. rexit 4. quaeremus, petemus 5. colueratis 6. clauserint 7. ludebam
8. reddidisti 9. scribet 10. ascenderamus 11. reliqueritis 12. poscunt 13. cecidi 14. mittes
15. creverat 16. legerimus 17. pellitis 18. cognoscebant 19. dicam 20. solveras 21. verterit
22. tradimus 23. edebatis 24. presserunt 25. ieceram 26. posueris 27. emit 28. bibebamus
29. tetigistis 30. vincent 31. cepero 32. agebas, faciebas, gerebas 33. cecidit 34. constituemus
35. cesseratis 36. cucurrerint (If you still feel unsure about the verbs retranslate them into English.)

Exercise I:
1.vendere 2.cadere 3.frangere 4.credere 5.dividere 6.compelling 7.bibere 8. ascendere
9. facere, agere 10. bellum gerere 11. rogare, orare, postulare, quaerere, petere, poscere

Exercise J:
> 3S (say) dicit, dicet, dicebat, dixit, dixerat, dixerit
> 2S (do) agis, ages, agebas, egisti, egeras, egeris
> 3S (defeat) vincit, vincet, vincebat, vicit, vicerat, vicerit
> 1S (warn) moneo, monebo, monebam, monui, monueram, monuero
> 1S (rule) rego, regam, regebam, rexi, rexeram, rexero
> 3S (leave) discedit, discedet, discedebat, discessit, discesserat, discesserit
> or 3S (relinquit, relinquet, relinquebat, reliquit, reliquerat, reliquerit)

or   3S   (abit, abibit, abibat, abiit, abierat, abierit)
     1P (put) ponimus, ponemus, ponebamus, posuimus, posueramus, posuerimus
     3P (carry) gerunt, gerent, gerebant, gesserunt, gesserant, gesserint
     2P (lead) ducitis, ducetis, ducebatis, duxistis, duxeratis, duxeritis
     1S (rise) surgo, surgam, surgebam, surrexi, surrexeram, surrexero
     3P (collect) cogunt, cogent, cogebant, coegerunt, coegerant, coegerint
     2S (hand over) tradis, trades, tradebas, tradidisti, tradideras, tradideris
     3P (defend) defendunt, defendent, defendebant, defenderunt, defenderant, defenderint
     1P (teach) docemus, docebimus, docebamus, docuimus, docueramus, docuerimus
     2S (see) vides, videbis, videbas, vidisti, videras, videris

Exercise K:

1. audire - you had heard 2. iacere - I lay 3. iacere - I threw 4. venire - to have come
5. nescire - I don't know who, someone 6. oboedire - he used to obey 7. venire - come! I have come 8. erudire - we will educate 9. aperire - they opened 10. finire - finish! 11. sentire - you are feeling 12. scire - you knew 13. impedire - they hinder 14. munire - we will have built

Exercise L:

1. We will not leave the town. 2. What did the good boy say after dinner? 3. We could find no food. 4. The master ordered this, the slave only obeyed. 5. The girl learned what she desired. 6. When will we come to your country house? 7. Did you sleep well yesterday? 8. Which of you drank the wine? 9. I ought to return the book which you wrote; I have read it. 10. What are you doing? I am sending a letter to a girlfriend (friendly girl).

Exercise M:

1. I want; I fly (volare) 2. to carry 3. almost 4. you want (Sg.) 5. I carry; Abl. or Dat. of ferus,a,um, wild 6. Dat. or Abl. of ferrum,i, iron 7. you want (Pl.) 8. he brought 9. she removes 10. (having been) carried; Nom. or Acc. of latus,a,um, wide.

Exercise N:

1. What do you want? I want to see you. 2. Tullia wanted to read the new book. 3. Marcus, bring water into the house! 4. Don't touch me! Don't shout! 5. Why has the meal which was on the table been removed? 6. The children must learn in school; certainly they would rather play.
7. Animals differ from humans by language and reason. (We hope that humans are the ones who have both of them.) 8. The wicked man carried the farmer's money away.

Reading 1 : Hercules

Hercules was the son of Alcmena and Jupiter, who often came to earth in various shapes and seduced women. Therefore Juno, the queen of the gods, held a grudge against Alcmena and wanted to kill Hercules (who was) still small. Hercules and his twin brother Iphicles slept in Alcmena's bedroom on a large shield. In the middle of the night the angry Juno sent two serpents. The serpents entered the bedroom and slithered to the shield. They moved the shield a little and woke the boys from sleep. Iphicles, a timid boy, cried out loudly. But Hercules, a strong boy, feared nothing. He suddenly grasped the serpents and squeezed them with great force. In this way he killed them. Alcmena heard the clamor and woke Amphitryon, her husband, from sleep. He grabbed a sword and hurried to the boys. However, when he came to the shield, he saw wonderful things: Hercules was laughing and showed him the dead serpents.

As a young man Hercules learned many things. He exercised his body and was strong. But he did not study music with the same diligence: He was a lazy musician. One time his music teacher, named Linus, admonished him, because he did not want to play the lyre. Hercules smashed the lyre and killed the teacher.

When Hercules was a man, he fought in war and led the Thebans into battle. After the victory Hercules led the troops back to their home. The Thebans were very happy. Creon, the king of the

Thebans, gave Hercules his daughter in matrimony. They led a happy life with their children. But suddenly Hercules fell into madness. Juno had sent this madness, because she hated Hercules. The demented Hercules killed his children.

Later the madness left Hercules and he felt great pain for his great crime. Therefore he hastened to the Delphic Oracle and asked for punishment for himself from Apollo. Pythia, the priestess of Apollo, ordered Hercules to proceed to the realm of Eurystheus and serve him, an evil tyrant, for ten years. This man demanded from Hercules to execute twelve labors. In many books of famous poets we can read about these deeds.

Hercules puer premit collum serpentis.

Reding 2: Stories for the Master

The slave of a master of old used to tell his master five stories every day. Without the stories the master could not sleep. One night great worries moved the master; even after eight stories he was not able to sleep. Therefore he begged for yet another eight stories, and the slave was not pleased, because he was very tired. "What you desired has already been done, master," he said to his master. Answered the master: "The stories you told me indeed were many, but small. I want a long story, which consists of many words."

Then the slave began: "Once upon a time there was a farmer who had a lot of money. In town he bought many sheep with his money. He led the sheep back and came to a big river, which on this day had a large amount of water. The farmer did not see either bridges or ships; therefore he was not able to lead the sheep across the river. Finally he came upon a little boat which could hold two sheep and ferry them across."

When he had said these words, the slave was silent. The master wanted to hear the end of the story and begged the slave: "Tell me the rest of your story!"

He answered: "The river is deep and wide, the boat is small, and there are many sheep. When the farmer has led all his sheep across the river, I will finish the story which I have begun."

Reading 3: Daedalus and Icarus

Daedalus was a famous Greek architect. With his son Icarus he went to the island of Crete, where Minos, a well-known king, lived. Minos kept a wild animal in his palace, by the name of Minotaurus; he was half man and half bull. For this animal Daedalus made a big labyrinth, in which Minotaurus lived. When Daedalus had finished the labyrinth, Minos forced him to remain on Crete, because other people should not know about the secret labyrinth.

Daedalus and Icarus were miserable, because they wanted to return to their homeland. But water surrounded the island of Crete on all sides, and without a ship they could not get away. Daedalus, the famous architect, said: "Minos owns the island and the water and the ships, but he does not own the air; we will go away through the air."

He took small, medium-sized, and big feathers and joined them with wax; in this way he made wings for himself and for his son. He put the wings on his son's back and balanced him in the wings. Then he adjusted his wings on himself and said the following words to his son: "Fly behind me, I will lead you. Don't go up to the higher air, near the sun; for the hot sun will touch your wings and dissolve and tear them. And don't fly down to the lower air, next to the water, because the water will touch your wings and make them heavy, and you will fall into the water. Fly in the middle and look at me!"

They left the island early, and Daedalus led Icarus. They flew above the water, and saw islands and forests, farmers and slaves, horses and donkeys. The men and women on the islands looked at them, as they were flying, and believed them to be gods. Father and son drove their wings, and the distance between them and the unpleasant island grew. But Icarus had learned to fly well and lusted for the high heavens. "Come on, father, let's go!" he said and began to race and to go up. "Keep on the middle road!" Daedalus begged him, "there is great danger!"

But Icarus did not hear his father. He was able to fly, he wanted to conquer the air, and soon he ascended to the high heaven, free like a bird, next to the sun and near to the gods. But the sun touched Icarus and melted the wax and broke the wings. Suddenly Icarus fell into the water and died. Sad Daedalus looked for his son, but he could not find him. From poor Icarus this water took its name: the **Icarian Sea.**

Summary:

1. Consonant 2. No 3. -i- 4. -e- 5. -bi- 6. reduplication

10

VERBS: THE PASSIVE VOICE
DEPONENTS

GERMANIC LANGUAGES II

On its way to becoming Proto-Germanic, the Indo-European source language went through a unique phonetic change, which linguists often call the Germanic Sound Shift or the Great Consonant Shift. This sound shift was discovered by the Grimm brothers, Jakob and Wilhelm, who are best known for their collection of fairy tales, but who were really philologists. Between them they spoke and read some 43 languages, among them Sanskrit. In their honor the Germanic Sound Shift is also called GRIMM'S LAW.

The manifestations of Grimm's Law are what distinguishes Germanic languages most obviously from Romance languages, or from Greek. This sound change involved 9 consonants and took place in a sort of round robin way. The PIE initial consonants /p/, /t/, and /k/ turned into Germanic /f/, /th/, and /h/. Since now 3 consonants were missing, so to speak, they were supplied by PIE /b/, /d/, /g/ changing into Germanic /p/, /t/, and /k/. Now, however, 3 different consonants were lacking. They in turn were supplied by PIE /bh/, /dh/, and /gh/ (probably consonants pronounced with a puff of breath after them, or 'aspirated') turning into Germanic /b/, /d/, and /g/. Now the set was complete again, as far as Proto-Germanic was concerned. The loss of the PIE aspirated consonants seemed of no importance, as indeed they were lost in most other branches also. Germanic had gained /f/, /th/, and /h/ to make up for them anyway.

The following graph summarizes Grimm's Law. In it the groups of consonants outside of the circle are Indo-European, those inside the circle are Germanic. There is no good explanation of why these changes occurred, why only in Germanic, or when. The process was a gradual one, however, and may have taken between 500 and 1000 years.

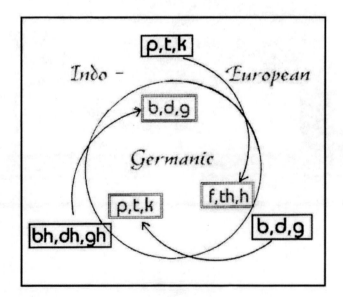

Chapter 10:   VERBS : THE PASSIVE VOICE; DEPONENTS

The **passive** voice developed from the Indo-European medium voice (still preserved in Greek), which had the meaning "I do something to, or for myself." The passive voice then extends this idea to "something is done to me." Or, expressing it differently: in the **active** someone or something (the subject) does something to, or acts upon, an object. In the **passive** the subject is acted upon by an agent, who may or may not be mentioned. Many actions or ideas can be expressed either in the active or passive.

Examples:

Active			**Passive**		
Subject	**acting on**	**object**	**Subject**	**being acted on**	**by agent**
The explorer	saw	a lion.	The lion	was seen	by the explorer.
			The explorer	was eaten	by the lion.
The explorer	cursed	the lion.			
			The lion	was eaten	by a crocodile.
The lion	gave the crocodile	indigestion.	The crocodile	was given indigestion	
An explorer will shoot the crocodile.		etc.			(by the lion)

In English all **passive** forms are **compound**, or **periphrastic** (which means "more than one word," and comes from the Greek for "talking around"). They must have two components:
1. a form of the verb **to be**, such as "is, is being, was, will be, has been."
2. a **past participle (passive)**, or **PPP** (past participles are always passive!),
   such as "ask**ed**, see**n**, throw**n**, stol**en**, lov**ed**."

("Ask**ing**, see**ing**, lov**ing**" are **present** participles (active) They do **not** make a passive.)
If one of the two components is missing, the form is not passive !
Examples:

Passive	**Active**
he **is asked**	he asks
he **is being asked**	he is asking
we **were asked**	we were asking
we **were caught**	we caught
The horse **was caught**.	We were catching horses.
The answer **had been given**.	We had given the answer.
The students **were tortured**.	The teacher tortured them.
The students **were being educated**.	The students were being silly.
We **are fenced** in.	We are great.
We **were given** an answer.	We were giving an answer.
He **was asked** questions.	He had asked questions.
The questions **were asked**.	The questions were hard.
We **will be asked** questions.	We will be asking questions.
He **will have been told** by Tuesday.	He will have told us by Thursday.

EXERCISE A:	Decide whether the following sentences are passive or not. If they are not passive, indicate which component is missing:

___ 1. We will be invited.   ___ 2. We will be there.

___ 3. We will be eating at nine.   ___ 4. It had to be done.

___ 5. They have been defeated.   ___ 6. He has been eating.

___ 7. He has eaten.   ___ 8. He is being grilled.

___ 9. He is being stupid.   ___ 10. This book was written by Virgil.

THE PASSIVE ENDINGS

For the passive we need a new set of endings.
The **passive** forms of the **present, imperfect,** and **future** are **synthetic,** that means one word only.
The set of passive endings is the same for present, imperfect, and future.

	Sg	Pl
1.	**-or (-r)**	**-mur**
2.	**-ris**	**-mini**
3.	**-tur**	**-ntur**

Here is the **present passive** of **portare** and **docere:**

		portare		docere
Sg	1. pórt **or**	I am (being) carried/taught	1. dóce **or**
	2. portá **ris**	you are carried/taught	2. docé **ris**
	3. portá **tur**	he/she/it is carried/taught	3. docé **tur**
Pl	1. portá **mur**	we are carried/taught	1. docé **mur**
	2. portá **mini**	you are carried/taught	2. docé **mini**
	3. portá **ntur**	they are carried/taught	3. docé **ntur**

Imperfect

Sg	1. portá **ba r**	I was (being), I used to be,	1. docé **ba r**
	2. porta **bá ris**	carried/taught	2. doce **bá ris**
	3. porta **bá tur**	etc.	3. doce **bá tur**
Pl	1. porta **bá mur**		1. doce **bá mur**
	2. porta **bá mini**		2. doce **bá mini**
	3. porta **bá ntur**		3. doce **bá ntur**

Future

Sg	1. portá **bo r**	I will be carried/taught	1. docé **bo r**
	2. portá **<u>be</u> ris**		2. docé **<u>be</u> ris**
	3. portá **bi tur**		3. docé **bi tur**
Pl	1. portá **bi mur**		1. docé **bi mur**
	2. porta **bí mini**		2. doce **bí mini**
	3. porta **bú ntur**		3. doce **bú ntur**

The person **by whom** something is done is expressed by the preposition **a (ab)** + **ablative**, for instance:

Pueri laudabantur **a magistro**.   The boys were praised by the teacher.
Femina portabitur **ab equo**   The woman will be carried by the horse.

It is not sensible for some verbs to be put into the passive, because of their meaning (often they are intransitive, i.e. they have no direct object), for instance **flere, gaudere, ambulare**. Go through your verb lists and find other examples!

PASSIVE INFINITIVES

The **present passive infinitive** for the first, second, and fourth conjugations is formed by replacing the final **-e** of the active infinitive with **-i** :

amare --> amari   (to be loved)   monere --> moneri (to be warned)   audire --> audiri   (to be heard)
parare --> parari   (to be prepared)   docere --> doceri (to be taught)   munire --> muniri (to be built)
captare --> captari (to be caught)   salutare --> salutari (to be greeted)

The present passive infinitive of **third conjugation** verbs is formed by replacing the final **-ere** of the active infinitive with just **-i** :

capere --> capi   ponere --> poni
ducere --> duci   solvere --> solvi
mittere --> mitti   vincere --> vinci

This makes the passive infinitive one syllable shorter than the active infinitive and, regretfully, quite similar to the 3rd principal part, (the 1st person Singular perfect). Compare: vici (I have defeated) - vinci (to be defeated); cepi - capi; misi - mitti. Only verbs with identical present and perfect stem have the same form: (solvere) solvi - solvi; (defendere) defendi - defendi; (emere) emi - emi.

EXERCISE B: Translate:

1. Oppidum parvum non delebitur.
2. Docebamur a bono magistro.
3. Cena paratur ab ancilla.
4. Bestiae ferae timebantur a nautis.
5. Cras invitaberis ab amicis.
7. Frumentum datur equis.
8. Multae fabulae ab avo nostro narrabantur.
9. Avus narrabat multas fabulas.
10. Ob bellum oppida occupabuntur.
11. Movebitisne vaccas ex horto?
12. A magistro rogabar.
13. Exspectamur ab avo.
14. A domino monentur servi.
15. Britannia tenebatur a Romanis.

The passive of the third and fourth conjugation is formed in the same way; the ending for the 3rd person Plural present is **-untur**:

Present	Imperfect	Future
1. dúc or	ducé ba r	dúc a r
2. dúc e ris (!)	duce bá ris	duc é ris (!)
3. dúc i tur	duce bá tur	duc é tur
1. dúc i mur	duce bá mur	duc é mur
2. duc í mini	duce bá mini	duc é mini
3. duc úntur	duce bá ntur	duc é ntur
1. cápi or	capi é ba r	cápi a r
2. cáp e ris	capi e bá ris	capi é ris
3. cápi tur	capi e bá tur	capi é tur
1. cápi mur	capi e bá mur	capi é mur
2. capí mini	capi e bá mini	capi é mini
3. capi úntur	capi e bá ntur	capi é ntur
1. aúdi or	audi é ba r	aúdi a r
2. audí ris	audi e bá ris	audi é ris
3. audí tur	audi e bá tur	audi é tur
1. audí mur	audi e bá mur	audi é mur
2. audí mini	audi e bá mini	audi é mini
3. audi úntur	audi e bá ntur	audi é ntur

The **passive** of the **perfect, pluperfect,** and **future perfect** are **periphrastic** in Latin, just as they are in English; moreover they are composed of the same two forms as the English passive: a **past participle**, and a form of the verb **to be**.

THE PAST PPARTICIPLE PASSIVE (PPP)

This form, which constitutes the **fourth principal part**, is again, like the perfect stem, one that can be produced for regular verbs and must be memorized for irregular verbs.

1. Regular Verbs (First Conjugation)

The verbs of the first conjugation form the PPP by adding **-tus, -ta, -tum** to the present stem; they are then **declined** like **adjectives** of the first and second declension (e.g. bonus, bona, bonum):

    ama **tus**, ama **ta**, ama **tum**   (having been) loved
    porta **tus,** porta **ta**, porta **tum**   (having been) carried
The **four principal parts** are then:

    amo, amare, amavi, amatum (or: amatus)

    porto, portare, portavi, portatum (or: portatus)
Some books give the **masculine** form, portat**us**, some the **Supine**, portat**um**, which is the same as the neuter form of the PPP, as fourth principal part. In this book the **supine** is used **(-um)**

2. Irregular Verbs

Just like some perfect forms, some irregular PPPs follow certain patterns; a number of second conjugation and several fourth conjugation verbs, for instance, have PPPs ending in **-itus, -ita, -itum**. Whether they are listed in groups or not: **they must be memorized !**
Some verbs do not have a PPP, or fourth principal part, a fact which is related to their meaning. Most of them are intransitive (no object possible). Other verbs, though they are intransitive, have a PPP listed, since some of their compounds, which use the same PPP, may be transitive.

Examples of PPPs :

Second Conjugation		Third Conjugation	
Infinitive PR	**PPP**	**Infinitive PR**	**PPP**
docére	doctum	dúcere	ductum
vidére	visum	gérere	gestum
monére	monitum	tráhere	tractum
movére	motum	cúrrere	cursum
ridére	risum	pétere	petitum
respondére	responsum	sólvere	solutum
		cápere	captum
Fourth Conjugation		pónere	positum
audire	auditum	dícere	dictum
venire	ventum	tángere	tactum
munire	munitum	émere	emptum

EXERCISE C: Form the PPPs of the following **regular** Verbs, and, if possible, give English words that are derived from these fourth principal parts: (You may have to use prefixes for your English words.) Ex.: parare - paratum (*preparation*); stare - statum (*static*).

1. rogare	2. monstrare	3. salutare	4. spectare	5. cantare
6. invitare	7. exspectare	8. laudare	9. narrare	10. donare
11. vocare	12. occupare	13. orare	14. visitare	15. dare

These **participles** can be used in <u>three ways:</u>
    1. as **adjectives**, or as adjectival nouns
    2. to form the **passive** perfect, pluperfect, and future perfect
    3. in an **Ablative Absolute** construction

1. Participles as Adjectives:
Examples:
Magister **doctus** habitat in vico.   A learned teacher lives in the village.
               (Some PPPs have also taken on an adjectival meaning, e.g. doctus = learned)
Invitati non gaudebant.   The invited (people) were not happy.
Portavimus libros nobis donatos ad scholam.
          We carried the books (having been) given to us to school.
          or better: the books that had been given to us
The literal translation of the PPP is: 'having been found',' having been carried',' having been asked,' etc.; usually it is shortened to 'found', 'carried', 'asked'. In many cases a relative clause will be the best translation. ("The books that had been given to us ..".)
The usage of participles in Latin corresponds to that in English, where PPPs can also be used as participles and adjectives: All these items were found during the week. (Passive - Participle)
         Please put the lost and found things into this bin. (Adjective)

EXERCISE D: Say in Latin: (use participles given on previous page)

    1. a learned man
    2. the expected girls
    3. the stories that had been told [acc.]
    4. of the food having been put on the table
    5. fortified towns
    6. the bought things
    7. a cart dragged by horses
    8. children who were heard, but not seen
    9. the camp, which had been moved
   10. the things that had been done [use gerere]

 (4) four words (6) one word! (7) use **ab** for "by" (10) also one word

Of course, many Relative Clauses were used in Latin, as you have seen already; but the PPP was vastly preferred over short Relative Clauses in Latin - for one thing it saves so much space!

2. The Passive

To form the **perfect, pluperfect,** and **future perfect passive** you need only add the appropriate **ending** to the PPP (**m., f., n., Sg., Pl.**) and combine it with the **present, imperfect,** or **future** tenses of **esse:**

Perfect

Sg	1. portatus,a,um	sum	I have been carried, I was carried
	2. portatus,a,um	es	you have been carried, you were carried
	3. portatus,a,um	est	he/she/it has been, was carried
Pl	1. portat**i,ae,a**	sumus	we have been, were carried
	2. portat**i,ae,a**	estis	you have been, were carried
	3. portat**i,ae,a**	sunt	they have been, were carried

also:

Sg	1. doctus,a,um	sum	I have been, was taught
	2. doctus,a,um	es	
	3. doctus,a,um	est	
Pl	1. docti,ae,a	sumus	we have been, were taught
	2. docti,ae,a	estis	
	3. docti,ae,a	sunt	

and:

auditus,a,um	sum	I have been heard, was heard
captus,a,um	sum	I have been captured, was captured
ductus,a,um	sum	I have been led, was led

Literally the form **portatus sum** means of course **I am carried,** as a resulting state of something that was finished in the past. A better example is perhaps:

Porta clausa est. The door **has been** closed, and, as a result, now **is** closed.

However, it is better to translate these perfect forms with the English past tense (has been closed, was closed), to avoid confusion of **is closed** and **is being closed** (clauditur). If in doubt, go by the context.

3. The Ablative Absolute

This construction, which often takes the place of a dependent clause in Latin, most often consists of a noun and a **PPP**, both in the ablative. It will be explained in Chapter 12.

Pluperfect

	1. portatus,a,um	eram	I had been carried
Sg	2. portatus,a,um	eras	you had been carried
	3. portatus,a,um	erat	he/she/it had been carried
	1. portati,ae,a	eramus	we had been carried
Pl	2. portati,ae,a	eratis	you had been carried
	3. portati,ae,a	erant	they had been carried

Future Perfect

	1. portatus,a,um	ero	I will have been carried
Sg	2. portatus,a,um	eris	you will have been carried
	3. portatus,a,um	erit	he/she/it will have been carried
	1. portati,ae,a	erimus	we will have been carried
Pl	2. portati,ae,a	eritis	you will have been carried
	3. portati,ae,a	erunt	they will have been carried

!!! Remember that the **ending** for the future perfect active is **-erint**, while the 3rd person Plural future of **esse** is **erunt**. !!!

The other conjugations:

doctus,a,um	eram	I had been taught
doctus,a,um	ero	I will have been taught
ductus,a,um	eram	I had been led
ductus,a,um	ero	I will have been led
captus,a,um	eram	I had been taken
captus,a,um	ero	I will have been taken
auditus,a,um	eram	I had been heard
auditus,a,um	ero	I will have been heard

Notice that the **conjugated** parts of these verb tenses are whatever forms of **esse** are used; the **participles** themselves are **not** considered conjugated forms, because they lack two of the requisite five categories: they have number (Sg and Pl), tense (past) and voice (passive), but they don't have person (**amatus** can be **I, you, he, it** - anybody or anything masculine in the Singular), or mood (indicative, imperative, subjunctive). Participles thus are **declined**, just like adjectives. Similar to English, they stay the same for all compound tenses: **portati sumus, eramus, erimus - we have been, had been, will have been carried.**

| EXERCISE E: | Translate the sentences (don't forget to use a relative or other dependent clause when suitable!) : |

1. Cibus tactus non erat. _____

2. Multa facta sunt. _____

3. Oppidum muniebatur. _____

4. Asinus obstinatus ad stabulum tractus est. _____

5. Ubi dona empta ponentur? _____

6. Ea, quae dominus imperavit, gesta erunt, ubi redibit. _____

7. Nihil dictum est a pueris rogatis. _____

8. Spectata nobis non placebant, quamquam pauci ridebant. _____

9. Visitavimus villam a nautis occupatam, sed salutati non sumus. _____

_____

10. Capti equi ex stabulo cucurrerunt et non iam visi sunt. _____

11. Liberi videri, sed non audiri debent. _____

12. Sellae motae sunt. Ubi invenientur? _____

13. Gesta Romanorum clara sunt. _____

14. Libri poetarum Romanorum semper legentur. _____

15. Avus visitabatur a me et ab asino meo. _____

Principal Parts of Verbs Revisited:

First Conjugation:

amo, amare, amavi, amatum   to love
    (and most other first conjugation verbs)
except:
do, dare, dedi, datum   to give
    circumdare   to surround
(the other compounds of dare - tradere, vendere, etc. - are 3rd Conjugation verbs)
sto, stare, steti, (staturus)   to stand
    circumstare, circumstiti   to stand around
    obstare, obstiti   to stand against, oppose
    restare, restiti   to be left over
    constat (impersonal)**, constitit**   it is well known
    praestat(impersonal)**, praestitit**   it is better
iuvo, iuvare, iuvi, iutum   to help
lavo, lavare, lavi, lautum   to wash
veto, vetare, vetui, vetitum   to forbid, prevent

Second Conjugation:

debeo, debere, debui, debitum   to owe; ought, should, must
doceo, docere, docui, doctum   to teach
fleo, flere, flevi, fletum   to cry
habeo, habere, habui, habitum   to have
iaceo, iacere, iacui, --   to lie down
moneo, monere, monui, monitum   to warn
moveo, movere, movi, motum   to move
pareo, parere, parui, --   to obey
placeo, placere, placui, placitum   to please
respondeo, -dere, responsi, responsum   to answer
rideo, ridere, risi, risum   to laugh
sedeo, sedere, sedi, sessum   to sit
taceo, tacere, tacui, tacitum   to be silent
teneo, tenere, tenui, tentum   to have, hold
timeo, timere, timui, --   to be afraid, fear
valeo, valere, valui, valitum   to be strong, well
video, videre, vidi, visum   to see

Fourth Conjugation:

aperio, aperire, aperui, apertum   to open
audio, audire, audivi, auditum   to hear
comperio, comperire, comperi, compertum   to learn, find out
custodio, custodire, custodivi, custoditum   to guard
dormio, dormire, dormivi, --   to sleep
erudio, erudire, erudivi, eruditum   to teach, educate
finio, finire, finivi, finitum   to finish
impedio, impedire, impedivi, impeditum   to hinder
munio, munire, munivi, munitum   to build, fortify

nescio, nescire, nescivi, nescitum	to not know
oboedio, oboedire, oboedivi, oboeditum	to obey
punio, punire, punivi, punitum	to punish
reperio, reperire, repperi, repertum	to find
scio, scire, scivi, scitum	to know
sentio, sentire, sensi, sensum	to feel
venio, venire, veni, ventum	to come

Third Conjugation:

ago, agere, egi, actum	to do, drive
ascendo, ascendere, ascendi, ascensum	to ascend
bibo, bibere, bibi, --	to drink
cado, cadere, cecidi, casum	to fall
caedo, caedere, cecidi, caesum	to fell, cut down
cedo, cedere, cessi, cessum	to go, yield
claudo, claudere, clausi, clausum	to shut, close
cognosco, cognoscere, cognovi, cognitum	to find out, learn
cogo, cogere, coegi, coactum	to collect, compel
colo, colere, colui, cultum	to cultivate, tend
consisto, consistere, constiti, --	to consist
constituo, -tuere, constitui, constitutum	to set up, decide
contendo, contendere, -tendi, -tentum	to strive, struggle, hasten, contend
credo, credere, credidi, creditum	to believe
cresco, crescere, crevi, cretum	to grow
curro, currere, cucurri, cursum	to run
defendo, defendere, defendi, defensum	to defend
descendo, -scendere, -scendi, -scensum	to descend
dico, dicere, dixi, dictum	to say
disco, discere, didici --	to learn
divido, dividere, divisi, divisum	to divide
duco, ducere, duxi, ductum	to lead
edo, edere, edi, esum	to eat
emo, emere, emi, emptum	to buy
frango, frangere, fregi, fractum	to break
gero, gerere, gessi, gestum	to bear, carry (on, out)
instituo, -tuere, institui, institutum	to establish
iungo, iungere, iunxi, iunctum	to join
lego, legere, legi, lectum	to read
ludo, ludere, lusi, lusum	to play
mitto, mittere, misi, missum	to send
pello, pellere, pepuli, pulsum	to drive, push
peto, petere, petivi, petitum	to ask, beg, search, attack
pono, ponere, posui, positum	to put, place
posco, poscere, poposci, --	to demand
premo, premere, pressi, pressum	to press
quaero, quaerere, quaesivi, quaesitum	to ask, look for
reddo, reddere, reddidi, redditum	to give back, render
rego, regere, rexi, rectum	to rule, govern

relinquo, relinquere, reliqui, relictum	to leave behind
rumpo, rumpere, rupi, ruptum	to tear, break
scribo, scribere, scripsi, scriptum	to write
solvo, solvere, solvi, solutum	to loosen, pay, sail
tango, tangere, tetigi, tactum	to touch
traho, trahere, traxi, tractum	to pull, drag
vendo, vendere, vendidi, venditum	to sell
verto, vertere, verti, versum	to turn
vinco, vincere, vici, victum	to defeat
vivo, vivere, vixi, victum	to live
capio, capere, cepi, captum	to take, catch
cupio, cupere, cupivi, cupitum	to want, desire
conspicio, -spicere, conspexi, -spectum	to look at, see
facio, facere, feci, factum	to do, make
fugio, fugere, fugi, --	to flee
iacio, iacere, ieci, iactum	to throw
rapio, rapere, rapui, raptum	to grasp, snatch
incipio, incipere, coepi, coeptum	to begin
fero, ferre, tuli, latum	to bear, carry
eo, ire, ii, itum	to go
sum, esse, fui, --	to be
volo, velle, volui, --	to want
nolo, nolle, nolui, --	to not want
malo, malle, malui, --	to prefer, rather want

Scribit, legit, discit: mus doctus

Many English words were derived from the PPP, the fourth principal part of the verb; doing the next exercise should also help you learn the Verbs.

EXERCISE F: Answer the questions and give the infinitive of the verb (see example 1 and 2).

1. A **factory** is a place where things are _____. (facere)

2. You need **victuals** in order to _____. (vivere)

3. Your **diction** refers to how you _____ your words.

4. **Victory** for one party means _____ for the other.

5. In a **constitution** the rules for a country are _____.

6. **Claustro**phobia means a fear of _____ places.

7. A **missive** is something which has been _____.

8. In a **petition** people _____ for something.

9. You give **credit** to a person, because you _____ in his ability to pay.

10. A **dormitory** is a place to _____ in.

11. Measuring your **pulse** shows you the speed at which your blood is _____.

12. Your **tactile** sense is your sense of _____.

13. When your leg is **fractured**, it is _____.

14. A **date** is a day which has been _____ for a purpose.

15. A **relic** is something which has been _____ by time.

EXERCISE G:

Now explain the following words, in a way similar to that above (you may have to consult an English dictionary that gives the etymology or history of words)

punitive, monitor, visa (in a passport), cult, position, well-versed, ruptured, cognitive, case, rapture, solution.

EXERCISE H: Translate: (careful: not all are Passive!)

1. This story has already been told before.
2. The horses had never been touched by the children.
3. The boy was taught well. (2 possible tenses)
4. Those bad men will be driven out of Italy.
5. The stupid boys broke the windows of her house.
6. Nothing was done about the money by the farmers.
7. Their country used to be ruled by women.
8. It has been written: "He ascended into heaven."
9. She had been called, but he had answered.
10. The books will have been read: the children will read them.

EXERCISE I: Give synopses of:

2nd Pers. Sg. of **iacere**, *to throw*, in the active (six forms)
3rd Pers. Pl. of **videre**, *to see*, in the Passive (six forms; use feminine)
3rd Pers. Sg. of **rogare**, *to ask*, active and passive (12 forms; use masc.)

EXERCISE J: In the following table supply the missing active or passive form of the same tense, give the name of the tense, and translate the Passive form:

	Active	Passive	Tense	Translation of the Passive
1.	_____	moniti sumus	____	_____
2.	vocas	_____	____	_____
3.	spectabo	_____	____	_____
4.	_____	doctus eram	____	_____
5.	_____	occupati erunt	____	_____
6.	_____	captae estis	____	_____
7.	invitabatis	_____	____	_____
8.	laudaverat	_____	____	_____
9.	docuerimus	_____	____	_____

10. _____ amabitur   ____ _____

11. _____ cantata sunt   ____ _____

12. visitaveratis   _____   ____ _____

13. _____ salutamur   ____ _____

14. oppugnabant   _____   ____ _____

15. exspectabis   _____   ____ _____

16. presserunt   _____   ____ _____

17. _____ visus est   ____ _____

18. _____ audiebamini   ____ _____

19. mittemus   _____   ____ _____

20. _____ ponitur   ____ _____

21. vertebatis   _____   ____ _____

22. custodiet   _____   ____ _____

23. _____ quaereris   ____ _____

24. fregerat   _____   ____ _____

25. finiverint   _____   ____ _____

invitata eram   **occupatus sum**   **missa sum a patre tuo:**
                                                 redi domum !

DEPONENT VERBS

Deponent verbs are verbs that have "put down" (**deponere**), meaning dropped, their active forms and use their passive forms to express active meaning. They have only three principal parts and are found in all four conjugations:

Examples:
First Conjugation: hortor, hortari, hortatus sum, to encourage

Present

Sg	1. **hortor**	I encourage
	2. **hortaris**	you encourage
	3. **hortatur**	he/she/it encourages
Pl	1. **hortamur**	we encourage
	2. **hortamini**	you encourage
	3. **hortantur**	they encourage

Imperfect

Sg	1. **hortabar**	I encouraged, I used to encourage
	2. **hortabaris**	
	3. **hortabatur**	
Pl	1. **hortabamur**	
	2. **hortabamini**	
	3. **hortabantur**	

Future

Sg	1. **hortabor**	I will, shall, am going to encourage
	2. **hortaberis**	
	3. **hortabitur**	
Pl	1. **hortabimur**	
	2. **hortabimini**	
	3. **hortabuntur**	

Perfect

Sg	hortatus,a,um	sum	I have encouraged		hortati,ae,a	sumus	we have encouraged
	hortatus,a,um	es	you	Pl	hortati,ae,a	estis	you
	hortatus,a,um	est	he,she,it		hortati,ae,a	sunt	they

Pluperfect

Sg.	hortatus,a,um	eram	I had encouraged
Pl.	hortati,ae,a	eramus	we had encouraged
		etc.	

Future Perfect

Sg.	hortatus,a,um	ero	I will have encouraged
Pl.	hortati,ae,a	erimus	we will have encouraged
		etc.	

Infinitive Present: **hortari**
Infinitive Perfect: **hortatus,a,um esse**

Imperatives: **hortare ! hortamini!**
(The Singular imperative looks just as the active infinitive would, if there were any!)

These deponents can not express passive meaning. If you want to say "he was encouraged," you must use another verb, for instance **monere**.

The past participle passive (PPP) of deponents is the only past participle passive with an **active** meaning:
hortatus,a,um - having encouraged (**not**: having **been** encouraged)

First Conjugation Deponents

arbitror,arbitrari,arbitratus sum	to think	arbitration
conor,conari,conatus sum	to try	
hortor,hortari,hortatus sum	to encourage	exhort
imitor, imitari, imitatus sum	to imitate	*
laetor, laetari, laetatus sum	to be happy	Letitia
miror,mirari,miratus sum	to wonder	miracle
miseror, miserari, miseratus sum	to lament	misery
moror,morari,moratus sum	to hesitate, delay	moratorium
recordor,recordari,recordatus sum	to remember	recording
veneror,venerari,veneratus sum	to venerate	*
venor, venari, --	to hunt	venison
versor, versari, versatus sum	to be present, active	versed

Second Conjugation Deponents

fateor, fateri, fassus sum	to confess	
confiteor, confiteri, confessus sum	"	*
mereor, mereri, meritus sum	to deserve, merit	*
misereor, misereri, --	to pity	
polliceor, polliceri, pollicitus sum	to promise	
reor, reri, ratus sum	to think	rational
tueor, tueri, tutus sum	to protect	tutelage
vereor, vereri, veritus sum	to fear	revere
videor, videri, visus sum	to seem (or: to be seen)	

Third Conjugation Deponents

abutor, abuti, abusus sum	to abuse	*
aggredior, aggredi, aggressus sum	to attack	aggressor
defungor, defungi, defunctus sum	to die	defunct
fruor, frui, fructus sum (+ Abl.)	to enjoy	fruition
fungor, fungi, functus sum (+Abl.)	to perform	functional
gradior, gradi, gressus sum	to walk, step, stride	grade
labor, labi, lapsus sum	to glide	lapse
loquor, loqui, locutus sum	to speak	elocution
morior, mori, mortuus sum	to die	mortal
nanciscor, nancisci, nactus sum	to obtain, reach	
nascor, nasci, natus sum	to be born	native
nitor, niti, nisus (or nixus) sum	to lean on, try, shine	
obliviscor, oblivisci, oblitus sum	to forget	oblivious
patior, pati, passus sum	to suffer, permit	passive
proficiscor, proficisci, profectus sum	to set out, depart	
queror, queri, questus sum	to complain	querulous
sequor, sequi, secutus sum	to follow	persecution
ulciscor, ulcisci, ultus sum	to take revenge	
utor, uti, usus sum (+ Abl.)	to use	*
vescor, vesci, --	to feed on	

Fourth Conjugation Deponents

assentior, assentiri, assensus sum	to agree, assent	*
experior, experiri, expertus sum	to experience	*
largior, largiri, largitus sum	to give, donate	largesse
mentior, mentiri, mentitus sum	to tell lies	
molior, moliri, molitus sum	to move away, to toil	molecule
ordior, ordiri, orsus sum	to begin	order
orior, oriri, ortus sum	to rise, come about, from	orient
potior, potiri, potitus sum (+ Abl.)	to get possession of	potent

EXERCISE K: Translate:

1. patientur   _____
2. conabaris   _____
3. morata est   _____
4. mentiti erant   _____
5. loquere   _____
6. proficiscar   _____
7. polliceri   _____
8. videntur   _____
9. arbitrabuntur _____
10. conatus eram   _____
11. hortabar   _____
12. secuti erimus   _____

13. he has spoken_____
14. she will encourage   _____
15. will you try? _____
16. you have lamented   _____
17. I will promise _____
18. I had permitted   _____
19. they have departed _____
20. we used to think   _____
21. he seems   _____
22. The moon has risen.   _____
23. A boy was born._____
24. They reached land.   _____

SEMIDEPONENTS

These verbs are only partially deponents. They have active forms with the present stem and passive forms in the perfect, except for **reverti**, which is reversed.

audeo, audere, ausus sum	to dare	**audacious**
confido, confidere, confisus sum	to confide	*
fio, fieri, factus sum	to become, to be done	**fiat**
gaudeo, gaudere, gavisus sum	to be happy	**gaudy**
soleo, solere, solitus sum	to be used to	**obsolete**
revertor, reverti (Infinitive)		
reverti (Perfect)	to return	**revert**

The Present, Imperfect, and Future of fieri, to become.

		Present	Imperfect	Future
	1.	fio	fiebam	fiam
Sg	2.	fis	fiebas	fies
	3.	fit	fiebat	fiet
	1.	fimus	fiebamus	fiemus
Pl	2.	fitis	fiebatis	fietis
	3.	fiunt	fiebant	fient

These forms of **fieri** are used as the **Passive** of **facere**
The perfect passive is **factus sum** either way.

EXERCISE L: Translate the sentences:

1. Illa femina numquam questa est, quamquam misera

3. Quo ad usque abuteris patientia nostra?

4. Magister puerum hortabatur, sed puer amicum imitari non voluit.

5. Germani antiqui in silvis ursos urosque venabantur (Caesar called them "Aurochs", wild ox).

6. Quid in casa obliti estis? Libros nostros obliti sumus.

7. Hannibal cum triginta quinque milibus virorum et multis elephantis Alpes transgredi ausus est.

8. Servus mentitus erat, quod dominum suum verebatur.

9. Cras proficiscemur; hodie gaudemus et laetamur.

10. Avus vespero dormire solet, sed hodie multum loquitur.

11. Nauta servatus in patriam revertit.

12. Malo multum esse quam multum videri.

Wall of the Roman Imperial Thermae in Trier

LECTIO I: Malum Nuntium Affert - Bad News (Petrus Alfonsi)

Dominus quidam laetus de foro venit, quia multam pecuniam acceperat.
Et obviam iit servus Maimundus domino suo.
Ubi dominus eum vidit, solitos rumores audire noluit et dixit:
       "Cave! Ne fer mihi rumores malos!"
5   Servus: "Non dicam rumores malos - sed canis nostra parva Bispella
        mortua est."
Cui dominus: "Quomodo mortua est?"
Servus ait: "Asinus noster territus est et rupit funem suum et, ubi
        fugit, sub pedibus suis canem suffocavit."
10 Dominus: "Quid actum est de asino?"
    Servus: "In puteum cecidit et mortuus est."
    Dominus: "Quomodo territus est asinus?"
    Servus: "Filius tuus de solario cecidit - et mortuus est, et inde
        territus est asinus."
15 Dominus: "Quid agit mater eius?"
    Servus: "Prae nimio dolore mortua est."
    Dominus: "Quis custodit villam?"
    Servus: "Nemo, quod in cinerem versa est, et quidquid in ea erat."
    Dominus: "Quomodo combusta est?"
20 Servus: "Eadem nocte, qua domina mortua est, ancilla, quae vigilabat
        pro domina, oblita est candelam in cubiculo, et ita combusta
        est villa tota."
    Dominus: "Ancilla ubi est?"
    Servus: "Ipsa volebat ignem exstinguere, et cecidit trabs in caput eius
25   et mortua est."
    Dominus: "Tu quomodo abisti, quamquam servus tam piger es?"
    Servus: "Ubi vidi ancillam mortuam, effugi."

---

(2) obviam ire = obire; (3) solitus,a,um - customary; rumor,oris - gossip; (5) canis,is - dog; (8) funis,is (m.) - rope, cord; (9) pes,pedis - foot; (11) puteus,i - well, pit; (13) solarium,i - balcony; (16) nimius,a,um - too great; dolor,doloris (m.) - sorrrow; (18) cinis,cineris (m.) - ashes; (19) comburere (comburo, combussi, combustum) - to burn down, incinerate; (20) nox,noctis (f.) - night; vigilare - to watch; (21) candela,ae - candle; (24) ignis,is - fire; exstinguere - to extinguish; trabs, trabis - beam; caput,capitis (n.) - head.

Practice from the reading: perfect active and passive, deponents. Fill in the blanks:

1. Dominus de foro _____.
                           (came)

2. Servus ei obviam _____.
                       (went)

3. Dominus solitos rumores audire _____.
                                       (did not want)

4. Servus _____ : "Canis nostra _____.
             (said)   (died)

5. Asinus _____ et _____ suum funem.
            (got scared)   (broke)

6. Quid _____ de asino?
           (was done, happened)

7. _____ in puteum et _____.
       (he fell)   (died)

8. Filius tuus de solario _____ et _____.
                    (fell)   (died)

9. Villa _____ et in cinerem _____.
          (was burned)   (was turned)

10. Ancilla candelam in cubiculo _____.
                           (forgot)

11. Quomodo _____?
          (you got away)

12. Ubi _____ ancillam _____, _____.
      (I saw)   (dead)   (I fled)

Lectio II: A "Successful" Doctor's Visit (Martial)

Languebam, sed tu comitatus protinus ad me
Venisti centum, Symmache, discipulis.
Centum me tetigere manus aquilone gelatae.
Non habui febrem, Symmache, nunc habeo.

I was weak [languished], but you, Symmachus, came to me with one hundred disciples. One hundred hands touched me, ice-cold from the North wind. I had no fever; now I have one.

A Superior Detergent (Martial)

Tibur in Herculeum migravit nigra Lycoris,
Omnia dum fieri candida credit ibi.

To Tibur in Herculeum the black Lycoris migrated, since she believes that there everything turns white.

Lectio III: De Romulo et Remo (Livius)

Ante multos annos Numitor in Italia rexit, sed frater eius Amulius eum ex patria pepulit, filios eius cecidit et filiam, nomine Rheae Silviae, in Virginem Vestalem vertit. Hoc modo illa neque nubere neque liberos parere potuit. Dei autem hanc terram novam Italiam valere et mundum regere voluerunt. Ergo
(5) Mars, deus belli, Rheam Silviam amavit et illa geminos filios peperit. Amulius valde iratus erat et pueros in aquam iaci imperavit. Gemini in cistam positi sunt, sed haec cista in aqua fluitavit et ita pueri servati sunt. Lupa eos repperit et custodivit et coluit velut suos filios. Forte pastor eos apud lupam invenit et in suam casam tulit. Pastor et femina pueros secum servaverunt;
(10) geminos Romulum et Remum appellaverunt et eos erudiverunt.

Romulus et Remus, ubi viri facti sunt, oppidum magnum munire voluerunt in loco, in quo lupa eos coluerat. In hoc loco, prope Tiberim fluvium, septem colles steterunt. Ubi finiverunt oppidum, Romulus et Remus de imperio incerti erant et dixerunt: "Uter vir novum oppidum regere debet?" Deos
(15) rogare constituerunt.

Remus, qui stabat in Aventino cum amicis et sociis suis, six vultures vidit, sed Romulus, qui stabat in Palatino cum amicis et sociis, duodecim vultures vidit. Romulus et Remus autem non gaudebant, quod signum legere non potuerunt. Remus dixit vultures suos venisse priores, Romulus contra dixit
(20) numerum suorum duplicem esse. Utrumque virum socii sui salutaverunt. Tandem ad caedem verterunt et in pugna Remus caesus est.

Altera fabula narratur hoc modo: Romulus circum oppidum murum fecerat, et Remus lusit risitque et trans murum novum saluit. Tum Romulus iratus fuit et Remum cecidit. Postea dixit: "Quis vestrum item trans murum salire
(25) cupit? Ille eandem fortunam comperiet et morietur!" Ita Romulus oppidum solus rexit et oppidum de Romulo nomen suum cepit: ROMA.

---

(1) Numitor - (king of Alba Longa, a town built before Rome was); (3) Virgo Vestalis - (Vestal Virgins had to guard the holy fire and were not allowed to marry); nubere - to marry; (5) geminus,a,um - twin; (6) iaci - (don't confuse this form with the 3rd Principal Part **ieci ! iaci** is present passive infinitive - to be thrown; cista,ae - box; (7) fluitare - to float; lupa - female wolf; (8) pastor - shepherd; (9) servare - here: to keep; (10) appellare - to call; (12) Tiber - (the river in Rome); fluvius,i - river; (13) colles - hills; (14) uter,utra,utrum - which (of two); (16) Aventinus, Palatinus - (two of the seven hills if Rome); vultures - vultures (several types of birds were used for predicting the future); (19) priores - earlier, prior; (20) numerus,i - number; duplicem - double (refers to numerum); uterque, utraque, utrumque - both, each of two; (21) caedes,is - murder; (22) murus,i - wall; (24) item - likewise; (26) nomen - name.

A. Fill in the blanks:

1. In the **active** the subject acts on an _____.

2. In the **passive** the _____ is acted on by an agent.

3. Many actions can be expressed in the active or in the passive. Y/N _____

4. All English passive forms are compound. Y/N ____

5. Another word for compound (two or more words) is _____.

6. English passive forms must have two components: a form of the verb _____

     and a past _____.

7. The passive **infinitive** ends in the letter _____.

8. The passive infinitive is one syllable shorter than the active infinitive **only** in the _____ conjugation.

9. **PPP** means _____ _____ _____.

10. The **PPP** is the _____ principal part of a verb.

11. The three uses of the **participles** are: as _____; to form the _____;

     in an _____ _____ construction.

12. Participles are considered **conjugated** verb forms. Y/N _____

13. The participles of the _____ _____ conjugation are regular.

14. All verbs have **PPP**s. Y/N _____

15. **Deponents** have _____ forms with _____ meaning.

16. Deponents can**not** express passive meaning. Y/N _____

17. Deponents can occur in the (1st, 2nd, 3rd, 4th, all) conjugation(s). _____

18. Verbs like **audere** and **gaudere** are called _____.

B. Review the words:

fieri - audere - coeptum - solere - loqui - sequi - proficisci - reri - potiri - gaudere - polliceri - metiri - nancisci

C. Do not confuse:

quaerere - queri; malo - malus; facio - fio; audere - audire; morari - mori - mirari;

moratus - mortuus; nasci - nancisci; natus - nactus; venari - venerari - vereri;

casum - caesum - cessum ; miserari - misereri.

The Arena in Verona

Public Buildings and Institutions

The Forum

Every city had a forum, a central place for markets and large meetings, modelled on the Greek agora. On this square or oblong site there were temples, triumphal arches, and monuments. Around the square were arcades with shops, more temples, and basilicas, which were large business, court, and government buildings. All day long people met on the square, or indoors during inclement weather, to conduct business, discuss politics, give campaign speeches, or vote on laws.

Rome's first forum was the Forum Romanum; it was built on the former swamp valley between three hills, which the Etruscans had drained with the Cloaca Maxima. Since Rome's population grew ever larger, additional space was soon needed for business and government. First the original Forum Romanum was enlarged and added to by Caesar; later it was called the Forum Iulium. His son, the Emperor Augustus built another forum to the east, which was enlarged by Vespasian. Emperor Domitian constructed yet another forum, called the Transitorium, since it connected the fora of Caesar and Augustus.

Soon after that Emperor Trajan had another forum built, the largest and grandest of them. It was 300 meters long and 185 meters wide and was flanked by porticoes and a triple arch that led to the forum of Augustus. On one side there was a temple honoring Mars. It was built entirely of Carrara marble, and Caesar's sword was kept in it. Next to it there was a huge basilica, much larger than those built before, with a nave and four aisles divided by columns. Basilicas were places for people to meet, walk around, or conduct business, visit shops, government offices, banks, or money-lenders, similar to today's shopping-malls.

Foundations of a Basilica on the Forum Romanum

Then there were two libraries, one Greek, one Latin, where the main works in either language were collected. Between the libraries the Column of Trajan was erected, on which Trajan's conquest of Dacia (Romania) was commemorated in reliefs arranged in an upward spiral. There are 155 scenes with some 2500 figures in them; the length of the spiral is more than 200 meters. It can still be seen today in its original place.

Trajan's Column still stands on the site of the former Forum.

The Capitol (Campidoglio)

In modern American usage the Capitol is the seat of the Congress in Washington, or, respectively, the place where state legislatures meet. In Rome the Capitolium was a hill with two summits; one held a fortress and was called Arx; it enabled the Romans to control traffic both by land and by the Tiber River. On the Arx was a temple for Iuno Moneta. On the other summit, the Capitolium, stood the most important temple: that of Jupiter Optimus Maximus.

According to the historian Livy, this temple was inaugurated in 509 BC, the first year of the Roman Republic. The temple was adorned by a sculpture of Jupiter in a quadriga, made of terracotta by the Etruscan artist Vulca from Veii. Another statue of Jupiter made by Vulca stood inside; he carried a thunderbolt in his right hand, had a face painted in red, and was dressed in precious clothes. The temple burnt down numerous times, but was always rebuilt more splendidly. In the final version of AD82 the temple was covered with marble, the roof with gilded bronze tiles, and the doors with gold sheets; the statue of Jupiter was made of gold and ivory. These precious materials were carried off by the Goths when they sacked Rome.

There were many other structures on the Capitolium, such as the Tabularium, the State Archives, as well as smaller temples and statues. There was such a profusion of monuments, triumphal arches, statues, and busts at the time of Augustus that he had some of them moved to the Campus Martius. For the Romans the Capitolium symbolized the religious and political power of Rome. Other cities, like Ostia, Rome's harbour, soon had their own Capitolium area or building.

The Capitoline Square, today's Piazza del Campidoglio, was redesigned in 1536 by Michelangelo

The Public Baths

Romans had baths in their private houses and villas from earliest times on. There was even a public swimming pool in Rome, where people learned to swim. Being able to swim was considered the mark of a civilized person; of ignorant people it was said that "they do not know how to read or to swim." Some eight hundred years later Charlemagne still considered swimming the best exercise and had a large swimming pool built in his palace in Aachen.

Large public baths were constructed by several Roman emperors; among them the Baths of Trajan were considered the model for later ones, because of their design with a central complex, an enclosure with a peristyle and gardens, meeting places, and exercise rooms. The largest public baths were the Baths of Diocletian (298-306 A.D.), which covered more than 1 Million square feet and could accomodate over 2000 bathers. There are remnants, ruins, and foundations of Roman baths left all over the world, as for instance the Baths of Caracalla in Rome, the baths in the city of Bath, England, and the city of Trier, Germany, or those on the Greek island of Kos.

The Imperial Baths in Trier

Roman baths were heated with hypocaustum heating; they received their water by aqueduct and had elaborate drainage and ventilation systems. They consisted of several rooms: an unheated room for undressing (**Apodyterium**), a cold water pool (**Frigidarium**), a moderately heated transition room (**Tepidarium**), a rather warm room with pools and tubs for bathing or sweating (**Caldarium**), and sometimes a sauna-like hot room (**Laconicum, Sudatorium**). In addition there were often showers, rooms for oiling the body before exercise, conversation rooms, libraries, gymnasiums, porticoes, gardens, and stadiums. People met in baths to wash, talk, exercise, and conduct business. In early times there were separate facilities for men and women, but already at the time of Augustus communal facilities were the rule.

The water for the Roman bath in the city of Bath, England, has been supplied by nearby thermal springs since Roman times. It contains sulphur and other minerals and although swimming in it is healthful, it is very tiring and therefore limited to about twenty minutes.

Model of the interior of a bath.

The Porta Nigra in Trier

The entrance to the Forum Romanum

Chapter 10: Answers and Translations

Exercise A:

1. yes 2. no (no Past Participle) 3. no (no PP) 4. yes 5. yes 6. no (no PP) 7. no (no form of 'to be') 8. yes 9. no (no PP) 10. yes

Exercise B:

1. The small town will not be destroyed.
2. We used to be taught by a good teacher.
3. Dinner is being prepared by the maid.
4. The wild animals were feared by the sailors.
5. Tomorrow you will be invited by friends.
6. You were greeted by us.
7. Grain is given to the horses.
8. Many stories were told by our grandfather.
9. Grandfather told many stories. (not Passive!)
10. On account of the war towns will be besieged.
11. Will you move the cows out of the garden? (not Passive!)
12. I was asked by the teacher.
13. We are expected by grandfather.
14. The slaves are admonished by their master.
15. Britain was held by the Romans.

Exercise C:

1. rogatum (interrogate) 2. monstratum (demonstrate) 3. salutatum (salute) 4. spectatum (spectator) 5. cantatum (cantata) 6. invitatum (invitation) 7. exspectatum (expectation)
8. laudatum (laudatory) 9. narratum (narrative) 10. donatum (donation) 11. vocatum (vocation) 12. occupatum (occupation) 13. oratum (orator) 14. visitatum (visitation) 15. datum (date) (Some of these English words are actually derived from Latin nouns which in turn developed from these verbs.)

Exercise D:

1. vir doctus 2. puellae esxpectatae 3. fabulas narratas 4. cibi positi in mensam
5. oppida munita 6. empta 7. carrus ab equis tractus 8. liberi auditi, sed non visi
9. castra mota 10. gesta

Exercise E:

1. The food had not been touched.
2. Many things were done.
3. The town was being fortified.
4. The obstinate donkey was dragged to the stable.
5. Where will the gifts be put which have been bought?
6. The things, which the master ordered, will have been done, when he returns.
7. Nothing was said by the boys when they were asked.
8. What we watched (the watched things) did not please us, although
    a few people were laughing.

9. We visited the house occupied by the sailors, but we were not greeted.
10. The captured horses ran out of the stable and were not seen again.
11. Children ought to be seen, but not heard.
12. The chairs have been moved. Where will they be found?
13. The deeds of the Romans are famous.
14. The books of Roman poets will always be praised.
15. My grandfather was visited by me and my donkey.

Exercise F:
1. made 2. live 3. say 4. defeat 5. decided, set up 6. closed 7. sent 8. ask 9. believe
10. sleep 11. pushed, driven 12. touch 13. broken 14. set, given 15. left behind

Exercise H:
1. Haec fabula iam antea narrata est. 2. Equi nondum a liberis tacti erant. 3. Puer bene doctus est. (docebatur) 4. Illi viri improbi ex Italia expellebuntur. 5. Pueri stulti fenestras villae eius fregerunt. 6. Nihil ab agricolis de pecunia actum est. 7. Eorum patria a feminis regebatur.
8. Scriptum est: "Ascendit in coelum." 9. Illa vocata erat, sed ille responderat. 10. Libri lecti erunt: Liberi eos legent.

Exercise I:
iacis, iaces, iacebas, iecisti, ieceras, ieceris
videntur, videbuntur, videbantur, visae sunt, visae erant, visae erunt
rogat, rogabit, rogabat, rogavit, rogaverat, rogaverit
rogatur, rogabitur, rogabatur, rogatus est, rogatus erat, rogatus erit

Exercise J:

1. monuimus	(P)	we have been warned
2. vocaris	(PR)	you are called
3. spectabor	(F)	I will be looked at
4. docueram	(PQ)	I had been taught
5. occupaverint	(FP)	they will have been besieged
6. cepistis	(P)	you have been taken
7. invitabamini	(I)	you were invited
8. laudatus erat	(PQ)	he had been praised
9. docti erimus	(FP)	we will have been taught
10. amabit	(F)	she will be loved
11. cantaverunt	(P)	they were sung
12. visitatae eratis	(PQ)	you had been visited
13. salutamus	(PR)	we are greeted
14. oppugnabantur	(I)	they used to be attacked
15. exspectaberis	(F)	you will be expected
16. pressa sunt	(P)	they have been pressed
17. vidit	(P)	he has been seen
18. audiebatis	(I)	you were heard
19. mittemur	(F)	we will be sent
20. ponit	(PR)	it is put
21. vertebamini	(I)	you were being turned

22. custodietur	(F)	it will be guarded
23. quaeres	(F)	you will be asked
24. fractum erat	(PQ)	it had been broken
25. finiti erint	(FP)	they will have been finished

Exercise K:

1. they will suffer 2. you used to try 3. she has delayed 4. they had lied 5. speak! 6. I will set out
7. to promise 8. they seem 9. they will think 10. I had tried 11. I used to encourage
12. we will have followed 13. locutus est 14. hortabitur 15. conaberisne? 16. miseratus es
17. pollicebor 18. passa eram 19. profecti sunt 20. arbitrabamur 21. videtur
22. Luna orta est. 23. Puer natus est. 24. Terram nacti sunt.

Exercise L:

1. This woman has never complained, altough she has been miserable.
2. The Romans took possession of many lands.
3. Up to which point will you abuse our patience?
4. The teacher encouraged the boy, but the boy did not want to imitate his friend.
5. The ancient Germans hunted bears and mammoths in the woods. (Actually
   urus is an extinct species called Auerochs. Mammoths were long extinct by then.)
6. What have you forgotten in the house? We have forgotten our books.
7. Hannibal dared to cross the Alps with 35000 men and many elephants.
8. The slave had lied, because he feared his master.
9. Tomorrow we will depart; today we are happy and rejoice.
10. My grandfather usually sleeps in the evening, but today he is talking a lot.
11. The sailor who was saved returned to his homeland.
12. I had rather be much than seem much.

Reading 1 : Bad News

A certain master came back happy from the market, because he had received much money.
And there the slave Maimundus encountered his master.
When the master saw him, he wanted to avoid the customary gossip and said:
      "Watch out! Don't bring me any bad gossip!"
Slave: "I shall not tell bad gossip, but our little dog Bispella has died."
To him the master (said): "How did she die?"
The slave said: "Our donkey was frightened and broke his rope, and when
      he fled he suffocated the dog under his feet."
Master: "What happened to the donkey?"
Slave: "He fell into the well and died."
Master: "How did the donkey get scared?"
Slave: "Your son fell from the balcony and died, and thus the donkey got scared."
Master: "What is his mother doing?"
Slave: "She has died from too much grief."
Master: "Who is guarding the house?"
Slave: "Nobody, because it was turned into ashes, and whatever was in it."
Master: "How was it burned down?"

Slave: "The same night, in which the mistress died, the maid, who was keeping watch for the mistress, forgot the candle in the bedroom, and this way the whole house got burned."

Master: "And the maid, where is she?"

Slave: "She herself wanted to extinguish the fire, and a beam fell on her head, and she died."

Master: "How did you get away, although you are such a lazy slave?"

Slave: "When I saw the dead maid, I ran off."

Practice: Perfect Active and Passive

1. Venit 2. iit 3. noluit 4. ait or dixit; mortua est 5. territus est; rupit 6. actum est 7. cecidit; mortuus est 8. cecidit, mortuus est 9. combusta est; versa est 10. oblita est 11. abisti 12. vidi; mortuam; effugi

Reading 3 : Romulus and Remus

Many years ago Numitor ruled in Italy, but his brother Amulius drove him from his home, killed his sons, and turned his daughter, by the name of Rhea Silvia, into a Vestal Virgin. That way she could neither marry nor bear children. The gods, however, wanted this new country Italy to be strong and for it to rule the world. Therefore Mars, the war-god, made love to Rhea Silvia, and she bore twin sons. Amulius was very angry and ordered the boys to be thrown into the water. The boys were put into a box, but this box floated in the water, and so the boys were saved. A she-wolf found them and guarded them and cared for them like for her own sons. By chance a shepherd found them with the wolf and carried them to his hut. The shepherd and his wife kept the boys with them; they called the twins Romulus and Remus and brought them up.

When Romulus and Remus became men they wanted to build a large town in the place where the she-wolf had taken care of them. In this place, near the river Tiber, there stood seven hills. When Romulus and Remus had finished their town they were uncertain about its government and said: 'Which man shall reign over the new city?' They decided to ask the gods. Remus, who was standing on the Aventine (hill) with his friends and comrades, saw six vultures, but Romulus, who was standing on the Palatine with his friends and comrades, saw twelve vultures. But Romulus and Remus were not happy, because they could not read the sign. Remus said that his vultures had come earlier, Romulus contradicted that the number of his (vultures) was twice as large. To each man his allies paid homage. Finally they turned to murder, and during the fight Remus was slain.

Another story is told this way: Romulus had made a wall around the city, and Remus played and laughed and jumped over the new wall. Then Romulus was furious and killed Remus. Afterwards he said: 'Which of you also wishes to jump over the wall? He will meet the same fate and will die.' 'Thus Romulus reigned the town alone, and the town took its name from him: ROMA

Summary: 1. object 2. subject 3. yes 4. yes 5. periphrastic 6. to be; participle 7. -i 8. third 9. past participle passive 10. fourth 11. Adjectives; Passive; Ablative Absolute 12. no 13. 1st 14. no 15. Passive; Active 16. yes 17. all 18. Semideponentsi

11

NOUNS: THE THIRD DECLENSION

GERMANIC LANGUAGES III

The effect of Grimm's Law can be seen when comparing Latin words and their cognates in English and German. Keep in mind that these phonetic changes took place before there were the Latin and the Germanic languages. You might think of these groups as children of the same parents (PIE). The fact that the words are cognates is due to their being siblings, not to the fact that one brother (Germanic languages, e.g. English) would be derived from his sister (Latin, Romance languages). There are, however, many words in English which were derived from Latin, either directly, or by way of French, but this took place much later (as much as 3000 years later). By way of Grimm's Law you can easily distinguish between these 2 groups, since the later borrowing or derivation would not show the effects of the Germanic sound shift.

Latin		Germanic Cognate	Later borrowing from Latin or French
/p/	< >	/f/	
pater		father	paternal
		Vater (G; v = f) fader (Sw)	
pes		foot	pedal
/t/	< >	/th/	
tres		three	trilateral, tripartite
tu		thou, thee (/th/ was lost in other	
		modern Germanic languages)	
/k/	< >	/h/	
cor		heart	coronary, cordial
		Herz (G); hjerte (D, N)	
cornu		horn	cornea
/b/	< >	/p/	
labium		lip	labial
		Lippe (G), leppe (N)	
/d/	< >	/t/	
decem		ten	decimal
		tien (D)	
/g/	< >	/k/	
genu		knee	genuflect
		kne (N)	
granum		corn	granulate
/bh/ (Latin = f)	< >	/b/	
frater		brother	
		Bruder (G)	fraternal
ferre		bear	transfer
/dh/ (Latin = f)	< >	/d/	
facere		do, deed	fact
/gh/ (Latin = h)	< >	/g/	
hostis		guest, Gast (G)	host

Chapter 11   Nouns: The Third Declension

The third declension is the largest, containing a great number of nouns, which can be grouped according to their different **nominative** endings. Nouns of the third declension can be masculine, feminine, or neuter; in many instances their **gender** can be inferred from their **nominative ending**.

Here are some examples of third declension nouns, grouped by gender. The endings, which are characteristic for the gender, are in bold print. (Of course there are a number of exceptions.) Since in this declension the nominative is often shortened, and looks quite different from the rest of the cases, the **genitive** must also be given; it must be learned together with the nominative. Only from the **genitive** form can the **stem** of the noun be determined; it is found by removing the genitive ending **-is**.

masculine		feminine		neuter	
Nom.	**Gen.**	**Nom.**	**Gen.**	**Nom.**	**Gen.**
lab**or**,	laboris	libert**as**,	libertatis	flum**en**,	fluminis
lim**es**,	limitis	valetud**o**,	valetudinis	temp**us**,	temporis
sangu**is**,	sanguinis	rati**o**,	rationis	anim**al**,	animalis
hon**os**,	honoris	sal**us**,	salutis	rob**ur**,	roburis
vent**er**,	ventris	ur**bs**,	urbis	mar**e**,	maris
coll**is**,	collis	aur**is**,	auris (sorry!)	(and others)	

Examples of **noun stems:**

	genitive	stem	meaning (one of many)
labor,laboris	**labor is**	**labor-**	**work**
tempus,temporis	**tempor is**	**tempor-**	**time**
salus,salutis	**salut is**	**salut-**	**health**
auris,auris	**aur is**	**aur-**	**ear**
valetudo,valetudinis	**valetudin is**	**valetudin-**	**strength**
caput,capitis	**capit is**	**capit-**	**head**
venter,ventris	**ventr is**	**ventr-**	**stomach**
limes,limitis	**limit is**	**limit-**	**border**
urbs,urbis	**urb is**	**urb-**	**city**
vox,vocis	**voc is**	**voc-**	**voice**

Again: the **nominative** gives you the **gender** (with exceptions).

The **genitive** gives you the **stem** (without exceptions).

To these **stems** the following **endings** are added:

Masculine and Feminine Nouns   **Neuter Nouns**

Singular

N	---	---
G	-is	-is
D	-i	-i
A	-em	(= nominative)
Ab	-e	-e

Plural

N	-es	-a
G	-um (-ium)	-um (-ium)
D	-ibus	-ibus
A	-es	-a
Ab	-ibus	-ibus

Even though these endings look quite different from those of the first and second declensions, there are similarities.

1. Some cases end in characteristic consonants in every declension:
   -m for **accusative Singular** (puella**m**, amicu**m**, patre**m**)
   -s for **accusative Plural** (puella**s**, amico**s**, patre**s**)
   -i..s for dative and ablative Plural (puell**is**, amic**is**, patr**ibus**)

2. In the third declension there is syncretism in dative and ablative Plural (**-ibus**) and nominative and accusative Plural (**-es**). Neuter nouns have the customary syncretism of nominative and accusative Singular and Plural. (The ending for the Plural is **-a**)

The third declension is a **consonant declension**, just as the third conjugation is a consonant conjugation, and like the conjugation, the declension has some **i-stems** in it. They will be listed and declined separately, since there are few. In addition there are some **mixed stems**; they differ from the consonant stems only in the genitive Plural, where they take the ending **-ium**.

Since several endings in the first, second, and third declension are identical, but not necessarily the same case, (e.g. **-um, -i, -a, -is**) you must learn to which declension a noun belongs, in order to be able to tell in which case it is. This is most easily accomplished by learning the genitive of the noun together with the nominative. In the third declension, and **only in the third**, the **genitive always ends in -is.** Genitive Singular endings are not alike among any of the five declensions.

1. Consonant Stems
Paradigms: **pater,patris** (m.) *father*; **lex,legis** (f.) *law*; **tempus,temporis** (n.) *time*

		Masculine	Feminine	Neuter
	N	pater	lex	tempus
	G	patris	legis	temporis
Sg	D	patri	legi	tempori
	A	patrem	legem	tempus
	Ab	patre	lege	tempore
	N	patres	leges	tempora
	G	patrum	legum	temporum
Pl	D	patribus	legibus	temporibus
	A	patres	leges	tempora
	Ab	patribus	legibus	temporibus

2. Mixed Stems
Mixed stems use the ending **-ium** in the genitive Plural. They are:
  a. Equisyllabic nouns (= same number of syllables in the nominative and genitive Singular) ending in **-is,-is** or **-es,-is**, for instance:
    vallis,vallis *valley*; **classis,classis** *fleet;* **nubes,nubis** *cloud*
    Their genitive Plurals are vall**ium**, class**ium**, nub**ium**.
    Not belonging to this group are nouns like **miles,militis** *soldier*, because they are not equisyllabic.

  b. Nouns whose **stem** (genitive!) ends in **two consonants**, for instance:
    urbs,**urb**is *city,*   gen. Pl. urb**ium**
    pars,**part**is *part,*   part**ium**
    but not:
    lex,**leg**is *law*   leg**um**   (stem ends in 1 consonant)
    rex,**reg**is *king*   reg**um**

c. i - Stems

There are a few commonly used (and some less commonly used) i-stems:
animal,animalis (n.) *animal*; **mare,maris** (n.) *sea*; **vis** (f.) *force*; **turris,turris** (f.) *tower*
They are declined like this:

	N	animal	mare	vis	turris
	G	animalis	maris	--	turris
Sg	D	animali	mari	--	turri
	A	animal	mare	vim	turr**im**
	Ab	animal**i**	mar**i**	v**i**	turr**i**
	N	animal**ia**	mar**ia**	vires	turres
	G	animal**ium**	mar**ium**	vir**ium**	turr**ium**
Pl	D	animalibus	maribus	viribus	turribus
	A	animal**ia**	mar**ia**	vires	turres
	Ab	animalibus	maribus	viribus	turribus

Animal mirum fert mulierem

THIRD DECLENSION NOUNS LISTED IN GROUPS BY GENDER

A. Natural Gender

Masculine		
adulescens,adulescentis	young man	adolescent
artifex,artificis	artisan ("art maker")	artificial
auctor,auctoris	author	*
civis,civis	citizen	civic
comes,comitis	comrade	
consul,consulis	consul	*
dux,ducis	leader	duke
eques,equitis	knight	equestrian
frater,fratris	brother	fraternal
homo,hominis	man (as a species)	human
hospes,hospitis	host, guest	hospitality
hostis,hostis	enemy	hostile
imperator,imperatoris	general, emperor	imperial
iudex,iudicis	judge	judicial
iuvenis,iuvenis	young man	juvenile
leo,leonis	lion	leonine
maiores,maiorum (Pl)	ancestors	major
miles,militis	soldier	military
nepos,nepotis	grandson	nepotism
optimates,optimatum (Pl)	Nobles' Party	optimal
orator,oratoris	speaker	oratory
parentes,parentum (Pl)	parents	*
pater,patris	father	patriarch
patres,patrum	senators	
pedes,peditis	foot soldier	pedestrian
pontifex,pontificis	priest("bridge maker")	pontificate
populares,popularum (Pl)	People's Party	popular
rex,regis	king	regal, royal
scriptor,scriptoris	writer	script
senator,senatoris	senator	*
senex,senis	old man	senile

Masculine or Feminine		
augur,auguris	augur, soothsayer	augur
bos,bovis	ox, cow	bovine
canis,canis	dog	canine
custos,custodis	guard	custodian
obses,obsidis	hostage	
sacerdos,sacerdotis	priest/ess	
vates,vatis	prophet/ess	

Feminine		
coniunx,coniugis	wife, spouse	conjugal
mater,matris	mother	maternal
mulier,mulieris	woman	
soror,sororis	sister	sorority
uxor,uxoris	wife	uxorious
virgo,virginis	girl, young woman	virginal

Homo
homines docti - *learned men*
Homo est homini lupus. *Man is like a wolf to his fellow man.*
nemo, *nobody*, was contracted from **ne-homo**, *no man*.

Aetates Hominis : *The steps of existence in human life.*
Hoc modo Amos Comenius septem aetates hominis gradibus
ascendentibus et descendentibus repraesentat:

1 infans   2 puer   3 adulescens   4 iuvenis   5 vir   6 senex   7 silicernium
8 pupa   9 puella   10 virgo   11 mulier   12 vetula   13 anus decrepita

Comes comes from **cum** and **ire**; so he is actually a person who goes with you, a comrade, companion.

EXERCISE A: Since Latin is a verb-oriented language, many nouns are derived from verbs. Can you figure out from which verbs the following nouns have evolved?

1. orator
2. parentes
3. imperator
4. rex
5. dux
6. comes

7. scriptor
8. artifex, pontifex
9. custos
10. obses [remove the prefix!]
11. coniunx

Roman Official Life Around the Time of Cicero

consul, senator, patres, rex, praetor, quaestor, civis, populares, optimates, quirites

The two **consuls** were the highest officials of the Roman state. To be elected consul one had to be a free-born citizen, at least forty-three years of age, and had to have been **quaestor** and **praetor** already. Consuls were elected for one-year terms.

The eight **praetors**, also elected annually, were judicial officers, or judges. The praetor appointed 360 men for one year, from which the jury of 70 men for the trial was picked.

Twenty **quaestors** were financial officers, elected for a year. They managed the state treasuries, kept census lists and copies of official building contracts, took in taxes, and paid out money to state officers.

Optimates, the patricians, were the original citizens of Rome. Later a new class arose from those who had migrated to the city from other territories, those who could not make a life as farmers any longer, people conquered in war, and others. They were called **plebeians**, their party was the Populares. They had rebelled against the arrogant patricians and demanded more rights, a struggle that had continued for two hundred years.

A **civis** or Roman citizen, was any free-born Roman (later any Italian) over sixteen years of age. Cives could vote, but only in Rome. They were called **Populus Romanus**, or **Quirites**. Women, children, and foreigners could not be citizens.

The **senate** was an advisory body of three hundred to six hundred elders (**senes**), which had no power to make or enforce laws. The senators were usually addressed as **patres conscripti**. The elective and legislative functions were executed by the popular assemblies (**Comitiae**).

From the beginning of Rome's history to the end of the sixth century BC Rome was a monarchy, ruled by a king, **rex**. After the fall of the monarchy it became a republic.

EXERCISE B: Decline **mater, miles, consul**

B. Grammatical Gender

To facilitate your learning these nouns, they are grouped by endings. An asterisk with the derivations means that is identical with the English translation.

Masculine

1. -or,-oris -os,-oris

amor,amoris	love	amorous
clamor,clamoris	noise, clamor	*
dolor,doloris	pain, sorrow	doleful
error,erroris	error	*
flos,floris	flower	floral
honos (or honor),honoris	honor	*
labor,laboris	work	*
mores,morum (Pl)	character	
mos,moris	custom	moral
rumor,rumoris	rumor, reputation	*
terror,terroris	terror	*
timor,timoris	fear	timid

Exception: **arbor,arboris,** *tree,* is feminine, as are the names of all trees.

2. -es,-is; -is,-eris; etc. (not equisyllabic)

cinis,cineris	ashes	incinerate
limes,limitis	border, path	limit
occidens,occidentis	west	occidental
oriens,orientis	east	oriental
pes,pedis	foot	pedal
sal,salis	salt	saline
sanguis,sanguinis	blood	sanguine
sol,solis	sun	solar
vertex,verticis	top, vertex	*

3. -er,-is

aer,aeris	air	aerial
carcer,carceris	prison	incarcerate
imber,imbris	rain	
venter,ventris	belly, stomach	ventriloquist

Exceptions: **ver,veris (n.),** *Spring (the season);* **iter,itineris (n.),** *journey*

4. -is,-is; -es,is (equisyllabic)

collis,collis	**hill**	
crines,crinium (Pl)	**hair**	**crinoline**
finis,finis	**border, end**	**final**
fines,finium (Pl)	**territory**	
ignis,ignis	**fire**	**ignite**
mensis,mensis	**month**	**menstrual**
orbis,orbis	**circle, earth**	**orbit**
panis,panis	**bread**	**companion**
piscis,piscis	**fish**	**piscivorous**

Limes

The Limes was a Roman border and defense wall that stretched from the Rhine River to the Danube, about 550 kilometers in all. In the beginning it was only a braided fence, which was later replaced by wooden palisades. Finally a stone wall was added, up to nine feet high, fortified with watchtowers like the one shown here. The towers were spaced several thousand feet apart; the guards were able to communicate by fire or smoke signals. Troops were placed in garrisons like the *Saalburg* near Frankfurt. The Limes was designed to keep German tribes out of the Roman provinces.

Miles

Participants in a parade in France are dressed up as Roman soldiers.

Feminine

1. -o,-onis; -o,-inis

draco, -onis m.
dragon

Latin	English	Derivative
admiratio,admirationis	admiration	*
altitudo,altitudinis	height,altitude	*
ambitio,ambitionis	ambition	*
condicio,condicionis	condition	*
consuetudo,consuetudinis	habit	
coniuratio,coniurationis	conspiracy	conjure
dicio,dicionis	power	
factio,factionis	faction, party	*
fortitudo,fortitudinis	bravery	fortitude
legio,legionis	legion	*
libido,libidinis	violent desire, lust	libidinous
magnitudo,magnitudinis	size	*
multitudo,multitudinis	crowd	*
natio,nationis	nation	*
occasio,occasionis	occasion	*
opinio,opinionis	opinion	*
oratio,orationis	speech	*
origo,originis	source	origin
ratio,rationis	reason	rational
regio,regionis	region	*
religio,religionis	religion	*
seditio,seditionis	uprising	sedition
suspicio,suspicionis	suspicion	*
valetudo,valetudinis	health	valid

    Exceptions: ordo,ordinis (m.)   order, rank   *
         and - - >

2. -as,-tis

Vespertilio,onis m.
bat

Latin	English	Derivative
aestas,aestatis	summer	
aetas,aetatis	era, age	
auctoritas,auctoritatis	reputation, authority	*
calamitas,calamitatis	harm, misfortune	calamity
celeritas,celeritatis	speed, celerity	
civitas,civitatis	state	
crudelitas,crudelitatis	cruelty	*
cupiditas,cupiditatis	greed, passion	
difficultas,difficultatis	difficulty	*
dignitas,dignitatis	dignity	*
facultas,facultatis	ability, faculty	*
gravitas,gravitatis	gravity	*
humanitas,humanitatis	humanity	*
liberalitas,liberalitatis	generosity (liberal)	
libertas,libertatis	liberty	*

papilio,-onis m.
butterfly

paupertas,paupertatis	poverty	*
pietas,pietatis	duty, piety	*
potestas,potestatis	power	potestate
tempestas,tempestatis	weather, storm	tempest
veritas,veritatis	truth	veracity
voluntas,voluntatis	will	voluntary
voluptas,voluptatis	joy, pleasure	voluptuous

3. Consonant + s in the Nominative (also -x, which really = -cs or -gs)

ars,artis	art	artisan
arx,arcis	fortress, castle	
cohors,cohortis	cohort	*
fraus,fraudis	fraud	*
frons,frontis	face, forehead	frontal
gens,gentis	tribe	genteel
hiems,hiemis	winter	
laus,laudis (u=v)	praise	laudable
lex,legis	law	legal
lux,lucis	light	lucid
mens,mentis	mind	mental
merx,mercis	wares,goods	mercenary
mors,mortis	death	mortal
nex,necis	murder	internecine
nix,nivis	snow	Nivea
nox,noctis	night	nocturnal
pars,partis	part	impartial
partes,partium (Pl.)	party (political)	*
pax,pacis	peace	pacify
plebs,plebis	people, masses, citizens	plebeian
sors,sortis	fate, lot	assorted
urbs,urbis	city	urban
vox,vocis	voice	vocal

Exceptions:

pons,pontis (m.)	bridge	pontoon
mons,montis (m.)	mountain	*
fons,fontis (m.)	spring,fountain	font
dens,dentis (m.)	tooth	dental
grex,gregis (m.)	herd	gregarious

4. -us,-utis; -us,-udis; -us,-uris

iuventus,iuventutis	youth	
palus,paludis	swamp	paludism
pecus,pecudis	sheep, head of cattle	(cp. pecus,pecoris, pg.267)
salus,salutis	health	salutary
senectus,senectutis	old age	
servitus,servitutis	servitude	*

tellus,telluris	**earth**	**tellurium**
virtus,virtutis	**courage, fortitude, virtue**	**virtuous**

5. -i,-is; -es,-is (equisyllabic)

aedes,aedium (Pl.)	**building**	**edifice**
auris,auris	**ear**	**aural**
avis,is	**bird**	**avian**
caedes,is	**murder**	**homicide**
clades,is	**defeat**	
classis,is	**fleet**	
fames,famis	**hunger**	**famine**
fauces,faucium (Pl.)	**throat; gorge; entrance**	**faucet**
feles,is	**cat**	**feline**
navis,is	**ship**	**naval**
opes,opum (Pl.)	**help; wealth**	
preces,precum (Pl.)	**prayer**	**imprecation**
sitis,is (i-stem)	**thirst**	
turris,is (i-stem)	**tower**	**turret**
vallis,is	**valley**	*****
vestis,is	**clothing**	**vestment**
vires,virium (Pl.)	**force, troops**	
vis,vim,vi	**strength**	
vulpes,is	**fox**	

From PECUS comes the word **pecunia**, since cattle were used as means of payment. By way of the Germanic Soundshift (see Chapter 10) we got English **fee** and German **Vieh** (cattle) from the same Indo-European source

.

Venator venatur (watch out! Deponent verb!)

| | EXERCISE C: | Translate the phrases and sentences:

1. rara avis _____   2. Cave canem! _____

3. orbis terrarum _____

4. cuius regio eius religio _____

5. Honores mutant mores. _____

6. alma mater _____   7. Homini necesse est mori. _____

8. Hominis mores naturaque ex corpore, oculis, vultu, fronte cognoscuntur. (vultus - face)

_____

9. Plenus venter non studet libenter. (gladly, readily)

_____

10. Pars militum in Italiam non revertit; manserunt in finibus Graecorum.

_____

11. Leo habebat multos dentes acerbos et magnam vocem, quae nobis fecit terrorem.

_____

12. Est grex bovum in pratis nostris; satisne cibi invenire possunt?

_____

13. Hiems fert nivem. Debemus gerere multas vestes.

_____

14. Magna cum celeritate canes, fame coacti, in villam cucurrerunt.

_____

15. Ranae in palude vivere malunt. _____

16. Mens agitat molem. (molis,is - matter) _____

17. Tempestas orta est; iimus sub pontem et exspectavimus finem tempestatis.

_____

18. Honor est praemium (reward) virtutis. _____

19. Venter est magister artis. _____

20. Consuetudo est quasi altera natura _____

EXERCISE D: **Quid agunt?** (Match up right and left columns and write as sentences.)

1. canes	(a) pugnant	1 (o) 1. Canes edunt ossa.
2. feles	(b) orant	
3. aves	(c) visitant amicos	
4. avi	(d) gerunt bella	
5. parentes	(e) capiunt mures (mus, muris - mouse)	
6. imperatores	(f) narrant fabulas	
7. boves	(g) habent filios filiasque	
8. hospites	(h) multum loquuntur	
9. hostes	(i) faciunt artificia	
10. fratres	(j) custodiunt aurum	
11. scriptores	(k) edunt boves	
12. nepotes	(l) herbas edunt	
13. pisces	(m) amant sorores	
14. pontifices	(n) sedent in equis	
15. artifices	(o) edunt ossa	
16. custodes	(p) cantant in silvis	
17. milites	(q) audiunt avos	
18. leones	(r) scribunt libros	
19. oratores	(s) tacent	
20. equites	(t) Romanos non amant	

Neuter

1. -men,-minis

agmen,agminis	march, marching army	
carmen,carminis	song	Carmen
certamen,certaminis	competition	
crimen,criminis	crime	*
flumen,fluminis	river	flume
fulmen,fulminis	lightning	fulminate
nomen,nominis	name	nominal
numen,numinis	divine will, god	
omen,ominis	omen	*

2. -us,-eris; -us,-oris; -ur,-oris

corpus,corporis	body	corpse
decus,decoris	ornament	decorate
dedecus,dedecoris	shame	
facinus,facinoris	crime	
foedus,foederis	pact, alliance	federation
frigus,frigoris	cold	refrigerate
genus,generis	kind, type	genus
latus,lateris	side	bilateral
litus,litoris	coast	litoral
munus,muneris	present, task	munificent
onus,oneris	burden	onus
opus,operis	work	opus
pectus,pectoris	chest	pectoral
pecus,pecoris	cattle, herd, flock	
robur,roboris	strength	corroborate
scelus,sceleris	crime	
sidus,sideris	constellation (of stars)	sidereal
tempus,temporis	time	temporary
vulnus,vulneris	wound	invulnerable

3. Others

aes,aeris	ore, money	
animal,animalis	animal	*
caput,capitis	head	capital
conclave,conclavis	room	conclave
cor,cordis	heart	cordial
fas (not declined)	right	
nefas "	crime	nefarious
iter,itineris	journey, march	itinerary
ius,iuris	right, law	jurisdiction
lac,lactis	milk	lactose

mare,maris	sea	maritime
mel,mellis	honey	mellifluous
moenia,moenium (Pl.)	city walls	
os,oris	mouth, face	oral
os,ossis	bone	ossified
vas,vasis	container, vase	*

EXERCISE E: In the following sentences translate only the underlined words (in the appropriate case, of course):

1. A crowd of oxen does not scare me, but a crowd of people does.

2. The generals thought they could fulfil their ambitions only by force, not by their authority.

3. Many people do not like hot summers or cold winters.

4. Do you know the names of all your comrades?

5. Some orators have a habit of speech, but not of truth.

6. We wish peace to all men of good will.

7. Some philosophers consider poverty with dignity easier to bear; but it is a burden without pleasure.

8. Spring brings storms with lightning and rain.

EXERCISE F: **Translate:**

1. Tempora mutantur, et nos mutamur in illis

2. mens sana in corpore sano   3. Vinum est lac senum.

4. Caelum, non animum mutant, qui trans mare currunt. (Horace)

5. O tempora, o mores! Cicero dixit, ubi Catilinam ex urbe expellere voluit et orationem in Catilinam habuit.

6. Duas naves sub ponte vidimus, qui magna cum celeritate trans flumen transire voluerunt.

7. Cur equus iuxta fontem stabat? Siti coactus ad aquam descenderat et cum hominibus aquam bibere cupivit.

8. Amasne sororem meam? Referam parentibus amorem tuum, et pater te ex villa expellet.

9. Post mortem militis comites corpus eius ad carrum attulerunt.

10. Carmen poetae clari longum, sed non pulchrum erat.

11. Panem quotidianum (daily) da nobis hodie.

12. Ver redit optatum (longed-for) cum gaudio, flore decoratum purpureo (purple).   (Carmina Burana)

EXERCISE G: Fill in the chart:

	Nom.Sg.	Gen.Sg.	Nom.Pl.	Gender
1. bridge	pons	pontis	pontes	masculine
2. time				
3. ship				
4. song				
5. soldier				
6. journey				
7. bread				
8. general				
9. habit				
10. head				
11. body				
12. animal				
13. sister				
14. city				
15. sea				
16. mountain				
17. citizen				
18. state				

	Nom.Sg.	Gen.Sg.	Nom.Pl.	Gender
19. father				
20. king				
21. height				
22. custom				
23. sun				
24. power				
25. kind, type				
26. right, law				
27. ear				

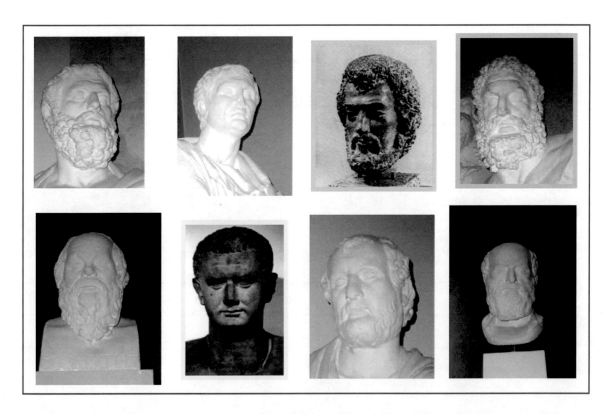

Capita diversa: imperator, pater, rex, miles, frater, cives, consul, eques, custos, iudex, philosophus, comes, scriptor, orator ...multi senes, pauci iuvenes

Lectio I : Puer Parvus

Sum puer parvus et bonus, nomine Marci, et habito in magna urbe cum patre, matre, sorore, fratreque. Sororis nomen est Iulia et nomen fratris est Marius. Narrabo vobis fabulam itineris nostri in nave.

Pater noster bonus convocaverat familiam et nuntiaverat: "Ad insulam navigabimus et spectabimus agros latos nostros. Multorum servorum dominus sum et volo confirmare servos, ubi laborant in agris."

Heri paravimus iter. Multa ad navem portavimus: frumentum, panem, pecuniam; duximus quoque equos et asinos. Ubi parati eramus, ad navem ambulavimus. Liberi non amamus naves et mare altum, et iter nostrum erat miserum. Navis angusta saluit in aqua magna cum celeritate, caelum erat nigrum, et fuimus captivi tempestatis et maris feri. Servavi equos et asinos magna cum virtute et demonstravi sorori animalia in mari. Dedimus equis amicis panem nostrum. Soror exclamavit: "Da, Marce, Mario panem!" Sed frater noster Marius erat aegrotus; stabat diu in nave, gemebat (moaned) "Male est mihi!" et exspectabat mortem.

Post tempus longum fuimus in terra et laudavimus grate deos deasque propter nostram fortunam: effugeramus mare horribile. Fortasse manebimus semper in insula...Liberate nos, di immortales, mari misero!

Navis et puer in tempestate

Lectio II : Anseres Custodiunt Capitolium (Gesta Romanorum)

Quarto saeculo Romani a Gallis ad Alliam flumen victi sunt. Tum Galli subito ad urbem Romam iter fecerunt. Romani ubi hostes venire senserunt, illis urbem tradere, sed arcem, Capitolium, defendere constituerunt. Viri, mulieres, liberi cum duce et militibus in arcem ascenderunt, sed senes, qui decora honoresque tulerunt, in villis
5 sederunt et ibi Gallos et mortem exspectaverunt.

Milites Gallorum intraverunt et senes ornatos et tranquillos invenerunt. Primo steterunt magna cum admiratione. Sed unus ex Gallis senui cuidam barbam vellicavit, et senex caput hostis pepulit. Miles iratus eum cecidit. Postea cuncti senes caesi sunt, et omnes villae incensae et in cinerem versae sunt.

10 Media nocte Galli Capitolium ascenderunt. Non locuti sunt, tacuerunt, et custodes eos audire non potuerunt. Etiam canes nihil audiverunt. Sed Galli anseres fallere non potuerunt. Clamaverunt et ululaverunt. Eorum clamore dux Romanorum e somno excitatus est et milites ad arma vocavit. Gallos de arce iecerunt et ita anseres arcem et incolas eius servaverunt.
15 Adhuc hodie Romani anseres in Capitolio tenent.

anser,anseris (m.) - goose (sacred to Juno); (1) Allia - (name of a river in Latium, which flows into the Ti- ber); (2) iter facere - to march; (7) barbam vellicare - to pull s.o.'s beard; (9) omnes - all; (10) medius,a,um - the middle, in the middle of; (12) fallere (fallo, fefelli) - to deceive; (12) ululare - to screech.

EXERCISE H: **Responde Latine:**

1. Quando Romani a Gallis victi sunt?
2. Ubi victi sunt?
3. Quando Galli a Romanis victi sunt? (not in this story)
4. Quid Romani agere constituerunt?
5. Quid Romani Gallis tradere voluerunt?
6. Quis arcem defendere debuit?
7. Quomodo visi sunt senes?
8. Quid senes exspectaverunt?
9. Cur unus ex senibus caput militis Galli pepulit? (use Pluperfect)
10. Qui occisi sunt?
11. Qui eos occiderunt?
12. Quid actum est de villis?
13. Quando Galli Capitolium ascenderunt?
14. Cur custodes Gallos audire non potuerunt?
15. Quem Galli fallere non potuerunt?
16. Qualem clamorem anseres fecerunt?
17. Quomodo dux e somno excitatus est?
18. Quomodo Galli repulsi sunt?
19. Quis servavit Capitolium?

Lectio III : Sententiae et Proverbia (various authors, proverbs, sayings)

1. Vox populi vox dei.

2. Salus populi suprema (highest) lex.

3. Necessitas dat legem.

4. ex libris suis

5. Dum colosseum stabit, Roma stabit;
   dum Roma stabit, mundus stabit.

6. Ubi bene, ibi patria.

7. Quid novi sub sole? Nihil novi sub sole.

8. Honos habet onus.

9. Tempora mutant mores.

10. Nomen est omen.

11. Nullum crimen sine lege.

12. Cibi <u>condimentum</u> fames.   spice

13. Invidia gloriae comes.

14. Civis Romanus sum.

15. Finis coronat (crowns) opus.

16. Contra vim mortis
    non est medicamen in hortis.

17. Mors certa, hora incerta.

18. Nil (= nihil) sine magno vita labore dedit mortalibus.

19. Homo doctus in se semper divitias (wealth) habet.

20. Summum (highest) ius, summa iniuria.

21. Mali principii (beginning) malus finis est.

22. nec caput nec pedes habere

23. maria montesque polliceri

24. Amor misceri (be mixed) cum timore non potest.

   .   .   .   .   .   .

25. Gaudia principium nostri sunt saepe doloris.
    (This is a Hexameter, a verse.)
    In prose the sentence could read:
    Gaudia saepe sunt principium nostri doloris.

An Epigram by Martial, comparing the teeth of Thais and Laecania:

  Thais habet nigros, niveos Laecania dentes.
  Quae ratio est? Emptos haec habet, illa suos.

And another one, about the physician/quack Diaulus:

  Nuper erat medicus, nunc est vespillo Diaulus.   (both Epigrams are Distichs
  Quod vespillo facit, fecerat et medicus.   see Metrics, Bk.2)

nuper - earlier; vespillo,onis - undertaker; et = etiam

Liberalitas aedificavit (et) donavit me,
nunc grata memoria (me) tenet servatque.

✶ ✶ ✶ ✶ ✶ ✶ ✶ ✶
✶ Riddle ✶
✶ ✶ ✶ ✶ ✶ ✶ ✶ ✶

Cut this sheet into syllables (you should, of course, copy it first), and form 9 (nine) nouns of the third declension from the pieces. The nouns are in different cases.

tis	ti	ta
ra	ra	ta
su	re	to
pe	pi	po

ca	ce	ges	mi	ni
car	le	bus	mi	ne
con	i	tem	no	ne
les	im	rum	ri	ri

Crafts and Trades

Many crafts were attested to in Rome and Pompeii, either in literature, or in stone-masonry reliefs found in shops, taverns, homes, and on tombs. One relief on the Column of Trajan shows a construction site; a blacksmith's and a butcher's tomb show them at work, a cutler's tomb shows him selling knives;

PISTOR - THE BAKER

The whole bread-making process was depicted on a baker's tomb: sowing and harvesting the grain, milling the flour, taking the bread out of the oven.

A baker selling bread

FULLO - THE CLOTHMAKER

SUTOR - THE COBBLER

LAPICIDA - THE STONEMASON

Products of Roman craftsmen

Roman glass

Iron vessels

**Terracotta pottery
(terra sigillata)**

Stone mason's art

If we broadly categorize the trades, there were people who worked with stone (quarry workers, stone cutters, stone masons, brick layers, mosaic artists, sculptors); with wood (carpenters, cabinet- makers, bridge-builders, well-makers, wood-cutters); with metals (miners, blacksmiths, bronze- smiths, goldsmiths, pipefitters, plumbers, mint-workers); with textiles and leather (weavers, fullers, dyers, tailors, shoemakers); with ceramics and glass; and with food.

The nobility considered only political life, the army, or country estates worthy of their station in life. Since the tradesmen then were mostly plebeians, who had no civic rights, they organized early into professional organizations, called "collegium," which protected their rights, represented them, invited them to social gatherings, and on occasion paid for their funeral; students were trained there as apprentices. The headquarters of the collegia were called "schola". In the beginning there were nine collegia: masons, dyers, shoemakers, goldsmiths, potters, tanners, blacksmiths, flute-players (!), and a ninth collegium for all other trades. Soon, however, trades became more specialized and the collegia subdivided. In later times many slaves and servants came to Rome in the wake of conquests. Powerful merchant groups formed corporations; they acquired slaves who were taught a trade, then their labor was sold, or else their owners employed them. This often meant unemployment for the plebeian tradesmen. All of the members of the collegia and the slaves had to work together, however, to bring about the construction of the gigantic buildings and monuments whose remnants can be seen up to this day.

One very old trade was that of the fuller (**fullo**), who treated and cleaned cloth, usually made of wool. First the cloth was soaked in urine to soften and shrink it. To this end the Emperor Vespasian allowed fullers to keep a bucket for collecting urine in front of their shops - for a fee, which served to strengthen the imperial coffers. When neighbors complained about the stench he commented with the words "Pecunia non olet" (Money doesn't smell bad). For the cleaning of the cloth a mixture of clay and soda was added, and the fullers walked on the cloth. To bleach the cloth it was spread on racks over fires containing sulphur. The resulting vapours made many fullers incurably ill. After that the cloth was combed and carded, dried, folded, and pressed in a large press. From this felt-like material they made hooded coats, blankets for horses, and shoes.

Glassmaking was also a venerable art. Early glass was pressed in forms, but already in the first century BC glass-blowing was introduced from Syria. A famous center for glass-making was Colonia Agrippina, today's Cologne.

artifex   ars   artificium

Chapter 11: Answers and Translations

Exercise A:
1. orare 2. parere (pario) 3. imperare 4. regere 5. ducere 6. ire 7. scribere 8. facere
9. custodire 10. sedere 11. iungere

Exercise C:
    1. a rare bird   2. Beware of the dog!   3. the world (circle of countries)
    4. whose country, his religion (Rule of the Westphalian Peace, after the Thirty Years War)
    5. Honors change the character.   6. the nourishing mother (your university)
    7. For man it is necessary to die. (Men, humans have to die.)
    8. People's character can be recognized from their body, eyes, face, and forehead.
    9. A full belly does not study gladly.
  10. A part of the soldiers did not return to Italy; they stayed in the territory of the Greeks.
  11. The lion had many sharp teeth and a loud voice, which caused us terror.
  12. There is a herd of cows in our meadows; can they find enough food?
  13. Winter brings snow. We have to wear many clothes.
  14. The dogs, compelled by hunger, ran with great speed into the house.
  15. Frogs prefer living in swamps.   16. Mind moves matter.
  17. A storm arose; we went under the bridge and waited for the end of the storm.
  18. Honour is the reward of courage.   19. The stomach is the master of art.
  20. Habit is like a second nature (another nature).

Exercise D:
1. Canes edunt ossa. (o)	2. Feles edunt mures. (e)
3. Aves cantant in silvis. (p)	4. Avi narrant fabulas. (f)
5. Parentes habent filios filiasque. (g)	6. Imperatores gerunt bella. (d)
7. Boves herbas edunt. (l)	8. Hospites visitant amicos. (c)
9. Hostes Romanos non amant. (t)	10. Fratres amant sorores. (m)
11. Scriptores scribunt libros. (r)	12. Nepotes audiunt avos. (q)
13. Pisces tacent. (s)	14. Pontifices orant. (b)
15. Artifices faciunt artificia. (i)	16. Custodes custodiunt aurum. (j)
17. Milites pugnant. (a)	18. Leones edunt boves. (k)
19. Oratores multum loquuntur. (h)	20. Equites sedent in equis. (n)

Exercise E:
    1. multitudo bovum...multitudo hominum
    2. Imperatores...ambitiones...vi...auctoritate
    3. Multi homines (or just: multi)...aestates...hiemes
    4. ...nomina...comitum
    5. ...oratores...consuetudinem orationis...veritatis
    6. ...pacem...hominibus bonae voluntatis
    7. ...paupertatem cum dignitate...onus sine voluptate
    8. Ver fert tempestates cum fulminibus et imbre.

Exercise F:
1. Times change, and we change with them.   2. a healthy mind in a healthy body 3. Wine is the milk of old men.   4. Those who run across the sea change the sky, not their mind.   5. O times, o customs! said Cicero when he wanted to drive Catiline out of the city and held a speech (invective) against Catiline.   6. We saw two ships under the bridge, who wanted to cross the river with great speed.   7. Why was the horse standing next to the spring? Compelled by thirst it had descended to the water and wanted to drink water with the people.   8. Do you love my sister? I will tell my parents about your love, and my father will kick you out of the house.   9. After the death of the soldier the comrades carried his body to a cart.   10. The poem of the famous poet was long, but not beautiful.   11. Today give us our daily bread.   12. Longed-for Spring returns with joy, decorated with a purple flower.

Reading I: A Small Boy
I am a small and good boy by the name of Marcus and I live in a large city with my father, mother, sister and brother. My sister's name is Julia and my brother's name is Marius. I will tell you the story of our journey in a ship.
Our good father had called the family together and announced: "We will sail to the island and look at our extensive fields. I am the master of many slaves, and I want to support the slaves, when they work in the fields."
Yesterday we prepared for the journey. We carried many things to the ship: grain, bread, money; and we also led horses and donkeys there. When we were prepared, we walked to the ship. We children do not like ships and the high sea, and our journey was miserable. The narrow ship jumped in the water with great speed, the sky was black, and we were captives of the storm and the wild sea. I guarded the horses and donkeys with great courage and showed my sister the animals in the sea. We gave our bread to the dear horses. My sister exclaimed: "Marcus, give Marius some bread!" But our brother amrius was sick; he stood a long time in the ship, moaned "I feel sick," and was expecting death. After a long time we were on land and gratefully praised the gods and goddesses because of our fortune: we had escaped the horrible sea! Maybe we will remaim on the island forever...
Liberate us, immortal gods, from the miserable sea!

Reading II: The Geese Guard the Capitol
In the 4th century the Romans were defeated by the Gauls near the river Allia. Then the Gauls suddenly marched towards Rome. When the Romans felt that the enemy was coming, they decided to hand over to them the city, but to defend the fortress, the Capitol. Men, women, and children, with their leader and with soldiers, climbed up to the fortress, but the old men, who were wearing their decorations and medals, sat in the houses and there awaited the Gauls and death.
The Gallic soldiers entered and came upon the dressed-up and calm old men. First they stood in great admiration. But one of the soldiers pulled a certain old man by the beard, and the old man hit the enemy on the head. The angry soldier killed him. Afterwards all the old men were killed, and the houses were burnt and turned into ashes.
In the middle of the night the Gauls climbed up to the Capitol. They did not speak, they were silent, and the guardians could not hear them. Even the dogs heard nothing. But the Gauls could not deceive the geese. They screeched and howled. By their clamor the leader of the Romans was awakened from sleep and called the soldiers to arms. They threw the Gauls down from the fortress, and in this way the geese saved the fortress and its inhabitants.
To this day the Romans keep geese on the Capitol.

Exercise H:
1. Quarto saeculo victi sunt.   2. Ad Alliam flumen victi sunt.   3. In bello Gallico, a Caesare victi sunt. 4. Constituerunt Gallis urbem tradere, sed arcem defendere. Constituerunt viros, mulie- res, liberos in arcem mittere.   5. Urbem Romam tradere voluerunt.   6. Dux cum militibus, viri, mulieres arcem defendere debuerunt.   7. Senes ornati et tranquilli visi sunt.   8. Senes mortem exspectaverunt. 9. Senes caput militis pepulit, quod miles senui barbam vellicaverat.
10. Omnes senes occisi sunt.   11. Milites Gallorum eos ceciderunt. 12. Omnes villae incensae et in cinerem versae sunt.   13. Galli media nocte Capitolium ascenderunt.   14. Galli audiri non potuerunt, quod tacuerunt et non locuti sunt. 15. Galli anseres fallere non potuerunt.   16. Anseres clamaverunt et ululaverunt.   17. Dux clamore anserum e somno excitatus est.   18. Romani eos de arce iecerunt.
19. Anseres servaverunt Capitolium.

Reading III: Sentences and Proverbs
1. The voice of the people (is) the voice of God.
2. The well-being of the people is the highest law.
3. Necessity gives the law.   4. from his books (name plate for book)
5. While the colosseum stands, Rome will stand; while Rome stands, the world will stand.
6. Where (you feel) good, there is your home.
7. What's new under the sun? Nothing new under the sun.
8. Honor carries a burden.   9. Times change customs.
10. The name is an omen. (Your name says something about you.)
11. No crime without law.   12. Hunger is the spice of the food.
13. Envy (is) the companion of glory.   14. I am a Roman citizen.
15. The end crowns the work.
16. Against the force of death there is no medicine in the gardens.
17. Death is sure, the hour unsure.
18. Life has not given anything to mortals without great labor.
19. An educated man always has great wealth in him.
20. The highest law (is sometimes) the greatest wrong.
21. A bad beginning has a bad end.
22. to have neither head nor feet (to be half-baked)
23. to promise the seas and the mountains
24. Love can not be mixed with fear.   25. Joys are often the beginning of our pain
26. Thais has black, Laecania white teeth.
    What is the reason? The latter has bought ones, the former her own.
27. Recently he was a doctor, now Diaulus is an undertaker.
    What the undertaker does, the doctor had done also.
    (or: What he does as an undertaker, he also had done as a doctor i.e., bring
    people under the earth.)

Riddle:
1. capita   2. consules   3. reges   4. celeritatis   5. carmine (carminibus)   6. nominibus (nomine)
7. itineri   8. imperatorum   9. tempora (endings of 7, 8, and 9 can be switched)

12

VERBS: PARTICIPLES: GERUNDIVE
ABLATIVE ABSOLUTE
PERIPHRASTIC CONSTRUCTIONS

ENGLISH AND LATIN 1

If the speakers of Germanic in Northern Europe ever spoke one unified language, they did not do so for very long. After several generations, sometime before the Christian Era, they began migrating again and their dialects gradually developed apart to the point where they became different languages. One group moved to Southeastern Europe, to the area of today's Bulgaria. Since they originated at the island of Gotland (today in Sweden), they called themselves, or were called, **Goths**. They became Christians, and their bishop Wulfila translated the Bible for them from Greek into Gothic, about 350 A.D. This is the oldest Germanic document in existence. Its most extensive and most beautiful copy is kept in Uppsala, Sweden, and is called the **Codex Argenteus**, because of its magnificent silver cover. Because of the Goths' vicinity to Greece the writing uses a number of Greek or Greek-inspired letters. The Gothic language became extinct in the 6th century, together with its people. So did another East Germanic language, Vandalic.

The North Germanic branch in its oldest written form is called Old Norse. Its documents date from the 9th century. There are, however, inscriptions and a few manuscripts which are much older. They were written in Runes, an alphabet used in Scandinavia, Germany, and the British Isles. Nobody knows where the alphabet came from, but it is believed that it was derived from the Roman alphabet during the first centuries of our era, when there were a number of Roman cities and camps in the Rhine area.

The Western group of Germanic languages divided into the speakers of High and Low German (this being a geographical name - high, as in the southern mountains, low, as in the northern flatlands). The tribes who migrated to England, the Angles, Saxons, and Jutes, spoke a Low German dialect.

A sample of Gothic from the Codex Argenteus

Chapter 12:   VERBS : PARTICIPLES, GERUNDIVE,
ABLATIVE ABSOLUTE; PERIPHRASTIC CONSTRUCTIONS

Participles are formed from verbs, but they do **not** serve as **conjugated** verb forms, because they have no person or mood categories; rather they are **adjectives**, or **adjectival nouns**. They can, however, be combined with conjugated forms of the verb **esse** to produce verb forms or constructions. These forms are all **periphrastic**: they use more than one word.

Participles exist in the **present**, the **past**, and the **future**. six participles would be needed to cover active and passive for present, past, and future, but there are only three, or four, if one includes the gerundive, as we do here. They are distributed as follows:

	Active	Passive
Present	**Present Participle**	--
Past	--	**Past Participle**
Future	**Future Participle**	**Gerundive**

This does not mean that some ideas can not be expressed in Latin, it only means that Latin uses different forms to express them.

1. You have already learned the **past participle passive**, or **PPP**, as the fourth principal part of the verb, and as a component in the periphrastic forms of the passive (P, PQ, FP). Remember again that the PPP is, as its name already tells you, generally **passive** in meaning:

portatus,a,um	(having been) carried
deletus,a,um	(having been) destroyed
missus,a,um	(having been) sent
captus,a,um	(having been) taken
auditus,a,um	(having been) heard

But what if one wants to say: "Having destroyed the town of Carthage, Scipio left for Rome" or "Having tried force to no avail, they resorted to deceit"? (This latter refers to the Trojan horse.)
There are two possibilities in Latin for expressing past **active** participle concepts:

a) You can hope to find a **deponent verb** with the appropriate meaning.
   The (passive) forms of deponents you have learned so far have **active meaning**, for instance,
       conatur - *she tries*; mentiti sunt - *they lied*; pollicebaris - *you used to promise*.
   This holds also for their past participles, for example:
       conatus - *having tried*   profectus - *having departed*
       pollicitus - *having promised*   aggressus - *having attacked*

(But remember that in turn you can not produce a passive meaning with these verbs, such as "having **been** attacked," "having **been** promised," "having **been** tried.")

Therefore remember:

Active Verbs --> past participle meaning is **passive**

Deponent Verbs --> past participle meaning is **active**

b) Failing to find a deponent verb you must change the whole sentence into a **passive sentence**,
For instance:

Having destroyed the town of Carthage...

---> The town of Carthage having been destroyed...

Having tried force... ---> Force having been tried...

Changing the sentence to the passive also changes the **subject** of the sentence. This leaves the participial part of the sentence somewhat isolated as far as the function within the sentence is concerned. Latin takes care of this by putting the **participle** and its accompanying **noun(s)** in the **ablative** and not even attempting to integrate it into the rest of the sentence. This construction is called an **Ablative Absolute**. (See part two of this chapter)

EXERCISE A: Translate the participles as active or passive forms according to the type of verb:
(The endings do not affect the translation here; they are just to show you that different endings are possible, and necessary, in contexts.) Give the Infinitive of each verb!

1. hortatus	2. positum
3. mentiti	4. tactum
5. sensum	6. usus
7. oblita	8. iuncti
9. relictus	10. moratum
11. fracta	12. caesus
13. confessus	14. secuti
15. esum	16. gesta
17. locutus	18. quaesita
19. redditum	20. questi

2. The form of the **future active participle** is derived from the past participle and looks quite similar to it; however, it is always **active** in meaning, and it is usually translated as "about to...," or "going to...."
To form the future participle replace the -us,-a,-um of the past participle with **-urus,-ura,-urum**

(captus) -->	**capturus,a,um**	about to take, going to take
(portatus) -->	**portaturus,a,um**	about to, going to, carry
(doctus) -->	**docturus,a,um**	about to, going to, teach
(auditus) -->	**auditurus,a,um**	about to, going to, hear

Interestingly, deponent verbs also form the future active participle, with an **active meaning**:

(hortatus) -->	**hortaturus,a,um**	about to, going to, encourage
(passus) -->	**passurus,a,um**	about to, going to, suffer
(mentitus) -->	**mentiturus,a,um**	about to, going to, lie

There are some **irregular** future participles; two common ones are:

(mortuus)	----> **moriturus,a,um**	about to, going to, die
(partus)	-----> **pariturus,a,um**	about to, going to, give birth

 **EXERCISE B:**　　　Say in Latin (remember to use **deponents** for **active** past participles, like "having forgotten"):

1. about to sleep
2. going to buy
3. about to sell
4. having been heard
5. having lamented
6. about to remember
7. having been snatched
8. having been born (two verbs - you can use nasci also, since it means 'to be born')
9. going to leave behind
10. about to throw
11. about to answer
12. having been attacked
13. having attacked
14. about to finish
15. having been believed

These participle forms can also be used as **adjectives**, a popular use in Latin, but not in English, where they sound very awkward ("The about-to-answering boys," "the (having been) attacked city"), and are usually replaced by relative clauses. (See chapter 10.)

With the help of these participles you can easily produce **conjugated verb forms:**
If you want to say not only "about to teach," but: "**She is** about to teach," or "**We were** about to leave town," you only need to use the appropriate form of **esse** (only present and imperfect are used) and add the correct ending for the person(s) to the future participle:

Doctur**a est**.	**She is** about to teach.
Urbem relictur**i eramus**.	**We were** about to leave town.

This **construction** consisting of the **future active participle** and the **conjugated verb** *to be* is called **active periphrastic construction,** or, in Latin, **coniugatio periphrastica activa.**

3. The **present participle** is formed from the present stem of the verb. It is similar in meaning to the present participle in English: *taking, doing, sending;* its meaning is always **active**. There is no periphrastic construction in Latin that uses the present participle, corresponding to the English progressive construction "they are eating, you were laughing, she will be asking." (At least, there is no such construction in classical Latin, although it does appear in vulgar and medieval Latin. How would one say "She is carrying" in classical Latin? Right: **portat**.)

However, the present participle is used in place of entire English clauses, such as "while they are (were) reading," "while eating," "when eating," "one who has given," "as they are (were) leaving," "although they are (were) carrying," etc. You see that the tense does not matter here; the present participle relates only an *...ing* action to the conjugated verb, as taking place at the same time - in whatever tense this happens to be.

To form the present participle take the **present stem** and add **-ns** for verbs of the first and second conjugations, and **-ens** for the third, third i- stems, and fourth conjugations:

portare	-->	porta-	**porta ns**	carrying, one who carries
docere	-->	doce-	**doce ns**	teaching
ducere	-->	duc-	**duc ens**	leading
capere	-->	capi-	**capi ens**	taking
audire	-->	audi-	**audi ens**	hearing

These participles are **declined** like **mixed nouns** of the **third** declension (ablative Singular **-e**, nominative and accusative neuter **-ia**, genitive Plural **-ium**) The forms are alike for all genders, with separate forms for the neuter in the accusative Singular and the nominative and accusative Plural (because they must have syncretism in these cases, and **-a** in the neuter Plural).

		Masc + Fem	Neuter	Masc + Fem	Neuter
	N	portans	(portans)	capiens	(capiens)
	G	portantis		capientis	
Sg	D	portanti		capienti	
	A	portantem	portans	capientem	capiens
	Ab	portante		capiente	
	N	portantes	portant**ia**	capientes	capient**ia**
	G	portant**ium**		capient**ium**	
Pl	D	portantibus		capientibus	
	A	portantes	portant**ia**	capientes	capient**ia**
	Ab	portantibus		capientibus	

Deponent verbs also have present participles, with **active** meaning:
Examples:

loquens,loquentis	speaking
arbitrans,arbitrantis	thinking
fatens,fatentis	confessing
morans,morantis	hesitating
moriens,morientis	dying
proficiscens,proficiscentis	departing
querens,querentis	complaining

All participles of deponents are thus active in meaning!

The participles of **ire, ferre, velle, malle, nolle:**

ire:	PR:	iens, **eu**ntis (**eu**nti, euntem, eunte, etc.)	going
	PPP:	itus,a,um (only for compound verbs)	---
	F:	iturus,a,um	about to go
ferre:	PR:	ferens,ferentis	carrying
	PPP:	latus,a,um	(having been) carried
	F:	laturus,a,um	about to carry
velle:	PR:	volens,volentis	wanting, wishing
		(no past or future)	
nolle:	PR:	nolens,nolentis	not wanting
malle:	PR:	malens,malentis	preferring

EXERCISE C: Translate the sentences:

1. Liberi flentes a magistro moniti sunt.
2. Vidimus solem orientem.
3. Canes latrantes [*bark*] mordere [*bite*] non possunt.
4. Nihil habenti nihil deest.
5. Pugnantem militem videbant.
6. Pugnantes militem videbant. (!)
7. Historiam obliviscentes eam revivere debent.
8. Cave Graecos dona ferentes!
   [Actually Vergil said: "**Timeo Danaos et dona ferentes**";
   Danaos = Graecos; et = etiam)
9. Diu sequebamur animalia per silvam fugientia.
10. Cito [*quickly*] currentes vos capiemus.
11. Omnibus viribus saliens vulpes uvas tangere non potuit.

4. The **gerundive** is a verbal **adjective** which modifies a noun. It is **passive** and **future** in meaning; in addition it implies the **necessity** of an action. It is translated as "to be made," (meaning "supposed to be made"), "to be captured," "to be praised," as something, that is to be done in the future.
The gerundive is formed by adding **-ndus, -nda, -ndum** to the present stem of first and second conjugation verbs, and **-endus, -enda, -endum** to the present stem of third, third i-stem, and fourth conjugation verbs.

Examples:

portare -->	**porta ndus,a,um**	to be carried
docere -->	**doce ndus,a,um**	to be taught
ducere -->	**duc endus,a,um**	to be led
capere -->	**capi endus,a,um**	to be taken
audire -->	**audi endus,a,um**	to be heard

The gerundive together with, and in the same case as, the noun it modifies is often called a **Gerundive construction**; it is used in all cases.

Like the future active participle, the gerundive can also be combined with a form of **esse**, to enable you to say in Latin "The boy **is** to be taught" or "must be taught"; "The city **was** to be destroyed" or "had to be destroyed." This construction is called **passive periphrastic construction**, or **coniugatio periphrastica passiva** (see later for other gerundive constructions):

Puer docendus est.	The boy is to be taught. / The boy must be taught.
Urbs delenda erat.	The city was to be destroyed. / The city had to be destroyed.

The gerundive of **deponent** verbs has **passive** meaning, just like that of all other verbs:

conandus,a,um	to be tried
verendus,a,um	to be feared
loquendus,a,um	to be spoken
patiendus,a,um	to be suffered
audiendus,a,um	to be heard.

The gerundive of **ire** is **eundus,a,um**; of **ferre, ferendus,a,um**

SUMMARY: You can now form the following **participial phrases**:

1. a running dog	canis currens	Present Participle Active
flying birds	aves volantes	**(PPA)**
the boy while (he was) reading (acc.)	puerum legentem	
2. bought goods	merces emptae	Past Participle Passive
words which have been said	verba dicta	**(PPP)**
finished books	libri finiti	
3. having admonished	hortatus,a,um	**(PPP)**
having promised **(Deponents only)**	pollicitus,a,um	with active meaning
having lied	mentitus,a,um	
4. parents about to ask	parentes rogaturi	Future Participle Active
women going to read (acc.)	mulieres lecturas	**(FPA)**
farmers about to work	agricolae laboraturi	
5. books to be read	libri legendi	**Gerundive**
work to be done	labor faciendus	
girls to be praised	puellae laudandae	

-ns- and **-nt-**	=	Present Participle Active ("-ing")
-tus, -ta, -tum	=	PPP (Present Participle <u>Passive</u> or Deponent Active (Past)
-turus, -tura, -turum	=	Future Participle Active ("about to")
-nd-	=	Gerundive Future Passive ("to be..-ed")

Distinguish **-nt-** and **-nd-** !

EXERCISE D:	For the following participles give their tense (PPP, Present, Future), indicate whether their meaning is active or passive, and translate:

Form , Tense   Active/Passive   Translation

1. salutandus _____

2. ferentes _____

3. videndae _____

4. cessuri _____

5. mirata _____

6. puniendos _____

7. custodienda _____

8. relicta _____

9. nixus _____

10. obliti _____

11. rupturum _____

12. loquentium _____

13. divisa _____

14. tracturus _____

15. solutas _____

16. solvendas _____

17. petentibus _____

18. coacturae _____

19. venerati _____

20. recordatus _____

EXERCISE E:	Form these participles and gerundives in Latin:

1. friends to be saved   _____

2. the dogs while eating   _____

3. broken ships   _____

4. soldiers about to kill   _____

5. the house having been sold   _____

6. years to be remembered   _____

7. occupied towns   _____

8. generals about to lead   _____

9. horses supposed to be led   _____

10. the table which was moved   _____

11. having obtained (m., Pl.) the ships   _____

12. having forgotten (f., Sg.) the books   _____

13. defeated footsoldiers   _____

14. the expected Spring (season)   _____

15. for [ad] the journey to be made [facere]   _____

16. for [ad] these matters to be carried out   _____

****

Summary of Constructions Using Participles and Gerundives

The Participium Conjunctum and Participium Absolutum

1. The Participium Coniunctum:

   Examples:

Imperatores **regnantes** multa templa aedificaverunt.   The reigning emperors built many temples.
                              While the emperors were reigning, they built many temples.
         Regnantes modifies **imperatores,** the subject of the sentence.

Canes **expulsi** fortiter latrare coeperunt.   The expelled dogs began to bark loudly.
                         After the dogs were kicked out, they began to bark loudly.
         Expulsi modifies **canes,** the subject of the sentence.

Vidimus milites **mortuos.**   We saw the dead ("having died") soldiers.
            Mortuos modifies **milites,** the direct object of the sentence. (Mori = deponent)

2. The Participium Absolutum:

A **participium absolutum** is a participle that is disconnected from the sentence structure (absolvere, *to loosen, disconnect*); in other words, it does not relate to any part of the main sentence. (If it does, it is a **participium coniunctum**, and it modifies a part of the sentence.) The present participle implies an action going on at the same time, the past participle a previous one.

Since the participium absolutum usually occurs in the **ablative**, it is often called **Ablativus Absolutus** (Ablative Absolute). It consists of two words in the ablative, whose grammatical connection to the rest of the sentence is quite loose, and whose subject is different from the subject of the main sentence. Most frequently the two words used are a participle and a noun:

urbe capta;   canibus latrantibus

Occasionally two nouns are used:

Caesare imperatore.

The literal translation of the Ablative Absolute is somewhat clumsy, for example:

urbe capta	the city having been taken
Caesare imperatore	Caesar being general
canibus latrantibus	the dogs (being) barking

Therefore the Ablative Absolute is best rendered with a dependent clause. If you choose this option (a wise decision!), the clause can be introduced with conjunctions such as who, which, while, when, because, although for a present participle, and with after, who, which, when, because, althoug, for a past participle. Occasionally an active participle translation will work. Use your linguistic judgment and common sense!

Examples: **Urbe capta** incolae satis aquae non habebant.

After (because) the city had been taken, the inhabitants did not have enough water.

Urbe capta has no function in the main sentence and uses a different subject (the city).

Canibus latrantibus fures in villam divitis incesserunt.

While the dogs were barking, thieves broke into the rich man's house.

Although the dogs were barking...

Canibus latrantibus does not constitute a part of the main sentence. (subject: the dogs)

Caesare imperatore Romani multas victorias obtinuerunt.

While Caesar was general, the Romans won many victories.

Caesare imperatore exercitus ad victoriam ducetur.

If (when, because, etc.) Caesar is general, the army will be led to victory.

These sentences show that the present participle occurs at the same time as the main verb; therefore the translation can be **was** or **is**, depending on the time of the main verb. The same is true for two nouns.

EXERCISE F: Read the following sentences and decide whether the underlined participle is a **participium conjunctum** (the participle is part of the main sentence = same subject) or an **ablative absolute**, (the participle is not part of the main sentence (different subj.)

	Conjunctum	Absolutum
1. After the money had been <u>collected</u>, the quaestor left.	___	___
2. He left, <u>collecting</u> the money on the way.	___	___
3. Since the enemies were <u>attacking</u> the city, the people left.	___	___
4. The <u>shouting</u> senators frightened everybody.	___	___

	Conjunctum	Absolutum
5. Everyone was frightened by the <u>shouting</u> senators.	——	——
6. Because the people were <u>frightened</u>, the senators left.	——	——
7. The girl held the <u>wounded</u> dog with both hands.	——	——
8. Since the dog was <u>barking</u>, the girl held him with a leash.	——	——
9. The boy fell into the water while his brother was <u>playing</u> on the bridge.	——	——
10. <u>Having encouraged</u> the soldiers, the general began to fight	——	——
11. Give the bread to the girl who is <u>standing</u> there.	——	——
12. After the kings had been <u>driven</u> out, Rome became a Republic.	——	——

EXERCISE G: **Ablative Absolute :** Translate, using dependent clauses. The basic translation for the PPP: **after ....had (been)...**   for the PPA: **while...is (was) ...ing**

1. Aedificiis cunctis incensis...(After all the buildings had been burned down...)
2. Patre adstante... (While the father was (is) standing by...)
3. Tempestate orta...
4. Caesare consule...
5. Pace facta...
6. Navibus fractis...
7. Libris taedium ferentibus lectis...
8. Animalibus ferissimis repulsis...
9. His rebus constitutis...
10. Die constituta...
11. Dux huic imperavit, ut, omnibus rebus exploratis, ad se veniret.
12. Omnibus feminis liberisque ab urbe remotis senes adventum Gallorum exspectabant.
13. His omnibus rebus gestis pueri arbitrati sunt suum opus confectum esse.
14. His rebus ita constitutis ei, qui sorte delecti erant, in interiorem partem insulae profecti sunt.
15. Omnibus rebus ad iter paratis navem solverunt.
16. Milites capti gladios in manibus tenentes in urbem ducebantur. [P. conjunctum!]
17. Itinere viginti milium passuum facto exercitus castra aggressus est.
18. Mutato nomine de te fabula narratur. (Horace) [use 'although']
19. Mari tranquillo naves portum nacti sunt.
20. Orgetorix, Marco Messala Marco Pisone consulibus, regni cupiditate inductus, coniurationem nobilitatis fecit. (Caesar)

---

(1) incendere (incendo, incensi, insensum) - to burn; (7) taedium,i - boredom;
(8) ferissimus,a,um - (superlative) the wildest, very wild; (10) dies,diei (5th Declension) - day;
(11) ut ad se veniret - (**ut** with subjunctive of venire) **that** he should come; ad se - to him (i.e. dux);
        explorare - to explore;
(14) deligere - to choose
(15) omnibus = cunctis; navem solvere - to sail;
(17) iter facere - to march;
(18) mutare - to change;
(20) Orgetorix - (name of a Helvetian leader);
        M.M. M.P consulibus - Since both consuls are mentioned with both names, **et** is not used.

The Coniugatio Periphrastica Activa

This construction consists of a **future active participle** and a form of **esse** (Present, Imperfect). It differs from the plain Future Tense in that it expresses the idea of being immediately at the beginning of an action, "about to" do something, "going to," and also "intending to" do something.

Examples:

Liberos doct**urus sum**.	**I am** about to teach the children. (I = a man)
Libros lect**uri sumus**.	**We intend** to read the books.
Domum relict**ura est**.	**She is** going to leave the house.
Canis te mors**urus erat**.	The dog **was about** to bite you.
Vir nos rogavit, quid fact**uri essemus**.	The man asked us, what **we were** going to do. (Subjunctive)

The Coniugatio Periphrastica Passiva

This construction is formed with the **gerundive** and the conjugated verb **esse** (present, imperfect, future). It expresses the **necessity** of an action, something which "must" be, "has to" be, "is to" be, or "ought to" be done. The **person** who must do something (the agent, if there is one) stands in the **dative**, so what you are actually saying is: The book to me is (one) to be read = I must read the book. But if there is already a dative object, the personal agent is in the ablative with ab, as in the passive.

Examples: (compare to sentences in active periphrastic above)

Liberi **mihi** doc**endi** sunt.	**I** must teach the children.
Libri **nobis** leg**endi** erant.	**We** had to read the books.
Domus **ei** relinqu**enda** erit.	**She (he)** will have to leave the house.
Hoc faci**endum** est.	This has to be done. (is to be done, must be done.)

EXERCISE H: Translate, using active or passive periphrastics:

1. She intends to send the letter.   _____

2. She must send the letter.   _____

3. We ought to leave town.   _____

4. They were about to start a war.   _____

5. The horses must be led to the pasture.   _____

6. Are you going to prepare (m.) dinner?   _____

7. I have to finish the work today.   _____

8. The house will have to be sold.   _____

Other Constructions with the Gerundive

Gerundive constructions can be used in all cases:

> in the **accusative** with **ad**, to show **purpose**;
> in the **genitive** with **causa** or **gratia** ("for the sake of," postpositive prepositions);
> in the **dative** as **indirect object**;
> in the **ablative** as expression of **means by which** something is done.

Examples:

In urbem veni **ad libros legendos**.	I came to the city *in order to read books.*
In urbem veni **librorum legendorum causa**.	I came to the city *for the sake of reading books.*
Libris legendis multum didici.	*By reading books* I have learned much.
Magnam curam da **libris legendis**!	Give great care *to reading books!*

 **EXERCISE I:**   Participles and Gerundives.   Translate::

1. Audiendi sunt senatores.

2. Si nihil boni dici potest, tacendum est.

3. Parentibus a liberis parendum est.

4. Romani liberos suos servis Graecis educandos dederunt.

5. Nobis cedendum non est; amici e periculo servandi sunt.

6. Pyramus et Thisbe parietem inter domos suas ad oscula danda aperire voluerunt.

7. Atticus Ciceroni ex patria fugienti pecuniam dedit. (Nepos)

8. Qui timens vivet, liber non erit umquam. (Horace)

9. Verbum semel emissum volat irrevocabile. (Horace)

10. Asia victa, dux Romanus servos multos in Italiam misit. (Pliny)

11. Ceterum censeo Carthaginem delendam esse.

12. Roma locuta, causa finita.

13. His constitutis rebus, nactus idoneam ad navigandam tempestatem,

    Caesar tertia fere vigilia naves solvit equitesque in ulteriorem

    partem progredi et naves conscendere et se sequi iussit. (Cicero)

---

(6) paries,etis - wall; domus,-us (f.) - house (see Ch.13); osculum,i - kiss; (8) umquam - ever;
(11) ceterum - otherwise, as for the rest; Carthaginem - (translate 'that Carthage...').
(13) idoneus,a,um - suitable; naves conscendere - to board the ships.

THE GERUND

The **gerund** is introduced at this time, because its forms are related to those of the **gerundive**. The gerund is, however, neither a **participle** nor an a**djective**, but a **noun,** precisely: a **verbal noun** (a noun made from a verb**)**. The gerund supplies the cases of the infinitive, much the same as it does in English:

   to talk (nom.), **of talking** (gen.), **for talking** (acc., at least in Latin), **by talking** (abl.).

The sentence 'Errare human**um** est' - *To err is human* - shows that the infinitive (= nominative) is neuter.

The forms of the **gerund** are thus identical to those of the **gerundive, neuter, Singular.**
  The   The nominative of the gerund is the infinitive of the verb.

N	portare	to carry, carrying
G	portandi	of carrying
D	portando	to carrying
A	(ad) portandum	(for) carrying, to carry
Ab	portando	by, with, through carrying

Examples:

    In cubiculum itura sum **ad dormiendum**. *I am about to go to the bedroom for sleeping (to sleep).*
    Edendo, exercendo, discendo crescimus.
       By eating we grow (bigger), by training we grow (stronger), by studying we grow (smarter).
    In urbem venimus **ad emendum cibum**. *We went into the city to buy food.* (for buying = gerund;
    food = direct object, acc.; or: **ad cibum emendum** = acc. object and gerundive)

This last sentence shows that in many instances the difference between gerund and gerundive is blurred. The sentences with the gerundive from the previous page could also be expressed with the gerund, with the difference that in most cases the endings would not be the same, since we are then dealing with two nouns. Compare:

Gerundive		Gerund
In urbem veni **ad libros legendos**.	or	In urbem veni **ad libros legendum**.
		ad legendum libros.
(for the books to be read)		(for reading what: books - direct object, acc)
In urbem veni **librorum legendorum causa**.	or	In urbem veni **libros legendi causa**.
Libris legendis multum didici.	or	**Libros legendo** multum didici.
		(possibly also: **Librorum legendo..**)

If there is no object, the gerund must be used. (See examples, first and second sentence.)
Both constructions were quite popular in Latin writing; the translation is the same for both.

The Supine

This verbal noun of the fourth Declension, which is formed like the PPP, has only two forms:
> the accusative, ending in **-um**, is used to show a purpose (yes, one more way;
>> the Romans, it seems, were quite purposeful people.)
> the ablative, ending in **-u**, occurs mostly after some adjectives, such as
>> facilis (easy), difficilis (difficult), incredibilis (incredible), mirabilis
>> (wondersome), utilis (useful), optimus (the best). (For these and other third
>> declension adjectives see chapter 14.)

Examples with the **accusative:**
Legatos miserunt imperatorem consult**um**.   They sent envoys in order to consult the general.
Spectat**um** veni<u>u</u>nt; veni<u>u</u>nt spect<u>e</u>ntur ut <u>ip</u>sae. (Ovid)
(Read aloud, putting the stress on the underlined syllables.)
                                        They come in order to see; they come to be seen themselves.
(In the dependent clause the conjunction **ut** [*so that, in order to*] is buried in the middle, for reasons
of meter [Hexameter], and also to make possible the juxtaposition ...veniunt; veniunt...)

These purpose clauses could be, and commonly are, expressed with either a (relative or general)
purpose clause (**qui** or **ut** are used with the subjunctive, see ch.15 and 16) or a Gerundive of Purpose
with ad:

> Legatos miserunt **ad** imperatorem **consulendum**.   (Gerundive of Purpose)
> (Legatos miserunt, **qui** imperatorem **consulerent**.)   (Relative Purpose)
> (Legatos miserunt, **ut** imperatorem **consulerent**.)   (General Purpose)

Examples with the **ablative** of the supine:
> turpe vis**u**   ugly to see
> mirabile dict**u**   amazing to tell; amazingly
> Hoc est facile intellect**u**.   This is easy to understand.
> Fabulae eius sunt difficiles credit**u**.   His tales are hard to believe.

Lectio I : Uvae Acerbae (Secundum Phaedrum)

Vulpes fame vexata uvam de vite alta pendentem petebat.

Eam omnibus viribus saliens attingere non potuit et discedens dixit:

"Nolo hanc uvam; nondum maturuit."

(1) vexare - to torment; vitis,is (f.) - grape vine; pendére,-eo,pependi - to hang; (2) attingere (tangere) - to reach; (3) maturescere,maturesco,maturui) - to ripen.

EXERCISE J: Fill in the participles:

Vulpes fame _____ petebat uvam _____.
                  (vexed)   (hanging)

Omnibus viribus _____ eam attingere non potuit.
                    (jumping)

_____ dixit: "Nolo ...."
    (leaving)

Now with relative clauses instead of participles:

Vulpes, quae fame _____, uvam petebat,
                    was vexed (Imperf.)
quae de vita alta _____. Quamquam
                    was hanging
omnibus viribus _____, eam attingere non
                  (he) jumped
potuit et dixit, dum _____: "Nolo .....
                      (he) walked away

Note the difference in the number of words needed for the two versions!

Uva maturuit

Lectio II : De Lupo et Agno (Secundum Paedrum)

Ad rivum eundem lupus et agnus venerant, siti compulsi. Superior stabat lupus, longeque inferior agnus. Tum lupus mente improbo incitatus iniuriae causam intulit: "Cur" inquit "mihi bibenti aquam fecisti turbulentem?"
Laniger contra timens dixit: "Quomodo possum, quaeso, facere, quod quereris,
5 lupe? A te decurrit ad me hausta aqua."
Repulsus ille veritatis viribus dixit: "Ante sex menses male dixisti mihi."
Respondit agnus: "Equidem natus non eram."
"Pater hercle tuus ibi" ait lupus "male dixit mihi." Atque ita correptum lacerat iniusta nece.
10 Haec fabula scripta est propter illos homines, qui fictis causis innocentes opprimunt.

(1) rivus,i - stream; eundem - (Watch out! This is not a form of eundus,a,um, - it has no form ending in -em - but a form of idem,eadem,idem - the same); compulsus,a,um - driven; sitis,is - thirst; superior, inferior - further up, further down; (2) incitare - to incite; iniuriae causam inferre - lit: to carry in the cause of harm = to start a quarrel; (4) laniger - (from lana,ae - wool, and gerere, to bear): wool-bearer; meaning the lamb; quomodo - in which way, how ?; quaeso - I beg you, 'pray'; (5) haustus,a,um - used-up; (7) equidem - not even; hercle - by Hercules! (8) correptus,a,um - the snatched one, i.e.the lamb; lacerare - to tear up; (9) nex,necis - murder; (10) fingere (fingo, finxi, fictum) - to shape, fashion, invent.

EXERCISE K: Find the infinitives of these participles, and tell what they modify in the reading above.

A. Past Participles (PPP):

Example:	from:	modifies:
compulsi	<-- compellere	lupus et agnus

1. incitatus	_____	_____
2. hausta	<-- haurire	_____
3. repulsus	_____	_____
4. natus (eram)	_____	_____
5. correptum	<-- corripere	_____
6. scripta	_____	_____
7. fictis	_____	_____

B. Present Participles:

1. bibenti	_____	_____
2. timens	_____	_____

Lectio III : Samii et Spartiatae (Erasmus)

Legatis Samiorum longa oratione auxilium petentibus Spartiatae responderunt: "Prima obliti sumus, postrema non intelleximus, quod prima non recordati sumus."

(1) legatus,i - envoy; (2) postremus,a,um - the last, latter (prima,postrema here supply perhaps: verba; intellegere (intellego, intellexi, intellectum) - to understand. Read together: Legatis Samiorum...petentibus. What case is it?

Lectio IV: De Thesauro Agricolae (Poggio Bracciolini)

Agricola morti vicinus, qui divitias non habuit pro filiis suis, excitare animos eorum voluit ad assiduum laborem. Convocavit igitur eos et ita locutus est: "Mox a vobis, filii mei, discedam; omnes, quas habeo, opes in vinea nostra vobis sunt quaerendae." Paulo post mortuus est.
5 Tum filii, quod credebant patrem in vinea thesaurum abscondisse, totam vineae humum effoderunt. Thesaurum quidem non invenerunt, sed, humo fodiendo subacta, vites uberrimos fructus tulerunt.

Thesaurus,i - treasure; (1) vicinus,a,um - close to, neighbouring (+ Dat.); divitiae,arum (Pl.) - riches; (2) assiduus,a,um - diligent, hard; (3) opes,opum - means, wealth; vinea,ae - vineyard; (5) abscondere (abscondo,abscondi,absconsum) - to hide, squirrel away; (6) humus,i (**f.**) - soil, earth; effodere (effodio,efffodi,effossum) - to dig out or up; quidem - it is true; fodiendo - by digging; humo subacta - (Ablative Absolute); (7) subigere (subigo, subegi,subactum) - to drive up from below, to work, plough; vitis,is - vine; uber,ubera,uberum - ample, generous; uberrimus: very ample.

EXERCISE L: In Lectio IV find examples of the following:

1. passive periphrastic construction: _____

2. PPP as part of the perfect of a deponent: (there are two) _____

3. Ablative Absolute: _____

4. past active infinitive: _____

5. present active infinitive: _____

Lectio V : Diabolus Servat Vineam   (Secundum C.de Heisterbach)

Anno praeterito vindemiae tempore cellarius monasterii de Lacu vineam duobus servis custodiendam commisit. Quadam nocte alter servus vigilias nocturnas omittere volens diabolum ioculariter vocavit et dixit: "Veni, diabole, custodi hanc vineam, et ego tibi praemium dabo."

5 Vix verba compleverat, et ecce diabolus affuit dicens: "Praesto sum. Quid igitur dabis mihi, si vineam custodivero?" Et ille: "Corbem uvis plenam, sed una condicione: si quis intraverit ab ea hora, qua dies et nox separantur, usque ad ortum diei, collum eius franges, neque propriam neque alienam personam excipiens." Quod diabolus promisit, et ubi servus, quasi de vinea securus, intravit in domum, cellarius illi ait: "Quare non es in vinea?" **10** Servus respondit: "Socium meum ibi reliqui," diabolum notans. Cellarius autem cogitans de altero servo iratus ait: "Vade cito, quia solus non sufficit ille."

Iit servus et speculam, quae erat extra vineam, cum socio ascendit. Circa medium noctis motum quasi hominis in vinea ambulantis audiverunt, et alter servus, qui pactum constitutum non cognovit, ait: "Aliquis est in vinea." Respondit alter: "Sede! Ego **15**.descendam et videbo." Descendit, et vineam foris circumiens vestigia hominis non repperit; ergo custodem suum, diabolum, adesse cognovit.

Mane socio pactum aperuit, et, corbem uvis plenam diabolo pro praemio dare volens, uvas iuxta vitem aliquam iecit et discessit. Et rediens paulo post cum socio ne unam quidem uvam ibi repperit.

(1) praeteritus,a,um - last, gone-by; vindemia,ae - gathering of grapes; cellarius,i - (wine) cellar master; monasterium,i de Lacu - the monastery at Maria Laach in Germany; vinea,ae - vineyard; committere - to hand over, entrust; (2) alter,altera,alterum - the other; alter...alter... - the one, the other; (3) diabolus,i - devil; ioculariter - jokingly;
(4) praemium,i - reward; (5) complere (compleo, complevi, completum) - to complete; ecce - there, look there!; praesto - at hand, ready; (6) corbis,is (f.) - wicker basket;
(7) qua - (Abl. of means) by which; ortum,i - beginning; dies,diei - day; collum,i - neck; proprius,a,um - known, acquainted; (8) excipere (<-- capere) - to except; quod = id;
(9) domus,us (f.) - house; ait - he says, he said; quare - why, for what reason; socius,i - comrade; (10) notare - to mean; (11) cito - quickly; sufficere - to be enough;
(12) specula,ae - high, vantage point; (13) motus,us - movement; (14) aliquis - some one
(15) foris - outside; vestigium,i - trace, track; (17) mane - early in the morning;
(18) ne...quidem - not even.

EXERCISE M:

List all the participles in Lectio V, and indicate whether they are present, past, or future participles, or gerundives: (Some nouns look like participles, e.g., motus, movement)

	Participle	Type
1.	_____	_____
2.	_____	_____
3.	_____	_____
4.	_____	_____
5.	_____	_____
6.	_____	_____
7.	_____	_____
8.	_____	_____
9.	_____	_____
10.	_____	_____
11.	_____	

Liberi legentes   **Libri legendi**   **Puer lecturus**

R e v i e w

1. What happened here? The adjectives seem to have gotten mixed up! Switch them and theit cases!)

Equi **alti** obliti officium cum liberis **antiquis** ad ludendum ex horto **valido** praeter casam **angustam** in viis **laetis** oppidi nostri **magni** per flumen **album** ad silvas **pulchra** cum celeritate cucurrerunt.

_____

_____

_____

2. Can you tell these words and forms apart? Translate!

a) potamus - portamus

b) iacuerunt - iecerunt

c) paravisti - paruisti

d) maneo - moneo - munio

e) partum - paratum

f) videt - vidit - videtur

g) potui - posui

h) fere - ferre

i) adfuit - afuit - adiit

j) constiterunt - constituerunt

k) bellus,a,um - bellum,i

l) cado - caedo - cedo

m) vicit - vixit

n) cepistis - coepistis

o) duci - duxi

p) audio - audeo

q) petentis - petendis

r) quaerere - queri

s) miserari - misereri

t) moror - morior

u) foedus,eris - foedus,a,um

v) secundus,a,um - secundum

w) auris - aurum

x) servo - servio

y) nex - nix - nox

z) portus - porta

3. Finish the snake! You can use nouns, verbs, adjectives, adverbs, in any form or case.
   The last letter of one word is the beginning letter of the next (In the narrrow bands)

ROMAN TECHNOLOGY

The Romans used highly sophisticated technology, some of which they took from the Etruscans or the Greeks, but much of which they perfected or developed themselves. The Romans were not as interested as the Greeks in scientific research and theory, but more in their applications. Their greatest achievements were in architecture, shipbuilding, hydraulics, heating systems, road construction, water supply construction, machine building, and weaponry.

Many of the techniques and technical apparatus presented here were described by Vitruvius in his book *De Architectura.*

Orbiculum (Pulley)
Supposedly invented by Archimedes it was used for a variety of tasks, among them spreading the huge **velarium** (sun-sail) over the spectators in the Colosseum.

Tolleno (Crane)
An early picture of a crane was found in Pompeii.

Catapulta (Catapult)
This war machine, also invented by Archimedes, was able to hurl arrows and other projectiles with great force over long distances.

Antlia (Pump)
A wheel or belt with buckets or other containers, which at the summit deposited water in a chute. It was powered by people or animals. (See title page of this chapter.)

Libella (Plum line)
This assembly was used for surveying.

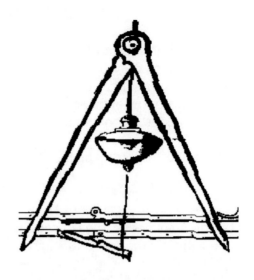

Ctesibica Machina (Hydraulic Press)
This type of machine, invented by the Alexandrinian Ctesibius, was used to power the hydraulic organ and water clocks (klepsydra), among other things. Plato is reputed to have built such a water clock, in which pipes sounded the hours by means of hydraulic air compression. Although the original treatise by Ctesibius has been lost, his system was described by several people, including Hero of Alexandria, and the Arabic scientist Muristus.

There was a cistern that was capable of holding one thousand pints of water. Within the cistern was an inverted funnel whose bottom was immersed in the water. Wind pipes, attached to air-bags or to pistons, and powered by bellows, were passed through the cistern into the funnel. When the bellows were blown the air passed through a non-return valve into the air-bag and from there into the funnel. The water within the funnel was depressed by the air and thereby forced to the outside of the funnel, where it became a stabilizer for the air pressure needed to blow the pipes of the hydraulic organ.

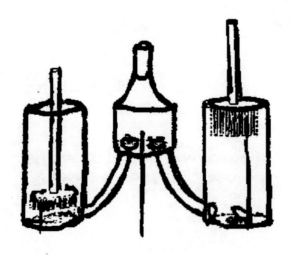

The <u>Velarium</u> or Sun-Sail of the Colosseum

The **velarium** was a huge sun-sail that provided shade for all of the approximately 50.000 spectators the Colosseum held. The mechanism is described in detail by L. B. da Maso in his book <u>Rome of the Caesars</u>.

The whole contraption centered on a big ring in the middle (which was left open, like a skylight). To this ring the ropes were attached that held up the velarium. First the ring was raised from the arena with ropes that ran through pulleys at the top of poles (3) and from the pulleys to the outside where they were attached to 160 large blocks of stone, which surrounded the Colosseum (4). Each of these blocks had a winch fastened to it (5). These 160 winches were turned in unison to the beating of time, and thus the ring was raised. Then the ends of the ropes were tied to the poles (7).

Then a second set of ropes was unfurled from each of the poles, on a lower level than the first rope (8); they were tied to each other and tightened by other pulleys and winches (10) until they reached the central ring. Altogether they formed a kind of spider-web which held up the canvas sections of the velarium. Da Maso writes:

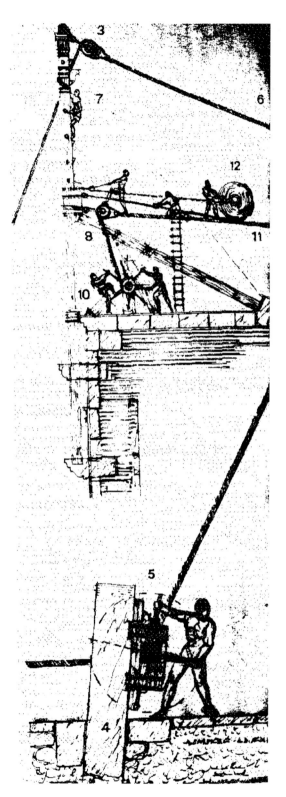

> Only sailors who were extremely expert in handling rigging were capable of carrying out such a vast and complex operation, which also required training of the greatest precision ... in measuring and placing the various parts of the velarium and the machinery...in the distribution of the men and tasks and their timing. The detachment of one hundred sailors from the fleet of Misenum, who lived in barracks near the amphitheatre, must have been employed exclusively in the maintenance of the velarium: at least a thousand others were needed to raise and lower it, and they arrived on ships twice a year either at the mouth of the Tiber or at Rome's river port. If all these requirements are taken into account, along with the enormous surface of the velarium, the huge weight of the ropes and sails and the static and dynamic problems created by resistance and tension, it must be concluded that raising the canopy was a much more difficult undertaking than erecting an obelisk.

(Rome of the Caes.,p.76. Translation M. Hollingworth)

Chapter 12 : Answers and Translations

Exercise A: (several possible translations are given for the first two examples; similar translations are possible for all examples.
1. having encouraged (**or:** one who has encouraged; after he had encouraged; although, because, when he had encouraged; etc.) 2. [having been] placed (**or:** something which has (had) been placed; after it had been placed; although/ when/ because it had been placed; etc.) 3. having lied 4. touched 5. [having been] felt 6. having used 7. because she had forgotten 8. those who had been joined 9. left behind 10. having delayed 11. what had been broken 12. the murdered man 13. having confessed 14. when they had followed 15. because it had been eaten 16. the things which have been carried on (the deeds) 17. having spoken 18. after they had been sought 19. that which was returned 20. having complained; those who had complained.

Infinitives: 1. hortari 2. ponere 3. mentiri 4. tangere 5. sentire 6. uti 7. oblivisci 8. iungere 9. relinquere 10. morari 11. frangere 12. caedere 13. confiteri 14. sequi 15. edere 16. gerere 17. loqui 18. quaerere 19. reddere 20. queri

Exercise B: (all endings nom. Sg. masc.)
1. dormiturus 2. empturus 3. venditurus 4. auditus 5. miseratus, questus 6. recordaturus 7. raptus 8. partus, natus 9. relicturus 10. iacturus 11. responsurus 12. petitus 13. aggressus 14. finiturus 15. creditus

Exercise C:
   1. The crying children were admonished by the teacher.
   2. We saw the rising sun.
   3. Barking dogs can not bite.
   4. He [to him] who has nothing, nothing is lacking.
   5. They saw a fighting soldier.
   6. While they were fighting they saw a soldier.
   7. Those who forget history must relive it.
   8. Beware of the Greeks bearing gifts. (I fear the Greeks even if they bring gifts.)
   9. For a long time we followed the animals that were fleeing through the forest.
  10. If we run quickly, we will catch you.
  11. Although he jumped with all his strength, the fox was not able to touch the grapes.

Exercise D:
   PPP = Past Participle Passive; PPDep. = Past Participle of Deponent;
   Fut.P = Future Participle; Pres.P = Present Participle; Ger. = Gerundive

1. Ger., Passive - to be greeted	2. Pres.P, Active - carrying
3. Ger., Passive - to be seen	4. Fut.P, Active - about to yield
5. PPDep., Active - having wondered	6. Ger., Passive - to be punished
7. Ger., Passive - to be guarded	8. PPP, Passive - (having been) left behind
9. PPDep., Active - having tried	10. PPDep., Active - having forgotten
11. Fut.P, Active - about to break	12. Pres.P, Active - of those who had been speaking
13. PPP, Passive - divided	14. Fut.P, Active - about to drag
15. PPP, Passive - having been paid	16. Ger., Passive - to be paid
17. Pres.P, Active - to the begging	18. Fut.P, Active - about to compel
19. PPDep., Active - having venerated	20. PPDep., Active - having remembered

Exercise E:
1. amici servandi 2. canes edentes 3. naves fractae 4. milites caesuri 5. villa vendita 6. anni recordandi 7. oppida occupata 8. imperatores ducturi 9. equi ducendi 10. mensa mota 11. naves [= Acc.!] nacti 12. oblita libros 13. pedites victi 14. ver exspectatum 15. ad iter faciendum 16. ad eas [has] res gerendas.

Exercise F:
    1. **A**   2. **C** 3. **A** 4. **C** 5. **C** 6. **A** 7. **C**
    8. **A**   9. **A** 10. **C** 11. **C** 12. **A**

Exercise G:
    1. After all buildings had been burned...
    2. While the father was standing near...
    3. A storm having arisen...
    4. When Caesar was consul...
    5. After peace had been made...
    6. Because the ships had been broken...
    7. When the boring [boredom bringing] books had been read...
    8. The very wild animals having been driven back... After the *wildest* animals had been...
    9. After these things had been decided...
    10. After the day was decided on...**or** on the decided day
    11. The leader ordered him that after all things had been explored, he should come to him.
    12. When all women and children had been removed from the city,
       the old men awaited the arrival of the Gauls.
    13. After all these things had been done, the boys considered their work to be done.
    14. When these things had been decided in such a way, those who had been
       chosen by lot departed for the interior part of the island.
    15. When all things had been prepared for the journey, they sailed off.
    16. The captured soldiers used to be led into the city holding swords in their hands.
    17. Having marched 20 miles the army attacked the camp. (**or** After a march of 20
       miles had been made...)
    18. Although the name has been changed, the story is about you.
    19. The sea being calm, the ships reached the port.
    20. When M.Messala and M.Piso were consuls, Orgetorix, led by the desire
       for power, started a conspiracy of the nobility.

Exercise H:
    1. Litteras missura est.
    2. Litterae ei mittendae sunt.
    3. Urbs nobis relinquenda est.
    4. Bellum coepturi (**or** inituri) erant.
    5. Equi ad pratum ducendi sunt.
    6. Cenam paraturus es?
    7. Opus mihi hodie conficiendum est.
    8. Villa vendenda erit.

Liber lectus

Exercise I:
1. The senators must be heard.
2. If nothing good can be said, one should be silent.
3. Parents must be obeyed by their children.
4. The Romans gave their children to Greek slaves to be educated.
5. We must not yield; our friends must be saved from danger.
6. Pyramus and Thisbe wanted to open the wall between their houses for kisses to be given.
7. Atticus gave Cicero, who was fleeing from his homeland, money.
8. He who lives in fear will not ever be free.
9. A word once sent out flies irretrievably.
10. After Asia was defeated, the Roman leader sent many slaves to Italy.
11. As for the rest (**or**: by the way) I believe that Carthage ought to be destroyed.
12. Rome has spoken, the matter is finished.
13. After these things had been decided, when he had obtained suitable weather for sailing, Caesar sailed at nearly the third hour and ordered the cavalry to proceed into the outer part and to board ships and follow him.

Reading 1 : Sour Grapes
A fox tormented by hunger sought a grape hanging from a high grapevine. Although he was jumping with all his might he could not attain it, and while leaving, he said: "I don't want this grape; it is not yet ripe." [it has not yet ripened.]

Reading 2 : The Wolf and the Lamb
The wolf and the lamb had come to the same river, compelled by thirst. The wolf stood higher up (the river), far further down, the lamb. Then the wolf, incited by his wicked mind, started a quarrel: "Why," he said, "have you made the water turbulent to me, while I am drinking?" The wool-bearer contradicted fearfully: "How, pray, can I do what you are complaining about, wolf? From you the used-up water runs down to me."
Repelled by the forces of truth, that one (the wolf) said: "Six months ago you spoke badly to me." Answered the lamb: "I had not even been born." "By Hercules," said the wolf, "then your father cursed at me." And thus he tore up the snatched (lamb) in unjust murder.
This story is written on account of those people who oppress the innocent with made-up charges (causes).

Exercise K:
1. incitatus <-- incitare   lupus
2. hausta   <-- (haurire)   aqua
3. repulsus   <-- repellere   ille
4. natus   <-- nasci   ego
5. correptum <-- (corripere)   agnum
6. scripta   <-- scribere   fabula
7. fictis   <-- fingere   causis

1. bibenti   <-- bibere   mihi
2. timens   <-- timere   laniger
(turbulens and innocens have become adjectives)

Reading 3 : The Samians and the Spartans

To the envoys of the Samians who were begging help in a long speech the Spartans responded: "The first part (of your speech) we have forgotten, the last part we did not understand, because we did not remember the first."

Reading 4 : The Farmer's Treasure

A farmer close to death, who had no wealth for his sons, wanted to excite their minds toward diligent labour. Therefore he called them together and spoke to them like this: "Soon I will leave from you, my sons; all the riches I have you must seek in our vineyard." A little later he died.

Then the sons, because they thought that their father had squirreled away a treasure in the vineyard, dug up the entire soil of the vineyard. It is true that they did not find a treasure, but since the soil had been worked thoroughly by digging, the vines bore ample fruit.

Exercise L:

1. omnes opes vobis sunt quaerendae
2. locutus est or mortuus est
3. humo fodiendo subacta
4. abscondisse
5. excitare

Reading 5 : The Devil Guards a Vineyard

Last year, at the time of the grape harvest, the cellar master of the monastery Maria Laach entrusted a vineyard to two servants to be guarded. On a certain night one of the servants, wanting to skip the nightly vigil, for a joke called the devil and said: "Come, devil, guard this vineyard, and I will give you a reward."

He had hardly completed the words, and see, there was the devil who said: "I am ready. So what are you going to give me, if I guard the vineyard?" And he [said]: "A wicker basket full of grapes, but on one condition: if anyone enters from that hour by which day and night are separated until daybreak [rise of the day], you will break his neck, excepting neither a familiar nor a strange person." The devil promised this, and when the servant, as if sure about the vineyard, entered the house, the cellar master said to him: "Why are you not in the vineyard?" The servant answered: "I left my companion there," meaning the devil. The cellar master, however, thinking about the other servant said angrily: "Go quickly, because he alone is not sufficient."

The servant went and together with his comrade ascended a vantage point, which was outside of the vineyard. Around the middle of the night they heard a movement like that of a man walking in the vineyard, and the other servant, who did not know about the pact which had been decided, said: "Someone is in the vineyyard." The other answered: "Sit down! I will go down and see." He descended, and going around the vineyard on the outside, he did not find any tracks of a person; therefore he knew his custodian, the devil, to be there.

In the morning he disclosed [opened] the pact to his comrade, and, wanting to give the devil a wicker basket full of grapes for a reward, he threw the grapes next to some vine and left. And returning a little later with his companion, he found not even one grape [left] there.

Exercise M:

1. custodiendam   Gerundive   to guard, for guarding
2. volens   Present Participle   wanting, because he wanted
3. dicens   Present Participle   etc.
4. excipiens   Present Participle
5. notans   Present Participle
6. cogitans   Present Participle
7. ambulantis   Present Participle (Gen.)
8. constitutum   PPP
9. circumiens   Present Participle
10. volens   Present Participle
11. rediens   Present Participle

Review:

1. Equi validi obliti officium cum liberis laetis
ad ludendum ex horto pulchro praeter casam
albam in viis angustis oppidi nostri antiqui
per flumen altum ad silvas magna cum
celeritate cucurrerunt.

2. a) we drink - we carry; b) they lay - they threw;
c) you prepared - you obeyed;
d) I remain - I warn - I build; e) born - prepared;
f) she sees - she saw - it seems;
g) I was able - I have put;
h) almost - to bring, carry; i) he was present - he was away - he went toward; j) they came
to a halt - they decided; k) pretty - war; l) I am falling - I am felling, killing - I am ceding;
m) he conquered - he lived; n) you took - you began (Pl); o) to be led - I have led
p) I hear - I dare; q) seeking (gen. Sg. of PPA) - to the ones to be sought (dat. or abl. Pl.
of gerundive); r) to ask - to complain; s) to lament - to pity; t) I am delaying - I am dying;
u) treaty - ugly; v) the second, favorable - according to; w) ear - gold; x) I save - I serve;
y) murder - snow - night; z) harbor - gate.

3. Example:
cap**u**t - **t**ime**t** - **t**empu**s** - **s**alu**s** - **s**eder**e** - **e**disti - **i**tiner**a** - **a**nima**l** - **l**up**o** - **o**men (et cetera, et
cetera...)

13

NOUNS: 4TH AND 5TH DECLENSIONS

ENGLISH AND LATIN 2

Before the Angles and Saxons migrated from Scandinavia, they and other Germanic tribes had come into contact with merchants from Italy, mostly in the Rhine area, and with Roman traders, who ventured to their lands to offer them goods such as foods which they could not grow themselves, spices, exotic materials for making clothes, and jewelry. The activities of these traders are attested to by Caesar, who, as a military man, considered them a mixed blessing. In his **Commentarii de Bello Gallico** he wrote of the Belgian tribe that they were the bravest of all, "because they are the furthest removed from the sophistication and highly civilized lifestyle of the Roman provinces, and they only seldom meet traders, who would offer them goods leading to a decadent lifestyle."

But most people were, of course, desirous of new things, and there was then a need for new words to fit the new objects and ideas. These words were taken from Latin. Examples of these early borrowings (in their modern English form) are *wine* (from **vinum**), *cheese* (**caseus**), *plum* (**prunum**), *butter* (**butyrum**), *kettle* (**catinus** or **catillus**), *gem* (**gemma**). Christianity was introduced also, but met with a lukewarm reception. Nevertheless some words were retained early on, though they had mostly been taken from Greek, like *bishop* and *church* (**episcopus, kyriake**)

The Romans had been ruling Britain since 43 B.C., driving back or subjugating the Celts, whom they had found there. But contrary to the development in Gaul and Spain, where the Roman conquerors imposed their language, Latin did not become the language of Britain. Instead people continued to speak Celtic. Moreover, a number of tribes were never conquered; they had merely retreated to Scotland and Wales, whence they kept attacking the Roman forces. In addition, the Angles and Saxons raided the eastern coast of Britain with increasing frequency. By the 4th century the bulk of the Roman legions had to be deployed elsewhere in the Empire, and in 410 A.D. the last Roman ruler left Britain.

According to the Venerable Bede, an 8th century historian, in 449 the Celtic king Vortigern called on the Jutes, from Jutland (today´s southern Denmark) to help him fight the Picts. The Jutes never returned to the continent, but settled in England, as did the Angles and Saxons. Over the next one hundred years the Celts were driven back or killed,   and a Germanic language, English, established itself in Britain.

Chapter 13:   NOUNS : FOURTH AND FIFTH DECLENSION

Compared to the first, second, and especially the third declensions, the fourth declension has few nouns, and the fifth declension only a handful.

Nouns of the fourth or u-declension, end in -us, as does their genitive. (The **-u-** is short in the nominative, and long in the genitive.) Most nouns of the fourth declension are **masculine**.

Example: **portus,portus,** *harbor*

	Sg	Pl
N	port**us**	port**us**
G	port**us**	port**uum**
D	port**ui**	port**ibus**
A	port**um**	port**us**
Ab	port**u**	port**ibus**

The characteristic **-u-** appears in all cases except the dative and ablative Plural.

By now you know nouns ending in **-us** (Nom.) in three declensions: second, third, and fourth.
To decide in which Declension they belong, you must look at the Genitive.
    2nd Declension: -us,   Genitive: **-i**   amicus, amic**i**
    4th Declension: -us,   Genitive: **-us**   manus, man**us**
    3rd Declension: -us,   Genitive: anybody's guess: -utis, -udis, -oris, -eris, etc. ,
                   but always with the ending -is (only in the third Declension)

EXERCISE A: Give the **declension** of each noun (2, 3, or 4)

1. manus,-us   ____   2. litus,-oris   ____

3. casus,-us   ____   4. captivus,-i   ____

5. exercitus,-us   ____   6. nervus,-i   ____

7. genus,-eris   ____   8. vulnus,-eris   ____

9. virtus,-tutis   ____   10. murus,-i   ____

11. mus,muris   ____   12. habitus,-us   ____

13. adventus,-us   ____   14. socius,-i   ____

15. passus,-us   ____   16. onus,-eris   ____

The noun **domus** (feminine), 4th declension, forms some cases according to the 2nd Declension:

	Sg.		Pl.	
N	domus	pulchra	domus	pulchrae
G	domus	pulchrae	domuum	pulchrarum
			(or dom**orum**)	
D	domui	pulchrae	domibus	pulchris
A	domum	pulchram	dom**os**	pulchras
			(or domus)	
Ab	dom**o**	pulchra	domibus	pulchris

Neuter:
cornu,us   *horn*

	Sg		Pl	
N	corn**u**	clarum	corn**ua**	clara
G	corn**us**	clari	corn**uum**	clarorum
D	corn**u**	claro	corn**ibus**	claris
A	corn**u**	clarum	corn**ua**	clara
Ab	corn**u**	claro	corn**ibus**	claris

Domus pulchrae
dearum et deorum

Vocabulary:

Masculine

1. **adventus,us**	arrival	**advent**
2. **aestus,us**	heat, ocean tide	**estuary**
3. **aquaeductus,us**	water supply, aqueduct	*
4. **arcus,us**	bow	**arc,arcade**
5. **aspectus,us**	sight, appearance	**aspect**
6. **casus,us**	case	*
7. **consulatus,us**	consulate, office of the consul	*
8. **conventus,us**	gathering	**convention**
9. **cursus,us**	run, race	**course**
10. **equitatus,us**	cavalry	
11. **eventus,us**	result, event	*
12. **exercitus,us**	army	**exercise**
13. **fructus,us**	fruit	*
14. **gradus,us**	step, rank	**grade**
15. **habitus,us**	appearance, dress	**habit**
16. **ictus,us**	blow, hit	
17. **impetus,us**	attack, impetus	
18. **iussus,us**	order	**iussive**
19. **lacus,us**	lake	*
20. **magistratus,us**	magistrate	*
21. **metus,us**	fear	
22. **motus,us**	movement, excitement	**motion**
23. **passus,us**	step, foot (measure)	**passage**
24. **portus,us**	harbour	**port**
25. **quietus,us**	rest, sleep	**quiet**
26. **saltus,us**	jump	**somersault**
27. **senatus,us**	senate	*
28. **sensus,us**	sense, feeling	*
29. **sinus,us**	bay,curve,bosom	**sine,cosine**
30. **situs,us**	location	**site**
31. **spiritus,us**	spirit, ghost	*
32. **strepitus,us**	noise	**obstreperous**
33. **tumultus,us**	uprising, unrest	**tumultuous**
34. **usus,us**	use	*
35. **versus,us**	verse	*
36. **victus,us**	life support, life style	**victuals**
37. **vultus.us**	face	

Feminine

38. **domus,us**	house	**domesticate**
39. **manus,us**	hand; band of men	**manual**
40. **porticus,us**	colonnade, arcade	**portico**
41. **quercus,us**	oak tree	**quercine**
42. **Idus,uum (Pl.)**	Ides of a month	*

EXERCISE B: Fourth Declension Nouns: Translate these phrases!

1. adventus Dei _____   2. tempus adventus patris _____

3. casus belli _____   4. cursus pedum _____

5. impetus peditum equitatusque _____

6. duo milia passuum (mille passus = one mile) _____

7. quindecim portus _____

8. Senatus Populusque Romanus (SPQR) _____

9. vultu laeto _____

10. patri et filio et spiritui sancto _____

11. metus mortis _____   12. uno ictu _____

13. habitus senatoris _____   14. iussu imperatoris _____

15. tumultus in casa _____   16. fructus laboris _____

17. aestus aestatis _____   18. Lacus Lemannus_____

19. Quercus Germanis sacra erat. _____

20. Multi aquaeductus ab Romanis aedificati sunt. _____

21. Poetae versus faciunt. _____

22. Magno strepitu anseres Capitolium servaverunt. _____

23. Libri mihi usui sunt. _____

24. Magno saltu gallus territus vulpem fugere conatus est.

_____

25. Incolae improbi provinciae adventum magistratuum metu exspectabant.

_____

26. Manus manum lavat. _____

There are also some fourth declension nouns derived from the verb **ire**; their meaning corresponds to the meaning of the verb. Can you guess:

> **interitus,us -**
> **obitus,us (obituary) -**
> **exitus,us -**
> **aditus,us -**
> **abitus,us -**
> **transitus,us -**
> **initus,us (also: initium,i - beginning)**

EXERCISE C: Say in Latin:

1. We had a sense of disaster. _____

2. Can't we have (some) rest? Must we suffer the noise and uproar?

_____

3. My friend walked with me (for) five miles because of my fear.

_____

4. Have you found out the names of the ports of Italy?

_____

5. There was a gathering of the animals, in which the lion declared himself to be king.

_____

6. The result of the long war was the same as it always is: many attacks, many dead, many wounds, much fear.

_____

7. Who ordered the aqueducts in Italy to be built? Many were put there by the order of the emperors.

_____

8. In the heat of the summer we cultivated our fields; in the winter we will eat the fruits of our labour.

_____

(1) disaster = harm, misfortune;
(5) use **dicere** for *declare*; translate the rest literally, with *king* in the accusative: you have actually got an indirect statement here!
(6) *as* = ut;
(7) to be built: passive infinitive present;
(8) *in the heat, in the winter*: use no preposition, just Ablative.

Eventus pugnae: multi vulnerati, multae lacrimae

The Fifth Declension

The fifth is also called the **e-declension**. With the exception of **dies** and its conpound **meridies**, which are masculine, all its nouns are **feminine**. The declension goes as follows:

dies festus, *the feast day*

	Sg.			Pl.	
N	di **es**	festus	di **es**	festi
G	di **ei**	festi	di **erum**	festorum
D	di **ei**	festo	di **ebus**	festis
A	di **em**	festum	di **es**	festos
Ab	di **e**	festo	di **ebus**	festis

res nova, *new thing, news*

	Sg		Pl	
N	**res**	nova	**res**	novae
G	**rei**	novae	**rerum**	novarum
D	**rei**	novae	**rebus**	novis
A	**rem**	novam	**res**	novas
Ab	**re**	nova	**rebus**	novis

Vocabulary:

1. **dies,diei (m.)**	day	**diary**
2. **meridies,meridiei (m.)**	Midday,south	**meridian**
3. **res,rei**	thing,matter	**reality**
4. **spes,spei**	hope	**despair**
5. **fides,fidei**	faith, belief	**fidelity**
6. **acies,aciei**	battle line	
7. **pernicies,perniciei**	destruction,downfall	**pernicious**
8. **facies,faciei**	appearance,face,figure	*****
9. **species,speciei**	sight,figure,appearance	**species**

As similar as they look, the English word "day" is not derived from **dies**, but rather from the Anglo-Saxon **dag. Dies** in turn is related to (the goddess) **Diana**.

Meridies is used in English: **a.m.**, ante meridiem, and **p.m.**, post meridiem.

EXERCISE D: In the space before each noun in column A, write the letter of its form from column B:

A   B

____ 1. specie   a. Genitive Singular

____ 2. passuum   b. Dative or Ablative Plural

____ 3. portam   c. Nominative Singular

____ 4. periculi   d. Genitive Plural

____ 5. hortos   e. Nominative or Accusative Plural

____ 6. potestati   f. Ablative Singular

____ 7. rebus   g. Vocative Singular

____ 8. capita   h. Dative Singular

____ 9. domine   i. Accusative Plural

____ 10. multitudo   j. Dative or Ablative Singular

____ 11. amico   k. Accusative Singular

EXERCISE E: Give the following forms:

1. Abl. Sg. of **iter**: _____

2. Nom. Pl. of **tempus**: _____

3. Abl. Pl. of **res**: _____

4. Gen. Sg. of **salus**: _____

5. Dat. Sg. of **urbs**: _____

6. Acc. Sg. of **vis**: _____

7. Gen. Pl. of **vir**: _____

8. Gen. Pl. of **vis**: _____

9. Acc. Pl. of **manus**: _____

10. Dat. Pl. of **miles**: _____

11. Abl. Sg. of **causa**: _____

12. Nom. Pl. of **dies**: _____

13. Acc. Sg. of **flumen**: _____

14. Acc. Sg. of **liber** (book): _____

15. Acc. Pl. of **nomen**: _____

16. Acc. Sg. of **civitas**: _____

17. Abl. Pl. of **avus**: _____

18. Dat. Sg. of **avis**: _____

19. Acc. Pl. of **pes**: _____

20. Acc. Pl. of **pedes**: _____

Feles Romana parva sub arcu Romano

Lectio : Fabula de Pyramo et Thisbe (secundum Ovidium)
This prose version of Pyramus and Thisbe stays very close to Ovids original, which is in Hexameters. The set off lines are quotes from Ovid's original.

Pyramus et Thisbe, alter iuvenis pulcher, altera puella praelata, quas oriens habuit, tenuerunt domos contiguas in urbe, ubi Semiramis dicitur muros et hortos munivisse. Cognoscebant alter alteram; tempore crevit amor. Nubere voluerunt, sed patres vetuerunt. Quod non vetare potuerunt: ambo ardebant
5 amore. Publice loqui non permittebantur; sed paries intra duas domos fissa erat. Amantes fissum invenerunt et iter vocis fecerunt. Ibi eorum verba transire solebant.

Sed amantes laeti non erant. Ubi steterunt hinc Thisbe, Pyramus illinc, dicebant: "Invide paries, quid amantibus obstas? Cur non sinis nos toto
10 corpore iungi, aut, hoc si nimium, cur non pates ad oscula danda? Neque sumus ingrati; debemus tibi gratias, quod verbis nostris dedisti transitum ad aures amicas." Talia locuti de situ diverso dixerunt "Vale" et oscula tacita non pervenientia quisque dedit.

> Postera nocturnos aurora removerat ignes,
15 > solque pruinosas radiis siccaverat herbas

Coierunt ad solitum locum. Primo multum questi sunt de condicione sua, tum constituerunt: "Fallemus custodes et excedemus ex urbe." Conventuri erant ad statuam Nini sub arbore, quae stabat prope fontem. Haec arbor, plena niveis pomis, erat morus.

20 > Pacta placent; et lux, tarde discedere visa,
> praecipitatur aquis, et aquis nox exit ab isdem.

---

(1) praelatus,a,um - loveliest, most preferred (from praeferre); (2) contiguus,a,um - adjoining; urbe - the city is Babylon, founded by Ninus, where Queen Semiramis had the Hanging Gardens built, one of the seven wonders of the ancient world; (3) nubere - to marry; (4) vetare, (veto, vetui) - to forbid; ardere - to burn; (6) findo, (fidi, fissum) - to split, crack; fissum,i - crack; (9) invidus,a,um - hateful; quid - why? sinere - to allow;
(10) patére - to stand, lie open; osculum,i - kiss; (12) diversus,a,um - different, separate;
(14) (two of the original Hexameter verses) posterus,a,um - next; aurora,ae - dawn;
(15) pruinosus,a,um - dewy; siccare - to dry; radius,i - ray; (17) fallere - to deceive;
(18) niveus,a,um - snow-white; (19) pomum,i - fruit; morus,i (f.) - mulberry tree; (20) tarde - late; (21) praecipitatur aquis - sinks into the water; isdem = eisdem: ab eisdem aquis

Nocte Thisbe exiit ex domo, fefellit suos, pervenit ad statuam et sedit sub arbore dicta. Amor faciebat eam audacem. Venit autem leo ore cruentato, qui occiderat bovem, depositurus sitim in aqua fontis. Thisbe eum vidit ad radios
25 lunae et timens fugit in antrum obscurum; dumque fugit, velamina reliquit. Leo ferus rediens de fonte ea invenit et laniavit ore cruentato.

Post puellam egressus, Pyramus ad locum dictum venit et ibi vestigia leonis feri vidit. Tum velamina quoque tincta sanguine repperit, sed puellam non videre potuit. Nimis territus se ipsum accusavit.
30 "Una nox", inquit, "perdet duos amantes, e quibus illa fuit digna longa vita. Est mea culpa, mea anima est nocens, ego te, miseranda, delevi. Ego non veni huc prior, sed iussi te venire in loca plena metu. Venite, leones, et divellite meum corpus;
et scelerata fero consumite viscera morsu!

35 Sed timidi est solum mortem desiderare." His verbis velamina Thisbes sustulit et secum portavit ad arborem. Ut oscula et lacrimas dedit vesti notae, gladium strinxit et dixit: "Accipe nunc quoque meum sanguinem!"

Quoque erat accinctus, demisit in ilia ferrum.

Tum moriens ferrum traxit ex vulnere Pyramus et iacuit humi. Sanguis saluit
40 alte et tinxit muri pendentia poma nivea purpureo colore.

Tum Thisbe exiit ex antro, quod amatum iuvenem fallere non voluit. Pyramum quaesivit ad narranda pericula, quae vitaverat. Ubi eum fere mortuum repperit, flere coepit, corpus amatum tenuit et clamavit: "Pyrame, quis te mihi cepit? Pyrame, responde! Tua cara Thisbe te vocat. Audi et aperi oculos
45 clausos!" Audiens nomen Thisbes Pyramus oculos morte gravatos aperuit, visaque illa eos recondidit et mortuus est.

(23) audax,audacis - bold (here Accusative); cruentatus,a,um - bloody; (24) deponere sitim - to quench one's thirst; (25) antrum,i - cave; obscurus,a,um - dark; velamen,inis -veil;
(26) ea (velamina); laniare - to tear up; (27) vestigium,i - track; (28) tingere (tingo, tinxi, tinctum) - to dye; (29) nimis - too much; accusare - to accuse; (30) dignus,a,um - worthy (with Ablative); (31) culpa,ae - fault; nocens - harmful; (32) prior - earlier; divellere - to tear up; (34) 'And consume my guilty flesh with your fierce bite!' (35) timidi est - it is (the part) of a coward; desiderare - to desire; (37) gladium stringere - to draw one's sword; (38) quoque = et quo - and with which (sword); accinctus - girded; ferrum - here: sword; 'And he rammed the sword with which he was girded into his entrails'; (39) humi - on the ground;
(40) pendere (pendeo, pependi) - to hang down; purpureus,a,um - purple; color,-oris - color;
(42) vitare - to avoid; (45) Thisbes - (Genitive of Thisbe); gravare - to weigh down;
(46) recondidit - he closed them again.

Postquam Thisbe velamina sua cognovit et gladium rubrum sanguine vidit, "Tua manus", inquit, "et amor te perdidit, infelix. Mihi quoque est manus valida, mihi est amor. Hic dabit vires in vulnera. Sequar te mortuum, et dicar
50 esse causa et comes mortis tuae." Tum parentibus locuta est:

"Hoc tamen amborum verbis estote rogati,
O multum miseri, meus illiusque parentes,
ut quos certus amor, quos hora novissima iunxit,
componi tumulo non invideatis eodem."

55 Tum locuta est arbori: "Tu, arbor, quae tegis miserabile corpus unius amantis, et quae mox tectura es corpora duorum, tene signum caedis et semper habe poma atra, pro memoria geminae mortis." Dixit, et aptato gladio sub pectus incubuit ferro, quod adhuc tepidum erat a caede.

Vota tamen tetigere deos, tetigere parentes;
60 nam color in pomo est, ubi permaturuit, ater,
quodque rogis superest, una requiescit in urna.

(47) postquam - after; (48) infelix - unhappy (one); mihi est - I have; (49) hic = amor; in vulnera - for wounds; (51) estote rogati - be asked; (53) ut ... non invideatis - that you may not begrudge; quos = eos, quos; novissimus,a,um - most recent; (54) tumulus,i -grave. (55) tegere (tego, texi, tectum) - to cover; (57) ater,atra,atrum - dark, black; gemi-nus,a,um - twin; aptare - to adjust; (58) incubuit here: she threw herself; tepidus,a,um -warm; (59) votum,i - vow; tetigere - (the ending -ere is often used instead of -erunt (Perfect), especially in poetry; (60) permaturescere, (permaturui) - to ripen; (61) rogis - from the funeral-pyres; requiescere - to rest; urna,ae - urn.

The Castel di Angelo in Rome was the tomb of Emperor Hadrian

A: Fill in the blanks:

1. The gender of most nouns of the fifth (-e) declension is _____.

2. The ending **-us** occurs _____ times in the fourth declension.

3. The gender of most nouns of the fourth (-u) declension is _____.

4. The **M.** in **a.m.** and **p.m.** stands for _____.

5. **Quercine** refers to an _____ _____.

6. The letters **SPQR** stood for _____.

B: Do not confuse:

portus - porta; aestus - aestas; casus - casa; dies - deus - diu.

William Shakespeare: A Midsummer Night's Dream

(Act I, Scene 2)   (In this scene a group of traveling actors prepares for a performance at the Duke's court, that is, the spectators Theseus and Demetrios, and others.)

Bottom: First, good Peter Quince, say what the play treats on; then read the names of the actors; and so grow to a point.

Quince: Marry, our play is, "The most lamentable comedy, and most cruel death of Pyramus and Thisby."

Bottom: A very good piece of work, I assure you, and a merry. Now, good Peter Quince, call forth your actors by the scroll. Masters, spread yourselves.

Quince: Answer as I call you. Nick Bottom, the weaver.

Bottom: Ready. Name what part I am for, and proceed.

Quince: You, Nick Bottom, are set down for Pyramus.

Bottom: What is Pyramus? A lover, or a tyrant?

Quince: A lover that kills himself, most gallant, for love.

Bottom: That will ask some tears in the true performing of it: if I do it, let the audience look to their eyes...

Quince: Francis Flute, the bellows mender.

Flute: Here, Peter Quince.

Quince: Flute, you must take Thisby on you.

Flute: What is Thisby? A wandring knight?

Quince: It is the lady that Pyramus must love.

Flute: Nay, faith, let not me play a woman. I have a beard coming.

Quince: That's all one. You shall play it in a mask, and you may speak as small as you will.

Bottom: An (if) I may hide my face, let me play Thisby too. I'll speak in a monstrous little voice, "Thisne, Thisne!" "Ah Pyramus, my lover dear! Thy Thisby dear, and lady dear!"

Quince: No, no; you must play Pyramus: and, Flute, you Thisby.

Bottom: Well, proceed.   (...)

Quince: ... Snug, the joiner; you, the lion's part. And I hope here is a play fitted.

Snug: Have you the lion's part written? Pray you, if it be, give it to me, for I am slow of study.

Quince: You may do it extempore, for it is nothing but roaring.

Bottom: Let me play the lion too. I will roar that I will do any man's heart good to hear me. I will roar, that I will make the Duke say, "Let him roar again, let him roar again."

Quince: And you should do it too terribly, you would fright the Duchess and the ladies, that they would shriek; and that were enough to hang us all.

All: That would hang us, every mother's son.

Bottom: I grant you, friends, if you should fright the ladies out of their wits, they would have no more discretion but to hang us: but I will aggravate my voice so that I will roar you as gently as any sucking dove; I will roar you an 'twere any nightingale.

Quince: You can play no part but Pyramus; for Pyramus is a sweet-faced man; a proper man as one shall see in a summer's day; a most lovely, gentlemanlike man; therefore you must needs play Pyramus.

(Act III, Scene 1)

Bottom: There are things in this comedy of Pyramus and Thisby that will never please. First, Pyramus must draw a sword to kill himself; which the ladies cannot abide. How answer you that?

Snout: By'r lakin, a parlous fear.

Starveling: I believe we must leave the killing out, when all is done.

Bottom: Not a whit. I have a device to make all well. Write me a prologue, and let the prologue seem to say, we will do no harm with our swords, and that Pyramus is not killed indeed; and for the more better assurance, tell them that I Pyramus am not Pyramus, but Bottom the weaver. This will put them out of fear.

Quince: Well, we will have such a prologue...

Snout: Will not the ladies be afeared of the lion?

Starveling: I fear it, I promise you.

Bottom: Masters, you ought to consider with yourselves. To bring in - God shield us! - a lion among ladies, is a most dreadful thing. For there is not a more fearful wild fowl than your lion living; and we ought to look to't.

Snout: Therefore another prologue must tell he is not a lion...

Quince: Well, it shall be so. But there is two hard things; that is, to bring the moonlight into a chamber; for you know, Pyramus and Thisby meet by moonlight...Then there is another thing: we must have a wall in the great chamber; for Pyramus and Thisby, says the story, did talk through the chink of a wall...

Bottom: Some man or other must present Wall...

        . . . .   Act V, Scene 1

Wall: In this same interlude it doth befall
That I, one Snout by name, present a wall;
And such a wall, as I would have you think,
That had in it a crannied hole or chink,
Through which the lovers, Pyramus and Thisby,
Did whisper often very secretly.
This loam, this roughcast, and this stone, doth show
That I am that same wall; the truth is so;
And this the cranny is, right and sinister,
Through which the fearful lovers are to whisper...

Lion: You, ladies, you, whose gentle hearts do fear
The smallest monstrous mouse that creeps on floor,
May now perchance both quake and tremble here,
When lion rough in wildest rage doth roar.
Then know that I, as Snug the joiner, am
A lion fell, nor else nor lion's dam;
For, if I should as lion come in strife
Into this place, 'twere pity on my life.

     Theseus: A very gentle beast, and of good conscience...   [*Enter Thisby.*]

Thisby: This is old Ninny's tomb. Where is my love?

Lion: Oh -   [*The lion roars. Thisby runs off.*]

     Demetrius: Well roared, Lion.
     Theseus: Well run, Thisby. ..   [*The lion shakes Thisby's mantle, and exit.*]
     Theseus: Well moused, lion.   .

From:The complete works of William Shakespeare, Nelson and Sons, London 1925

Funeral Rites

Roman religions did not have much of an afterlife concept, except the mythological ideas taken over from the Greeks. But they developed a number of funeral rites and practices, which somehow assumed that the dead were resting in their graves or still walking among the living, albeit in disembodied form. When people died, there were a number of customary steps to follow: first they were called by their name; then washed, dressed nicely, and perfumed; then they lay in state in the atrium of the house for several days. The outside of the house was hung with pine branches, to show the family's bereavement. Before the funeral a small coin, an **obolus**, was put into the dead person's mouth, with which to pay the ferry-man who ferried the dead over the river **Styx** to the underworld, to **Hades**.

People could not be buried within the city walls, so grave sites were located along the big roads leading to and from Rome, like the **Via Appia**. Bodies were more often cremated than buried, together with some of their belongings; then the urns with the ashes were stored in a **columbarium** (which actually means *pigeon coop*). Poor people were often put into mass graves, and to prevent this indignity many people joined funeral clubs, which would take care of appropriate burials. Wealthy people had elaborate grave sites with big monuments, or mausoleums. Probably the largest of these is the Mausoleum of the Emperor Hadrian, today's **Castel di Angelo**, in Rome. In later times sarcophagi became quite common. These stone tombs were adorned not only on the outside with commemorative reliefs and likenesses, but also on the inside with replicas of furniture and household items, again pointing to the belief that the dead stayed there for some time to come and wanted to be among their familiar and comfortable things. During feast days food was sacrificed and put near the graves, as a symbolic gesture.

The interior of a sarcophagus with (stone) replicas of furnishings.

Famous persons had a long procession of people accompanying them to their burial site, often by way of the Forum, where a eulogy was held. Shakespeare has **Marc Antony** give such a funeral speech in his ***Julius Caesar***, (III,2) a speech that was, however, not without hidden malice and attacks on Caesar's murderers:

> Friends, Romans, countrymen, lend me your ears.
> I come to bury Caesar, not to praise him.
> The evil that men do, lives after them,
> The good is oft interred with their bones;
> So let it be with Caesar. The noble Brutus
> Hath told you Caesar was ambitious;
> If it were so, it was a grievous fault,
> And grievously hath Caesar answered it.
> Here, under leave of Brutus, and the rest - For Brutus is an honourable man,
> So are they all, all honourable men -
> Come I to speak at Caesar's funeral.
> He was my friend, faithful, and just to me;
> But Brutus says, he was ambitious, And Brutus is an honourable man. . .
> You all did see, that on the Lupercal
> I thrice presented him a kingly crown,
> Which he did thrice refuse. Was this ambition?
> Yet Brutus says, he was ambitious; And sure he is an honourable man.
> I speak not to disprove what Brutus spoke,
> But here I am to speak what I do know;
> You all did love him once, not without cause,
> What cause withholds you then to mourn for him?
> O judgment, thou art fled to brutish beasts,
> And men have lost their reason. Bear with me;
> My heart is in the coffin here with Caesar,
> And I must pause, till it come back to me. . .
> If you have tears, prepare to shed them now.
> You all do know this mantle, I remember
> The first time Caesar put it on. . .
> Look, in that place ran Cassius' dagger through.
> See what a rent the envious Casca made.
> Through this the well-beloved Brutus stabbed. . .
> For Brutus, as you know, was Caesar's angel.
> Judge, o you gods, how dearly Caesar loved him.
> This was the most unkindest cut of all;
> For when the noble Caesar saw him stab,
> Ingratitude, more strong than traitor's arms,
> Quite vanquished him. Then burst his mighty heart. . .

Soliloquies and Speeches from the Plays of William Shakespeare, The Peter Pauper Press, Mount Vernon 1960

Many Romans memorialized their relatives and friends in more or less heartfelt sentiments inscribed on gravestones. Here are some examples:

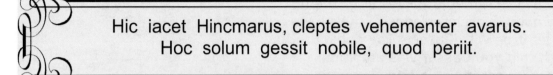

Hic iacet Hincmarus, cleptes vehementer avarus.
Hoc solum gessit nobile, quod periit.

Here lies Hincmarus, a mighty greedy thief.
His only noble act was that he died.
(Johannes Scotus Eriugena)

**Positus est hic Leburna magister mimariorum,
qui vixit annos plus minus centum.
Aliquotiens mortuus sum, sed sic numquam.**

Here was placed Leburna, the master of mimes,
who lived more or less one-hundred years.
Many a times I have died, but never like this.
(from Yugoslavia)

OLV   AN   XII
ET   FVSCINVS   AN
XVI   FVSCI   FILI
HIC   SITI   SUNT

[Olus Annorum XII et Fuscinus Annorum XVI Fusci Filii Hic Siti Sunt.]
Olus, age 12, and Fuscinus, age 16, the sons of Fuscus, are buried here.
Olus, "cabbage head," and Fuscinus, "the little dark one," were typical slave names..
(This inscription was found in Augst, Switzerland.)

The following inscription for a wealthy Roman woman was written in the somewhat archaic Latin of the 2nd Century BC

> Hospes, quod deico paullum est. Asta ac pellege:
> Heic est sepulcrum hau pulcrum pulcrai feminae.
> Nomen parentes nominarunt Claudiam.
> Suom mareitum corde deilexit suo.
> Gnatos duos creavit, horunc alterum
> in terra linquit, alium sub terra locat.
> Sermone lepido tum autem incessu commodo.
> Domum servavit, lanam fecit. Dixi. Abei!

> Stranger, what I say is short. Stay and read it through:
> Here is the not very beautiful grave of a beautiful woman.
> Her parents named her with the name Claudia.
> Her husband she loved from her heart.
> Two sons she has born, of whom the one
> she leaves on the earth, the other one she has placed under the earth.
> She was of gracious speech and decorous demeanour.
> She kept the house, she spun wool. I have spoken. Go away!

Tombstone for a small girl. She is shown with her doll, her favorite clothes, and her pet goose.

And finally this terse statement made by an obviously relieved husband:

> IACET
>
> TACET
>
> PLACET

FUNERAL SITES

The Pyramid of Cestius in Rome

A family's tomb
with scenes from their lives

Chapter 13: Answers and Translations

Exercise A:
1. (4) 2. (3) 3. (4) 4. (2) 5. (4) 6. (2) 7. (3) 8. (3) 9. (3)
10. (2) 11. (3) 12. (4) 13. (4) 14. (2) 15. (4) 16. (3)

Exercise B:
1. the arrival of God (Advent) 2. the time of father's arrival 3. a case of war 4. a foot race 5. an attack of infantry and cavalry 6. two miles 7. fifteen harbors 8. The Senate and the People of Rome 9. with a happy face 10. to the Father and to the Son and to the Holy Ghost 11. fear of death 12. with one blow 13. senatorial dress 14. by the order of the general 15. uproar in the house 16. the fruits of hard work 17. the heat of summer 18. Lake Geneva 19. The oak tree was sacred to the Germans. 20. Many aqueducts were built by the Romans. 21. Poets make verses. 22. With great noise the geese saved the Capitol. 23. The books are of use to me. 24. With a big jump the terrified rooster tried to escape the fox. 25. The wicked inhabitants of the province awaited the arrival of the magistrates with fear. 26. One hand washes the other.

Exercise C:
1.Sensum calamitatis habuimus. 2.Nonne quietum habere possumus? Nobisne strepitus tumultusque patiendi sunt? 3. Amicus meus mecum quinque milia passuum ambulavit propter metum meum. 4. Cognovisti nomina portuum Italiae? 5. Erat conventus animalium, in quo leo dixit se esse regem. 6. Eventus belli longi erat idem ut semper est: multi impetus, multi mortui, multa vulnera, multus metus. 7. Quis aquaeductus in Italia muniri imperavit? Multi ibi positi sunt iussu imperatorum. 8. Aestu aestatis agros nostros colebamus; hieme fructus laboris nostri edemus.

Exercise D:
1. f 2. d 3. k 4. a 5. i 6. h 7. b 8. e 9. g 10. c 11. j

Exercise E:
1. itinere 2. tempora 3. rebus 4. salutis 5. urbi 6. vim 7. virorum 8. virium 9. manus
10. militibus 11. causa 12. dies 13. flumen 14. librum 15. nomina 16. civitatem
17. avis 18. avi 19. pedes 20. pedites

Reading : Pyramus and Thisbe
Pyramus and Thisbe, the one a beautiful young man, the other the loveliest girl which the Orient had, held adjoining houses in the city, where Semiramis is said to have built walls and gardens. They knew each other; their love grew with time. They wanted to marry, but their fathers forbade it. What they could not forbid: both of them burned with love. They were not allowed to speak (to each other) in public; but the wall between the two houses was cracked. The lovers found the crack and made a passage for their voices. In this place their words used to go across.

But the lovers were not happy. When they stood, here Thisbe, there Pyramus, they said: "Hateful wall, why do you stand in the way of the lovers? Why do you not allow us to be joined with our whole body, or, if this is too much, why are you not open so that we can give each other kisses? (for kisses to be given) Neither are we ungrateful: we owe you thanks, because you have given our words a passage to friendly ears." Having spoken such things from their separate places they said "Farewell," and each gave silent kisses, which did not pass through.

> The next dawn had removed the nightly fires,
> and the sun with its rays dried the dewy grass.

They came together to the accustomed place. First they complained much about their condition, then they decided: "We will deceive our custodians and go away from the city." They were going to meet at the statue of Ninus under a tree, which stood close to a spring. The tree there, full of snow-white fruit, was a mulberry tree.

> The pact pleased them; and the light, seeming to leave late,
>
> sank into the water, and from the same waters rose the night. (actually Present Tense)

At night Thisbe went out of her house, deceived her family, came to the statue and sat under the appointed tree. Love made her bold. There came, however, a lion with a bloody mouth, who had killed an ox, about to quench his thirst in the water of the spring. Thisbe saw him by the rays of the moon and fearfully fled into a dark cave; while she fled, she left behind her veil. The wild lion returning from the spring found it and tore it up with his bloody mouth. Having left after the girl, Pyramus came to the agreed-upon place and saw there the traces of the wild lion. Then he also found the veil dyed with blood, but he could not see the girl. Quite terrified he accused himself:

"One night," he said, "will destroy two lovers, of which she was worthy of a long life. It is my fault, my soul is harmful, I have destroyed you, miserable woman (to be lamented). I did not come here first, but ordered you to come to a place full of terror. Come, you lions, and tear up my body;

> and consume my guilty flesh with your fierce bite!

But it is for a coward only to wish for death." With these words he picked up Thisbe's veil and carried it with him to the tree. As he gave kisses and tears to the familiar garment, he drew his sword and said: "Receive now also my blood!"

> And he rammed the sword with which he was girded into his entrails.

Then, dying, Pyramus pulled the sword out of his wound and lay on the ground. The blood spurted high and dyed the hanging snow-white fruit of the mulberry tree with purple color.

Then Thisbe came out of the cave, because she did not want to disappoint the beloved youth. She looked for Pyramus, to tell him of the dangers which she had avoided. When she found him, almost dead, she began to cry, held the beloved body and exclaimed: "Pyramus, who has taken you from me? Pyramus, answer! Your dear Thisbe is calling you. Listen, and open your closed eyes!" When he heard the name of Thisbe, Pyramus opened his eyes, which were weighted down by death, and after he had seen her, he closed them again and died.

After Thisbe recognized her veil and saw the sword red with blood, she said: "Your hand and your love have destroyed you, unhappy man. I also have a strong hand, I have love. It will give me strength for wounds. I will follow you in death, and I will be said to be the cause and the companion of your death." Then she spoke to her parents:

> "This, however, be asked by the words of both,
>
> O very miserable people, you and his parents,
>
> that you may not begrudge them, whom certain love and the
>
> most recent hour has joined, to be put into the same grave."

Then she spoke to the tree: "You, tree, who is covering the lamentable body of one lover, and who soon will cover the bodies of two, keep a sign of the killing, and always have black fruit, as a memory of the twin deaths." She said this, and having placed the sword under her chest, she threw herself on the iron (sword), which was still warm from the killing.

> The vows, however, touched the gods, touched the parents;
>
> for the color of the fruit is black, when it has ripened,
>
> and what is left from the funeral pyres, rests together in one urn.

Summary: 1. feminine 2. four 3. masculine 4. meridiem 5. oak tree
6. Senatus Populusque Romanus

14

ADJECTIVES : 3RD DECLENSION
COMPARATIVE; SUPERLATIVE

ENGLISH AND LATIN 3

The first record of the English language dates from around 600, when the Anglo-Saxons were converted to Christianity and learned the Latin alphabet. Whatever had been written down before that time had either been lost or was written in Runes. Serious scholars, such as the historian Bede, wrote in Latin. In the ninth century the West Saxon king Alfred the Great translated, or had translated, a number of books from Latin into English; this period of English, extending until 1100, is now called OLD ENGLISH. Again a number of words had to be borrowed from Latin to express the new ideas. Among them are angel (angelus), candle (candela), radish (radix), and school (schola). On the whole, however, the vocabulary remained Germanic.

A comparison between two versions of the Lord's prayer shows this state of the language, compared with modern English. The first is in **West Saxon**, from the 10th century, and uses few words derived from Latin; the other is in Latin, from the **Vulgate,** a Latin translation of the Bible. Some modern English derivatives are given in parantheses underneath, so you can see, how Latinized the English vocabulary has become. In this text the letter **Þ** ('thorn') represents both voiced and voiceless th.

Faeder ure, Þu Þe eart on heofonum: si Þin nama gehalgod.
(father our thou that art   heaven   thine name hallowed)
Tobecume Þin   rice. GeweorÞe bin willa on eorÞan swa swa on heofonum.
(to come   thine 'Reich'   thine will   earth   so   heaven)
Urne daegwamlican hlaf sielle us to daege.
(Our   daily   loaf sell us to-day)
And forgief us ure   gyltas, swa swa we forgiefaÞ urum gyltendum.
(forgive us our   guilt   forgive our   'guilters')
And ne gelaed Þu us on costnunge, ac   alies us of yfele.
(lead thou us   'costly'   'loosen'   evil)

Pater noster, qui es in caelis: sanctificetur nomen tuum.
(paternal   celestial sanctify   nominal)
Adveniat   regnum   tuum. Fiat   voluntas tua, sicut in caelo, et in terra.
(advent interregnum)   ('fiat' voluntary   celestial   terrestrial.)
Panem nostrum quotidianum da nobis hodie.
(companion   quotidien   date   )
Et dimitte nobis debita nostra, sicut et nos dimittimus debitoribus nostris.
(dismiss   debt   ) (dismiss   debtors)
Et ne nos inducas in temptationem, sed libera nos a malo.
(induce   temptation   liberate   mal-)

Chapter 14:   **ADJECTIVES OF THE THIRD DECLENSION;**
THE COMPARISON OF ADJECTIVES
(COMPARATIVE AND SUPERLATIVE)

In addition to adjectives declined in the first and second declension (bonus, malus, validus, etc.) there are adjectives that are declined like **third declension i-stems** (turris, mare). As was the case for the present participle, these adjectives must have separate forms for the neuter in the accusative Singular and the nominative and accusative Plural, in order to produce the syncretism required for neuters. There are three kinds of adjectives, distinguished by the number of endings they have in the nominative Singular:

    a) one ending for M, F, and N
    b) two endings, one for M and F, one for N
    c) three endings, one each for M, F, and N

Aside from the nominative Singular, all three groups of adjectives are declined alike.

Examples:

    a) **potens (potentis)** *powerful* (one ending for M, F, and N)
There are many adjectives in this group. Their genitive has to be given so that one can see the stem. In this book it will be placed in parentheses, so as not to confuse it with feminine and neuter nominative endings, which will be given for the other groups.

	Sg		Pl	
	Masc. + Fem.	Neuter	Masc. + Fem.	Neuter
N	potens		potentes	potent**ia**
G	potentis		potent**ium**	
D	potenti		potentibus	
A	potentem	potens	potentes	potent**ia**
Ab	potent**i**		potentibus	

Notice the **-i** in all endings but the accusative Singular M and F, where it has been weakened to an **-e**. Notice especially the ablative Singular, which ends in **-i** for adjectives, but in **-e** for nouns and for the present participle! This means syncretism in the dative and ablative Singular for these adjectives. (In which declensions does this occur also?) (In the second declension - domin**o** - , the third i-stems - mar**i** - , and the fourth neuter - corn**u** - well, there all Singular cases but the genitive are the same anyway.)

b) **brevis, breve** *short* (one ending for M and F, one for N)

Most third declension ajectives belong in this group. They are usually listed like this: **brevis, e**

	Sg			Pl	
	Masc. + Fem.	Neuter		Masc. + Fem.	Neuter
N	brevis	breve		breves	brevia
G	brevis			brevium	
D	brevi			brevibus	
A	brevem	breve		breves	brevia
Ab	brevi			brevibus	

c) **celer, celeris, celere** *swift, fast* (one ending each for M, F, and N)

This group has few adjectives in it; just like the **-er** adjectives of the first and second declension, some of them keep the **-e-** in all forms, and some of them drop it (acer,acris,acre):

	Sg			Pl	
	Masc.	Fem.	Neuter	Masc. + Fem.	Neuter
N	celer	celeris	celere	celeres	celeria
G		celeris		celerium	
D		celeri		celeribus	
A	celerem		celere	celeres	celeria
Ab		celeri		celeribus	

!!! It is especially important to learn all three nominative forms of adjectives ending in **-er**, since there are some in both declensions:

	Declension	
miser,misera,miserum	(1 + 2, keeps -e-)	miserable
sinister,sinistra,sinistrum	(1 + 2, drops -e-)	left
celer,celeris,celere	(3; three endings, keeps -e-)	swift
acer,acris,acre	(3; three endings, drops -e-)	sharp
pauper (pauperis)	(3; one ending, keeps -e)	poor

Note: Some adjectives, most importantly **vetus, dives, pauper,** and **princeps** (these are all nominatives with one ending) follow the **consonant declension**; that means ablative Singular **-e** (divite, paupere, vetere, principe), nominative and accusative Plural **-a** (vetera, divita, paupera, principa), and genitive Plural **-um** (divitum, veterum, pauperum, principum). Since this declension is also followed by all comparatives of adjectives (see below),it is given here:

| | Sg | | Pl | |
	Masc. + Fem.	Neuter	Masc. + Fem.	Neuter
N	vetus		veteres	vetera
G	veteris		veterum	
D	veteri		veteribus	
A	veterem	vetus	veteres	vetera
Ab	vetere		veteribus	

Compare this to
  a. the declension of **celer** and **potens**
  b. the declension of **portans**

Note and remember the differences! There will be a devilish exercise at the end of this chapter

Kitchen stove and pots

VOCABULARY of Adjectives, Third Declension:

acer,acris,acre	sharp, bitter, sour	acrimonious
absens (absentis)	absent, away	*
atrox (atrocis)	terrible	atrocious
audax (audacis)	bold	audacious
Brevis,e	short	brevity,brief
celer,celeris,celere	fast, quick	celerity
civilis,e	civil, of a citizen	*
communis,e	common	*
crudelis,e	cruel	*
demens/amens (dementis)	crazy	demented
difficilis,e	difficult	*
diligens (diligentis)	diligent	*
dissimilis,e	dissimilar	*
dives (divitis)	rich	
dulcis,e	sweet	dulcimer
facilis,e	easy	facility
familiaris,e	of the family	familiar
felix (felicis)	happy	felicity
ferox (ferocis)	wild	ferocious
fortis,e	strong, brave	forte
gravis,e	heavy, serious	grave
humilis,e	humble	humility
ingens (ingentis)	huge, enormous	
innocens (innocentis)	innocent	*
levis,e	light	levity
mollis,e	soft	mollify
omnis,e	every, each, all	omnipotent
par (paris)	equal	parity
pauper (pauperis)	poor	pauper
potens (potentis)	powerful	potent
praesens (praesentis)	present	*
princeps (principis)	first, foremost	principle
prudens (prudentis)	prudent	*
qualis,e	of what kind	quality
saluber,salubris,salubre	healthful	salubrious
sapiens (sapientis)	wise	sapient
similis,e	similar	*
suavis,e	sweet, smooth	suave
talis,e	of such a kind	
terribilis,e	terrible	*
utilis,e	useful	utility
vehemens (vehementis)	vehement	*
velox (velocis)	fast, speedy	velocity
vetus (veteris)	old	inveterate
viridis,e	green	viridescent

EXERCISE B: Match adjectives and nouns by case and number and give their meaning:

Letter   Translation

__j__ 1. tempestate   a. fortes   _____

_____ 2. homo   b. gravia   _____

_____ 3. virorum   c. ingens   _____

_____ 4. milites   d. velocis   _____

_____ 5. puero   e. omnes   _____

_____ 6. puellae   f. brevibus   _____

_____ 7. pericula   g. sapiens   _____

_____ 8. porta   h. audaci   _____

_____ 9. stellas   i. veterum   _____

_____ 10. viis   j. vehementi   _____

EXERCISE C: Give a Latin adjective, with the appropriate ending, to fit each description:

1. Haec animalia terrent et devorant alia animalia et parvos homines; sunt _____.

2. Illi pueri sunt gemini; videntur _____.

3. Uvae maturae non sunt acres, sed _____.

4. Viae, quae non sunt longae, sunt _____.

5. Puer, dum non abest, est _____.

6. Homines, qui multam pecuniam habent, sunt _____.

7. Homo, cui pecunia deest, est _____.

8. Res, quae faciliter portari potest, est _____.

9. Homo, qui cogitare aut ratione uti non potest, est _____.

10. Vere arbores fiunt _____.

EXERCISE D: Read and translate the following sayings and proverbs, or, if possible, give a corresponding English proverb. Some of these sayings are originally Greek, but for many Romans, Greek was their second language, just as many Greeks knew Latin. Generally Latin was supposed to be derived from Greek.

1. Ars longa, vita brevis. (Hippocrates)
2. Difficile est satiram non scribere. (Juvenal)
3. Dulce et decorum est pro patria mori. (Horace, and just about every general, leader, and government)
4. Felix, qui potuit rerum cognoscere causas. (Vergil)
5. Fortes fortuna adiuvat. or: Fortuna iuvat audaces. (Terence)
6. Fortiter in re, suaviter in modo. (Aquaviva)
7. Levis sit tibi terra! (Euripides; said at births and funerals)
8. Quidquid agis, prudenter agas, et respice finem! (*Gesta Romanorum*)
9. Molli bracchio tractari se vult. (Cicero)
10. Praesenti ne crede fortunae! (Livius)
11. Praesente medico nihil nocet.
12. Praeter speciem sapiens est.
13. primus omnium; primus inter pares.
14. utile dulci (Horace)
15. Qualis rex, talis grex. Qualis vir, talis oratio.
16. Sat celeriter fit, quidquid fit satis bene. (Suetonius)
17. Nihil est ab omni parte beatum. (Horace)
18. Non ovum tam simile ovo, quam hic illi est. (Quintilianus)
19. Omne principium grave.
20. Omnia mea mecum porto.
21. Omnia sunt inter eos communia.
22. Omnium rerum principia parva sunt. (Cicero)
23. Omnia vincit Amor. (Vergil)
24. Non est ad astra mollis e terra via. (Seneca)
25. Omnes amantes amentes.

---

(3) decorus,a,um - proper, becoming; (7) sit - may (it) be! (Subjunctive Present of esse); (8) agas - may you do (Subjunctive Present of agere); respicere (respicio, respexi, respectum) - to consider; (9) bracchium,i - arm; tractare - to treat; (10) Compare the cases of 'praesenti' and (11) 'praesente'; praesens,tis is not an adjective, but a participle, of prae-esse, to be present; this can be seen from the Ablative ending -e; together with medico this makes an Ablative Absolute (while...); praesenti on the other hand is part of the Adjective; (12) praeter speciem - beyond his looks; in other words: he is not as....; (16) sat = satis; (18) ovum,i - egg; (19) principium,i = initium,i; (24) astra = stellas.

The Comparative and Superlative of Adjectives

Adjectives have three degrees: **positive, comparative,** and **superlative**. The **positive**, or basic form, is what you have learned this far. The **comparative** is, as the name implies, for comparison: something, or someone, is tall**er**, small**er**, bett**er**, **more** beautiful, or **more** stupid than something or someone else. The **superlative** denotes the best, fastest, oldest, most extravagant, most interesting.

The Comparative:
All regular Latin adjectives you have learned this far form their **comparative** by the same pattern. (The irregular ones will have to be memorized, just like English **good - better - best**). No matter in which declension they are originally, you add the endings **-ior** (M and F), and **-ius** (N) to the stem; (the stem is the genitive form minus the ending.) These comparatives are then declined like **consonant stems** of third declension adjectives (vetus), with two endings in the nominative.

Examples:

Nominative	*Genitive*	*Stem*	*Comparative*	
pulcher,pulchra, pulchrum	pulchri	pulchr-	pulchr **ior**, pulchr **ius**	*more beautiful*
carus,a,um	cari	car-	car **ior**, car **ius**	*dearer*
potens	potentis	potent-	potent **ior**, potent **ius**	*more powerful*
longus,a,um	longi	long-	long **ior**, long **ius**	*longer*
celer,celeris celere	celeris	celer-	celer **ior**, celer **ius**	*faster*

The Neuter ending **-ius** is also used for the adverb of the comparative: **celerius,** *more quickly,* **pulchrius,** *more beautifully,* **fortius,** *more strongly.*

Declension of the comparative:

		Sg		Pl	
		Masc. + Fem.	Neuter	Masc. + Fem.	Neuter
N		celerior	celerius	celeriores	celerior**a**
G		celerioris		celerior**um**	
D		celeriori		celerioribus	
A		celeriorem	celerius	celeriores	celerior**a**
Ab		celeriore		celerioribus	

EXERCISE E: Give the opposite of each phrase (same case, change adjectives only):

1. longiora itinera
2. similiores liberi
3. pauperiores viri
4. suavius vinum
5. stultioribus hominibus
6. graviora onera
7. difficiliora opera
8. angustiorem viam

Note further:

1. Latin does not distinguish between "long**er**" and "**more** beautiful" by the length of the adjective, like English does. Almost all adjectives have the same comparative. There are a few (those with a vowel before the ending **-us**, e.g., **arduus,a,um; idoneus,a,um**), which form their comparative by using the word **magis**, more.

2. The comparative, besides serving for comparison, can also be used to express a degree: *rather difficult* (**difficilior, ius**), or *too high* (**altior, ius**). These English translations should be used, when there is no comparison made.

3. When comparing, in Latin there are two methods to express the comparison:
        a) **quam**, meaning "than", requires that the nouns or pronouns compared be in the same case.
(or, differently expressed, the nouns before and after **quam** must be in the same case.)
        Examples:

Frater tuus est long**ior** quam **tu**.	Your brother is taller than you.
Cognovi **canem** fort**iorem** quam **leonem**.	I know a dog stronger than a lion.
Pecuniam dabo **viro** pauper**iori** quam **illi**.	I will give the money to a man poorer than he.

The particle **quam**, together with **tam**, is also used for the comparisons of equals:

Frater tuus est **tam longus quam soror tua**.	Your brother is as tall as your sister.

        b) If the noun or pronoun following "than" is in the nominative or accusative, you can omit the **quam** and put the noun or pronoun in the **ablative of comparison:**:

Mea soror prudent**ior te** est. (quam tu)	My sister is smarter than you.
Meus canis pulchr**ior tuo** est. (quam tuus)	My dog is more beautiful than yours.
Cognovi canem fort**iorem leone**. (quam leonem)	I know a dog stronger than a lion.

Of course you can always use the **quam** construction (watching the case), but you must familiarize yourself with the ablative of comparison also, since this construction is quite popular with Latin authors.

 **EXERCISE F:**   Translate:

    1. the shorter road
    2. the higher mountain
    3. The mountain is too high.
    4. The river is too deep.
    5. more useful languages
    6. rather useful words
    7. a rather long journey
    8. by a stronger man
    9. with rather difficult things
  10. This bread is too old.
  11. My sister is bolder than my brother.
  12. I know no girl more beautiful than she.
  13. The prize [praemium,i] is given to a horse swifter than this one.
  14. This river is longer than that one.
  15. I read a book whose author seemed wiser than all the others.

The Superlative

The Superlative is formed in three ways:

1. All adjectives ending in **-er**, regardless of declension, add the first and second declension ending **-rimus, a, um** to the **nominative masculine Singular**, **not to the stem**:

pulcher -	**pulcherrimus,a,um**	the most beautiful; most, very beautiful
celer -	**celerrimus,a,um**	the swiftest; most, very swift
pauper -	**pauperrimus,a,um**	the poorest; most, very poor

2. The following six adjectives ending in **-lis** add **-limus, a, um** to the **stem**:

facilis -	**facillimus,a,um**	the easiest; most, very easy
difficilis -	**difficillimus,a,um**	the most difficult; very difficult
similis -	**simillimus,a,um**	the most similar;very similar
dissimilis -	**dissimillimus,a,um**	the most dissimilar
humilis -	**humillimus,a,um**	the humblest;very humble
gracilis -	**gracillimus,a,um**	the most graceful, very graceful

3. All other adjectives (except the irregular ones and those compared with **magis**) add the endings **-issimus, a, um** to the **stem**:

altus -	**altissimus,a,um**	the highest, deepest; most, very high, deep
longus -	**longissimus,a,um**	the longest; most, very long
brevis -	**brevissimus,a,um**	the shortest; etc.
notus -	**notissimus,a,um**	the best, most known
utilis -	**utilissimus,a,um**	the most useful

All these superlatives are declined like adjectives of the first and second declension. (Remember to get the **stem** of third declension adjectives from the genitive!)
The superlative can be translated into English as "the swiftest," "most beautiful," "**very** rich," and so on.

EXERCISE G: Supply the superlative and its meaning:

1. sapiens -
2. mollis -
3. audax -
4. acer -
5. dulcis -
6. prudens -
7. stultus -
8. miser -
9. laetus -
10. acerbus -
11. potens -

Irregular Comparatives and Superlatives

bonus,a,um	good	melior,melius	better	optimus,a,um	best
malus,a,um	bad	peior,peius	worse	pessimus,a,um	worst
magnus,a,um	big	maior,maius	bigger	maximus,a,um	biggest
parvus,a,um	small	minor,minus	smaller	minimus,a,um	smallest
multum (Adv.)	much	plus (pluris) (+ Genitive)	more	plurimum	most
multi,ae,a	many	plures,plura	more (Pl.)	plurimi,ae,a	most (Pl.)

Comparatives and Superlatives of Prepositions, or Adjectives lacking a Positive:

exterior,ius	outer	extremus,a,um	outermost, last	(extra)
interior,ius	inner	intimus,a,um	innermost	(intra)
superior,ius	higher	supremus,a,um or summus,a,um	highest, the top of	(supra)
inferior,ius	lower	infimus,a,um or imus,a,um	lowest, the bottom of	(infra)
prior,ius	earlier	primus,a,um	first, foremost	----
posterior,ius	later	postremus,a,um	last	(post)
proprior,ius	closer	proximus,a,um	closest, next	(prope)
ulterior,ius	farther	ultimus,a,um	farthest, last	(ultra)
deterior,ius	less, worse	deterrimus,a,um	the least, worst	----

These comparatives have special meanings:

citerior	on this side }	often used in reference to the Alps
ulterior	on the other side }	
iunior	younger	
senior	older	

EXERCISE H: Translate the sentences:

1. Postquam Androcles spinam ex pede leonis removit, leo gratissimus erat.
2. Leo est fortior urso, sed ursus est fortior vulpe.
3. Nihil melius est quam libertas, nihil peius quam servitus.
4. Iam temporibus antiquis nautae audacissimi ad extremas partes mundi navigaverunt.
5. In Alpibus montes pulcherrimi sunt; summus mons Alpium in Gallia est.
   (Scisne nomen huius montis? Lingua Latina appellatur "Mons Albus.")
6. Sisyphus semper saxum in summum montem volvebat, et semper saxum in infimum partem montis cadebat.
7. Quid enim stultius (est) quam incerta pro certis habere, falsa pro veris? (Cicero)
8. Summum ius, summa iniuria.   9. Maximum remedium irae mora est. (Seneca)
10. Video meliora proboque; peiora facio.

---

(1) postquam (ubi) - when, after (in Latin always with perfect tense, but in English pluperf.: "after A. had..."); spina,ae - thorn; (6) volvere (volvo, volvi, volutum) - to roll; (7) habere - to consider, hold; (9) mora,ae - delay; (10) probare - to approve.

EXERCISE I: Decide from which comparative or sperlative adjectives the underlined English words are derived, and how they got their meaning:

1. <u>ulterior</u> motives
2. Mother <u>Superior</u>
3. a <u>prior</u> engagement
4. to <u>ameliorate</u> the situation
5. a <u>pejorative</u> expression
6. <u>deteriorating</u> living quarters
7. an economic <u>summit</u>
8. the <u>prime</u> suspect
9. <u>Minimalism</u>
10. a <u>nonplussed</u> expression
11. a graceful <u>minuet</u>
12. an <u>intimate</u> confession
13. to give an <u>ultimatum</u>
14. <u>proximity</u> to school
15. written for <u>posterity</u>

EXERCISE J: Give the declensions of:

Sg	celer,is,e (Positive)	capiens,-ntis (Present participle)	vetus (veteris) (Positive, consonant stem)	celerior,-oris (Comparative)
N				
G				
D				
A				
Ab				
Pl.				
N				
G				
D				
A				
Ab				

EXERCISE K: (The horrible one): Give the ablative Singular, the nominative and accusative Plural neuter, and the genitive Plural of the following:

	Ablative Singular	Nominative and Accusative Pl Neuter	Genitive Plural
1. celer			
2. pauper			
3. miser			
4. miserior			
5. sequens			
6. prudens			
7. praesens			

(Participle of praeesse!)

8. princeps

9. acer

10. acrior

11. audax

Iron wood stove

Lectio I : Septem Viri Dormientes

Imperator Decius Christianos severissime puniebat; pauci odium eius fugerunt.

In urbe Epheso septem viri pii erant, qui milites Decii effugere cupiebant. Pecuniam secum portantes ex oppido exierunt et in antrum fugerunt. Cum esuriebant, unus ex eis in urbem mittebatur ad cibos emendos. Aliquando compererunt se a Decio quaeri, et a
5 Deo petiverunt maximam constantiam. Tum, curis confecti, somno capti sunt. Milites imperatoris viderunt eos in antro dormientes, et aditum muro clauserunt.

Post ducentos annos vir quidam prope illum locum domum aedificavit et illum murum rescidit. Ea re septem viri e somno excitati sunt. Statim unus ex eis ad oppidum missus est ad cibos emendos. Sed pecunia, quam habebat, mercatoribus ignota erat. Multi
10 homines concurrerunt et, ut vir timuit, milites eum ad imperatorem ducere voluerunt. Sed mox comperit imperatorem ante duo saecula mortuum esse. Tum narravit se temporibus Decii in antrum fugisse; et admiratio omnes cepit.

(1) Decius - Emperor from AD 249 to 251 A.D.; odium,i - hatred; (3) antrum,i - cave; cum - when; esurire - to be hungry; (5) constantia,ae -steadfastness; conficere (-ficio, -feci, -fectum) - to finish, wear out; (6) murus,i - wall; (8) rescindere (rescindo, rescidi, rescissum) - to tear down; (9) mercator,-oris - merchant; (11), (12) mortuum esse, fugisse - these infinitives are part of ACI (accusative cum infinitive) constructions, also called 'Indirect Statements'; change the literal translation *to have...* to a clause beginning with "that," the standard translation of Indirect Statements (see also Ch.17, part 2, vol.2). (11) se - (the accusative of the ACI; refers back to *narravit* - that he)

Lectio II   Ex Laboribs Herculis

Hercules ab Eurystheo iussus est Hydram capere et occidere. Hoc animal erat ingens serpens aqualis quod vixit in magno palude. Monstrum habebat corpus canis et multa capita, quae immortalia esse dicebantur. Longo itinere facto Hercules paludem invenit et Hydram in aqua latentem conspexit. Magna vi monstrum horribile una manu rapuit et
5 altera manu capita eius caedere conabatur. Quotiens tamen unum caput ceciderat, totiens duo nova capita statim in eodem loco crescebant. Hercules multas horas frustra laborabat; munus finire non potuit et ab eo destitit. Altera ratio ei invenienda erat. Tandem constituit ignem accendere et colla Hydrae urere in eo loco, unde capita nova oriebantur. Hoc modo Hydram interficere potuit. Eam ad regiam Eurysthei trahere non voluit, quod rex homo
10 timidus erat et perpetuo mortem suam exspectabat.

(2) aqualis - water... (actually **Hydra** means water snake, from Greek hydor, water; from there we get hydrant, hydraulic, etc); (4) latere,-eo,-ui - to hide; (6) frustra - in vain ('frustrate'); (5) quotiens - as (how) often; totiens - so often; (8) accendere,-cendi,-censum to light, ignite (not to be confused with **asc**endere); collum,i - neck; urere,uro,ussi,ussum - to burn, scorch; (10) perpetuo - continuously, perpetually.

Narratur Eurystheum ab Hercule alium difficillimum laborem postulavisse. Stabulum regis Augeae ei purgandum erat. Augeas, qui eo tempore in Elide rexit, in stabulo lato tria milia bovum tenebat. Hoc stabulum ne umquam purgatum erat; igitur incredibiliter squalidam et sordidam speciem offerebat. Eurystheus imperavit Herculi: "Hoc stabulum hodie
15 purgare debes!" Putabat autem hoc officium uno die confici non posse. Sed Hercules primo cogitabat breve tempus in mente suo, deinde omnibus viribus fossam viginti quattuor pedum effodit, per quam aquam de montibus ad murum stabuli duxit. Postquam murum rescidit, aqua in stabulum ruit et squalorem expulit. Hoc modo tota stabula purgata sunt et contra opinionem omnium labor confectus est.

(2) Augias - king of Elis: purgare - to clean,purge; (3) squalidus,a,um - dirty,filthy,squalid; (4) sordidus,a,um - filthy, sordid; (7) effodere - to dig out; postquam - (always uses perdect. but should be given as pluperfect in English: "after he had..." (8) rescindere - to tear down; ruere,ruo,rui - to rush, dash; expulit - (from expellere: verbs do not reduplicate if they have a prefix).

Lectio III : Erasmus Narrat Fabulas

Tonsor loquax
Archelaus, rex Macedonum, tonsori garrulo roganti "Quomodo te rado, o rex?" "Tacitus" inquit.

Quid est homo?
5 Plato sic definiverat hominem: 'Homo est animal bipes sine pennis.' Ei definitioni dum discipuli Platonis applauderunt, Diogenes gallum pennis ac plumis nudatum produxit in scholam: "Ecce", inquiens, "hic est homo Platonis!" Itaque definitioni adiectum est 'latis unguibus', quod aves tales ungues non habent.

Quando edere debemus
10 Aliquis Diogenem rogat: "Qua hora alicui prandendum est?" Roganti "Si dives est", inquit, "cum vult, si pauper, cum potest."

Cave !
Quidam in publico gerens longam trabem per imprudentiam percusserat Diogenem statimque ex more dixit: "Cave!" At Diogenes "Cur?" inquit, "me vis iterum percutere?"

(1) tonsor,oris - barber; (2) garrulus,a,um - talkative; radere - to shave; tacitus,a,um - quiet; (5) definire - to define; bipes - biped; penna,ae - feather; (6) nudatus,a,um - denuded; producere - to carry forth, produce; (7) adicere - to add; unguis,is - (finger or toe) nail; (10) prandere - to eat; (11) cum - whenever; (13) trabs,trabis - wooden beam; imprudentia,ae - carelessness; percutere (percutio,percussi,percussum) - to hit.

And a pun about Erasmus and Martin Luther: (A hexameter)

Dum leo Martinus, tu solum doctus **eras mus**.

.   .   .   .   .   .

Furnishings

Furniture in many Roman houses was built-in: niches and closets served for storage, or, as did stone consoles, for display. Sometimes even beds, tables, and chairs were made of brick or masonry.

Furniture made of wood, marble, or bronze was kept to a minimum, since even in rich people's houses the rooms were comparatively small. One important piece of furniture was the **Lectus.** With a mattress of straw or wool, and blankets, it served for sleeping; in the dining room it was used for reclining at meals. Three lecti were arranged like a horseshoe in the **Triclinium,** the dining-room. The larger beds offered space for three people each; the number of diners was supposed to be, as the author Varro said, no fewer than the Graces (three) and no more than the Muses (nine). There was either one large table or several small ones, made of wood, marble, or bronze.

Fresco in a Roman house

Other furnishings included chairs (**Sella**), some of them collapsible, stools (**Subsella**), portable heaters, bronze coal pans, large and small oil lamps made of pottery or bronze, and small house altars for the **Lares,** the family gods. From paintings we know that there was also a profusion of carpets, curtains, tablecloths, blankets, pillows, and wallhangings.

The most popular containers were wooden boxes or chests (**Cista**), or sometimes safe-like heavy containers made of wood and metal (**Arca**). There were also armoires, free-standing closets (**Armaria**) with decorated wooden doors. City dwellers liked to secure their houses with heavy doors and locks with large keys.

In the kitchen there were hearths fired with coal or lignite, on which cooks and slaves prepared food in earthenware or bronze containers. The pottery dishes broke very easily, but they were quite inexpensive; as a matter of fact, the amphoras used to import oil, wine, or Spanish fishsauce (**Garum**) were considered throwaway packaging.

**Man seated
in a cane chair**

The rooms of many people's houses were decorated by artworks. Most prominent were frescoes, which often served to give the illusion of perspective and distance and thus made the rooms seem larger than they were. There were also floor mosaics and marble inlays. In addition there could be statues, busts, water basins, vases, and even collections of objects, such as coins.

Illusion painting

Poor people had to do with a lot less, as we can read in Martial's description of a poor man's eviction for non-payment of rent.

"He took a little bed with three legs and a table with two legs with him, a lamp, a bucket made of cherry-wood; from the side of a dilapidated chamber pot the urine was dripping; the neck of an amphora followed a cooking-pot covered with rust ..."

(Martial, XII, 32, 11ff.)

Chapter 14 : Answers and Translations

Exercise A:

frater	felix	equus	celer	condicio	difficilis
fratris	felicis	equi	celeris	condicionis	difficilis
fratri	felici	equo	celeri	condicioni	difficili
fratrem	felicem	equum	celerem	condicionem	difficilem
fratre	felici	equo	celeri	condicione	difficili
fratres	felices	equi	celeres	condiciones	difficiles
fratrum	felicium	equorum	celerium	conditionum	difficilium
fratribus	felicibus	equis	celeribus	condicionibus	difficilibus
fratres	felices	equos	celeres	condiciones	difficiles
fratribus	felicibus	equis	celeribus	condicionibus	difficilibus
puella	fortis	mare	ingens	stabulum	humile
puellae	fortis	maris	ingentis	stabuli	humilis
puellae	forti	mari	ingenti	stabulo	humili
puellam	fortem	mare	ingens	stabulum	humile
puella	forti	mari	ingenti	stabulo	humili
puellae	fortes	maria	ingentia	stabula	humilia
puellarum	fortium	marium	ingentium	stabulorum	humilium
puellis	fortibus	maribus	ingentibus	stabulis	humilibus
puellas	fortes	maria	ingentia	stabula	humilia
puellis	fortibus	maribus	ingentibus	stabulis	humilibus

Exercise B:

(j)	1. tempestate vehementi	in a forceful storm
(g)	2. homo sapiens	*
(i)	3. virorum veterum	of old men
(a)	4. milites fortes	brave soldiers (Nom. or Acc.)
(h)	5. puero audaci	to the bold boy, from the bold boy
(d)	6. puellae velocis	of the swift girl
(b)	7. pericula gravia	grave dangers
(c)	8. porta ingens	a gigantic door
(e)	9. stellas omnes	all stars (Acc.)
(f)	10. viis brevibus	by short roads, to short roads

Exercise C:
1. ferocia 2. similes 3. dulces 4. breves 5. praesens 6. divites 7. pauper 8. levis 9. amens (demens) 10. virides

Exercise D:
1. Art is long, life is short.
2. It is difficult not to write a satire.
3. It is sweet and fitting to die for your fatherland.
4. Happy is he who can know the causes (or sources) of things.
5. Fortune helps (favors) the strong (or bold).

6. Strong in the matter, sweet in the mode.
7. May the earth be light for you.
8. Whatever you do, may you do it prudently, and consider the outcome!
9. He wants to be treated with a soft arm (kid gloves).
10. Don't trust present fortune. (present = adjective)
11. When the doctor is present nothing can do harm. (present = participle)
12. He is wise beyond his appearance. (He is not as stupid as he looks.)
13. First among all (men). First among equals.
14. (To combine) the sweet with the useful.
15. Like the king, like his herd. (As the king, so his herd.)
    Like the man, like his speech. (As the man, so his speech.)
16. Sufficiently quickly is done that, which is done well.
17. Nothing is in all parts happy.
18. An egg is not as similar to another egg as this person is to that one.
19. All beginnings are difficult.
20. I carry all my belongings with me.
21. They consider all things among them common (property).
22. The beginnings of all things are small.
23. Love conquers all.
24. The road from earth to the stars is not comfortable.
25. All lovers are crazy.

Exercise E:
1. breviora itinera 2. dissimiliores liberi 3. divitiores viri 4. acerbius vinum 5. sapientioribus hominibus 6. leviora onera 7. faciliora opera 8. latiorem viam

Exercise F:
1. via brevior 2. mons altior 3. Mons est altior. 4. Flumen est altius. 5. linguae utiliores
6. verba utiliora 7. iter longius 8. a viro fortiore 9. rebus difficilioribus 10. Hic panis est veterior.
11. Soror mea audacior est fratre meo. (...audacior est quam frater meus.) 12. Non cognovi puellam pulchriorem ea. (pulchriorem quam eam) 13. Praemium datur equo celeriori quam huic.
14. Hoc flumen longius est quam illud. (longius est illo) 15. Librum legi, cuius auctor sapientior visus est ceteris (auctoribus). [sapientior quam ceteri (auctores)]

Exercise G:
1. sapientissimus - very wise, the wisest
2. mollissimus - the softest, ...
3. audacissimus - the boldest
4. acerrimus - very sharp
5. dulcissimus - very sweet
6. prudentissimus - the most careful
7. stultissimus - very stupid
8. miserrimus - most miserable
9. laetissimus - the happiest
10. acerbissimus - very bitter
11. potentissimus - very powerful

Exercise H:
1. When Androcles had removed the thorn from the lion's foot, the lion was very grateful.
2. The lion is stronger than the bear, but the bear is stronger than the fox.
3. Nothing is better than freedom, nothing worse than serfdom. (nihil = neuter)
4. Already in old times very daring sailors sailed to the outermost parts of the world.
5. In the Alps there are very beautiful mountains; the highest mountain of the Alps is in Gaul. (Do you know the name of this mountain? In Latin it is called "White Mountain" - and in French, "Mont Blanc.")
6. Sisyphus was forever rolling a rock to the top of the mountain, and always the rock fell back to the bottom of the mountain.

7. For what is more stupid than to accept uncertainty in place of certainty, falsehood instead of truth? (uncertain things, false things, etc.)
8. The highest law is sometimes the greatest (or highest) injustice.
9. The greatest remedy for anger is delay.
10. I see better things, and I approve; (then) I do worse things.

Exercise I:

1. ulterior (motives beyond those easily visible)
2. superior (on a higher level of the hierarchy)
3. prior (an engagement made earlier)
4. melior (to make the situation better)
5. peior (an expression which makes the person seem worse)
6. deterior (they get worse)
7. summus (the highest representatives meet)
8. primus (the foremost suspect)
9. minimus (art or music using a very small amount of material)
10. plus (this shows that you are perplexed and can say no more)
11. minus, minutus (a dance with rather small steps)
12. intimus (it bares your innermost thoughts)
13. ultimus (giving a last chance)
14. proximus (in the very near neighborhood)
15. posterior (for the people who were born later)

Exercise J:

celer,eris,ere	capiens	vetus	celerior, celerius
celeris	capientis	veteris	celerioris
celeri	capienti	veteri	celeriori
celerem, ere	capientem, capiens	veterem, vetus	celeriorem, celerius
celeri	capiente	vetere	celeriore
celeres, celeria	capientes, capentia	veteres, vetera	celeriores, celeriora
celerium	capientium	veterum	celeriorum
celeribus	capientibus	veteribus	celerioribus
celeres, celeria	capientes, capientia	veteres, vetera	celeriores, celeriora
celeribus	capientibus	veteribus	celerioribus

Exercise K:

1. celeri, celeria, celerium
2. paupere, paupera, pauperum
3. misero/a, misera, miserorum/arum
4. miseriore, miseriora, miseriorum
5. sequente, sequentia, sequentium
6. prudenti, prudentia, prudentium
7. praesente, praesentia, praesentium
8. principe, principa, principum
9. acri, acria, acrium
10. acriore, acriora, acriorum
11. audaci, audacia, audacium

Reading 1 : The Seven Sleepers

The emperor Decius punished Christians severely; few escaped his wrath. In the city of Ephesus there were seven pious men, who wanted to escape the soldiers of Decius. Carrying money with them they left the city and fled into a cave. When they were hungry, one of them was sent to the city in order to buy food (for food to be bought). One time they learned that they were being sought by Decius, and they begged God for the greatest steadfastness. Then, worn out by cares, they were overtaken by sleep. The soldiers of Decius saw them sleeping in the cave and closed the entrance with a wall.

After two hundred years a certain man built a house near this place and tore down the wall. By this action the seven men were woken up from their sleep. Immediately one of them was sent into town to buy food. But the money he had was unknown to the merchants. Many people ran together and, as the man feared, the soldiers wanted to lead him to the emperor. But soon he found out that the emperor had died two centuries ago (he found out the emperor to have died) Then he told (them) that he had fled into the cave at Decius' times; and amazement captured all people.

Reading II: From the Labors of Hercules

Hercules was ordered by Eurystheus to catch the Hydra and kill her. This animal was a huge water serpent, which lived in a swamp. The monster had the body of a dog and many heads which were said to be immortal. After a long journey Hercules found the swamp and caught sight of the Hydra hiding there. With great force he grasped the horrible monster with one hand and with the other tried to cut off its heads. But however often he had cut off one head, so often two heads grew immediately in the same place. Hercules labored for many hours in vain; he could not finish the task and left off it (desisted from it). He had to find another plan. Finally he decided to light a fire and to scorch the necks of the Hydra in the places from which the new heads grew (rose). In this way he was able to kill the Hydra. He did not want to drag it back to the palace of Eurystheus, because the king was a fearful man and continuously expected his death.

It is told that Eurystheus demanded another very difficult labor from Hercules. He had to clean the stables of Augeas. Augeas, who at that time ruled Elis, kept three thousand cattle in a huge stable. This stable had never been cleaned; therefore it presented an incredibly sordid and filthy sight. Eurystheus ordered Hercules: "You must clean this stable today!" He believed that this task could not be carried out in one day. But Hercules first thought for a short time in his mind, then, with all his strength he dug a ditch of twenty-four feet, through which he led water down from the mountains to the wall of the stable. After he had torn down the wall, the water rushed into the stable and pushed the dirt out. In this way the stables were cleaned and the labor was finished.

Lectio III: Erasmus Tells Stories

The garrulous barber

Archelaus, the king of Macedonia, when a verbose barber asked him, "How shall I shave you, oh king?" said to him "Quietly".

What is man?

Plato had defined man this way: "Man is a two-legged animal without feathers." When the students of Plato applauded this definition, Diogenes brought a chicken, stripped of its feathers and downs, to school, saying: "Behold, here is Plato's man." Therefore to the definition was added "with wide finger and toe nails," because birds don't have nails of this kind.

When should we eat?

Someone asked Diogenes: "At what hour must someone eat?" He said to the questioner (questioning person): "If he is rich, whenever he wants to, if he is poor, whenever he is able to."

Watch out!

Some man carrying a long wooden beam in public had through carelessness struck Diogenes and right away said from habit: "Watch out!" "Why?" said Diogenes, "do you want to hit me again?"

Erasmus and Luther

'   '   '   '   '   '

While a lion was Martin, you only a much learned mouse were.

15

SUBJUNCTIVE 1: MAIN SENTENCE
CVM, VT

ENGLISH AND LATIN 4

The most extensive influx of Latin into English took place after the Norman Conquest of 1066. The Normans were originally 'North-Men', Scandinavians who had migrated to France (Normandy) and taken on the Romance language of their surroundings which they brought to England. In the beginning English and French were spoken concurrently, the one by the subjected people, the other by the ruling class. As new administrative and executive structures were imported, together with cultural, religious, philosophical, and scientific concepts, new French words came along with them; these either joined the English words and coexisted with them, usually with somewhat different meaning, or they replaced them. Thus most words in the English language which relate to administration (*government, state, authority, people, power, country*), or to law (*jurisprudence, court, judge, crime, accuse, defend*) are derived from Latin, usually by way of French. In many cases the Germanic / English word could not be pushed out because it was too firmly entrenched. Examples are **king, queen, lord, lady, window, thief, steal.**

A number of words came into English twice, once directly from Latin, once through French. This fact accounts for 'doubles' such as these:

Latin	from Latin	from French
regalis,e	regal	royal
conceptum (concipere)	concept	conceit
dominio,onis	dominion	dungeon
factio,onis	faction	fashion
defectum (deficere)	defect	defeat
senior	senior	Sir
poena	penal	punish
regulare	regulate	rule
computare	compute	count
fides,ei	fidelity	faith, fay

Often Latin words were borrowed for a specific, restricted denotation or grammatical concept. In the case of the familiar domestic and wild animals, for instance, the English words continued to be used: **pig, cow, calf, deer.** The meat from these animals, however, which was used for preparing dishes mostly at court and for the upper classes, took on French names: *porc, beef, veal, venison.*
Similarly, for many English nouns in use to this day: **mind, sun, moon, town, country, garden, mouth,** the corresponding Adjectives were borrowed from Latin: *mental, solar, lunar, urban, rural, horticultural, oral.*

Many English and Latin words coexist peacefully, such as **old** and *ancient,* although there is usually a difference in meaning. Some words represent a synthesis of Latin and Germanic parts, e.g. *Common*wealth, *beauti*ful, *grand*father, or *gentle*man.

Chapter 15 :   **SUBJUNCTIVE I - IN MAIN SENTENCE;**
SUBJUNCTIVE IN DEPENDENT CLAUSES; CUM, UT

This far you have learned two of the three **moods** in Latin: the **indicative** for **statements**, and the **imperative** for **commands**. The third mood, the **subjunctive**, is used widely in Latin and it has been difficult to avoid it so far. Though it may be possible to express nearly all thoughts without using the Subjunctive, it is quite impossible to express them idiomatically, succinctly, or elegantly, in other words, the way the Romans did. The Subjunctive occurs in both independent (main) and dependent clauses:

1. In main or independent clauses, it describes a statement contrary to fact, a wish, or a possibility or potential.

2. In dependent clauses the subjunctive mood can also express contrary to fact statements, but more generally it is used to express ideas like purpose, doubt, fear, result, circumstances, or time when something happened, as well as to express indirect questions and indirect commands. The English equivalents of most of these sentences are in the indicative. It is therefore quite important to understand the concepts or circumstances that require Latin subjunctive.

He would be king, if he were not so stupid.

should
I (could) have danced all night.

If my grandmother had wheels,
she would be a bus.

Let them eat cake !

They would have devoured the whole pie,
but we took it away.

Would you shut up, please!

The Subjunctive Forms

To be able to understand and write the subjunctive, you must learn some new forms. This is a matter of learning the rules of **subjunctive stem formation**, since they are the same for all four conjugations. To these stems you add the endings you already know. (Remember that there are two endings for the 1st person Sg.: -o and -m; for the subjunctive use **-m**. The ending for the 3rd person Plural is **-nt** for all Conjugations.) This is not as bad as it seems; besides they are the last of all forms to be learned, verb or noun! There are four tenses which have subjunctive forms. Neither the future nor the future perfect form a subjunctive, presumably because the future is already doubtful and irreal anyway. This may also explain the fact that in the third and fourth conjugations the 1st person Sg. of the subjunctive and the 1st person future are identical.

1. The present subjunctive is characterized by the vowel **-a-**, which is **added to the stem**, before the ending. This works well for all conjugations but the first, which already has an **-a-**. Therefore in the **first** conjugation the stem **-a-** is replaced by an **-e-**.

		1-portare	2-docere	3-ducere	3i-capere	4-audire	
A	1.	port **e** m	doce **a** m	duc **a** m	capi **a** m	audi **a** m	
C	2.	port **e** s	doce **a** s	duc **a** s	capi **a** s	audi **a** s	**Sg**
T	3.	port **e** t	doce **a** t	duc **a** t	capi **a** t	audi **a** t	
I	1.	port **e** mus	doce **a** mus	duc **a** mus	capi **a** mus	audi **a** mus	
V	2.	port **e** tis	doce **a** tis	duc **a** tis	capi **a** tis	audi **a** tis	**Pl**
E	3.	port **e** nt	doce **a** nt	duc **a** nt	capi **a** nt	audi **a** nt	
P	1.	port **e** r	doce **a** r	duc **a** r	capi **a** r	audi **a** r	
A	2.	port **e** ris	doce **a** ris	duc **a** ris	capi **a** ris	audi **a** ris	**Sg**
S	3.	port **e** tur	doce **a** tur	duc **a** tur	capi **a** tur	audi **a** tur	
S	1.	port **e** mur	doce **a** mur	duc **a** mur	capi **a** mur	audi **a** mur	
I	2.	port **e** mini	doce **a** mini	duc **a** mini	capi **a** mini	audi **a** mini	**Pl**
V	3.	port **e** ntur	doce **a** ntur	duc **a** ntur	capi **a** ntur	audi **a** ntur	
E							

	esse	ire	ferre	ferre (Passiv)	fieri	velle	
1.	**sim**	eam	feram	ferar	fiam	**velim**	
2.	**sis**	eas	feras	feraris	fias	**velis**	**Sg**
3.	**sit**	eat	ferat	feratur	fiat	**velit**	
1.	**simus**	eamus	feramus	feramur	fiamus	**velimus**	
2.	**sitis**	eatis	feratis	feramini	fiatis	**velitis**	**Pl**
3.	**sint**	eant	ferant	ferantur	fiant	**velint**	

Deponents use passive forms only (with active meaning). Examples from all conjugations:

	1- conari	2-misereri	3-uti	3i-pati	4-experiri	
1.	coner	miserear	utar	patiar	experiar	
2.	coneris	miserearis	utaris	patiaris	experiaris	**Sg**
3.	conetur	misereatur	utatur	patiatur	experiatur	
1.	conemur	misereamur	utamur	patiamur	experiamur	
2.	conemini	misereamini	utamini	patiamini	experiamini	**Pl**
3.	conentur	misereantur	utantur	patiantur	experiantur	

EXERCISE A: Write the present subjunctive form that corresponds to the indicative form given:

Example: audit --> **audiat**; amo --> **amem**

   1. video

   2. arbitraris

   3. dat

   4. iaciunt

   5. it

   6. movemur

   7. ponis

   8. fers

   9. estis

   10. punis

EXERCISE B: For each form write the tense, mood, and infinitive:

	Tense	*Mood*	*Infinitive*	*Translation*
Examples: **amet**	Present	Subjunctive	amare	he/she should like
vincet	Future	Indicative	vincere	he will conquer

   1. videt

   2. vidit

   3. ponit

   4. ponent

   5. ponant

   6. ponuntur

   7. portentur

   8. portantur

   9. velit

   10. laudat

   11. debeat

   12. audiam (2!)

   13. audit

   14. det

   15. debet

   16. audiet

2. The imperfect subjunctive is formed by adding the same endings to the **infinitive** of the verb.

		1-portare	2-docere	3-ducere	3i-capere	4-audire
			Active			
Sg	1.	**portare** m	**docere** m	**ducere** m	**capere** m	**audire** m
	2.	portare s	docere s	ducere s	capere s	audire s
	3.	portare t	docere t	ducere t	capere t	audire t
Pl	1.	portare mus	docere mus	ducere mus	capere mus	audire mus
	2.	portare tis	docere tis	ducere tis	capere tis	audire tis
	3.	portare nt	docere nt	ducere nt	capere nt	audire nt
			Passive			
Sg	1.	**portare** r	**docere** r	**ducere** r	**capere** r	**audire** r
	2.	portare ris	docere ris	ducere ris	capere ris	audire ris
	3.	portare tur	docere tur	ducere tur	capere tur	audire tur
Pl	1.	portare mur	docere mur	ducere mur	capere mur	audire mur
	2.	portare mini	docere mini	ducere mini	capere mini	audire mini
	3.	portare ntur	docere ntur	ducere ntur	capere ntur	audire ntur

esse	ire	ferre	ferre (passive)	fieri	velle
			(only ferre has a passive)	(use *fiere as Infinitive)	

	esse	ire	ferre	ferre	fiere	velle	
1.	**esse** m	**ire**m	**ferre** m	**ferre** r	**fiere** m	**velle** m	
2.	esse s	ire s	ferre s	ferre ris	fiere s	velle s	**Sg**
3.	esse t	ire t	ferre t	ferre tur	fiere t	velle t	
1.	esse mus	ire mus	ferre mus	ferre mur	fiere mus	velle mus	
2.	esse tis	ire tis	ferre tis	ferre mini	fiere tis	velle tis	**Pl**
3.	esse nt	ire nt	ferre nt	ferre ntur	fiere nt	velle nt	

To form the **imperfect subjunctive of deponents** you must use their hypothetical infinitive active, which is identical to the imperative Singular form of the verb. To this the **passive set of endings** must be added. The **meaning** of the verb is still **active**. Remember that in the **third** (consonant) conjugation the infinitive passive is one syllable shorter than the infinitive active: pati - patere; aggredi - aggredere; etc.

Deponens Infinitive Act.		1-conari conare	2-vereri verere	3-loqui loquere	3i-pati patere	4-oriri orire	
	1.	**conare** r	**verere** r	**loquere** r	**patere** r	**orire** r	
	2.	conare ris	verere ris	loquere ris	patere ris	orire ris	**Sg**
	3.	conare tur	verere tur	loquere tur	patere tur	orire tur	
	1.	conare mur	verere mur	loquere mur	patere mur	orire mur	
	2.	conare mini	verere mini	loquere mini	patere mini	orire mini	**Pl**
	3.	conare ntur	verere ntur	loquere ntur	patere ntur	orire ntur	

3. The perfect and pluperfect subjunctives are formed from the **perfect stem** (active) and the PPP (passive). In the **perfect active** the endings are identical to those of the **future perfect**, with the exception of the 1st person Sg., which uses **-erim** instead of **-ero**. (This shows again the affinity between subjunctive and future: both are speculative.) The **passive perfect subjunctive** is periphrastic, just like the passive perfect indicative, and uses as its conjugated part the **present subjunctive** of **esse: sim, sis, sit,** etc.

		1-portare	2-docere	3-ducere	3i-capere	4-audire
				Active		
Sg	1.	**portav** erim	**docu** erim	**dux** erim	**cep** erim	**audiv** erim
	2.	portav eris	docu eris	dux eris	cep eris	audiv eris
	3.	portav erit	docu erit	dux erit	cep erit	audiv erit
Pl	1.	portav erimus	docu erimus	dux erimus	cep erimus	audiv erimus
	2.	portav eritis	docu eritis	dux eritis	cep eritis	audiv eritis
	3.	portav erint	docu erint	dux erint	cep erint	audiv erint

	Passive			
	PPP **Sg**		PPP **Pl**	
1-portare	portatus,a,um		portati,ae,a	
2-docere	doctus,a,um	1. **sim**	docti,ae,a	1. **simus**
3-ducere	ductus,a,um	2. **sis**	ducti,ae,a	2. **sitis**
3i-capere	captus,a,um	3. **sit**	capti,ae,a	3. **sint**
4-audire	auditus,a,um		auditi,ae,a	

	Sg Deponents (active meaning!)		**Pl**	
1-conari	conatus,a,um		conati,ae,a	
2-vereri	veritus,a,um	1. **sim**	veriti,ae,a	1. **simus**
3-loqui	locutus,a,um	2. **sis**	locuti,ae,a	2. **sitis**
3i-pati	passus,a,um	3. **sit**	passi,ae,a	3. **sint**
4-oriri	ortus,a,um		orti,ae,a	

		esse	ire	ferre	ferre (passive)	fieri	velle
Sg	1.	**fu** erim	**i** erim	**tul** erim	latus,a,um **sim**	factus,a,um **sim**	**volu** erim
	2.	fu eris	i eris	tul eris	latus,a,um sis	factus,a,um sis	volu eris
	3.	fu erit	i erit	tul erit	latus,a,um sit	factus,a,um sit	volu erit
Pl	1.	fu erimus	i erimus	tul erimus	lati,ae,a simus	facti,ae,a simus	volu erimus
	2.	fu eritis	i eritis	tul eritis	lati,ae,a sitis	facti,ae,a sitis	volu eritis
	3.	fu erint	i erint	tul erint	lati,ae,a sint	facti,ae,a sint	volu erint

The pluperfect subjunctive is, like the perfect, formed from the **perfect stem**; in the **active** a set of quite distinctive endings is added, which is plainly derived from the imperfect subjunctive of **esse** (essem, esses); in the passive **essem, esses** is used outright:

1-portare	2-docere	3-ducere	3i-capere	4-audire	
Active					
1. portav **issem**	docu issem	dux issem	cep issem	audiv issem	
2. portav **isses**	docu isses	dux isses	cep isses	audiv isses	**Sg**
3. portav **isset**	docu isset	dux isset	cep isset	audiv isset	
1. portav **issemus**	docu issemus	dux issemus	cep issemus	audiv issemus	
2. portav **issetis**	docu issetis	dux issetis	cep issetis	audiv issetis	**Pl**
3. portav **issent**	docu issent	dux issent	cep issent	audiv issent	
Passive					
1. portatus,a,um **essem**	(doctus,a,um	ductus,a,um	captus,a,um	auditus,a,um)	
2. portatus,a,um **esses**					**Sg**
3. portatus,a,um **esset**					
1. portat**i,ae,a** **essemus**	(docti,ae,a	ducti,ae,a	capti,ae,a	auditi,ae,a)	
2. portati,ae,a **essetis**					**Pl**
3. portati,ae,a **essent**					

Deponents: conatus,a,um essem - conati,ae,a essemus; secutus,a,um essem - secuti,ae,a essemus
etc.

esse	ire	ferre (Active)	ferre (Passive)		fieri		velle	
1. fu **issem**	i ssem	tul issem	latus,a,um	**essem**	factus,a,um	**essem**	volu issem	
2. fu **isses**	i sses	tul isses	latus,a,um	**esses**	factus,a,um	**esses**	volu isses	**Sg**
3. fu **isset**	i sset	tul isset	latus,a,um	**esset**	factus,a,um	**esset**	volu isset	
1. fu **issemus**	i ssemus	tul issemus	lati,ae,a	**essemus**	facti,ae,a	**essemus**	volu issemus	
2. fu **issetis**	i ssetis	tul issetis	lati,ae,a	**essetis**	facti,ae,a	**essetis**	volu issetis	**Pl**
3. fu **issent**	i ssent	tul issent	lati,ae,a	**essent**	facti,ae,a	**essent**	volu issent	

EXERCISE C:　　　Give the subjunctive of the following indicative forms: (use the same tense)

1. habuit
2. manseras
3. petebamus
4. volebat
5. vult
6. munitur
7. polliciti sunt
8. tacti erant
9. fecistis
10. rogabant
11. oboedivi
12. laudo
13. monetur
14. eramus
15. ferebatis
16. iacti sunt
17. dixerat
18. crevit
19. mentiebamini
20. navigant

The Subjunctive in Independent Clauses

In independent clauses the subjunctive has several important functions:

1. To express desire, or an order. This use resembles a command. It occurs in the **present tense** only. In English it is generally expressed with the words "let," "shall," "should," and it is called a **hortatory** or **iussive subjunctive** (from **hortari**, *to urge, encourage*, and **iubere**, *to order*). It is commonly directed towards the first and third person; for the second person the imperative is more suitable. The negative particle used is **ne.**

Examples:

Eamus.	Let's go. We should go.
Audiatur.	Let him be heard. He shall be heard.
Ne edant panem.	Do not let them eat the bread.
Gaudeamus igitur.	Therefore we should be happy.

2. To express possibility, or a somewhat doubtful, modest statement. In English this is often translated as "may," "might," or "would"; "might have" or "would have"; it is called **potential.** Closely related to it is the **concessive**, which, too, is translated as "may".

> Use:
>
> | | | |
> |---|---|---|
> | present (or perfect) subjunctive | for | present concepts |
> | imperfect subjunctive | for | past concepts |

Examples: **Present**

Aliquis dicat...	Someone might say...
Quis dubitet?	Who would doubt?
Dicas...	You (one) might say...
Putes..	You (one) might think...
Omnia possideat, non possidet aera Minos. (Ovid)	
	He may own everything, but Minos does not own the air.

The **past** occurs only in these expressions:

Crederes..., putares...	One might (could) have thought...
Videres..., cerneres...	One might (could) have seen...

3. To express wishes; in Latin a difference is assumed between wishes which can be realized and those which cannot. In English both are expressed by "May...," "I wish that..." or "Would that...".
In Latin the word **utinam** ("would that...") is commonly used for emphasis.
The negative Particle is **ne.**

> Use:
>
> | | |
> |---|---|
> | Present subjunctive for a wish in the present | that can be fulfilled |
> | Perfect subjunctive for a wish in the past | |
> | Imperfect subjunctive for a wish in the present | that cannot be fulfilled |
> | Pluperfect subjunctive for a wish in the past | |

Examples:

Felicior sis Marco!	*May you be happier than Marcus!*
Utinam illum diem videam!	*May I see that day! Wish I would see this day!*
Utinam ne cepissem pecuniam!	*If only I had not taken the money!*
Utinam mater viveret!	*I wish that my mother were still alive!*
Utinam omnes servare potuisses!	*If only you could have saved them all!*

So far the theory; in practice obviously the line between fulfillable and unfulfillable wishes tends to get blurred at times. We can only hope that Latin authors knew the difference.

4. To show a statement as contrary to fact, not real. This use of the subjunctive is actually more common in dependent clauses, for instance those using **si**, *if*.
There is no conditional form in Latin, as there is in English**:** "If I **had** money, I **would have** a car." - these two forms are the same in Latin: **haberem.** (Literally: *If I **would have** money, I **would have** a car.*)
The negative particle is **non**.

> **Use**:
> | **Imperfect** subjunctive | for | present time (!) | ("would") |
> |---|---|---|---|
> | **Pluperfect** subjunctive | for | past time | ("would have") |

Examples:

Facerem opus, sed occupata sum.	*I would do the work, but I am busy.*
Fecissem opus, si potuissem.	*I would have done the work, if I could have.*
Sine amicis vita tristis esset.	*Without friends life would be sad.*
Ad me venires, si posses.	*You would come to my house, if you could.*
Cur tacerem?	*Why should I be silent?*
Si tacuisses, philosophus mansisses. (Boetius)	

> If you had been silent, you would have remained a philosopher.
> (But you had to open your big mouth and show your ignorance.)

 **EXERCISE D:**   Say in Latin: (**use present subjunctive!**)

1. Let's eat and drink.   2. Let all be heard. (Two words; use 3rd person Pl.)

3. Let him have the body.   4. May he live.

5. May your will be done. [use fieri]   6. May we be happy.

7. You (Sg) might believe him to be a god. [Accusative, twice]

8. I wish I could believe! ("Could" is in the subjunctive, "believe" is in the infinitive!)

9. The window should not be broken.

10. Let her give them the food. [Careful with "them" !]

EXERCISE E: Translate into English and indicate whether the subjunctive is used in a main clause (MC) or a dependent clause (DC):

1. Utinam ne oblitus essem librum! [Why pluperfect?]

2. Si me monuisses, eum non oblitus essem.

3. Utinam omnes incolae patriae nostrae liberi fiant! [Why Present?]

4. Si omnia animalia orbis terrarum cognosceres, doctus dici posses.

5. Nihil faciamus irati, sed exspectemus unam horam!

6. Utinam pueri ne tam pigri essent! [Unfulfillable wish!]

7. Si liberi totum panem non edissent, mihi esuriendum non esset.

8. Audiantur omnes partes!

9. Si id certius scirem, tibi dicerem.

10. Si dives fieri vellem, magister non essem.

Si tacuisses, philosophus mansisses.

The Subjunctive in Dependent Clauses

There are many kinds of dependent clauses in which Latin syntax requires a subjunctive form to be used, although this may not be obvious from the English version. There are a great many types of subjunctive clauses, subordinating conjunctions, and grammatical terms. Of these we will cover here the most basic and frequent kinds. For more of them and the sequence of tenses see vol 2, ch. 16.

Two very common **subordinating conjunctions** usually requiring a subjunctive clause are **cum** and **ut**. You have encountered both words before, **cum** as a preposition with the ablative, and **ut** as a subordinating conjunction meaning **as** and using the indicative. When introducing dependent clauses, they have the following main functions and translations:

CUM	1. when, whenever, at the time when, while	(**temporal, iterative, circumstantial cum**)
	2. since, because	(**causal cum**)
	3. although, while (on the other hand)	(**concessive** or **adversative cum**)

:

1. Cum meaning "when" or "whenever"

If the clause refers to the present or future, **cum** is used with the **Indicative**:

Cum tacent, clamant. (Cicero)	When they say nothing, they are (really) shouting.
Cum in domo meo **eris**, te videbo.	When you are in my house, I will see you.
Cum talia **audimus**, timemus.	When we hear such things, we are afraid.
Cum avus de iuventute sua **narrat**, gaudet.	Whenever grandfather tells of his youth, he is happy.

When referring to a definite time in the past, or to a repeated action, **cum** is also used with the **indicative**:

Cum in urbem **venit**, eam vidi.   When she came to town, I saw her.
Cum Caesar in Galliam **venit**, ibi duae factiones erant.
                    [At the time] when Caesar came to Gaul, there were two factions there.
Cum avus de iuventute **narrabat**, gaudebat.
                    Whenever grandfather told of his youth, he was happy.

When the clause refers to a **time in the past** and describes the **circumstances** of the action of the main verb - usually a single past occurrence, rather than just a time frame - **cum** is used with the **imperfect** or **pluperfect subjunctive** (**circumstantial** or **historical cum**). This is very similar to the **causal cum** in showing the inner connection of two events and can often be thought of as "because."

Cum Caesar in Galliam **venisset**, Helvetii territi sunt.
                    When (or because) Caesar had come into Gaul, the Helvetians were scared.

Milites **cum vidissent** urbes deletas, redire non voluerunt.
> When the soldiers had seen the destroyed houses, they did not want to return.

Caesar **cum** a coniuratis **occisus esset**, sub statua Pompei iacuit.
> When Caesar had been killed by the conspirators, he lay at the foot of Pompey's statue.

2. Cum meaning "since" or "because"

This **cum** always takes the **subjunctive**.

Cum sors servorum miserrima **esset**, seditionem fecerunt.
> Since the lot of the slaves was miserable, they started an uprising.

Cum pecuniam invenire non **possis**, esurire debemus.
> Since you can not find the money, we have to go hungry.

3. Cum meaning "although" or "while"

This **cum** always takes the **subjunctive**. When cum means "although", the adverb **tamen** (yet, nevertheless) is often used in the main sentence; it need not be translated.

Socrates, **cum** innocens **esset**, tamen ab iudicibus damnatus est.
> Although Socrates was innocent, he was condemned by the judges.

Homo solus rationem habet, **cum** ceteris animalibus **desit**.
> Man alone has reason, while it is lacking in the other animals.

When the subject of the **cum**-clause and the main clause are identical, the subject often precedes the cum clause (see 'Socrates' above and Nr. 3 below). It has to be a separate word, though, not part of the verb.

 **EXERCISE F:**   Translate the sentences and choose the appropriate meaning of **cum**; some of them can be rendered in more than one way; choose according to your judgment:

1. Cum hostes venirent, milites in castra properaverunt.
2. Cum omnia scire videaris, me adiuvare potes.
3. Socrates, cum faciliter e custodia effugere potuisset, noluit.
4. Cum pueri ludere possunt, gaudent. [Indicative!]
5. Cum alii liberi magistrum orarent et implorarent, frater meus librum suum legebat.
6. Quae cum relata essent imperatori, magna voce risit.
7. Cum media nocte clamorem audirent, territi sunt.
8. Cum discipuli Platonis eius definitioni applauderent, Diogenes gallum nudatum produxit.
9. Cum leo praedam divisisset in tres partes, suam partem tertiam exspectabat
      et equus et asinus.
10. Servus, cum nulla hominis vestigia repperisset, tamen custodem suum adesse cognovit.
11. Quod cum diabolus promisisset et servus sero intravisset, ait ei dominus:
      "Quare non es in vinea?"
12. Vulpes, cum uvam omnibus viribus saliens attingere non posset, dixit:
      "Nolo hanc uvam."

Compare sentences (8), (10), (11), and (12) on the previous page to the indicative versions which first occurred in the stories! The subjunctive clauses are the originals.

While **cum** mostly demands your flexibility in translating, the conjunction **ut** poses a different challenge. It is always used with the subjunctive (unless it means **as**), and it can always be translated as **that,** or **so that**, (although not to the benefit of English style). The problem is knowing when to use this conjunction in Latin. Here are four types of dependent clauses using ut:

> **UT**   1. Purpose clauses
>   2. Indirect commands, demands, or requests
>   3. Result clauses
>   4. Clauses of fearing

1. Purpose Clauses: This is the most difficult clause to detect, because in English it occurs often in the form of an infinitive construction, and it is easily confused with real infinitive uses. The English conjunction "that" is of little help either, since this chamaeleon of a word has so many different functions. Compare the following types of English and Latin sentences:

a. True Infinitive Constructions (including ACI):

Constituimus domum relinquere.	We decided to leave the house.
	We decided that we would leave the house.
Virine agros emere possunt?	Can the men buy fields?
Si equos capere volumus, celerrime currere debemus.	
	If we want to catch the horses, we must run very fast.
Militem mortuum esse arbitratus est. (ACI)	He considered the soldier to be dead (to have died).
Speramus te valere.	We hope [for] you to be well. (ACI)
	We hope that you are doing well.

b. Purpose Constructions:

In these, the English infinitive expresses really an end, or purpose, and you can replace it with a clause starting with "in order to" (among others).
In Latin such phrases are introduced by **ut**, or by **ne**, if they are negative:

Tuli libros, **ut** eos **legerem**.	I brought the books to read them.
	... in order to read them.
	...[so] that I could read them.
Veniemus, **ut spectemus** villam tuam.	We will come to look at your house.
	...in order to look at your house.
	...that we may look at your house.
Teneo librum tuum, **ne** eum **obliviscas**.	I am holding your book, so you won't forget it.
	....in order for you not to forget it.

Distinguish clauses. Decide which of the following are purpose clauses (P) and which infinitive clauses (I).   Apply the 'in-order-to' test!

_____ 1. We hope to see you soon.

_____ 2. We came to see you.

_____ 3. We decided to see you.

_____ 4. We ran all the way to see you sooner.

_____ 5. We worked all day to finish the project.

_____ 6. We did not come here to do your work.

_____ 7. We think that you will be finished.

_____ 8. We can see that you won't be finished.

_____ 9. We are cooking some food to eat later.

_____10. We eat to live, we don't live to eat.

All other **ut-clauses** are comparatively easy to recognize, because the main clause has either a verb or an adverb or adjective in it to characterize the type of ut-clause.

2. Indirect Commands, Demands, or Requests have a verb in the main clause that does exactly one of these things, in which case the subordinate clause uses **ut**; or the verb prohibits or prevents you from doing it, then the subordinate clause starts with **ne :**

Some frequently used verbs are**:**   case for the person asked, ordered, etc.
                                                    (if other than accusative)

rogare - to ask	
orare - to ask, beg	
postulare - to demand (from s.o.)	**ab + Abl.**
imperare - to order	**Dative**
persuadere - to persuade	**Dative**
monere - to admonish	
hortari - to encourage, admonish	
adducere - to cause	
petere - to strive, beg	**ab + Abl.**
contendere - to strive	**(no person)**
niti - to strive	
efficere - to effect	
id agere - to plan	

> **id spectare** - to see to it
> **videre** - to see to it
>
> **impedire** - to hinder
> **prohibere** - to prevent
> **resistere** - to resist
> **cavere** - to guard

Examples:

Adducimur natura, **ut** multis hominibus prodesse **velimus**.

> We are caused by nature to want to help many people.

Omnibus viribus gladiator nitebatur, **ut** leonem **occideret**.

> The gladiator was trying with all his strength to kill the lion.

Hortor vos, **ne** fessi fiatis et agros **relinquatis**.

> I admonish you not to get tired and not to leave the fields.

Cavendum est, **ne** poena maior **sit** quam culpa.

> One has to watch out that the punishment not be greater than the crime.
> One has to guard against the punishment being greater than the crime.

3. Result clauses can also be detected quite easily, because they are "announced" in the main clause by a word meaning "so," "so...," or "such", like the following.

> **tam** - so   (modifies adjectives and adverbs)
> **sic** - so   (modifies verbs)
> **ita** - so   (modifies either)
>
> **tantus,a,um** - so great
> **talis,e** - of such a kind
> **totiens** - so often   \ **not declined**
> **tot** - so many   /

Furthermore, result clauses follow impersonal verbs of "happening" or "bringing something about" - namely a "result" - such as:

> **accidit**   it happens
> **evenit**   it happens, occurs
> **fit**   it comes about
> **fieri potest**   it can happen
> **factum est**   it came about, happened
> **sequitur**   it follows
> **necesse est**   it is necessary

The subjunctive clause is introduced by **ut**, the negative is **ut non**.

Examples:

Urbs **ita** deleta est, **ut** restitui **non possit**.	The city is so [heavily] destroyed that it cannot be rebuilt.
Nemo **tam** prudens est, **ut** omnia **sciat**.	Nobody is so wise that he knows everything.
Liberi aulam **totiens** iacebant, **ut frangeret**.	The children threw the jug so many times that it broke.

Cum omnes postul**ent** a nobis, ut fortes **simus**, **necesse est**, **ut** nihil **faciamus**.
    Although everyone is demanding from us that we be strong,
        it is necessary that we we do nothing.

4. Clauses of fearing are simply introduced by a verb meaning **to fear, to be afraid**, or the like. Since the dependent clauses following these verbs actually mean that something should **not** happen, the conjunction meaning "that" is **ne**, and its negative is **ne non** or - **ut**!

timere	to fear
metuere	to fear
vereri	to fear
periculum est	there is danger

Examples:

Timeo, **ne** pecuniam **amiserim**.	I fear that I have lost the money.
Vereor, **ne** amicus meus **non veniat**.	I am afraid my friend is not coming.
Vereor, **ut** amicus meus **veniat**.	

Periculum erat, **ne** Galli Capitolium **aggrederentur**.
        There was a danger that the Gauls might attack the Capitol.

EXERCISE H:	Translate the sentences: (Using the infinitive often makes the best translation.)

1. Vereor, ut quis me audiverit.

2. Impedit ira animum, ne possit videre verum.

3. Orpheus deos inferorum [of the Underworld] orabat, ut sibi Eurydicen redderent.

4. Laocoon Troianos monuit, ne donum Graecorum acciperent.

5. Cicero Catilinam persuadere voluit, ut urbem relinqueret.

6. Multi in theatrum eunt, non ut spectent, sed ut spectentur.

7. Atheniensis quidam tam dives fuisse dicitur, ut pecuniam non numeraret,

    sed metiretur. [numerare - to count; metiri - to measure]

8. Nonnullae stellae tam longe absunt, ut eas videre numquam possimus.

9. Medicus me monuit, ut cotidie ambularem et paulum ederem.

10. Accidit ut esset luna plena, quae daret nobis lucem.

Lecto I : Dolus Punitus 1 (Poggio Bracciolini)

Esuriens quondam vulpes ad gallum accessit, ut gallinas deciperet; illae enim gallo duce arborem altiorem, quo ei aditus non erat, ascenderant. Quem comiter cum salutavisset, "Quid in alto agis," inquit, "num nondum audivisti haec nova tam salutaria nobis?"

5 Gallus respondit: "Nequaquam, sed nuntia!"
"Huc accessi," inquit vulpes, "ut communicarem tecum gaudium. Animalium omnium consilium celebratum est, in quo pacem perpetuam inter se firmaverunt, ita ut, omni sublato timore, nulli iam ab altero aut insidiae aut iniuriae fieri possint, sed omnes pace et concordia fruantur. Licet unicuique, vel soli, quo velit, ire secure.

10 Descendite igitur, et communiter agamus hunc festum diem!"
Perspecta vulpis fallacia gallus: "Bonum," inquit, "affers nuntium et mihi gratum," et simul collum altius protendit prospicientique similis in pedes se erexit.
Tum vulpes: "Quid aspicis?" et gallus: "Duos magno cursu ore patulo advenientes canes."

15 Tum tremebunda vulpes: "Vale," inquit, "mihi fugiendum est, antequam illi advenerint," et simul coepit abire.
Hic gallus: "Quo fugis aut quid times, quoniam pace constituta nihil est timendum?"
"Dubito," inquit vulpes, "an canes isti audiverint decretum pacis."
Hoc modo dolo illusus est dolus.

dolus,i - cunning, trickery, deceit; (1) esurire - to be hungry; quondam - once (upon a time); accedere - to go to; decipere - to deceive; (2) comiter - politely; gallo duce - (Ablative Absolute) with the rooster as their leader; (**cum** is placed in the middle of the clause; this is a matter of style); (3) num - or by chance; (4) salutaris,e - healthful, advantageous; (5) nequaquam - not at all; (6) communicare - to share; (7) perpetuus - everlasting; celebrare - to make known, celebrate; firmare - to confirm; (8) omni sublato timore - (Ablative Absolute: after...); nulli ...possint - (What is the subject of possint? Therefore, what case is nulli?); insidiae,arum - ambush; (9) concordia,ae - harmony; vel - (here: even); (11) perspicere - to see through; fallacia - deceit, trickery; (12) collum,i - neck; protendere - to stretch out; prospicere - to look out into the distance; similis is followed by the Dative; in pedes se erigere - to rise up on tiptoes; (13) aspicere - to see; patulus,a,um - hanging open;
(15) tremebundus,a,um - shaking, trembling; (19) dubito an - I doubt whether (that)...; decretum,i - decision, treaty; (20) illudere - to mock, deride.

Lectio II: Dolus Punitus 2   (C.V. Heisterbach)

Prior quidam ordinis nostri, mortuo abbate suo, abbatiam petens, cum tempore electionis - sicut ceteri seniores - a visitatore de persona idonea interrogaretur, corde non columbino monachum quendam de domo eadem ob infamiam eiectum nominavit. Sciebat enim suam auctoritatem esse magnam et, si quem de conventu

5 nominaret, per hoc suam electionem posse infirmari et se in suo desiderio impediri. Factum est nutu, ut creditur, divino, ut ceteri eius exemplo eandem personam eligerent, cogitantes secum: "Prior noster oculus noster est, nec eam personam

nominavisset, si de illius innocentia ei non constaret."

Fortasse, si prior simpliciter ambulavisset, factus esset abbas. Ecce sic astutos et

10 dolosos punit etiam in praesenti Deus.

(1) prior,oris - prior, second to the abbot; ordo - here: monastic order; abbas,abbatis - abbot; abbatia,ae - office of the abbot; tempore - at the time; (2) idoneus,a,um - suitable; (3) columbinus,a,um - (Adjective from columba,ae - dove) - lily-white; monachus,i - monk;
eicere, eicio,eieci,eiectum - to throw out, kick out; (4) conventus,us - convent, monastery;
(5) infirmare - to weaken; desiderium,i - desire; (6) nutus,us - nod, will; ius exemplo - by his example, advice; (7) eligere - to elect; oculus,i - eye; (8) ei constat - he is sure; (9) ambulare - here: to proceed.

Translation Help: Translate the skeleton of the first sentence above as follows: Cum prior ordinis nostri... tempore electionis...a visitatore de persona idonea interrogaretur,...monachum quendam nominavit. Now fill in participial and other constructions:

mortuo abbate suo (Abl. Abs.); abbatiam petens (refers to? Subject!); (monachum quendam) de domo eadem ob infamiam eiectum; sicut ceteri seniores; corde non columbino.

EXERCISE I: In the readings above find examples of the following:

1. a purpose clause   _____

2. an Ablative Absolute   _____

3. a pluperfect subjunctive   _____

4. a present participle (nom.)   _____

5. a present participle (acc.)   _____

6. a present participle (dat.)   _____

7. a hortatory (iussive) subjunctive   _____

8. a gerundive   _____

9. a passive periphrastic construction _____

10. a circumstantial cum clause   _____

11. a result clause   _____

12. adverbs formed from adjectives   _____

Lectio III : Fabulae Parvae (There are no titles in Latin, English titles suggested here)

1. Old Wine

M. Cicero, cum apud Damasippium cenaret et ille mediocri vino posito diceret: "Bibite Falernum hoc; annorum quadraginta est", "Bene," inquit, "aetatem fert."

2. Too small

Cicero cum generum suum, exiguae staturae hominem, longo gladio accinctum vidisset: "Quis," inquit, "generum meum ad gladium alligavit?"

3. She Doesn't Age

5 Cicero, Fabia dicente triginta annos se habere: "Verum est," inquit, "nam hoc illam iam viginti annis audio."

4. The Miraculous Mattress

Quidam eques Romanus debuit et celavit magnum aes alienum, dum vixit. Quae cum relata sint Augusto, iussit servos sibi emere culcitam cubicularem in eius auctione. Mirantibus servis hanc rationem reddidit: "Mihi habenda est ad somnum illa culcita, in **10** qua ille vir, cum tantum deberet, dormire potuit."

5. A Rare Skill

Cum taurum in arenam misisset, et exisset ad eum feriendum venator, neque productum decies potuisset occidere, coronam venatori misit Gallienus; mussantibusque cunctis, quid rei esset, quod homo ineptissimus coronaretur, Gallienus per curionem dici iussit: "Taurum totiens non ferire dificillimum est."

6. A Bunch of Turkeys

15 Quidam abbas, cum cellarius deesset, dixit ad fratres suos: "Quem ego eligam ex numero istorum stultorum?" Cui unus ex grege: "Nonne abbatem antea invenimus ex istis stultis?"

---

(2) Falernum - a famous wine; (3) gener,i - son-in-law; exiguus,a,um - small, little; accingere - to gird; (4) alligare - to tie to; (5) Fabia was the first wife of Cicero's son-in-law Dolabella; (7) aes alienum - debt; (8) Augustus - (emperor); culcita cubicularis - bedroom mattress; (11) taurus,i - bull; ferire - to hit, kill; venator - hunter, bull-fighter; (12) productum - the (having been) led out, = taurum; decies - ten times; corona,ae - crown; Gallienus - (Roman Emperor AD 253 to 268); (13) mussare - to mutter; coronare - to crown; (14) curio,onis - herald; totiens - so many times; (15) cellarius,i - wine master; eligere - to choose.

Reading: An Early Vegetarian

In his *Metamorphoses* Ovid quotes an early proponent of a vegetarian lifestyle:
(Bk. 15, 75-142 excerpts):

"Take care, you mortals, not to disgrace your bodies with murderous food. After all there is the produce of the fields, there are the fruits of the trees,...grapes ripening on the vines; there are sweet herbs and others that can only become soft and mild when cooked. Neither the fluid milk is taken from you, nor the honey smelling of thyme blossoms. The earth gives abundant riches and offers peaceful food without murder and blood. Only animals eat meat, and not even all of them: Horses, sheep, cattle live off grass...Untamed animals like Armenian tigers, irascible lions, bears, and wolves enjoy the bloody food...But for humans it is criminal to chew miserably wounded animals with cruel teeth and as living beings live off the death of other living beings. Do you want to bring back the bad habits of the Cyclopes? [who ate human beings]
During the aera that we call the golden we were happy with fruits and vegetables and herbs and did not besmear our mouths with blood. At that time birds, rabbits,...fish all lived without fear and in peace.
When a useless innovator, whoever he was, envied the lions their food and devoured flesh as food, he prepared the way for crime...We may confess, without violating the heavenly order, to have killed animals that were threatening our lives. We should have killed them but we should not have eaten them.
Then the evil continued. First the pig supposedly deserved death as a sacrificial victim, because it had dug up the seeds of the field; then the goat was accused of chewing the vines and was slaughtered at the altars of Bacchus. At least these two can be said to have brought on their own downfall. But what was your fault, sheep, gentle small beasts, born to protect humans from the cold? You carry nectar in your udders and offer your wool for soft clothes; you help us more alive than dead. And what was the fault of the cattle - steers, oxen, cows - animals without fraud or deception, harmless, simple, born to tolerate labors. Is not he ungrateful and unworthy to receive the gift of the grain, that has managed to slaughter his field laborer, who has so often helped him plow the fields and bring in the harvest?
And people even used the gods as an excuse for their criminal acts and killed the unsuspecting steer in order to tear out his entrails and try to foretell the plans of the gods from them."

Ovid comments: This man was the first to raise a complaint against the custom of serving animals, especially domestic animals, as food, the first to open his mouth to speak words, which were wise, but were obviously not heeded or believed.

The man who had launched this fiery appeal was none other than the mathematician and philosopher Pythagoras! (Yes: $a^2 + b^2 = c^2$; he wrote this ca. 540 BC)

Food and Cooking

What the Romans ate depended, like so many other things, on their class and their wealth. In early times almost everybody ate simple foods: black bread, onions, cabbage, some meat, and the Roman national dish, a type of grits or polenta made with flour **(puls).** When the Romans came into contact with Eastern countries, they learned more refined recipes with different ingredients and condiments, such as pepper and cinnamon. Romans grew to like different kinds of bread and cake, and exotic fruit, such as dates, and they became used to fatty and highly spiced foods, which they varied with different sauces. One favorite sauce was the **liquamen** or **garum**, which was produced by marinating fish entrails and tails in brine, and letting them disintegrate and ferment in the sun, before boiling and thickening the sauce in pots. Notwithstanding their unpleasant smell Pompeiian and Spanish **garum** were famous all over the Mediterranean and imported to the northernmost parts of the empire.

In general Roman cooks liked to spice their dishes in the sweet and sour mode. Meat was sweetened with honey or fruits. Pepper was used for everything, even desserts. Here is a dessert recipe from the cookbook of Caelius Apicius:

> **Take green or ripe pitted fresh dates, fill them with pine nuts, or other nuts, and coarsely ground pepper; salt them on the outside; fry them in hot honey and serve them.**

Roman triclinium

For meat the Romans used poultry, lamb, pork, venison, rabbit, wild boar, partridge, pheasant, and several animal organs, such as liver, heart, kidneys, and stomachs. Beef was expensive and rarely used. Fish was eaten widely. Some specialties of the day are perhaps less to our contemporary taste, for instance dormice, shrews, cultivated snails, and udder or vulva of pig. (There are, however, still many places where pig´s knuckles, tails, ears, snouts, and stomachs are prized.) Here is a somewhat more exotic recipe:

Flamingo

**Pluck the flamingo, wash and dress, and put it into a pot.
Add water, salt, dill, and a little vinegar. When it is half cooked,
tie a bunch of leeks and coriander and add it.
Shortly before it is done, pour *defritum* in, to add color.
Into a mortar put pepper, caraway (or cumin) seeds,
coriander, laser root, mint, and rue, and grind them;
moisten with a little vinegar, add Jericho dates and a little
of the stock. Pour all into the pot, thicken with *amulum*.
(Put the bird on a platter), pour the sauce over it, and serve.
The same recipe can also be used for parrot.**

Note: **defritum** or **defrutum** was a kind of thick grape juice; **amulum** is starch

This recipe for ham is perhaps more to our modern taste (and means):

Ham

**Cook the ham with a lot of dried figs and three laurel [bay]
leaves. Remove the skin, make crosswise incisions, and fill
the cuts with honey. Then make a dough of flour and oil
and wrap the ham as with a skin. Bake in the oven until
the dough is done, take it out and serve it as it is.**

Meats and fish were never eaten without sauces. Of the nine chapters in the cookbook of Apicius two deal with sauces. Here is a sauce to be poured over sardines. Apicius did not believe in patronizing cooks by dwelling too much on the amount or proportion of the ingredients, so use your own judgment!

> **[Mix] pepper, privet [an herb], dried mint, cooked onion, honey, vinegar, and oil, and pour over the sardines; spread chopped hard-boiled egg over it.**

Foods that the Romans knew already include several types of pizza (soft and crispy), lasagne, sausages, cheese, and even ices: they were mixed from white flour, sweet wine, and snow from the mountains. During the summer the mountain snow also served to thin and cool the wine, which was kept in underground storage vaults. The Romans did not have sugar, potatoes, coffee, tea, oranges, or bananas. There was, however, a wide variety of vegetables and fruits: onions, green beans, peas, turnips, garlic, olives, leeks, apples, pears, plums, figs, dates, cherries, and nuts. Here is a modernized recipe for zucchini salad:

> **Slice zucchini lengthwise, fry the slices in very hot oil. Put them on paper towels to dry and serve with a sauce of wine, salt, and pepper. (Can also be served cold.)**

The Romans drank water, milk, and, of course, wine, which they thinned with water, and heated in the winter. The wine could also be spiced with honey or pepper. There was dessert wine, resinated wine, and, for the poor people, **posca**, a very refreshing mixture of vinegar and water, sweetened with a little honey.

The original three meals a day soon fell victim to hectic city life. There was breakfast (**ientaculum)** with bread, cheese, and leftovers from the day before. Lunch was grabbed somewhere in the city at one of the many taverns or foodstands. They offered sardines, olives, bread, sausages, pancakes, fruits, and sweets. Many people did not even bother with breakfast at home, but ate it out also. After going to the public bath in the afternoon people went home and ate dinner, around 3 or 4 in the afternoon **(cena).** They stretched out on their beds in the triclinium, and depending on the occasion, ate a simple meal consisting of antipasto and a main course of meat, or an elaborate banquet with a number of courses, which Martial described as **ab ovo usque ad mala**, *from the egg to the apples,* since the first course always had eggs and olives in it, and the last one sweets and fruit.

Here are 2 more recipes for desserts. Now you can prepare a Roman meal of several courses. (Your aunt´s parrot is off limits!)

Dulcia

Take fine wheat flour and cook in hot water to a very stiff puree [mash].
Spread this on a platter. After it is cold, cut small squares,
as with sweet pastry, and fry them in the best oil.
Take them out, drizzle them with honey, sprinkle with pepper and serve.
You will do better if you use milk instead of water.

Egg Creme (Tyropatia)

Take a sufficient amount of milk, according to the size of the pot,
and mix it with honey as for milk broth.
Add 5 eggs for 1/2 liter of milk, or 3 eggs for 1/4 liter of milk.
Mix until smooth, then pass the mixture through a strainer
into an earthenware pot (cumana) and cook it on a low flame.
When it is stiff, sprinkle with pepper and serve.

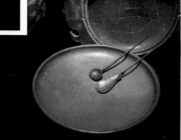

Jars, bowls, and plates
with spoons

Chapter 15 : Answers and Translations

Exercise A:
1. videam 2. arbitreris 3. det 4. iaciant 5. eat 6. moveamur 7. ponas 8. feras 9. sitis 10. punias

Exercise B: The choice of possible translations is arbitrary! You might want to try alternatives.

1.	Present, Ind.,	videre	he/she sees		2.	Perfect, Ind.,	videre	he/she saw, has seen
3.	Present, Ind.,	ponere	he/she places		4.	Future, Ind.,	ponere	they will put
5.	Present, Subj.,	ponere	they should put		6.	Present, Ind.,	ponere	they are (being) put
7.	Present, Subj.,	portare	let them carry		8.	Present, Ind.,	portare	they are carried
9.	Present, Subj.,	velle	she should want		10.	Present, Ind.,	laudare	he praises
11.	Present, Subj.,	debere	let him owe		12.	Present, Subj.,	audire	let me hear
						Future, Ind.,	audire	I shall hear
13.	Present, Ind.,	audire	she hears		14.	Present, Subj.,	dare	he should give
15.	Present, Ind.,	debere	she owes, ought to		16.	Future, Ind.,	audire	he/she will hear

Exercise C:
1. habuerit 2. mansisses 3. peteremus 4. vellet 5. velit 6. muniatur 7. polliciti sint 8. tacti essent 9. feceritis 10. rogarent 11. oboediverim 12. laudem 13. moneatur 14. essemus 15. ferretis 16. iacti sint 17. dixisset 18. creverit 19. mentiremini 20. navigent

Exercise D:
1. Edamus et bibamus! 2. Audiantur omnes. 3. Habeat corpus. 4. Vivat. 5. Fiat voluntas tua. 6. Gaudeamus. (or Laeti simus.) 7. Credas eum deum esse. 8. Utinam credere possim! 9. Ne frangatur fenestra. 10. Det eis cibum.

Exercise E:
1. If only I had not forgotten the book. (unfulfillable wish) MC
2. If you had reminded (or warned) me, I would not have forgotten it. DC, MC
3. Would that all inhabitants of our country were free! (Possibly fulfillable) MC
4. If you knew all the animals in the world, you could be called learned. DC, MC
5. Let us not do anything in anger, but let us wait for one hour. MC
6. If only the boys were not so lazy! MC
7. If the children had not eaten all the bread, I would not have to be hungry. DC, MC
8. Let all sides be heard! MC
9. If I knew more certainly, I would tell you. DC, MC
10. If I wanted to become rich, I would not be a teacher. DC, MC

Exercise F:
1. When the enemy came, the soldiers hurried into the camp.
2. Since you seem to know everything, you can help me.
3. Although Socrates could have escaped easily from prison, he did not want to.
4. When(ever) the boys can play, they are happy.
5. While the other children begged and implored the teacher, my brother read his book.
6. When these things were related to the emperor, he laughed in a loud voice.
7. When they heard a noise in the middle of the night, they were scared.
8. While the disciples of Plato applauded his definition, Diogenes produced a nude chicken.
9. When the lion had divided the loot into three parts, both the horse and the donkey expected their third (part).

10. Since the servant had found no traces of a man, he knew his custodian to be present.
11. When the devil had promised this and the servant had entered late,
    his master said to him: "Why are you not in the vineyard?"
12. Since the fox could not reach the grapes, although he was jumping with all his might,
    he said: "I don't want these grapes."

Exercise G:
1. I 2. P 3. I 4. P 5. P 6. P 7. I 8. I 9. P 10. P

Exercise H:
1. I am afraid (my) father has not heard me.
2. Anger prevents the mind from being able to see the truth.
3. Orpheus begged the gods of the underworld to give him back Euridice.
4. Laocoon warned the Trojans not to accept a gift from (of) the Greeks.
5. Cicero wanted to persuade Catiline to leave the city.
6. Many go to the theater, not to see, but to be seen.
7. A certain Athenian is said to have been so rich that he did not
   count his money, but measured it (in buckets).
8. Some stars are so far away that we will never be able to see them.
9. The physician admonished me to walk daily and to eat little.
10. It happened that there was a full moon, which gave us light.

Reading 1 : Cunning is Punished (1)
One time a fox who was hungry went to a rooster in order to deceive the hens; for they had, with the rooster as their leader, ascended a rather high tree, to which there was no access for him [the fox]. When he had greeted him politely, he said: "What are you doing up high? Or have you not yet heard this piece of news so advantageous to us?"
The rooster answered: "Not at all, but report!"
"I have come here," said the fox, "to share with you (great) joy. A plan of all the animals has been made known, in which they confirm eternal peace among themselves, so that, all fear having been put aside, there can no ambush or injury be done to any one from another, but all enjoy peace and harmony. It is permitted to everyone, even alone, to go securely to wherever he wants to. Come down, therefore, and let us celebrate together this festive day!"
Having seen through the deceit of the fox [the deceit of the fox having been seen through] the rooster said: "You bring good news and pleasing to me," and at the same time he stuck out his neck higher and rose up on tiptoes similar to one who is looking out into the distance.
Then the fox said: "What are you looking at?" and the rooster: "Two dogs arriving at top speed [great run] and with their mouths hanging open."
Then the trembling fox said: "Goodbye, I must flee, before they arrive," and at the same time he began to walk away.
At this point the rooster [said]: "Where are you running to, and what do you fear, since, with peace having been decided on, there is nothing to be feared?"
"I doubt," said the fox, "that those dogs there have heard about the peace treaty."
In this manner cunning was deceived by cunning.

Reading 2 : Cunning is Punished (2)

When a certain prior of our order, who was seeking the office of the abbot, after his abbot had died, at the time of the election - just like the other elders - was asked by a visitor about a suitable person [for the office], he nominated, with a less than lily-white heart, a certain monk from the same monastery, who had been kicked out because of his infamy. For he knew that his authority was great and that, if he nominated someone from the convent, through this, his election [bid] could be weakened and he would be hampered in his pursuits. It happened, however, as is believed, by divine will, that by his advice the others elected the self-same person, thinking unto themselves: "Our prior is our eye, and he would not have nominated this person if he were not sure of his innocence."

Perhaps, if the prior had proceeded simply, he would have been made abbot. Behold, in such a way God punishes even in the present the deceitful and cunning people.

Exercise I:

1. ut communicarem... gaudium; ut nulli...invidiae fieri possint, sed (ut) omnes...pace fruantur
2. perspecta vulpis fallacia; omni sublato timore; pace constituta; mortuo abbate suo
3. ambulavisset; salutavisset; nominavisset   4. esuriens; cogitantes; petens
5. advenientes   6. prospicienti
7. agamus   8. fugiendum, timendum
9. mihi fugiendum est; nihil est timendum   10. cum ... interrogaretur
11. ut ... eligerent   12. comiter; communiter; secure; altius

Reading 3 : Little Stories

1. When M. Cicero dined at the house of Damasippius and his host [ille] told him, after a mediocre wine had been placed [before him]: "Drink this Falernian; it is forty years old," he [Cicero] said: "It carries its age well."

2. When Cicero saw his son-in-law, a man of small stature, girded with a long sword, he asked: "Who tied my son-in-law to this sword?"

3. When Fabia said that she was thirty years old, Cicero said: "It is true, for I have heard it already for twenty years from her." (or: I hear her say...)

4. A certain Roman knight owed and hid great debts, while he was alive. When this was brought to the ears of Augustus, he ordered his slaves to buy for him the bedroom mattress at his [the knight's] estate auction. When the slaves were wondering, he gave them this reason: "I must have that mattress for my sleep on which this man, although he owed so much, was able to sleep."

5. After he had sent a bull into the arena and a bull-fighter had come out to kill him and had not been able to kill the bull, although it had been led out ten times, Gallienus gave the bull-fighter the [victory] crown; when all people muttered what kind of thing it was that the most inept man was being crowned, Gallienus had this announcement made through a herald: "To miss [not to hit] a bull so many times is very difficult."

6. When there was no wine master [or: the wine master was lacking], a certain abbot said to his brothers: "Whom shall I elect from the number of these idiots?" To him [said] one of the flock: "Haven't we earlier found an abbot from these idiots?"

APPENDIX   GRAMMAR

VERB CONJUGATIONS

1st (a-)	2nd (e-)	3rd (consonant)	3rd (i- stems)	4th (i)
portare, *to carry*	**docere,** *to teach*	**regere,** *to rule*	**capere,** *to take*	**audire,** *to hear*

Indicative Active

Present

I carry, am carrying	*I teach, am teaching*	*I rule, am ruling*	*I take, am taking*	*I hear, am hearing*	
do carry	*do teach*	*do rule*	*do take*	*do hear*	
1. port**o**	doce**o**	reg**o**	capi**o**	audi**o**	
2. port**as**	doc**es**	reg**is**	cap**is**	aud**is**	**Sg**
3. port**at**	doc**et**	reg**it**	cap**it**	aud**it**	
1. porta**mus**	doce**mus**	reg**imus**	capi**mus**	audi**mus**	
2. porta**tis**	doce**tis**	reg**itis**	cap**itis**	aud**itis**	**Pl**
3. port**ant**	doc**ent**	reg**unt**	capi**unt**	audi**unt**	

Imperative: port**a**! port**ate** !   doc**e**! doc**ete**!   reg**e**! reg**ite**!   cap**e**! cap**ite**!   aud**i**! aud**ite**!

Imperfect

I carried, was carrying,	*I taught, was teaching,*	*I ruled, was ruling,*	*I took, was taking,*	*I heard, was hearing,*	
used to carry	*used to teach*	*used to rule*	*used to take*	*used to hear*	
1. porta**bam**	doce**bam**	reg**ebam**	capi**ebam**	audi**ebam**	
2. porta**bas**	doce**bas**	reg**ebas**	capi**ebas**	audi**ebas**	**Sg**
3. porta**bat**	doce**bat**	reg**ebat**	capi**ebat**	audi**ebat**	
1. porta**bamus**	doce**bamus**	reg**ebamus**	capi**ebamus**	audi**ebamus**	
2. porta**batis**	doce**batis**	reg**ebatis**	capi**ebatis**	audi**ebatis**	**Pl**
3. porta**bant**	doce**bant**	reg**ebant**	capi**ebant**	audi**ebant**	

Future

I will carry	*I will teach*	*I will rule*	*I will take*	*I will hear*	
1. porta**bo**	doce**bo**	reg**am**	capi**am**	audi**am**	
2. porta**bis**	doce**bis**	reg**es**	cap**ies**	aud**ies**	**Sg**
3. porta**bit**	doce**bit**	reg**et**	cap**iet**	aud**iet**	
1. porta**bimus**	doce**bimus**	reg**emus**	capi**emus**	audi**emus**	
2. porta**bitis**	doce**bitis**	reg**etis**	cap**ietis**	aud**ietis**	**Pl**
3. porta**bunt**	doce**bunt**	reg**ent**	cap**ient**	aud**ient**	

Perfect

I (have) carried	*I (have) taught*	*I (have) ruled*	*I took, have taken*	*I (have) heard*	
1. portav**i**	docu**i**	rex**i**	cep**i**	audiv**i**	
2. portav**isti**	docu**isti**	rex**isti**	cep**isti**	audiv**isti**	**Sg**
3. portav**it**	docu**it**	rex**it**	cep**it**	audiv**it**	
1. portav**imus**	docu**imus**	rex**imus**	cep**imus**	audiv**imus**	
2. portav**istis**	docu**istis**	rex**istis**	cep**istis**	audiv**istis**	**Pl**
3. portav**erunt**	docu**erunt**	rex**erunt**	cep**erunt**	audiv**erunt**	

Plusquamperfect (Pluperfect)

I had carried	*I had taught*	*I had ruled*	*I had taken*	*I had heard*	
1. portav**eram**	docu**eram**	rex**eram**	cep**eram**	audiv**eram**	
2. portav**eras**	docu**eras**	rex**eras**	cep**eras**	audiv**eras**	**Sg**
3. portav**erat**	docu**erat**	rex**erat**	cep**erat**	audiv**erat**	
1. portav**eramus**	docu**eramus**	rex**eramus**	cep**eramus**	audiv**eramus**	
2. portav**eratis**	docu**eratis**	rex**eratis**	cep**eratis**	audiv**eratis**	**Pl**
3. portav**erant**	docu**erant**	rex**erant**	cep**erant**	audiv**erant**	

Future Perfect

I will have carried	*I will have taught*	*I will have ruled*	*I will have taken*	*I will have heard*	
1. portav**ero**	docu**ero**	rex**ero**	cep**ero**	audiv**ero**	
2. portav**eris**	docu**eris**	rex**eris**	cep**eris**	audiv**eris**	**Sg**
3. portav**erit**	docu**erit**	rex**erit**	cep**erit**	audiv**erit**	
1. portav**erimus**	docu**erimus**	rex**erimus**	cep**erimus**	audiv**erimus**	
2. portav**eritis**	docu**eritis**	rex**eritis**	cep**eritis**	audiv**eritis**	**Pl**
3. portav**erint**	docu**erint**	rex**erint**	cep**erint**	audiv**erint**	

Indicative Passive

Present

I am (being) carried	*I am (being) taught*	*I am (being) ruled*	*I am (being) taken*	*I am (being) heard*	
1. port**or**	doce**or**	reg**or**	capi**or**	audi**or**	
2. porta**ris**	doce**ris**	reg**eris**	cap**eris**	audi**ris**	**Sg**
3. porta**tur**	doce**tur**	reg**itur**	capi**tur**	audi**tur**	
1. porta**mur**	doce**mur**	reg**imur**	capi**mur**	audi**mur**	
2. porta**mini**	doce**mini**	reg**imini**	capi**mini**	audi**mini**	**Pl**
3. porta**ntur**	doce**ntur**	reg**untur**	capi**untur**	audi**untur**	

Imperative: **portare!** portamini! *(be carried!)* **docere!** docemini! *(be taught!)* **regere!** regimini *(be ruled!)* **capere!** capimini! *(be taken!)* **audire!** audimini! *(be heard!)* **Notice the Singular forms: like the activeinfinitive!**

Imperfect

I was, used to be carried	*I was taught*	*I was ruled*	*I was taken*	*I was heard*	
1. porta**bar**	doce**bar**	reg**ebar**	capi**ebar**	audi**ebar**	
2. porta**baris**	doce**baris**	reg**ebaris**	capi**ebaris**	audi**ebaris**	**Sg**
3. porta**batur**	doce**batur**	reg**ebatur**	capi**ebatur**	audi**ebatur**	
1. porta**bamur**	doce**bamur**	reg**ebamur**	capi**ebamur**	audi**ebamur**	
2. porta**bamini**	doce**bamini**	reg**ebamini**	capi**ebamini**	audi**ebamini**	**Pl**
3. porta**bantur**	doce**bantur**	reg**ebantur**	capi**ebantur**	audi**ebantur**	

Future

I will be carried	*I will be taught*	*I will be ruled*	*I will be taken*	*I will be heard*	
1. porta**bor**	doce**bor**	reg**ar**	capi**ar**	audi**ar**	
2. porta**beris**	doce**beris**	reg**eris**	capi**eris**	audi**eris**	**Sg**
3. porta**bitur**	doce**bitur**	reg**etur**	capi**etur**	audi**etur**	
1. porta**bimur**	doce**bimur**	reg**emur**	capi**emur**	audi**emur**	
2. porta**bimini**	doce**bimini**	reg**emini**	capi**emini**	audi**emini**	**Pl**
3. porta**buntur**	doce**buntur**	reg**entur**	capi**entur**	audi**entur**	

Perfect

I was carried, have been carried	*I was taught, have been taught*	*I was ruled, have been ruled*
portatus,a,um **sum, es, est**	doctus,a,um **sum, es, est**	rectus,a,um **sum, es, est**
portati,ae,a **sumus, estis, sunt**	docti,ae,a **sumus, estis, sunt**	recti,ae,a **sumus, estis, sunt**

I was taken, have been taken	*I was heard, have been heard*
captus,a,um **sum, es, est**	auditus,a,um **sum, es, est**
capti,ae,a **sumus, estis, sunt**	auditi,ae,a **sumus, estis, sunt**

Plusquamperfect (Pluperfect)

I had been carried	*I had been taught*	*I had been ruled*
portatus,a,um **eram, eras, erat**	doctus,a,um **eram, eras, erat**	rectus,a,um **eram, eras, erat**
portati,ae,a **eramus, eratis, erant**	docti,ae,a **eramus, eratis, erant**	recti,ae,a **eramus, eratis, erant**

I had been taken	*I had been heard*
captus,a,um **eram, eras, erat**	auditus,a,um **eram, eras, erat**
capti,ae,a **eramus, eratis, erant**	auditi,ae,a **eramus, eratis, erant**

Future Perfect

I will have been carried	*I will have been taught*	*I will have been ruled*
portatus,a,um **ero, eris, erit**	doctus,a,um **ero, eris, erit**	rectus,a,um **ero, eris, erit**
portati,ae,a **erimus, eritis, erunt**	docti,ae,a **erimus, eritis, erunt**	recti,ae,a **erimus, eritis, erunt**

I will have been taken	*I will have been heard*
captus,a,um **ero, eris, erit**	auditus,a,um **ero, eris, erit**
capti,ae,a **erimus, eritis, erunt**	auditi,ae,a **erimus, eritis, erunt**

Subjunctive Active

Present

I may, should carry	*I may, should teach*	*I may, should rule*	*I may, should take*	*I may, should hear*	
1. port**em**	doce**am**	reg**am**	capi**am**	audi**am**	
2. port**es**	doce**as**	reg**as**	capi**as**	audi**as**	**Sg**
3. port**et**	doce**at**	reg**at**	capi**at**	audi**at**	
1. port**emus**	doce**amus**	reg**amus**	capi**amus**	audi**amus**	
2. port**etis**	doce**atis**	reg**atis**	capi**atis**	audi**atis**	**Pl**
3. port**ent**	doce**ant**	reg**ant**	capi**ant**	audi**ant**	

Imperfect

I would carry	*I would teach*	*I would rule*	*I would take*	*I would hear*	
1. portar**em**	docer**em**	reger**em**	caper**em**	audir**em**	
2. portar**es**	docer**es**	reger**es**	caper**es**	audir**es**	**Sg**
3. portar**et**	docer**et**	reger**et**	caper**et**	audir**et**	
1. portar**emus**	docer**emus**	reger**emus**	caper**emus**	audir**emus**	
2. portar**etis**	docer**etis**	reger**etis**	caper**etis**	audir**etis**	**Pl**
3. portar**ent**	docer**ent**	reger**ent**	caper**ent**	audir**ent**	

Perfect

(Translate like Indicative Perfect)

1. portav**erim**	docu**erim**	rex**erim**	cep**erim**	audiv**erim**	
2. portav**eris**	docu**eris**	rex**eris**	cep**eris**	audiv**eris**	**Sg**
3. portav**erit**	docu**erit**	rex**erit**	cep**erit**	audiv**erit**	
1. portav**erimus**	docu**erimus**	rex**erimus**	cep**erimus**	audiv**erimus**	
2. portav**eritis**	docu**eritis**	rex**eritis**	cep**eritis**	audiv**eritis**	**Pl**
3. portav**erint**	docu**erint**	rex**erint**	cep**erint**	audiv**erint**	

Plusquamperfect (Pluperfect)

I would have carried	*I would have taught*	*I would have ruled*	*I would have taken*	*I would have heard*	
1. portav**issem**	docu**issem**	rex**issem**	cep**issem**	audiv**issem**	
2. portav**isses**	docu**isses**	rex**isses**	cep**isses**	audiv**isses**	**Sg**
3. portav**isset**	docu**isset**	rex**isset**	cep**isset**	audiv**isset**	
1. portav**issemus**	docu**issemus**	rex**issemus**	cep**issemus**	audiv**issemus**	
2. portav**issetis**	docu**issetis**	rex**issetis**	cep**issetis**	audiv**issetis**	**Pl**
3. portav**issent**	docu**issent**	rex**issent**	cep**issent**	audiv**issent**	

Subjunctive Passive

Present

I may, should be carried	*I may, should be taught*	*I should be ruled*	*I may be taken*	*I may, should be heard*	
1. port**er**	doce**ar**	reg**ar**	capi**ar**	audi**ar**	
2. port**eris**	doce**aris**	reg**aris**	capi**aris**	audi**aris**	**Sg**
3. port**etur**	doce**atur**	reg**atur**	capi**atur**	audi**atur**	
1. port**emur**	doce**amur**	reg**amur**	capi**amur**	audi**amur**	
2. port**emini**	doce**amini**	reg**amini**	capi**amini**	audi**amini**	**Pl**
3. port**entur**	doce**antur**	reg**antur**	capi**antur**	audi**antur**	

Imperfect

I would be carried	*I would be taught*	*I would be ruled*	*I would be taken*	*I would be heard*	
1. portar**er**	docer**er**	reger**er**	caper**er**	audir**er**	
2. portar**eris**	docer**eris**	reger**eris**	caper**eris**	audir**eris**	**Sg**
3. portar**etur**	docer**etur**	reger**etur**	caper**etur**	audir**etur**	
1. portar**emur**	docer**emur**	reger**emur**	caper**emur**	audir**emur**	
2. portar**emini**	docer**emini**	reger**emini**	caper**emini**	audir**emini**	**Pl**
3. portar**entur**	docer**entur**	reger**entur**	caper**entur**	audir**entur**	

Perfect *(Translate like indicative)*

portatus,a,um **sim, sis, sit**	doctus,a,um **sim, sis,** sit	captus,a,um **sim, sis, sit**
portati,ae,a **simus, sitis sint**	docti,ae,a **simus, sitis, sint**	capti,ae,a **simus, sitis, sint**
rectus,a,um **sim, sis, sit**	auditus,a,um **sim, sis, sit**	
recti,ae,a **simus, sitis, sint**	auditi,ae,a **simus, sitis, sint**	

Plusquamperfect (Pluperfect)

I would have been carried   *I would have been taught*   *I would have been ruled / taken*   *I would have been heard*

portatus,a,um **essem, esses, esset**   doctus,a,um / rectus,a,um / captus,a,um / auditus,a,um **essem, esses, esset**

portati,ae,a **essemus, essetis, essent**   docti,ae,a / recti,ae,a / capti,ae,a / auditi,ae,a **essemus, essetis, essent**

Note: In many instances the Latin subjunctive must be rendered as indicative in English.

Infinitives

	Active		Passive	
Present	portare	*to carry*	portari	*to be carried*
	docere	*to teach*	doceri	*to be taught*
	regere	*to rule*	regi	*to be ruled*
	capere	*to take*	capi	*to be taken*
	audire	*to hear*	audiri	*to be heard*
Perfect	portavisse	*to have carried*	portatus,a,um **esse**	*to have been carried*
	docuisse	*to have taught*	doctus,a,um **esse**	*to have been taught*
	rexisse	*to have ruled*	rectus,a,um **esse**	*to have been ruled*
	cepisse	*to have taken*	captus,a,um **esse**	*to have been taken*
	audivisse	*to have heard*	auditus,a,um **esse**	*to have been heard*
Future	portaturus,a,um **esse**	*to be about to carry*	portatum **iri**	*to be about to be carried* }
	docturus,a,um **esse**	*to be about to teach*	doctum **iri**	*to be about to be taught* }
	recturus,a,um **esse**	*to be about to rule*	rectum **iri**	*to be about to be ruled* }(unusual)
	capturus,a,um **esse**	*to be about to take*	captum **iri**	*to be about to be taken* }
	auditurus,a,um **esse**	*to be about to hear*	auditum **iri**	*to be about to be heard* }

Participles

	Active		Passive	
Present	portans, portantis	*carrying*		
	docens, docentis	*teaching*		
	regens, regentis	*ruling*		
	capiens, capientis	*taking*		
	audiens, audientis	*hearing*		
Perfect			portatus,a,um	*(having been) carried*
			doctus,a,um	*(having been) taught*
			rectus,a,um	*(having been) ruled*
			captus,a,um	*(having been) taken*
			auditus,a,um	*(having been) heard*
Future	portaturus,a,um	*about to carry*	portandus,a,um	*(required) to be carried*
	docturus,a,um	*about to teach*	docendus,a,um	*(required) to be taught*
	recturus,a,um	*about to rule*	regendus,a,um	*(required) to be ruled*
	capturus,a,um	*about to take*	capiendus,a,um	*(required) to be taken*
	auditurus,a,um	*about to hear*	audiendus,a,um	*(required) to be heard*

Supines

Accusative	portatum	doctum	rectum	captum	auditum
Ablative	portatu	doctu	rectu	captu	auditu

Gerunds

Nominative	(portare)	(docere)	(regere)	(capere)	(audire)	*to carry*
Genitive	porta**ndi**	doce**ndi**	rege**ndi**	capie**ndi**	audie**ndi**	*of carrying*
(Dative	porta**ndo**	doce**ndo**	rege**ndo**	capie**ndo**	audie**ndo**	*for carrying*)
Accusative	porta**ndum**	doce**ndum**	rege**ndum**	capie**ndum**	audie**ndum**	*carrying*
Ablative	porta**ndo**	doce**ndo**	rege**ndo**	capie**ndo**	audie**ndo**	*by carrying*

Deponent Verbs

Deponent verbs are conjugated like the passive of other verbs. They have active meaning for these passive forms. There are three active forms that deponent verbs have retained:

Present Participle

horta**ns**, horta**ntis**	pollice**ns**, pollice**ntis**	loquens, loque**ntis**	morie**ns**, morientis	mentie**ns**, mentie**ntis**
(encouraging)	*(promising)*	*(speaking)*	*(dying)*	*(lying)*

Future Participle Active

hortat**urus,a,um**	pollicit**urus,a,**um	locut**urus,a,um**	morit**urus,a,um**	mentit**urus,a,um**
(about to encourage)	*(about to promise)*	*(about to speak)*	*(about to die)*	*(about to lie)*

Future Infinitive

hortaturus,a,um esse	polliciturus,a,um esse	locuturus,a,um esse	moriturus,a,um esse	mentiturus,a,um esse

Semideponent Verbs

audeo, audere, ausus sum	*to dare*	**gaudeo, gaudere, gavisus sum**	*to be happy*
soleo, solere, solitus sum	*to be used to (doing)*		

Periphrastic Conjugations

The **active periphrastic** is used to express intended or future actions; it is formed with the **future participle active** and the verb **esse** and is translated as *I am going to carry, I am about to rule, I was about to hear, etc.* Examples: portaturus sum *(I am about to carry)* - doctura eram *(I was about to teach)* - recturus erit *(he will be about to rule)* - capturi essent *(they would want to take)* - auditurae fuissent *(they would have been going to hear)*

The **passive periphrastic** denotes an obligation, or necessity, something which must be done. It is formed with the **gerundive** (future participle passive) and the verb **esse**.

Examples: captandus est *(he must be taken)* - audiendus fuissem *(I would have had to be heard, I should have been heard)* - terra mihi regenda est *(the land must be ruled by me; I must rule the land)*.

Irregular Verbs

esse, *to be* **(sum, fui, futurus)**

Indicative

Present	Imperfect	Future	Perfect	Pluperfect	Future Perfect
I am	*I was*	*I will be*	*I have been, I was*	*I had been*	*I will have been*
1. **sum**	eram	ero	fui	fueram	fuero
2. **es**	eras	eris	fuisti	fueras	fueris
3. **est**	erat	erit	fuit	fuerat	fuerit
1. **sumus**	eramus	erimus	fuimus	fueramus	fuerimus
2. **estis**	eratis	eritis	fuistis	fueratis	fueritis
3. **sunt**	erant	erunt	fuerunt	fuerant	fuerint

Subjunctive

Present	*Imperfect*		*Perfect*	Pluperfect	
1. **sim**	essem	____	**fuerim**	**fuissem**	_____
2. **sis**	esses		**fueris**	**fuisses**	
3. **sit**	esset		**fuerit**	**fuisset**	
1. **simus**	essemus		**fuerimus**	**fuissemus**	
2. **sitis**	essetis		**fueritis**	**fuissetis**	
3. **sint**	essent		**fuerint**	**fuissent**	

Imperatives: **es! este!** *(be!)* **esto! estote!** *(you shall be)* **esto!** *(he shall be)* **sunto!** *(they shall be)*
Infinitives: **esse** *(to be)*, **fuisse** *(to have been)*, **futurus,a,um esse** *(to be about to be)*
Participle: **futurus,a,um**

> **posse,** *to be able to* (**possum, potui**)

Indicative

Present	*Imperfect*	*Future*	*Perfect*	*Pluperfect*	*Future Perfect*
I can	*I could*	*I will be able to*	*I have been able to*	*I had been able to*	*I will have been able to*
1. **possum**	**poteram**	**potero**	**potui**	**potueram**	**potuero**
2. **potes**	**poteras**	**poteris**	**potuisti**	**potueras**	**potueris**
3. **potest**	**poterat**	**poterit**	**potuit**	**potuerat**	**potuerit**
1. **possumus**	**poteramus**	**poterimus**	**potuimus**	**potueramus**	**potuerimus**
2. **potestis**	**poteratis**	**poteritis**	**potuistis**	**potueratis**	**potueritis**
3. **possunt**	**poterant**	**poterunt**	**potuerunt**	**potuerant**	**potuerint**

Subjunctive

1. **possim**	**possem**	_____	**potuerim**	**potuissem**	_____
2. **possis**	**posses**		**potueris**	**potuisses**	
3. **possit**	**posset**		**potuerit**	**potuisset**	
1. **possimus**	**possemus**		**potuerimus**	**potuissemus**	
2. **possitis**	**possetis**		**potueritis**	**potuissetis**	
3. **possint**	**possent**		**potuerint**	**potuissent**	

Infinitives: **posse** *(to be able)*, **potuisse** *(to have been able)*
Participle: **potens, potentis** *(to be) powerful*

> **ire,** *to go* (**eo, ii (ivi), itum**)

Indicative

Present	*Imperfect*	*Future*	*Perfect*	*Pluperfect*	*Future Perfect*
I go	*I went*	*I will go*	*I have gone*	*I had gone*	*I will have gone*
1. **eo**	**ibam**	**ibo**	**ii**	**ieram**	**iero**
2. **is**	**ibas**	**ibis**	**isti**	**ieras**	**ieris**
3. **it**	**ibat**	**ibit**	**iit**	**ierat**	**ierit**
1. **imus**	**ibamus**	**ibimus**	**iimus**	**ieramus**	**ierimus**
2. **itis**	**ibatis**	**ibitis**	**istis**	**ieratis**	**ieritis**
3. **eunt**	**ibant**	**ibunt**	**ierunt**	**ierant**	**ierint**

Subjunctive

	Present	*Imperfect*		*Perfect*	*Pluperfect*	
1.	**eam**	**irem**	_____	**ierim**	**issem**	_____
2.	**eas**	**ires**		**ieris**	**isses**	
3.	**eat**	**iret**		**ierit**	**isset**	
1.	**eamus**	**iremus**		**ierimus**	**issemus**	
2.	**eatis**	**iretis**		**ieritis**	**issetis**	
3.	**eant**	**irent**		**ierint**	**issent**	

Imperative: **i! ite!** *(go!);* Infinitives*:* **ire, isse (iise), iturus,a,um esse**
Participles: **iens, euntis** (Present); **itum** (Perfect); **iturus,a,um** (Future Active); **eundus,a,um** (Future Passive)

ferre, *to bring, carry* **(fero, tuli, latum)**

Indicative

Active:	*Passive*:
Present **fero, fers, fert, ferimus, fertis, ferunt**	**feror, ferris, fertur, ferimur, ferimini, feruntur**
Imperfect: **ferebam, ferebas, ...**	**ferebar, ferebaris, ...**
Future: **feram, feres, ...**	**ferar, fereris, feretur ...**
Perfect: **tuli, tulisti, ...**	**latus,a,um sum; lati,ae,a sumus, ...**
Pluperfect: **tuleram, tuleras ...**	**latus,a,um eram; lati,ae,a eramus, ...**
Future Perfect: **tulero, tuleris ...**	**latus,a,um ero; lati,ae,a erimus, ...**

Subjunctive

Present: **feram, feras, ...**	**ferar, feraris, ...**
Imperfect: **ferrem, ferres, ...**	**ferrer, ferreris, ...**
Perfect: **tulerim, tuleris, ...**	**latus,a,um sim; lati,ae,a simus, ...**
Pluperfect: **tulissem, tulisses, ...**	**latus,a,um essem; lati,ae,a essemus, ...**

Imperatives: **fer! ferte!**	**ferre! ferimini!**
Infinitives: **ferre, tulisse, laturus,a,um esse**	**ferri, latus,a,um ess, latum iri**
Participles: **ferens, ferentis; laturus,a,um**	**latus,a,um; ferendus,a,um**
Gerund: **ferre, ferendi, ...**	
Supine: **latum, latu**	

fieri, *to be made* **(fio, factus sum)**

Indicative	Subjunctive
Present: **fio, fis, fit, fimus, fitis, fiunt**	**fiam, fias, fiat, fiamus, fiatis, fiant**
Imperfect: **fiebam, fiebas, ...**	**fierem, fieres, ...**
Future: **fiam, fies, fiet, ...**	
Perfect: **factus sum, factus es, ...**	**factus sim, factus sis, ...**
Pluperfect: **factus eram, factus eras, ...**	**factus essem, factus esses, ...**
Future Perfect: **factus ero, factus eris, ...**	

Imperatives: **fi! fite!**
Infinitives: **fieri, factus,a,um esse, factum iri**
Participles: **factus,a,um**; **faciendus,a,um**
Gerund: **fieri, faciendi, ...**

velle, *to want*	**nolle**, *to not want*	**malle**, *to prefer*

Indicative

Present:

1. **volo**	1. **volumus**	1. **nolo**	1. **nolumus**	1. **malo**	1. **malumus**
2. **vis**	2. **vultis**	2. **non vis**	2. **non vultis**	2. **mavis**	2. **mavultis**
3. **vult**	3. **volunt**	3. **non vult**	3. **nolunt**	3. **mavult**	3. **malunt**

Imperfect:	**volebam, volebas...**	**nolebam,nolebas...**	**malebam,malebas**
Future:	**volam, voles..**	**nolam,noles..**	**malam,males...**
Perfect:	**volui, voluisti..**	**nolui,noluisti...**	**malui,maluisti...**
Pluperfect:	**volueram, volueras..**	**nolueram,nolueras...**	**malueram,malueras...**
Future Perfect:	**voluero, volueris..**	**noluero, nolueris...**	**maluero,malueris...**

Subjunctive

Present:

1. **velim**	1. **velimus**	1. **nolim**	1. **nolimus**	1. **malim**	1. **malimus**
2. **velis**	2. **velitis**	2. **nolis**	2. **nolitis**	2. **malis**	2. **malitis**
3. **velit**	3. **velint**	3. **nolit**	3. **nolint**	3. **malit**	3. **malint**

Imperfect:	**vellem, velles**	**nollem, nolles**	**mallem**
Perfect:	**voluerim**	**noluerim**	**maluerim**
Pluperfect:	**voluissem**	**noluissem**	**maluissem**
Imperative:		**noli! nolite!**	
Infinitive:	**velle, voluisse**	**nolle, noluisse**	**malle, maluisse**
Participles:	**volens, volentis**	**nolens, nolentis**	**malens, malentis**

Defective Verbs

These verbs are defective in that they have no present stem; they are used with the perfect stem only, albeit with the meaning of the Present: **odi** *(I hate);* **memini** *(I remember);* **coepi** *(I have begun; present:* **incipio***)*

Indicative

Perfect:	**odi**	**memini**	**coepi**
Pluperfect:	**oderam**	**memineram**	**coeperam**
Future Perfect:	**odero**	**meminero**	**coepero**

Subjunctive

Perfect:	**oderim**	**meminerim**	**coeperim**
Pluperfect:	**odissem**	**meminissem**	**coepissem**

Imperative:		**memento! mementote!**	
Participles:	**osus,a,um; osurus,a,um**		**coeptus,a,um; coepturus,a,um**
Infinitives:	**odisse; osurus,a,um esse**	**meminisse**	**coepisse; coepturus,a,um esse**

Other verbs: **aio,** *I say,* **ais, ait, aiunt; aiebam...; inquam, inquit,** *I say;* **queo, nequeo,** *I can (not):* conjug. like **eo.**

Impersonal verbs

licet mihi, *it is permitted;* **placet mihi,** *it pleases;* **oportet mihi,** *it is necessary, I must;* **paenitet me,** *I repent;* **pudet me,** *I am ashamed;* **piget me,** *it shames;* **taedet me,** *it disgusts;* **libet mihi,** *it suits, pleases me;* **decet,** *it is fitting, becoming;* **dedecet,** *it is not fitting, becoming;* **praestat,** *it is better;* **accidit, evenit, contingit, fit,** *it happens;* **interest, refert,** *it concerns;* **delectat, iuvat,** *it delights;* **accedit,** *it is added, in addition.*

NOUN DECLENSIONS

First (a) Declension

		Singular		**Plural**	
Nom	puella	*the girl, a girl, girl*	puellae	*(the) girls*
Gen	puellae	*of the girl, of a girl, the girl's, a girl's, girl's*	puellarum	*of (the) girls, (the) girls'*
Dat	puellae	*to the girl, to a girl, to girl*	puellis	*to (the) girls*
Acc	puellam	*the girl (Dir. Obj), a girl (D.O.), girl (D.O.)*	puellas	*(the) girls (D.O.)*
Abl	a puella	*by, from the girl, a girl, girl*	a puellis	*by, from (the) girls*

The vocative (o girl!) of first declension nouns is like the nominative.
The gender of the nouns is feminine, except nouns for male persons, which have natural masculine gender.
The dative and ablative Plural of **filia** and **dea** are **filiabus** and **deabus** (not to be confused with **filius** and **deus**).

Second (o) Declension

	Singular				**Plural**			
	masculine			**neuter**	**masculine**			**neuter**
	friend	*boy*		*gift*				
N	amicus	puer		donum	amici	pueri		don a
G	amici	pueri		doni	amicorum	puerorum		donorum
D	amico	puero		dono	amicis	pueris		donis
A	amicum	puerum		donum	amicos	pueros		dona
V	amice	puer		donum	amici	pueri		dona
Ab	ab amico	a puero		dono	ab amicis	a pueris		donis

The vocative of nouns ending in **-us** is **-e**, of nouns and names ending in **-ius**, it is **-i: amice, fili, Luci.** The vocative of **deus** is **deus** in the Singular, and **di** in the Plural. The Vocative of nouns ending in -er and -um is like the nominative.
The gender of nouns ending in **-us** and **-er** is masculine, of those ending in **-um** neuter. Trees are feminine: **populus,i** *(f.) (poplar-tree)*; **ficus,i** *(f.) (fig-tree).*

Third Declension (Mixed Consonant and -i)

	Consonant Stems		**Singular** **(masculine and feminine)**		**I - Stems**	
N	labor	pater	civitas	pes	urbs	civis
G	laboris	patris	civitatis	pedis	urbis	civis
D	labori	patri	civitati	pedi	urbi	civi
A	laborem	patrem	civitatem	pedem	urbem	civem
Ab	labore	patre	civitate	pede	urbe	cive

			Plural			
N	labores	patres	civitates	pedes	urbes	cives
G	laborum	patrum	civitatum	pedum	urb**ium**	civ**ium**
D	laboribus	patribus	civitatibus	pedibus	urbibus	civibus
A	labores	patres	civitates	pedes	urbes	cives
Ab	laboribus	patribus	civitatibus	pedibus	urbibus	civibus

Neuter nouns:

<table>
<tr><td></td><td colspan="5" align="center">Consonant Stems</td><td colspan="3" align="center">I - Stems</td></tr>
<tr><td></td><td colspan="8" align="center">Singular</td></tr>
<tr><td>N</td><td>tempus</td><td>flumen</td><td>genus</td><td>caput</td><td>iter</td><td>mare</td><td>animal</td><td>turris (fem.)</td></tr>
<tr><td>G</td><td>temporis</td><td>fluminis</td><td>generis</td><td>capitis</td><td>itineris</td><td>maris</td><td>animalis</td><td>turris</td></tr>
<tr><td>D</td><td>tempori</td><td>flumini</td><td>generi</td><td>capiti</td><td>itineri</td><td>mari</td><td>animali</td><td>turri</td></tr>
<tr><td>A</td><td>tempus</td><td>flumen</td><td>genus</td><td>caput</td><td>iter</td><td>mare</td><td>animal</td><td>turrim</td></tr>
<tr><td>Ab</td><td>tempore</td><td>flumine</td><td>genere</td><td>capite</td><td>itinere</td><td>mari</td><td>animali</td><td>turri</td></tr>
<tr><td></td><td colspan="8" align="center">Plural</td></tr>
<tr><td>N</td><td>tempora</td><td>flumina</td><td>genera</td><td>capita</td><td>itinera</td><td>maria</td><td>animalia</td><td>turres</td></tr>
<tr><td>G</td><td>temporum</td><td>fluminum</td><td>generum</td><td>capitum</td><td>itinerum</td><td>marium</td><td>animalium</td><td>turrium</td></tr>
<tr><td>D</td><td>temporibus</td><td>fluminibus</td><td>generibus</td><td>capitibus</td><td>itineribus</td><td>maribus</td><td>animalibus</td><td>turribus</td></tr>
<tr><td>A</td><td>tempora</td><td>flumina</td><td>genera</td><td>capita</td><td>itinera</td><td>maria</td><td>animalia</td><td>turres (is)</td></tr>
<tr><td>Ab</td><td>temporibus</td><td>fluminibus</td><td>generibus</td><td>capitibus</td><td>itineribus</td><td>maribus</td><td>animalibus</td><td>turribus</td></tr>
</table>

Fourth (u) Declension

<table>
<tr><td></td><td colspan="3" align="center">Singular</td><td colspan="3" align="center">Plural</td></tr>
<tr><td>N</td><td>portus</td><td>manus</td><td>cornu (neuter)</td><td>portus</td><td>manus</td><td>cornua</td></tr>
<tr><td>G</td><td>portus</td><td>manus</td><td>cornus</td><td>portuum</td><td>manuum</td><td>cornuum</td></tr>
<tr><td>D</td><td>portui</td><td>manui</td><td>cornu</td><td>portibus</td><td>manibus</td><td>cornibus</td></tr>
<tr><td>A</td><td>portum</td><td>manum</td><td>cornu</td><td>portus</td><td>manus</td><td>cornua</td></tr>
<tr><td>Ab</td><td>portu</td><td>manu</td><td>cornu</td><td>portibus</td><td>manibus</td><td>cornibus</td></tr>
</table>

The gender of fourth declension nouns is **masculine**, with the exception of **manus** and **domus**, which are **feminine**, and **cornu**, which is **neuter**.

Domus can also use some forms of the second declension: gen.Sg: domus or domi; dat. Sg. domui or domo; gen. Pl: domuum or domorum; acc. Pl: domus or domos.

Fifth (e) Declension

<table>
<tr><td></td><td colspan="3" align="center">Singular</td><td colspan="3" align="center">Plural</td></tr>
<tr><td>N</td><td>dies</td><td>res</td><td>species</td><td>dies</td><td>res</td><td>species</td></tr>
<tr><td>G</td><td>diei</td><td>rei</td><td>speciei</td><td>dierum</td><td>rerum</td><td>specierum</td></tr>
<tr><td>D</td><td>diei</td><td>rei</td><td>speciei</td><td>diebus</td><td>rebus</td><td>speciebus</td></tr>
<tr><td>A</td><td>diem</td><td>rem</td><td>speciem</td><td>dies</td><td>res</td><td>species</td></tr>
<tr><td>Ab</td><td>die</td><td>re</td><td>specie</td><td>diebus</td><td>rebus</td><td>speciebus</td></tr>
</table>

Irregular Nouns:

<table>
<tr><td>N</td><td>vis (force)</td><td>deus (god)</td><td>nemo, (nobody)</td><td>Iuppiter</td></tr>
<tr><td>G</td><td>--</td><td>dei</td><td>(nullius)</td><td>Iovis</td></tr>
<tr><td>D</td><td>--</td><td>deo</td><td>nemini</td><td>Iovi</td></tr>
<tr><td>A</td><td>vim</td><td>deum</td><td>neminem</td><td>Iovem</td></tr>
<tr><td>Ab</td><td>vi</td><td>deo</td><td>(nullo)</td><td>Iove</td></tr>
<tr><td></td><td></td><td></td><td></td><td></td></tr>
<tr><td>N</td><td>vires</td><td>dei, dii, di</td><td colspan="2">Indeclinable nouns (Singular only):</td></tr>
<tr><td>G</td><td>virium</td><td>deorum, deum</td><td colspan="2">fas (right), nefas (wrong), nihil (nothing),</td></tr>
<tr><td>D</td><td>viribus</td><td>deis, diis, dis</td><td colspan="2">mille (one thousand)</td></tr>
<tr><td>A</td><td>vires</td><td>deos</td><td colspan="2"></td></tr>
<tr><td>Ab</td><td>viribus</td><td>deis, diis, dis</td><td colspan="2">nemo misses some forms which are replaced by nullus.</td></tr>
</table>

ADJECTIVES

Adjectives of the First and Second Declension

	M	F	N		M	F	N
	Singular				**Singular (-er, drops the -e)**		
N	bonus	bona	bonum		pulcher	pulchra	pulchrum
G	boni	bonae	boni		pulchri	pulchrae	pulchri
D	bono	bonae	bono		pulchro	pulchrae	pulchro
A	bonum	bonam	bonum		pulchrum	pulchram	pulchrum
Ab	bono	a bona	bono		pulchro	pulchra	pulchro

	M	F	N		M	F	N
	Plural				**Plural**		
N	boni	bonae	bona		pulchri	pulchrae	pulchra
G	bonorum	bonarum	bonorum		pulchrorum	pulchrarum	pulchrorum
D	bonis	bonis	bonis		pulchris	pulchris	pulchris
A	bonos	bonas	bona		pulchros	pulchras	pulchra
Ab	bonis	bonis	bonis		pulchris	pulchris	pulchris

Adjectives with Special Declension

	M	F	N	M	F	N	M	F	N
N	unus	una	unum	uter	utra	utrum	alter	altera	alterum
G	unius	**unius**	unius	utrius	**utrius**	utrius	alterius	**alterius**	alterius
D	uni	**uni**	uni	utri	**utri**	utri	alteri	**alteri**	alteri
A	unum	unam	unum	utrum	utram	utrum	alterum	alteram	alterum
Ab	uno	una	uno	utro	utra	utra	altera	altero	altera

Like **unus**, *one*; **uter**, *which of two*; and **alter**, *the other*; the following adjectives are declined: **alius,alia,aliud**, *other, another*; **ullus, ulla, ullum**, *any*; **nullus, nulla, nullum**, *none*; **uterque, utraque, utrumque**, *each of two, both*; **neuter, neutra, neutrum**, *neither of two*; **solus, sola, solum**, *alone, only, single*; **totus, tota, totum**, *whole, entire, all*. *Their other forms are those of* **bonus** *and* **pulcher**

Adjectives of the Third Declension — Singular

	Three endings			Two endings			One ending		
	M	F	N	M F	N		M F	N	
N	celer	celeris	celere	brevis	breve		potens		
G		celeris		brevis			potentis		
D		celeri		brevi			potenti		
A	celerem	celerem	celere	brevem	breve		potentem	potens	
Ab		celeri		brevi			potenti		

Plural

	M	F	N	M F	N		M F	N	
N	celeres	celeres	celeria	breves	brevia		potentes	potentia	
G		celerium		brevium			potentium		
D		celeribus		brevibus			potentibus		
A	celeres	celeres	celeri	breves	brevia		potentes	potentia	Ab
		celeribus		brevibus			potentibus		

The number of endings concerns only the nominative and accusative Sg and Pl. All the other cases have only one (the same) ending. One exception is the (nominative) and accusative of adjectives with one ending: they have to have two endings, to accomodate syncretism of nominative and accusative of the neuter (see above potens).

The adjectives **vetus,veteris; pauper,pauperis; dives,divitis; and princeps,principis** are not i-stems and have these different endings: in the ablative Singular **-e**; in the nominative Plural neuter **-a**; in the genitive Plural **-um**.

Declension of the Present Participle

	Sg		Pl	
	M F	**N**	**M F**	**N**
N	portans		portantes	portant**ia**
G	portantis		portant**ium**	
D	portanti		portantibus	
A	portantem	portans	portantes	portant**ia**
Ab	portante (-i)		portantibus	

When present participles are used as adjectives their ablative Singular ending is **-i**. Example: praesente - praesenti.

COMPARISON OF ADJECTIVES

Regular comparison

Positive	Comparative	Superlative
altus,a,um	altior, altius	altissimus,a,um
fortis,e	fortior, fortius	fortissimus,a,um
brevis,e	brevior, brevius	brevissimus,a,um
potens (potentis) (genitive)	potentior, potentius	potentissimus,a,um
audax (audacis) (gen.)	audacior, audacius	audacissimus,a,um
pulcher, pulchra, pulchrum	pulchrior, pulchrius	pulcherrimus,a,um
facilis,e	facilior, facilius	facillimus,a,um

Irregular comparison

bonus,a,um	melior, melius	optimus,a,um
malus,a,um	peior, peius	pessimus,a,um
magnus,a,um	maior, maius	maximus,a,um
parvus,a,um	minor, minus	minimus,a,um
multus,a,um	-----, plus	plurimus,a,um
multi,ae,a	plures, plura	plurimi,ae,a

The following adjectives and adverbs are almost exclusively used in comparison

(extra)	exterior, exterius	extremus,a,um
(intra)	interior, interius	intimus,a,um
(infra)	inferior, inferius	infimus,a,um
(post)	posterior, posterius	postremus,a,um
(supra)	superior, superius	supremus,a,um
(prae, pro)	prior, prius	primus,a,um
(prope)	propior, propius	proximus,a,um
(ultra)	ulterior, ulterius	ultimus,a,um

Declension of the Comparative

	M F	N	M F	N	N	M F	N
	Singular		**Plural**		**Singular**	**Plural**	
N	celerior	celerius	celeriores	celeriora	plus	plures	plura
G	celerioris		celerior**um**		pluris	plur**ium**	
D	celeriori		celerioribus		------	pluribus	
A	celeriorem	celerius	celeriores	celeriora	plus	plures	plura
Ab	celeriore		celerioribus		plure	pluribus	

Some adjectives, mostly those ending in **-eus, -ius,** -and **-uus** use **magis** *(more)* and **maxime** *(most)* for comparison: idoneus, *suitable;* **magis** idoneus, *more suitable;* **maxime** idoneus, *most suitable.*

NUMERICAL ADJECTIVES

	M	F	N		M F	N	N
N	duo	duae	duo		tres	tria	milia
G	duorum	duarum	duorum		trium		milium
D	duobus	duabus	duobus		tribus		milibus
A	duos	duas	duo		tres	tria	milia
Ab	duobus	duabus	duobus		tribus		milibus

Other numbers

Roman Numeral	Cardinals	Ordinals (all declined)	Arabic Numeral	Roman Numeral	Cardinals	Ordinals (all declined)	Arabic Numeral
I	unus,a,um	primus (,a,um)	1	XL	quadraginta	quadragesimus	40
II	duo,ae,o	secundus	2	L	quinquaginta	quinquagesimus	50
III	tres,ia	tertius	3	LX	sexaginta	sexagesimus	60
IV	quattuor	quartus	4	LXX	septuaginta	septuagesimus	70
V	quinque	quintus	5	LXXX	octoginta	octogesimus	80
VI	sex	sextus	6	XC	nonaginta	nonagesimus	90
VII	septem	septimus	7	C	centum	centesimus	100
VIII	octo	octavus	8				
IX	novem	nonus	9				
X	decem	decimus	10				

Roman Numeral	Cardinals	Ordinals	Arabic Numeral	Roman Numeral	Cardinals	Ordinals	Arabic Numeral
XI	undecim	undecimus	11	CC	ducenti,ae,a	ducentesimus	200
XII	duodecim	duodecimus	12	CCC	trecenti (ae,a)	trecentesimus	300
XIII	tredecim	tertius decimus	13	CCCC	quadringenti	quadringentesimus	400
XIV	quattuordecim	quartus decimus	14	D	quingenti	quingentesimus	500
XV	quindecim	quintus decimus	15	DC	sescenti	sescentesimus	600
XVI	sedecim	sextus decimus	16	DCC	septingenti	septingentesimus	700
XVII	septendecim	septimus decimus	17	DCCC	octingenti	octingentesimus	800
XVIII	duodeviginti	duodevicesius	18	DCCCC	nongenti	nongentesimus	900
XIX	undeviginti	undevicesimus	19	M	mille	millesimus	1000
XX	viginti	vicesimus	20				

Roman Numeral	Cardinals	Ordinals	Arabic Numeral
XXI	viginti unus / unus et viginti	vicesimus primus / unus et vicesimus	21
XXII	viginti duo / duo et viginti etc.	vicesimus secundus / duo et vicesimus etc.	22
XXVIII	duodetriginta	duodetricesimus	28
XXIX	undetriginta	undetricesimus	29
XXX	triginta	tricesimus	30

POSSESSIVE ADJECTIVES

meus,a,um *my, mine*

tuus,a,um *your, yours*

suus,a,um *his, her, hers, its* (**reflexive**)
eius *his, her, hers, its* (**not reflexive**)

noster, nostra, nostrum
our, ours

vester, vestra, vestrum
your, yours

suus,a,um *their, theirs* (**reflexive**)
eorum, earum, eorum *their, theirs* (**not reflexive**)

ADVERBS

Adverb Formation

1st and 2nd declension: add **-e** to the adjective's stem: altus **--> alte**, *highly, deeply;* miser **--> misere**, *miserably;*
pulcher **--> pulchre**, *beautifully*

3rd declension: most adjectives: add **-iter** to the stem: brevis **--> breviter**, *shortly;* celer **--> celeriter**, *quickly;*
acer (acris) **--> acriter** *(sharply).* But: audax **--> audacter**.

Adjectives ending in **-ns**: add **-er** to the stem: sapiens (sapientis) **--> sapienter** *(wisely).*

Regular Comparison

alte, *highly*	**altius**, *more, rather, too, quite highly*	**altissime**, *most, very highly*
celeriter, *quickly*	**celerius**, *more, rather, too, quite quickly*	**celerrime**, *most, very quickly*

Irregular Comparison

bene, *well*	**melius**, *better*	**optime**, *very well*
male, *badly*	**peius**, *worse*	**pessime**, *very badly*
multum, *much*	**plus**, *more*	**plurimum**, *most*
parum, *little*	**minus**, *less*	**minime**, *not at all, least*
magnopere, *greatly*	**magis**, *more, rather*	**maxime**, *very greatly, especially*
prope, *near*	**propius**, *nearer*	**proxime**, *nearest, recently*
saepe, *often*	**saepius**, *more often*	**saepissime**, *most often*
diu, *for a long time*	**diutius**, *longer*	**diutissime**, *for the longest, a very long time*

PRONOUN DECLENSIONS

Personal Pronouns

	1st Pers. Sg		2nd Pers. Sg		1st Pl		2nd Pl		3rd Pers. Reflexive Sg and Pl
N	ego	*I*	tu	*you*	nos	*we*	vos	*you*	-----
G	mei	*of me, of mine*	tui	*of you, of yours*	nostri / nostrum	*of us, of ours*	vestri / vestrum	*of you, of yours*	sui
D	mihi	*to me*	tibi	*to you*	nobis	*to us*	vobis	*to you*	sibi
A	me	*me*	te	*you*	nos	*us*	vos	*you*	se / sese
Ab	a me	*by me*	a te	*by you*	nobis	*by us*	vobis	*by you*	se / sese

Also: **mecum**, *with me;* **tecum**, *with you;* **nobiscum**, *with us;* **vobiscum**, *with you.*

3rd Person Pronoun

	M		F		N		M		F	N
			Singular						**Plural**	
N	is	*he, it*	ea	*she, it*	id	*it*	ei	*they*	eae	ea
G	eius	*of him, of it his, its*	eius	*of her, it her, its*	eius	*of it, its*	eorum	*of them, their*	earum	eorum
D	ei	*to him, to it*	ei	*to her, to it*	ei	*to it*	eis	*to them*	eis	eis
A	eum	*him, it*	eam	*her, it*	id	*it*	eos	*them*	eas	ea
Ab	ab eo	*by him, by it*	ab ea	*by her, by it*	eo	*by it*	ab eis	*by them*	eis	eis

Is, ea, id can also function as demonstrative pronoun: **eae terrae** *(these countries);* **eos viros** *(those men).*

Demonstrative Pronouns and Adjectives : hic, haec, hoc: *this, these;* ille illa illud: *that,those;* iste: *that one there*

	M	F	N
		Singular	
N	hic	haec	hoc
G		huius	
D		huic	
A	hunc	hanc	hoc
Ab	hoc	hac	hoc
		Plural	
N	hi	hae	haec
G	horum	harum	horum
D		his	
A	hos	has	haec
Ab		his	

	M	F	N
		Singular	
N	ille	illa	illud
G		illius	
D		illi	
A	illum	illam	illud
Ab	illo	illa	illo
		Plural	
N	illi	illae	illa
G	illorum	illarum	illorum
D		illis	
A	illos	illas	illa
Ab		illis	

	M	F	N
		Singular	
N	iste	ista	istud
G		istius	
D		isti	
A	istum	istam	istud
Ab	isto	ista	isto
		Plural	
N	isti	istae	ista
G	istorum	istarum	istorum
D		istis	
A	istos	istas	ista
Ab		istis	

	the same	Singular	
N	idem	eadem	idem
G		eiusdem	
D		eidem	
A	eundem	eandem	idem
Ab	eodem	eadem	eodem
		Plural	
N	eidem / idem	eaedem	eadem
G	eorundem	earundem	eorundem
D		eisdem / iisdem	
A	eosdem	easdem	eadem
Ab		eisdem / iisdem	

	Singular		
N	ipse *he himself*	ipsa *she herself*	ipsum *it itself*
G		ipsius	
D		ipsi	
A	ipsum	ipsam	ipsum
Ab	ipso	ipsa	ipso
	Plural		
N	ipsi	ipsae	ipsa
G	ipsorum	ipsarum	ipsorum
D		ipsis	
A	ipsos	ipsas	ipsa
Ab		ipsis	

Relative Pronoun and Interrogative Adjective: *who, which, that*

		Sg				Pl	
N	qui	quae	quod	qui	quae	quae
G		cuius		quorum	quarum	quorum
D		cui			quibus	
A	quem	quam	quod	quos	quas	quae
Ab	qui	qua	quo		quibus	

Interrogative Pronoun

quis *who?*   quid *what?*
 cuius *whose, of what?*
 cui *to whom, to what?*
quem *whom?* quid *what?*
quo *by whom? through what?*

Indefinite Pronouns

M F	N	
aliquis / quis aliquid / quid	*anyone, anything*
quisquam quidquam	*anyone, anything*
quispiam quidpiam	*anyone, anything, some*
quisquis quidquid	*whoever, whatever*
quivis quidvis	*anyone / anything you wish*
quilibet quidlibet	*anyone / anything you please*
quisque quidque	*each, every*
quidam quiddam	*a certain one / thing*

Indefinite Adjectives

M	F	N
aliqui	aliqua	aliquod
quisquam		quidquam
quispiam	quaepiam	quodpiam
quivis	quaevis	quodvis
quilibet	quaelibet	quodlibet
quisque	quaeque	quodque
quidam	quaedam	quoddam

quicumque, quaecumque, quodcumque *whoever, whatever*

These pronouns are declined like **quis, quid** and **qui, quae, quod.**

Appendix 2

Latin - English Vocabulary

(The number indicates the lesson in which the word first appears.)

A

ab (a) 3 (Ab)	from, away from, since
abesse 4	to be away
abire 4	to go away
abuti 10	to abuse
ac 1	and
accidit 15	it happens
acer,acris,acre 14	sharp, cutting, vehement, zealous
acerbus,a,um 6	acid, bitter, sharp, sour
acies,ei *f* 13	battle line
ad 3 (A)	to, towards, at, near, until
adducere 15	to cause, lead to, influence
adesse 4	to be near, present
adhuc 5	up to now
adire 4	to approach, go to(ward)
aditus,us 13	approach, access
(ad)iuvare	to help, assist
admiratio,onis *f* 11	admiration
adulescens,centis *m* 11	young man
advenire	to arrive
adventus,us *m* 13	arrival
adversus,a,um 6	adverse, facing; hostile
aedes,aedium *f* Pl 11	building, house
aes,aeris *n* 11	copper, ore, money
aestas,tatis *f* 11	summer
aestus,us *m* 13	heat; ocean tide, surf
aetas,aetatis *f* 11	age, era, epoch
ager,agri 3	field
agere 9	to do, drive
aggredi 10	to attack
agmen,minis *n* 11	army in marching order
agricola,ae *m!* 2	farmer
albus,a,um 6	white
aliquis,aliquid	someone, anyone,-thing
alius,a,um (G: alius)	another, the other
alter,a,um (G: alterius)	the other (of two)
altitudo,dinis *f* 11	height
altus,a,um 6	high, deep
amare 1	to love, like
amarus,a,um 6	bitter

ambitio,-onis *f* 11	ambition, running for office
ambo 7	both
ambulare 1	to walk
amica,ae 2	friend (female)
amicus,i 3	friend (male)
amor,amoris *m* 11	love
ancilla,ae 2	maid, servant
angustus,a,um 6	narrow
animal,alis *n* 11	animal
annus,i 3	year
ante 3 (A)	before, in front of
antea 5	before(hand)
antequam 5	before (Conj.)
antiquus,a,um 6	old, ancient
aperire 9	to open, uncover
apud 3 (A)	at (someone's), with
aqua,ae 2	water
aquaeductus,us 13	water supply, aqueduct
arbor,oris *f* 11	tree
arcus,us 13	bow
argentum,i 2	silver
ars,artis *f* 11	art, skill; quality
artifex,-ficis *m* 11	artist, artisan;tradesman, craftsman
arx,arcis *f* 11	fortress
ascendere 9	to climb, ascend
asinus,i 3	donkey
aspectus,us 13	sight, appearance
assentiri 10	to agree
at 5	but, moreover
atque 1	and
atrox (atrocis) 14	terrible
auctor,-oris *m* 11	author, authority
Auctoritas,tatis *f* 11	authority, influence, power,reputation
audax (audacis) 14	bold, daring
audere, ausus sum 10	to dare
audire 9	to hear
augur,uris *m* 11	augur, soothsayer
auris,is *f* 11	ear
aurum,i 2	gold
aut 5	or
aut...aut... 5	either...or...
autem 5	but, however
avus,i 3	grandfather

B

beatus,a,um 6	happy, wealthy
bellum,i 3	war

bellus,a,um 6	pretty
bibere (bibo) 9	to drink
bonus,a,um 6	good
bos,bovis *m/f* 11	cow, ox
brevis,breve 14	short

C

cadere 9	to fall
caedere 9	to cut down, kill
caedes,caedis *f* 11	killing, murder
caelum,i 3	heaven, air
caeruleus,a,um 6	blue
calamitas,tatis *f* 11	harm, misfortune, disaster, defeat
canis,is *m/f* 11	dog
canus,a,um 6	grey
capere 10	to take,grab, seize, catch, to take prisoner
captare 1	to grab, take, capture, reach for
caput,itis *m* 11	head, main ..., capital
carcer,eris *m* 11	jail, prison
carmen,minis *n* 11	song, poem
carrus,i 3	cart, carriage
carus,a,um 6	dear, expensive
casa,ae 2	hut, house
castra,orum Pl 3	camp
casus,us *m* 13	fall; case, chance
causa,ae 2	cause, argument, reason; lawsuit
cavere 15	to beware, guard
cedere 9	to go, yield
celer 14	quick, fast
celeritas,tatis *f* 11	speed
cena,ae 2	meal, dinner
certamen,inis *n* 11	fight, competition
certus,a,um 6	certain, sure, reliable
ceteri,ae,a (Pl) 6	the remaining, the rest
ceterum (Adv) 6	by the way, and for the rest
cibus,i 3	food
cinis,cineris *m* 11	ashes
circa / circum 3 (A)	around
citerior 14	on this side
civilis,e 14	civil, of a citizen, public
civis,is *m/f* 11	citizen
civitas,tatis *f* 11	state, citizenry; citizenship
clades,is *f* 11	defeat
clamare 1	to exclaim, shout, make noise
clamor,oris *m* 11	noise, clamor

clarus,a,um 6	clear, bright, famous
classis,is *f* 11	fleet
claudere 9	to shut, close, enclose
cogere 9	to collect, compel
cogitare 1	to think
cognoscere 9	to recognize, acknowledge, find out,learn
cognovisse 9	to know
cohors,-hortis *f* 11	cohort
colere 9	to cultivate, tend, care for
collis,is *m* 11	hill
color,coloris *m* 11	color
comes,-mitis *m* 11	comrade
communis,e 14	common, general, public
comperire 9	to learn
conari 10	to try
conclave,is *n* 11	room
condicio,-ionis *f* 11	condition; location
confidere 10	to trust, confide
confiteri 10	to confess
coniunx,coniugis f 11	wife, spouse
coniuratio,-ionis *f* 11	conspiracy
consentire 9	to agree
consilium,i 3	plan, advice
consistere 9	to stand, stop; consist of
conspicere 9	to look (at), see
constituere 9	to set up, decide
consuetudo,dinis *f* 11	habit; usage
consul,consulis *m* 11	consul
consulatus,us *m* 13	consulate, consul's office
contendere 9	to strive,struggle,hasten, to claim
contra 3 (A)	against
convenire 9	to come together, suit, fit; to be correct
conventus,us *m* 13	meeting
copia,ae 2	mass, a lot; amount, supply
cor,cordis *n* 11	heart
corpus,corporis *n* 11	body, corpse
cotidie 5	daily
cras 5	tomorrow
credere 9	to believe, trust
crescere 9	to grow
crimen,criminis *n* 11	accusation; crime
crines,crinium (Pl) 11	hair
crudelis,e 14	cruel
crudelitas,tatis 11	cruelty
cum (Conj.) 15	when, after, although, since, while, by...ing
cum, una cum (Ab) 3	with, together with
cuncti,ae,a (Pl) 6	all
cupere 9	to want, wish, desire

cupiditas,-tatis *f* 11	desire, passion
cupidus,a,um 6	greedy, desirous
currere 9	to run
cursus,us *m* 13	course, run, race
custodire 9	to guard
custos,custodis *m/f* 11	guard

D

dare 1	to give
de 3 (Ab)	(down) from, about, concerning
dea,ae 2	goddess
debere 1	to owe,ought to,have to; must
dedecus,dedecoris 11	shame
deesse (defui) 4	to be lacking, missing
defendere 9	to defend
defungi 10	to die, fulfill one's life
deinde 5	then, after that
demens (dementis)14	crazy, demented
dens,dentis m 11	tooth
descendere 9	to descend
deterior,ius 14	less, worse
deterrimus,a,um 14	the least, worst
dexter,dextra,-trum 6	right
dicere 9	to say
dicio,dicionis 11	power
dies,diei *m/f* 13	day
difficilis,e 14	difficult
difficultas,-tatis 11	difficulty
dignitas,-tatis *f* 11	worth, reputation, rank
diligens (diligentis) 14	diligent
discere 9	to learn
dissentire 9	to disagree, contradict
dissimilis,e 14	dissimilar
diu 4	for a long time
dives (divitis) 14	rich
dividere 9	to divide
docere 1	to teach
dolor,doloris 11	pain, sorrow
domi 8	at home
domina,ae 2	mistress (of the house)
dominus,i 3	master, lord
domo 8	from home
domum 8	towards home
domus,us *f* 13	house
donare 1	to give as a present
donum,i 3	present, gift
dormire 9	to sleep
draco,draconis *m* 11	dragon

ducere 9	to lead, pull, draw; consider
dulcis,e 14	sweet, lovely
dum 5	while, as long as
dux,ducis *m* 11	leader, general

E

ecce 5	see there!
edere 9	to eat
efficere 15	to accomplish, effect
ego 5	I, me
emere 9	to buy
enim 5	namely
eo 5	to there
epistula,ae	letter, epistle
eques,equitis *m* 11	horseman, knight
equitatus,us 13	cavalry
equus,i 3	horse
ergo 5	therefore, consequently
error,erroris *m* 11	error
erudire 9	to teach, educate
esse 7	to be
et 1	and
et...et... 5	both...and...
etsi 5	even if
evenit 15	it happens, occurs
eventus,us *m* 13	result, outcome, event
ex (e) 3 (Ab)	out of, since, following
exercitus,us *m* 13	army
exire 4	to go out of, leave
exitus,us 13	exit, outcome
experiri 10	to experience
exsistere	to come up, show oneself
exspectare 1	to wait for, expect
exterior,ius 14	outer
extra 3 (A)	outside of, besides
extremus,a,um 14	outermost, last

F

fabula,ae 2	story, fable, (stage) play
facere 9	to make, do
facies,ei f 13	appearance, form, face
facilis,e 14	easy
facinus,facinoris *n* 11	deed, crime
factio,factionis *f* 11	(small) party, clique
facultas,tatis 11	ability, opportunity, faculty
falsus,a,um 6	wrong, false
fames,famis *f* 11	hunger
familia,ae 2	family, household

familiaris,e 14	of the household, familiar, friendly
fas *n* (undeclined) 11	divine law, right
fateri 10	to confess
fauces,faucium *f* Pl 11	throat, narrows, gorge, entrance
feles,is *f* 11	cat
felix (felicis) 14	happy
femina,ae 2	woman
fere 5	almost
ferox (ferocis) 14	wild, spiteful
ferre (tuli,latum) 10	to bear, carry, bring; report
ferrum,i 4	iron, sword
ferus,a,um 6	wild, untamed
fessus,a,um 6	tired
festinare 1	to hurry, hasten
fides,ei *f* 13	faith,trust,promise, protection
fidus,a,um 6	faithful, reliable
fieri potest 15	it can happen
fieri,fio,factus sum	to become, be done
filia,ae 2	daughter
filius,i 3	son
fines,finium (Pl) 11	territory
finire 9	to finish, limit, end
finis,is *m* 11	border, limit, end
firmus,a,um 6	strong, firm
fit 15	it comes about
flavus,a,um 6	yellow
flere 1	to cry
flos,floris *m* 11	flower
flumen,fluminis *n* 11	flow, stream, river
foedus,a,um 6	ugly
foedus,foederis *n* 11	alliance, pact, treaty
fons,fontis *m* 11	source, spring, fountain
formosus,a,um 6	beautiful
fortasse 5	perhaps
forte 5	by chance
fortis,e 14	strong, brave
fortitudo,dinis *f* 11	strength, bravery
fortuna,ae 2	luck, fate, fortune
forum,i 3	market (place)
frangere 9	to break
frater,fratris m 11	brother
fraus,fraudis *f* 11	fraud, damage
frigus,oris *n* 11	cold
frons,tis *f* 11	forehead, face; front
fructus,us *m* 13	fruit, crop
frui [+Abl] 10	to enjoy
frumentum,i 3	grain
frustra 5	in vain
fugere 9	to flee

fulmen,minis *n* 11	lightning
fungi 10	to perform, ececute
fuscus,a,um 6	brown, dark
futurus,a,um 6	future

G

gallina,ae 2	hen
gallus,i 3	rooster
gaudere 1	to be happy
gaudium,i 3	joy
gens,gentis *f* 11	tribe, clan, people, race
genus,eris *n* 11	gender, race, sex, origin, class, kind, type
gerere 9	to carry on, bear, do
gracilis 14	graceful
gradus,us *m* 13	step, rank
gratus,a,um 6	grateful, pleasant, thankful
gravis,e 14	heavy, weighty, serious
gravitas,tatis *f* 11	gravity, dignity
grex,gregis *m* 11	herd, flock

H

habere 1	to have, hold, own
habitare 1	to live, dwell
habitus,us *m* 13	appearance, clothing,
herba,ae 2	grass, herb
heri 5	yesterday
hic 1	here
hic,haec,hoc 8	this
hiems,hiemis *f* 11	winter
hinc	from here
historia,ae	history, story
hodie 5	today
homo,hominis 11	man (as a species)
honos,honoris *m* 11	honor, prestige
hora,ae	hour
hortari 10	to encourage, admonish
hortus,i 3	garden
hospes,itis m 11	guest, host, stranger
hostis,tis *m* 11	enemy, adversary
huc	to this place, here
humanitas,tatis *f* 11	humanity, education
humilis,e 14	low, humble

I

iacére (iacui) 1	to lie (down)
iácere (ieci) 9	to throw

iam / non iam	already / not yet, no longer
ibi 1	here
ictus,us *m* 13	blow, hit
idem,eadem,idem	the same
Idus,uum (Pl) 13	Ides of a month
igitur 5	therefore
ignis,is *m* 11	fire
ignotus,a,um 6	unknown
ille,illa,illud 8	that, this
imber,imbris *m* 11	rain
imitari 10	to imitate
impedire 9	to hinder, prevent
imperare (+Dat) 1	to order, rule, command
imperator,-toris *m* 11	general, leader, emperor
imperium,i 3	empire,power,realm, order
impetus,us *m* 13	attack; violence
imprimis (Adv)	above all, especially
improbus,a,um 6	inferior, wicked
imus,a,um 14	lowest, the bottom of
in 3	Acc: into, onto, to, against
	Abl: in, on, at, during
incertus,a,um 6	uncertain
incipere 10	to begin
incola,ae *m!* 2	inhabitant
inde 5	from there
inferior,ius 14	lower, lesser
inferre	to carry in
infimus,a,um 14	the lowest, least, the bottom of
infra 3 (A)	under
ingens (ingentis) 14	huge, enormous
inire 4	to go in; to begin
initus,us 13	entrance, going in
iniustus,a,um 6	unjust
innocens,centis 14	innocent, harmless
inquit	he/she/it says, said
instituere 9	to teach, institute, begin, install, establish
insula,ae 2	island
inter 3 (A)	between, among
interdum 5	once in a while
interea 5	in the meantime
interesse 4	to be present, take part
interior,ius 14	inner
interire 4	to perish, go under, die
interitus,us *m* 13	downfall, destruction
intimus,a,um 14	innermost
intra 3 (A)	within
intrare 1	to enter
invenire 9	to come upon, find
invitare 1	to invite
ipse,ipsa,ipsum (G. ipsius)	himself, herself, itself
iratus,a,um 6	furious, angry
ire 7 10	to go
is, ea, id 5	he, she, it; this
iste,ista,istud 8	that one there
ita 5	so
itaque 5	therefore
item 5	likewise
iter,itineris *n* 11	march, journey, route
iterum 5	again
iubere	to order, threaten
iucundus,a,um 6	enjoyable, pleasant
iudex,iudicis *m* 11	judge
iungere 9	to join
iunior 14	younger
iurare	to swear an oath
ius,iuris *n* 11	right, law
iussus,us 13	order
iustus,a,um 6	just
iuvenis,iuvenis 11	young man
iuventus,-tutis *f* 11	youth, young age
iuxta 3 (A)	next to

L

labi 10	to slide, fall, glide
labor,laboris *m* 11	work, labor, trouble, suffering
laborare 1	work, suffer, toil
lac,lactis 11	milk
lacus,us *m* 13	lake
laetari 10	to be happy
laetus,a,um 6	happy
largiri 10	to give, grant, donate
latus,a,um 6	wide
latus,eris *n* 11	side, flank
laudare 1	to praise
laus,laudis *f* 11	glory, praise
lectus,i 3	bed, couch
legere 9	to read; collect; choose
legio,onis *f* 11	legion
leo,leonis *m* 11	lion
levis,e 14	light, slight, easy, careless
lex,legis 11	law
libenter 5	gladly
liber,libera,liberum 6	free
liber,libri 3	book
liberalitas,tatis *f* 11	generosity
liberi,orum *m* 3	children
libertas,tatis *f* 11	freedom, liberty
libido,libidinis *f* 11	violent desire, lust, greed
limes,itis *m* 11	border, border wall, path

lingua,ae 2	tongue, speech, language
littera,ae 2	letter (of the alphabet)
litterae,arum (Pl) 2	letter (epistle); science, literature
litus,litoris *n* 11	coast
longe 5	far, by far
longus,a,um 6	long
loqui 10	to talk, speak
ludere 9	to play
ludus,i 3	game, (stage) play, school
luna,ae 2	moon
lux,lucis *f* 11	light

M

magis 5	more
magis...quam	more...than
magister,tri 3	teacher
magistratus,us *m* 13	magistrate
magnitudo,dinis *f* 1	size
magnopere 5	very (much)
magnus,a,um 6	big, great, large
maior,ius 14	bigger, larger
maiores,um *m* Pl.	ancestors
malle 9	to prefer, rather want
malus,a,um 6	bad, wicked
mane 5	early
manere 7	to wait for, remain, stay, last, take (time)
manus,us *f* 13	hand, band of men
mare,is *n* 11	sea, ocean
mater,matris *f*	mother
maximus,a,um	largest
mel,mellis 11	honey
melior,ius	better
memoria,ae 2	memory, remembrance
mens,mentis *f*	brain, mind, spirit, reason, thought
mensa,ae 2	table
mensis,is *m* 11	month
mentiri 10	to tell a lie
merere 10	to earn, deserve
meridies,ei *m* 13	south; midday
merx,mercis *f*	wares, goods
metuere (metui) 15	to fear
metus,us *m* 13	fear
meus,a,um	my
miles,militis *m*	soldier
minimus,a,um	smallest
minor,us	smaller

minus / minime (Adv)	less / least
mirari	to wonder
mirus,a,um 6	wonderful, strange
miser,era,erum 6	unhappy, miserable, poor
miserari 10	to lament
misereri 10	to pity
mittere 9	to send, throw, let go
modus,i 3	measure, way, method
moenia,-ium *n* (Pl) 11	city walls
moliri 10	to move, undertake, toil
mollis,e 14	soft
monere 1	to warn, admonish
mons,montis *m* 11	mountain
monstrare 1	to show
morari 10	to hesitate, delay
mores,um *m* (Pl) 11	character
mori 10	to die
mors,mortis *f* 11	death
mos,moris *m* 11	custom, use; Pl character
motus,us *m* 13	movement, excitement
movere 1	to move, cause, influence
mox 5	soon
mulier,mulieris 11	woman
multitudo,inis *f* 11	amount, mass, crowd
multum 5	much
multus,a,um 6	much, many
mundus,i 3	world, universe
munire 9	to build, fortify
munus,muneris *n* 11	task; gift; office

N

nam 5	for, because
nancisci 10	to obtain, reach
narrare 1	to tell, recount
nasci 10	to be born
natio,nationis *f* 11	nation, people, tribe
natura,ae 2	nature
nauta,ae 2	sailor
navigare 1	to sail
navis,is *f* 11	ship
necesse est 15	it is necessary
nefas *n* (not decl.) 11	impiety, sin, crime abomination
negare	to deny, negate;say that not
nemo	no one
nepos,otis *m* 11	grandson
neque 5	and not
neque...neque... 5	neither...nor...
nescire 9	to not know
neuter, neutra, neutrum	neither (of two)

nex,necis *f* 11	killing, murder
niger,nigra,nigrum 6	black
nihil	nothing
nimis (Adv)	too much, too
nisi 5	if not; unless; except
niti 10	to lean on, try, shine, strive
nix,nivis *f* 11	snow
nobilis,e 14	noble
nobilitas,tatis 11	nobility, upper class
nolle 9	to not want
nomen,nominis *n* 11	name
nondum 5	not yet
non solum..sed etiam	not only...but also...
nos 5	we
noster,nostra,-trum 6	our
notus,a,um 6	known
novus,a,um 6	new, young
nullus,a,um 7	no, none
numen,numinis *n* 11	divine will, god
numquam 5	never
nunc 1	now
nuntius,i 3	messenger, message

O

ob 3 (A)	on account of
obesse 4	to be against, harm
obire 4	to go toward, meet;
obitus,us 13	meeting; death
oblivisci 10	to forget
oboedire 9	to obey
obses,obsidis *m/f* 11	hostage
occasio,onis *f* 11	occasion
occidens,-dentis *m* 11	evening, west
occupare 1	to occupy, lay siege to
officium,i 3	task, duty, office
olim 5	once upon a time
omen,ominis *n* 11	omen
omnis,e 14	each, all, every
onus,oneris *n*	burden
operire 9	to cover, close, hide
opes,opum *f* (Pl) 11	help, means, riches
opinio,onis *f* 11	opinion, reputation
oppidum,i	town
oppugnare 1	to attack, storm
optimates,ium *m* (Pl)11	aristocrats, patriots, Nobles' Party
optimus,a,um 14	best
opus,operis *n* 11	work
orare 1 15	to ask, pray, beg, speak
oratio,onis *f* 11	speech

orator,oratoris *m* 11	speaker, orator
orbis,orbis 11	circle, sphere, earth
ordiri 10	to begin
ordo,dinis *m* 11	class, standing, order, rank
oriens,orientis *m* 11	morning, east
origo,originis *f* 11	origin, source, beginning
oriri 10	to rise, come about
os,oris *n* 11	mouth, face
os,ossis 11	bone

P

paene 5	almost
panis,is *m* 11	bread
par (paris) 14	equal
parare 1	to prepare
parentes,um *m* (Pl)11	parents
parére (parui) 1	to obey
párere 9	to bear, bring forth; acquire
paries,parietis *m* 13	wall (of a house)
pars,partis *f* 11	part, share
partes,ium *f* (Pl) 11	political party (large)
parvus,a,um 6	small
passus,us *m* 13	span; pace; step, foot (measure)
pater,patris *m* 11	father
pati 10	to suffer, allow, tolerate
patres,-trum *m* (Pl) 11	senators, city fathers
patria,ae 2	fatherland, home
pauci,ae,a (Pl) 6	few
paulatim 5	gradually
paulo 5	(by) a little
paulo post 5	a little later
pauper (pauperis) 14	poor
paupertas,-atis *f* 11	poverty
pax,pacis *f* 11	peace
pectus,pectoris *n* 11	chest; heart, soul
pecunia,ae 2	money
pecus,pecoris *n* 11	cattle, herd, flock
pecus,pecudis *f* 11	head of cattle; sheep
pedes,peditis *m* 11	footsoldier, infantrist
peior,ius 14	worse
pellere 9	to push, drive, expel
per 3 (A)	through, during, by means of
periculum,i 3	danger
periculum est 15	there is danger
perire 4	to perish, die
pernicies,iei *f* 13	destruction, ruin, downfall
persuadere (+Dat) 15	to persuade, convince
pes,pedis *m* 11	foot

pessimus,a,um 14	worst
petere (ab+Abl) 9	to ask, beg, seek, attack, strive
pietas,pietatis *f* 11	duty, piety
piger,pigra,pigrum 6	lazy, slow
piscis,is *m* 11	fish
placere (placuit) 1	to please
plebs,plebis *f* 11	people, middle class, citizens
plenus,a,um 6	full
plures,a (Pl) 14	more
plurimi,ae,a (Pl) 14	most
plurimum (Adv) 14	most
plus (pluris) 14	more
poeta,ae *m* 2	poet
polliceri 10	to promise
ponere 9	to put, place
pons,pontis *m* 11	bridge
pontifex,-ficis *m* 11	priest (lit.: bridge maker)
populares,ium *m* (Pl) 11	People's Party
populus,i 3	people
portare 1	to carry, bring
porticus,us 13	colonnade, arcade
portus,us *m* 13	harbor
poscere 9	to demand
posse 4	to be able
post 3 (A)	after, behind
postea 5	later, afterwards
posterior,ius 14	later
postquam 5	after
postremo 5	lastly, finally
postremus,a,um 14	the last, least
postulare (ab+Ab) 15	to demand (from someone)
potare 1	to drink
potens (potentis) 14	powerful, mighty
potestas,tatis *f* 11	power of office; possibility
potiri (+Ab) 10	to take power, to take possession of
prae 3 (Ab)	before
praeesse (+D) 4	to be in charge
praeter 3 (A)	past, besides
praeterea 5	besides
praeterire 4	to pass over, omit
pratum,i 3	meadow, pasture
preces,-cum *f* (Pl) 11	request, prayer
premere 9	to press, urge
primo, primum 5	at first
primus,a,um 14	first, foremost
princeps,cipis *m* 14	the first, leader
prior,ius 14	earlier
priusquam 5	before

pro 3 (Ab)	before, for, instead of, in relation to, on behalf of
procul (Adv)	far
prodesse 4 7	to be for, be of use
profecto (Adv) 5	indeed
proficisci 10	to set out, depart, march
prohibere 15	to prevent, prohibit
prope 3 (A)	near
properare 1	to run, hurry
proprior,ius 14	closer
propter 3 (A)	on account of;
proximus,a,um 14	the closest, next
prudens (prudentis)14	prudent, wise
puella,ae 2	girl
puer,i 3	boy
pugna,ae 2	fight
pugnare 1	to fight
pulcher,chra,chrum 6	beautiful
punire 9	to punish

Q

quaerere 9	to ask, seek, look for
qualis,e 14	of what kind
quam 5	how, as, than
quamquam 5	although
quasi 5	just as, as if
-que; neque 1	and; and not
quercus,us 13	oak tree
queri 10	to complain
qui,quae,quod 8	who, which, that
quia 5	because
quicumque,quaecumque, quodcumque	whoever, everyone who
quid 1 5	what
quidam,quaedam,quoddam (Adj.)	a certain
quidam,quiddam	a certain (one) (noun)
quietus,us 13	rest, sleep
quis 1 5	who
quisquam,quicquam	someone, anyone,-thing
quisque,quidque	every one
quo 1	where to
quod 1	because
quondam 5	once upon a time
quoniam 5	because
quoque 1	also

R

rapere 9	to grasp, seize, rob

raro 5	seldom	sedere 17	to sit
ratio,rationis *f* 11	reason, deliberation, calculation,bill, method	seditio,onis *f* 11	uprising
		sedulus,a,um 6	industrious
recordari 10	to remember	semper 1	always
reddere 9	to make into, give back	senator,oris *m* 11	senator
redire 4	to go back, return	senatus,us *m* 13	senate
regere 9	to rule, govern	senectus,tutis *f* 11	old age
regio,regionis *f* 11	(lit: a king's) land, region	senex,senis *m* 11	old man
religio,onis *f* 11	religion, belief, cult	senior 14	older
relinquere 9	to leave behind	sensus,us 13	sense, reason, feeling
reliquus,a,um 6	the rest (of)	sentire 9	to feel, think
reperire 9	to find	sequi 10	to follow
reri 10	to think, calculate	sequitur 15	it follows
res,rei *f* 13	matter, thing; situation	sero 5	(too) late
resistere 15	to resist	serva,ae 2	slave, servant (female)
respondere 17	to answer	servare 1	to keep, protect, guard, save
reverti 10	to return		
rex,regis *m* 11	king	servitus,tutis *f* 11	servitude, slavery
ridere 17	to laugh, smile	servus,i 3	slave, servant (male)
robur,roboris *n* 11	strength, force	severus,a,um 6	severe, strict, serious
rogare 1	to ask, beg	si 5	if
roseus,a,um 6	pink	sic (with verbs) 5	so
ruber, -bra, -brum 6	red	sicut 5	just as, like
rumor,oris *m* 11	noise; rumour, reputation	sidus,eris *n* 11	star, constellation of stars
rumpere 9	to tear, break		
		silva,ae 2	forest
S		similis,e 14	similar
		simul 5	at the same time
sacer,sacra,sacrum	holy; cursed	sine 3 (Ab)	without
sacerdos,dotis *m/f* 11	priest(ess)	sinister,-tra,-trum 6	left
saepe 5	often	sinus,us *m* 13	bay, gulf, cove, curve
sal,salis 11	salt	sitis,is *f* 11	thirst
salire 9	to jump	situs,us *m* 13	location, situation
saltus,us 13	jump	socius,i 3	comrade, ally
salubris,e 14	healthful, salutary	sol,solis *m* 11	sun
salus,salutis *f* 11	health, salvation	solere,solitus sum 10	to be used to doing s.th.
salutare 16	to greet	solum 5	alone, only
salutatio,-ionis *f* 1	greeting, salutation	solvere 9	to loosen, pay, sail
sanguis,sanguinis *f* 11	blood	soror,oris *f* 11	sister
sanus,a,um 6	healthy, sane, reasonable	sors,sortis *f* 11	lot, fate
sapiens,tis 14	reasonable, wise	species,ei *f* 13	sight, form, appearance
satis 5	enough	spectare 1	to look at
scelus,sceleris *n* 11	crime	spes,spei *f* 13	hope
scire 9	to know	spiritus,us *m* 13	spirit, breath, life
scribere 10	to write	stabulum,i 3	stable, barn
scriptor,scriptoris *m*	writer, author	stare (steti,statum) 7	to stand
secundum 3 (A)	along, according to	statim 5	immediately
secundus,a,um 6	opportune; second, following	stella,ae 2	star
		strepitus,us *m* 13	noise, clamor, thunder
securus,a,um 6	careless, secure	studiosus,a,um 6	zealous, studious, busy, industrious
sed 1	but		
		studium,i 3	zeal

stultus,a,um 6	stupid, foolish
stupidus,a,um 6	stupid
suavis,e 14	sweet, smooth
sub 3	Acc: under, close to, to the foot of
	Abl: under, close to, at the foot of
subito 1	suddenly
summus,a,um 14	the highest; the top of
super / supra 3 (A)	above, beyond
superesse 4	to be left over, remain;
superior,ius 14	further up
supremus,a,um 14	the highest, the top of;
last	
suspicio,ionis f 11	suspicion
suus,a,um 6	his, her, its, their

T

tacere 1	to be silent
talis,e 14	of such a kind
tam 15	so
tam...quam... 5	as...as...
tamen 5	nevertheless
tandem 5	finally
tangere 9	to touch
tantum (Adv.) 5	so much, only
tantus,a,um 15	so great
tellus,telluris f 11	earth
tempestas,tatis f 11	(thunder)storm, weather; time
templum,i	temple
tempus,temporis n 11	time; circumstances
tenere 1	to hold, keep
terra,ae 2	land, earth
terribilis,e 14	terrible
timere 1	to fear, be afraid
timidus,a,um 6	timid
timor,oris m 11	fear
toga,ae	toga, outer garment
tollere 9	to raise, remove
tot 15	so many
totiens 15	so often
totus,a,um 7	whole, entire, complete
tradere 9	to hand down, over
trahere 9 10	to pull, drag
trans 3 (A)	across, to the other side
transgredi 10	to cross
transire	to go across
transitus,us m 13	crossing
tu 5	you
tuba,ae 2	trumpet, tuba
tueri 10	to protect

tum 5	then, at that time
tumultus,us m 13	noise, uproar
turris,turris f 11	tower
tuus,a,um 6	your (Sg)

U

ubi 1 5	where, when(ever); as often as; as soon as
ubique 5	everywhere
ulterior,ius 14	further, on the other side
ultimus,a,um 14	furthest, last
ultra 3 (A)	beyond, on the other side
undique 5	from everywhere
unde 1	from where
usque ad 3 (A)	up to
usus,us m 13	use
ut (with indicative) 5	as
ut (w. subjunctive) 15	that, so that, in order to
uter,utra,utrum	which (of two)
uterque,utraque, utrumque	each one (of two), both
uti (+Ab) 10	to use
utilis,e 14	useful
uva,ae 2	grape
uxor,oris f 11	wife

V

vacca,ae 2	cow
vacuus,a,um 6	empty
valde (Adv)	very much
vale!	farewell!
valere 1	to be healthy, strong, valid, powerful
valetudo,dinis f 11	condition, health
validus,a,um 6	healthy, strong
vallis,is f 11	valley
vas,vasis 11	container, vase
vates,is m/f 11	seer, prophet(ess)
vehemens (-ntis) 14	vehement, energetic, violent
vel 5	or
velle 9	to want
velox (velocis) 14	fast, speedy, quick
velut 5	just as, like
venari 10	to hunt
vendere 9	to sell
venerari 10	to adore, venerate
venire 9	to come
venter,ventris m 11	stomach, belly

ventus,i 3	wind
ver,veris *n* 11	**Spring** (the season)
vere, vero 5	**indeed, in truth; but**
vereri 10	**to be in awe, venerate;fear**
veritas,veritatis *f* 11	**truth**
vero / verum 5	**but; in truth; moreover**
versari 10	**to be present, be active**
versus,us *m* 13	**verse**
vertere 9	**to turn**
vertex,icis *m* 11	**top of the head, vertex**
verus,a,um 6	**true, real, genuine**
vesci	**to feed on**
vesper,i 3	**evening, Evening Star**
vester,-tra,-trum 6	**your (Pl)**
vestis,is f 11	**clothing**
vetus (veteris)14	**old, aged**
via,ae 2	**way, road**
vicinus,a,um 3	**neighboring, next to;**
vicinus,i 3	**neighbor**
victus,us 13	**life style, means of life, necessities**
vicus,i 2	**village**
videre 1	**to see, to see to it**
videri 10	**to seem, to appear, to seem right**
villa,ae 2	**farmhouse, country house, estate**
vincere 9	**to defeat, vanquish**
vinum,i 3	**wine**
vir,i 3	**man**
vires,virium *f* 11	**physical strength; forces; troops, army**
virgo,virginis *f* 11	**girl, young woman**
viridis,e 14	**green**
virtus,virtutis *f* 11	**excellence, bravery, courage, manliness**
vis (vim, vi) *f* 11	**strength, force; amount, a lot**
visitare 1	**to visit**
vita,ae 2	**life**
vivere 10	**to live**
vix 5	**hardly, barely**
vocare 1	**to call, name**
volare 1	**to fly**
voluntas,tatis *f* 11	**will, wish**
voluptas,tatis *f* 11	**fun, joy, enjoyment,**
vos 5	**you (Pl.)**
vulnus,vulneris *n* 11	**wound, injury**
vulpes,is *f* 11	**fox**
vultus,us *m* 13	**face, facial expression, mien**

The Captoline she-wolf nursing the
twins, Romulus and Remus.
(The twins are actually a later addition
to the statue.)

ENGLISH - LATIN VOCABULARY

Abbreviations:
Verbs are listed without "to". To clarify ambiguities
N = Noun, **V** = Verb, **A** = Adjective, **Adv** = Adverb;
Other information is added, such as cases after
prepositions or verbs (A = Accusative; Ab = Ablative
D = Dative)

A

ability	facultas,tatis; potestas,tatis *f*
able, be able	posse
about	de (Ab)
above	super / supra (A);
above all	imprimis (Adv)
absent, away	absens,absentis
abuse	abuti (abusus)
a certain one N	quidam. quiddam
a certain one A	quidam, quaedam, quoddam
accept	accipere (io,cepi,ceptum)
accomplish	impetrare, efficere
according to	secundum (A)
on account of	ob (A)
acid	acerbus; acer,acris,acre
acknowledge	cognoscere
acquire	comparare, parere (io,peperi,partum)
across	trans (A)
act	agere (egi,actum), facere (feci factum), se gerere(gessi,-stum) V; factum,i N
add	addere (-didi,-ditum)
admiration	admiratio,onis *f*
admire	admirari
admonish	(ad)monere (-eo,-ui), hortari
adverse	adversus
adversary	adversarius,i; hostis,hostis *m*
advice	consilium
be afraid	timere
after	post (A); cum (Conj.) postquam (Conj.)
after(ward)	postea, deinde (Adv.)
against	contra (A)
be against	obesse
age, era	aetas,aetatis *f*
agree	consentire (-sensi,-sensus)
all, every	omnis,e; cuncti,ae,a (Pl)

all people	omnes,omnium
all things	omnia,omnium
alliance	societas,tatis *f*
allow	permittere (misi,missum), pati (passus)
ally	socius,i
almost fere (Adv); paene (Adv)	
already	iam
also	etiam, quoque
although	quamquam, cum (Conj.)
always	semper
amazing	mirus,a,um
ambush	insidiae,arum Pl
and	et, ac, atque, -que
both...and...	et...et...
and not	neque
animal	animal,animalis *n*
another one	alius,a,um (Gen. alius)
answer	respondere (eo,pondi,ponsum)
anyone,-thing	quisquam,quicquam, aliquis,aliquid
appear	apparere (-ui,-itum)
appearance	aspectus,us, species,ei *f*; facies,ei *f*
applaud	plaudere (plausi,plausum)
apply	adhibere (-eo,-ui,-itum)
approach	appropinquare, accedere, adire
aqueduct	aquaeductus,us *m*
area	fines,finium *m* Pl.
arms	arma,orum Pl
army	exercitus,us *m*, vires,virium
around	circa / circum (A)
arrival	adventus,*us m*
art, skill	ars,artis *f*
artist, artisan	artifex,-ficis
as	ut (Ind.)
as...as...	tam...quam...
ascend	ascendere
ashes	cinis,cineris *m*
ask, beg	rogare, quaerere (quaesivi, situm) petere (ab + Abl)
assembly	conventus,us *m*
associate	socius, comes,comitis
at (someone's)	apud (A)
at home	domi
at first	primo, primum
at last	postremo, tandem
at night	noctu
at the foot of (where)	sub (Ab)

at, near	ad (A), in (Ab)	before	ante (A), prae, coram (Ab),
attack	aggredi (-gressus); petere	before(hand)	antea, ante, prius (Adv.)
attempt	temptare, conari	before	antequam, priusquam
avoid	vitare	beg	rogare, precari
away from	ab (a) (Ab)	begin	committere (misi, missum)
			incipere (-io, coepi, coeptum)

B

			incohare, inire (eo, ii, itum)
		beginning	initium, i; origo, originis *f*
bad	malus, a, um		principium, i
battle, fight	proelium, i	behind	post (A)
be	esse (sum, fui, futurus)	believe	arbitrari, credere
be able	posse (possum, potui)		(-didi, -ditum)
be absent, away	abesse (absum, afui)	bend	flectere (flexi, flexum)
be present	adesse (adsum, affui); versari	besides	praeterea (Adv); ceterum
be obvious	apparere (-ui, -itum)		(Adv); praeter (A)
be fixed	constare (constiti)	betray	indicare; prodere, tradere
be lacking	deesse (defui);		(prodo, prodidi, proditum)
	deficere (feci, fectum)	better, best	melior, ius; optimus, a, um
be in need of	egere (egeo, egui)	between	inter (A)
be mistaken	errare	beware	cavere (-eo, cavi, cautum)
be in charge	praeesse (sum, fui) (+D)	beyond	ultra (A); super / supra (A)
be of use	prodesse (prosum, fui)	big	magnus, a, um
be used to	solere (solitus sum)	bigger, larger	maior, ius; ~est maximus, a, um
be afraid	timere (-eo, timui)	bill, sum	ratio, rationis *f*
be done	fieri (fio, factus sum)	bird	avis, is *f*
be in the future	fore (= futurum esse)	bitter	amarus, a, um
be happy	gaudere (-eo, gavisus), laetari	black	niger, nigra, nigrum
be upset	indignari	blindly	temere (Adv)
be born	nasci (natus)	blood	sanguis, sanguinis *f*
be left over	restare (resto, stiti), superesse	blue	caeruleus, a, um
be silent	tacere (-eo, ui, itum)	boast	gloriari
be empty, void	vacare	body, corpse	corpus, corporis n
be strong	valere (eo, ui)	bold, daring	audax (audacis)
be sold venire	(ven<u>eo</u>, venii; from ire)	bone	os, ossis *n*
	(Passive of vendere, sell)	book	liber, libri
	venire (venio, veni) come	border	finis, is *m*
bear	ferre (fero, tuli, latum);	border wall	limes, itis *m*
	perferre; gerere (gessi, gestum)	both	ambo, ae, o
	pati (ior, passus); tolerare	both...and...	et...et...
bear (zool.)	ursus, i N	boy	puer, i
beast	bestia, ae	brave	fortis, e
beat	verberare	bravery	fortitudo, dinis *f*; virtus, tutis *f*
beautiful	pulcher, chra, chrum,	bread	panis, is *m*
	formosus, a, um	break	frangere (fregi, fractum)
because	quod, quia; quoniam; cum	Bridge	pons, pontis *m*
become	fieri (fio, factus sum)	bring	portare, ferre (fero, tuli, latum)
become used to	consuescere (consuevi)		

bring forth	proferre; gignere (genui, genitum); edere (edidi,editum)	century	saeculum,i
brother	frater,fratris *m*	certain, sure	certus,a,um
brown	fuscus,a,um	chain, bind	vincire (-io,vinxi,vinctum)
build	aedificare; construere (struxi,structum), erigere (erexi,erectum)	chair	sella,ae
		chance	casus,us *m*
		change	mutare
bull	taurus,i	character	mores,um *m* Pl
burn	urere (ussi,ustum); ardere (-eo,arsi)	chest; heart	pectus,pectoris *n* ; cor,cordis *n*
		children	liberi,orum *m*
business	negotium,i	choose	legere (legi,lectum) ; diligere (dilexi,dilectum)
busy	studiosus,a,um		
but	sed; at, tamen, autem, vero/verum	circle, (earth)	orbis,is (terrarum) *m*
		citizen	civis,is *m/f* ; privatus,a,um
buy	emere (emi,emptum)	citizenry	civitas,tatis *f*, plebs,plebis *f*
by	ab (Ab), ad, apud, iuxta, prope, per (A); (Ablative alone)	city walls	moenia,moenium *n* Pl
		city	urbs,urbis *f*, oppidum,i
by the way	ceterum (Adv)	civil, public	civilis,e
by chance	forte (Adv.)	claim, affirm	affirmare, contendere (-tendi,-tentum)
by means of	per (A)		
		class, rank	ordo, ordinis *m*
		clear, bright	clarus,a,um

C

calculate	reri (reor, ratus)	clever	callidus,a,um
call, name	appellare, vocare	client	cliens,clientis
camp	castra,orum *n* Pl	climb	ascendere (-cendi,-censum)
can	posse (possum, potui)	close, shut	claudere (clausi,clausum)
capital	caput,capitis *m*	close to	prope (A)
care for	curare; colere (colui,cultum)	closer	propior,ius
care	cura,ae	clothing	vestis,is *f*
carpenter	faber,fabri	coast	litus,litoris *n*
carry, bring	portare; ferre (fero,tuli,latum)	cold	frigus,oris *n* ; frigidus,a,um, gelidus,a,um
carry away	auferre (abstuli,ablatum)		
carry oneself	se gerere (gessi,gestum)	collapse	ruere (rui,rutum)
carry across	transferre (-tuli,-latum) transportare	collect	colligere (-legi,-lectum) cogere (coegi,coactum)
carry in	inferre (intuli,illatum)	color	color,coloris *m*
cart	carrus,i	come	venire (io,veni,ventum)
case	casus,us *m*	come into existence	exsistere (exstiti)
cat	feles,is *f*	come about	oriri (ior,ortus)
catch	capere (-io,cepi,captum)	come to help	subvenire (io,veni,ventum)
cattle, herd,	pecus,pecoris, *n* ; grex,gregis *m*	command	imperare; iubere(eo,iussi,ssum) imperium; iussum,i; decretum,i
cause	causa,ae N; impellere (impuli, -pulsum), adducere (-duxi,-ductum)		
		common	communis,e
		complain	queri (questus)
cease	cessare; desinere (desii, desitum)	complaint	querela,ae
censor	censor,censoris *m*	compute	computare
centurion	centurio,centurionis *m*	condemn	damnare/ condemnare
		condition	condicio,condicionis *f*

confess	confiteri,(-fiteor,-fessus) fateri (-eor,fassus sum)		**D**
confuse	turbare, confundere (-fudi,-fusum)	daily	cottidianus,a,um
conquer	vincere, vici, victum	danger	periculum,i;
consent	consensus,us N *m*; consentire V (-sentio,sensi,sensum)	dangerous	periculosus,a,um
		dare	audere (ausus)
consider	considerare;ducere (duxi,ductum)	daughter	filia,ae (Dat.+Abl.Pl.:filiabus)
		day	dies,diei *m/f* , *by day* interdiu, *from day to day* in dies *some day* aliquando
consist of	constare; consistere (constiti)		
conspiracy	coniuratio,coniurationis *f*		
consul	consul,consulis *m*	dead	mortuus,a,um;
consulate, consul's office consulatus,us *m*		death	mors, mortis *f*
consume	consumere (sumpsi,sumptum)	dear	carus,a,um
contain	continere (-eo,-ui,tentum)	deceive	fallere (fefelli) ; decipere (-io,-cepi,-ceptum)
continent	continens,ntis (terra) *f*		
continue	pergere (rexi,rectum)	decide	constituere(-tuo,-tui,-tutum); iudicare, decernere (decrevi)
continuous	continuus,a,um		
conversation	colloquium,i	decree	decretum,i
convince	persuadere (-eo,-suasi,-suasum) (+Dat)	deed	actum,i
		deer	cervus,i
cost	constare (constiti)	defeat	superare; vincere (vici,victum)
Council	conciilium,i	defend	defendere (fendi,fensum)
country	rus,ruris *n* ;	defendant	reus,i
in, to, from the country ruri, rus, rure		delay	mora,ae; morari
country house villa,ae		deliberate	deliberare
courage	animus,i ; virtus,virtutis *f*	deliberation	deliberatio,onis; consultatio
cow	vacca,ae; *cow, ox* bos,bovis *m/f*	delight	delectare
crazy	amens, demens (dementis)	demand (from s.o.) postulare (ab + Ab); poscere (poposci)	
create	creare		
crime	crimen,criminis *n* , facinus, facinoris *n* , scelus,sceleris *n*	demented	amens, demens (dementis)
		deny	negare
cross	crux,crucis *f*	depart	discedere (-cessi,-cessum)
crowd	turba,ae; multitudo,inis *f*	descend	descendere (-ndi,-nsum)
cruel	crudelis,e	desert V	deficere (-feci,-fectum), deserere (-serui,-sertum)
cruelty	crudelitas,crudelitatis *f*		
cry	flere (-eo,flevi,fletum)	desire	desiderare, cupere (-io,-ivi); cupiditas,cupiditatis *f*
cult	religio,onis *f*		
cultivate	colere (colui,cultum)	despair	desperare
cultivation	cultus,us *m* ; cultura,ae	despise	contemnere (tempsi,temptum)
cunning, tricky callidus,a,um; dolus,i N		destroy	delere (-eo,levi,letum)
curia, senate, city hall curia,ae		devastate	vastare
curse	maledicere (-dixi,-dictum)	die	mori (-ior, mortuus); interire; perire (pereo, perii)
cursed	sacer,sacra,sacrum		
custom	mos,moris *m*	different	diversus,a,um
cut	secare (secui)	difficult	difficilis,e
cut down	caedere(cecidi,caesum) occidere (occidi,occisum)	dig	fodere (fodi,fossum); *dig out* effodere (-fodi,-fossum)

diligence	diligentia,ae
diligent	diligens (diligentis)
diminish	minuere (-ui,-utum)
disagree	dissentire (-sensi,-sensum)
disaster	calamitas,tatis *f*
discover	invenire (-io, veni,-ventum),
	reperire (-io,repperi,repertum)
discuss	disputare
	disserere (-serui,-sertum)
disease	morbus,i
dispute	disputare
dissimilar	dissimilis,e
diverse	varius,a,um
divide	dividere (-do,divi̱si,visum), *not*
	related to videre (eo,vi̱di,visum)
divine	divinus,a,um; divus,a,um
do	facere (-io,feci,factum); *do, drive*
	agere (egi,actum)
dog	canis,is *m/f*
donkey	asinus,i
door	ianua,ae
doubt	dubitare; dubium,i
dragon	draco,draconis *m*
drink	bibere (bibo); potare
drive	pellere (-lo,pepuli,pulsum); ~ *out*
	expellere (expuli); ~*back* repellere
duty	officium,i ; munus,muneris *n*
dwell	habitare

E

each one	quisque, quidque N;
	quisque, quaeque, quodque Adj
(of two)	uterque, utraque, utrumque
ear	auris,is *f*
earlier	prior,ius
early	mane
earth	terra,ae ; tellus,telluris *f*
earthbound	terrestris,is
east	oriens,orientis *m*
easy	facilis,e; *easily* facile
eat	edere (edi,esum)
educate	educare
either...or...	aut...aut...
eloquence	eloquentia,ae
embrace	amplecti (amplexus)
emperor	imperator,toris *m*

empire	regnum,i ; imperium,i
empty	vacuus,a,um
encourage	monere (-eo,-ui,-itum)
end	finire (finivi,itum); finis,is *m*
enemy (collect.)	hostis,is; hostes,hostium Pl
enemy (personal)	inimicus,i
enjoy	frui (fructus) +Abl.
enormous	ingens (ingentis)
enough	satis (Adv)
enter	intrare
entrance	fauces,cium *f* Pl , ostium,i
envoy	legatus,i
envy	invidere (-eo,vidi,visum)
	invidia,ae N
equal	par (paris)
error	error,erroris *m*
escape	effugere (effugio,effugi)
especially	imprimis (Adv)
establish	instituere(tui,tutum)
evening,	vesper,i
Evening Star	
every day	cot(t)idie
every	omnis,e; *every one* quisque;
everyone who	qui-, quae-, quodcumque
example	exemplum,i
excel	praestare (praesto, praestiti)
excellent	optimus,a,um; egregius,a,um;
	praeclarus,a,um
except	nisi
excite	excitare
excuse	excusare
exercise	exercere (-eo,exercui)
exhibit	exponere (-posui,-positum)
exile	exsilium,i
exist	exsistere (exstiti)
expect	exspectare
expel	pellere (pepuli,pulsum)
expense, cost	sumptus,us *m*
expensive	carus,a,um
explain	explicare,exponere(posui,itum)
extinguish	exstinguere (-tinxi,-tinctum)
eye	oculus,i

F

fable	fabula,ae
face	vultus,us *m*

fact	factum,i
fail	deficere(deficio,-feci,-fectum), Deesse(desum,defui)
faith	fides,ei *f*
faithful	fidelis,e; fidus,a,um
fall	cadere (cecidi,casum)
false	falsus,a,um
fame, glory	gloria,ae; fama,ae; laus,laudis *f*
family	familia,ae; gens,gentis *f* ; genus,generis *n*
famous	clarus,a,um celeber,celebris,celebre
far	procul (Adv.) ; longe
farewell!	vale!
farmer	agricola,ae *m* ! , rusticus,i
farmhouse	villa,ae
farthest, last	ultimus,a,um
fast	celer,is,e
father	pater,patris *m*
fatherland	patria,ae
fault	culpa,ae
fear	metuere (uo,metui), timere (eo,timui), vereri (eor,veritus); timor,oris *m*, metus,us *m* N
feed on	vesci,vescor, --
feel	sentire (io,sensi)
feel pain	dolere (eo,dolui)
feeling	sensus,us
few	pauci,ae,a Pl
field	ager,agri
fight	pugna,ae; pugnare
fill	complere (-eo,-plevi,-pletum)
find	invenire (io,veni,ventum) reperire (io,repperi,repertum)
find out	cognoscere (-novi,cognitum)
finger	digitus,i
finish	conficere (-ficio,-feci,-fectum); finire (io,finivi,finitum)
fire	ignis,is *m* ; *fire, arson* incendium,i
firm	firmus,a,um
first	primus,a,um
fish	piscis,is *m*
fitting, it is f.	decet (decuit)
flee	fugere (-io,fugi,fugitum)
fleet	classis,is *f*
flock, herd	grex,gregis *m* , pecus,pecoris *n*
flow	fluere (fluxi)
flower	flos,floris *m*
fly	volare
follow	sequi (secutus)
food	cibus,i ; victus,us *m*
foot	pes,pedis *m*
for a long time	diu
for, on behalf of	pro (Ab)
forbid	vetare (vetui)
force	coercere(-eo,coercui); cogere (coegi,coactum); vis (vim, vi) *f* N
forest	silva,ae
forget	oblivisci (oblitus)
forgive	ignoscere (novi,notum)
fortify	munire (ivi,itum)
fortress	arx,arcis *f*
fortune	fortuna,ae
found	condere (-didi,-ditum); *from the founding of Rome (753)* ab urbe condita
fountain	fons,fontis *m*
fox	vulpes,is *f*
free	liber,libera,liberum; liberare
friend	amicus,i (male); amica,ae (female)
friendly	amicus,a,um
friendship	amicitia,ae
frighten	terrere (-eo,terrui,-itum)
frog	rana,ae
from	ab, a, ex, e, de (Ab);
from home	domo
from here	hinc
from then on	inde
from where	unde
full	plenus,a,um
furious, angry	iratus,a,um
fury, anger	ira,ae
future	futurus,a,um

G

garden	hortus,i
gate	porta,ae
general	imperator,toris
get, obtain	nancisci (nactus)
girl	puella,ae; virgo,virginis *f*
give	dare (do, dedi, datum),
give back	reddere (reddidi,redditum)

give as a present	donare	handle	tractare
gladiator	gladiator,gladiatoris *m*	hang	pendere (-eo,pependi)
gladly	libenter	happen	accidere (accidi); fieri;
glory	gloria,ae	it happens	accidit
go	ire (eo,ii,itum), se conferre	happy	beatus,a,um, felix (felicis),
	(contuli,collatum)		laetus,a,um
go back and forth	commeare	harbor	portus,us *m*
go across	transire (-eo,-ii,-itum)	hard	durus,a,um
go to(ward)	adire (-eo,-ii,-itum)	hardly, barely	vix (Adv) ; haud
go away	discedere (cessi,cessum);	harm	nocere (eo,ui), obesse(sum,fui)
	abire (-eo,-ii,-itum)		detrimentum,i , iniuria,ae,
go out	egredi (-ior,egressus);	hasten	contendere (-tendi,-tentum);
	excedere (-cessi,-cessum);		properare, festinare
	exire (-eo,-ii,-itum)	hasten to help	succurrere (succurri,cursum
go in	ingredi (ior,gressum); inire	hate	odium,i ; odisse
go back	redire (-eo,-ii,-itum)	have	habere, tenere (-eo,-ui)
go, yield	cedere (-cessi,-cessum)	have to	debere (-eo,ui,itum)
go, stride	vadere (vado)	have, own	esse + Dat.
god	deus,i ; *goddess* dea,ae	he,she,it; this	is, ea, id
gods below	inferi,orum Pl	head, main	caput,capitis *m*
gods in heaven	superi,orum Pl	healthy	sanus,a,um
gold	aurum,i	hear	audire (-ivi,-itum)
good	bonus,a,um (melior,optimus)	heart	cor,cordis *n*
Goods	bona *n* Pl, res *f* Pl	heaven, air	caelum,i ; heavenly caelestis,e
grain	frumentum,i	heavy	gravis,e
grandfather (grandmother)	avus,i (avia,ae)	height	altitudo,-tudinis *f*
grape	uva,ae	help	(ad)iuvare (-iuvi,-iutum),
grass	herba,ae		auxiliari; auxilium, subsidium
grateful	gratus,a,um	hen	gallina,ae
great	magnus,a,um, (maior, maximus);	herb	herba,ae
	ingens,ingentis,	here	hic; *be here* adesse (adsum,-fui)
so great	tantus,a,um;	hesitate	dubitare , morari
as great as	tantum..quantum	high, deep	altus,a,um
green	viridis,e	himself, herself etc	ipse (Gen ipsius)
greet	salutare	hinder	impedire (-io,-ivi,-itum), obesse
grey	canus,a,um	his, her, its, their	eius; suus,a,um (reflexive)
ground	solum,i	hit, beat	verberare
grow	crescere (crevi,cretum)	hold	tenere (teneo, tenui),
guard	(con)servare, custodire (io,ivi);		obtinere (obtineo,obtinui)
	custos,custodis *m/f* N	hold off	arcere (arceo,arcui)
guest	hospes,hospitis *m/f*	hold back	retinere (eo,ui,tentum)
guilt, fault	culpa,ae	holiday	festus (dies) *m*
		home	patria,ae; domus,us *f*, tectus,i
H		honey	mel,mellis *n*
		honor	honos (honor),honoris *m*
habit	consuetudo,dinis *f*	honorable	probus,a,um, honestus,a,um
hand	manus *f*		

hope	spes,spei *f* ; sperare
horn	cornu,us *n*
horror	horror,horroris *m*
horrible	horribilis,e
horse	equus,i
host	hospes, hospitis *m*
Hostage	obses,obsidis *m/f*
hot	calidus,a,um
hour	hora,ae
house	domus,us *f*, tectum,i; villa,ae
house, hut	casa,ae
household	familia,ae
how	quam; *how far* quam longe;
how long	quam diu
how many	quot
how often	quotiens
human, humane	humanus,a,um
hunger	fames,famis *f*
hurry	festinare, properare

I

I, me	ego
Ides of a month	Idus,uum Pl.
if	si ; *if not* nisi; *if only* utinam
ill	aeger,gra,grum, aegrotus,a,um
imitate	imitari
immortal	immortalis,e
implore	implorare
impose	imponere (posui,positum)
in front of	ante (A)
in vain	frustra (Adv.)
in, into, onto to, against	in (A)
in, on, at, during	in (Ab)
in order to	ut (Subj)
inactive	iners (inertis); *inactivity* inertia
increase	augere (-eo,auxi,auctum), crescere (crevi,cretum)
indeed	profecto (Adv.)
inflame	incendere (-cendi,-censum)
inform	certiorem facere (io,feci)
inhabit	incolere (incolui)
inhabitant	incola,ae *m* !
injure	violare
inner	interior,ius

innermost	intimus,a,um
intend to do	facere in animo habere; facturus esse
interrupt	intermittere
into, onto	in (A)
invite	invitare
iron	ferrum,i
Irritate	lacessere (lacessivi,lacessitum)
island	insula,ae
it happens	accidit (accidit)
it is known	constat
it is said	dicunt
it can happen	fieri potest
it comes about	fit
it pleases	libet (libuit), placet
it is permitted	licet (licuit)
it is necessary	necesse est, opus est, oportet (oportuit)
it follows	sequitur

J

join	iungere (iunxi,iunctum)
journey	iter,itineris *n*
joy	gaudium,i ; laetitia,ae
judge	iudex,iudicis *m* , iudicare
judgment	iudicium,i
jump	saltus,us *m*; salire (salui,saltum)
just	iustus,a,um
justice	iustitia,ae
keep	tenere (-eo,tenui)

K

kill	caedere (cecidi,caesum), interficere (io,feci,fectum), necare
killing	caedes,caedis *f*, nex,necis *f*
kind, type	modus,i , genus,generis *n*
king	rex,regis *m*
kitchen	culina,ae
know	scire (scivi, scitum), cognovisse, intellegere (-lego,-le<u>x</u>i,lectum);
not know	nescire (-io,-ivi); ignorare
known	notus,a,um
know	novisse (novi,notum)
knowledge	scientia,ae

L

labor	labor,oris *m*
lack	carere (-eo,carui); deesse
lamb, sheep	agnus,i
lament	miserari
land	terra,ae
language	lingua,ae
large	magnus,a,um (maior,maximus)
last	extremus,a,um, supremus,a,um/summus
late(r)	serus,a,um,
a little later	paulo post
late, too late	sero (Adv.)
laugh	ridere (-eo,risi,risum)
law	lex,legis *f*
lawsuit	causa,ae
lay waste to	vastare
lazy, slow	piger,pigra,pigrum
lead, pull	ducere (duxi,ductum)
lead to	adducere, perducere
lead war	bellum gerere
lead out	educere
lead across	traducere (duxi,ductum)
lead forward	producere
lead back	reducere (duxi,ductum)
leader	dux,ducis *m*, princeps,principis
learn	discere (disco,didici), cognoscere (cognovi)
learned	doctus,a,um; eruditus,a,um
leave	discedere (cessi,cessum)
leave behind	relinquere (reliqui,relictum), deserere (deserui,desertum)
left over	reliquus,a,um
left (not right)	sinister,sinistra,sinistrum
legion	legio,onis *f*
less/ least	minus/ minime (Adv)
lessen	minuere (minui,minutum)
let	permittere (misi,missum), sinere (sivi,situm)
letter (of the alphabet)	littera,ae
letter (epistle)	litterae,arum, epistula,ae
literature	litterae,arum Pl
liberty	libertas,tatis *f*
lie (down)	iacere (-eo,iacui)
lie hidden	latere (lateo,latui)
lie open	patere (pateo,patui)

life	vita,ae
lift up	erigere (erexi,erectum), tollere (sustuli,sublatum)
light	lux,lucis *f*, (not heavy) levis,e
lion	leo,leonis *m*
little, a l.	paulum, parum (Adv)
live	vivere (vixi,victum)
live, alive	vivus,a,um;
locate	locare
location	locus,i
long	longus,a,um
look at	spectare, conspicere (-spexi,-spectum)
look down on	despicere (-io,-spexi,-ctum)
look at	perspicere (-io,-spexi,-ctum)
look for	quaerere (-sivi,-situm)
look out	prospicere (-io,-spexi,-spectum)
lose	amittere (amisi, amissum), perdere (perdidi,perditum)
lose hope	animum demittere
lot, fate	sors,sortis *f*
love	amor,amoris *m*
love	diligere (dilexi,lectum)
love, like	amare

M

magistrate	magistratus,us *m*
maid	ancilla,ae
make	facere (facio,feci,factum),
be made	fieri (fio,factum esse)
make into	reddere (reddidi,redditum)
man (as a species)	homo,hominis *m*
man	vir,i,
young man	adulescens, adulescentis
manner	modus,i; ratio,-onis; consuetudo,-tudinis
many	multi,ae,a
march	proficisci (profectus)
market (place)	forum,i
mass, a lot	copia,ae, multitudo,dinis *f*
master, lord	dominus,i
meadow	pratum,i
meal, dinner	cena,ae
measure	metiri (mensus)
meeting	conventus,us *m* concursus,us; *m* contio,contionis *f*

memory	memoria,ae		new	novus,a,um
merchant	mercator,mercatoris *m*		next to	iuxta (A)
message,messenger	nuntius,i		next	proximus,a,um
method	modus,i		night	nox,noctis *f*
middle	medius,a,um		no one	nemo,neminis
might	potentia,ae		no, none	nullus,a,um
mighty	potens (potentis)		noble	patricius,a,um; nobilis,e
military	militaris,e		noise	clamor,oris *m*; strepitus,us
milk	lac,lactis *n*		not	non, haud; *or not* annon; *not at*
mind	mens,mentis *f*; ratio, onis *f*			*all* minime; *not...even* ne...quidem
mistress of the house	domina,ae		not only...but also...	non solum...sed etiam...
moderate	moderatus,a,um		not know	ignorare; nescire (-scio,-scivi)
money	pecunia,ae		not want	nolle (nolo,nolui)
month	mensis,is *m*		nothing	nihil (N)
moon	luna,ae		number	numerus,i
more	plus (pluris), plures,a Pl			
more/ most	magis/ maxime			
most of the time	plerumque (Adv)			
most (people, things) plurimi,ae,a Pl				

O

mother	mater,matris *f*		oak tree	quercus,us *f*
mountain	mons,montis *m* !		obey	parere (eo,parui); oboedire
mouse	mus,muris *m/f*			(oboedivi); obsequi (obsecutus)
mouth, face	os,oris *n*		observe	observare
move	movere (eo,movi,motum)		obtain	adipisci (adeptus sum);
movement	motus,us *m*			nancisci (nanctus); obtinere
much, many	multus,a,um (plus,plurimum)		occasion	occasio,onis *f*
must	debere (-eo,ui,itum)		occupy	occupare
my	meus,a,um		ocean	mare,is *n*
myself, yourself, him/herself etc. ipse,ipsa,ipsum			of the state	publicus,a,um
	(Gen. ipsius)		of what kind	qualis,e
			of such a kind	talis,e

N

			offend	offendere (fendi,fensum)
			offer	offerre (obtuli,oblatum)
name	nomen,nominis *n*		office	officium,i ; munus,muneris *n*
name	nominare		often	saepe; multum (Adv)
nation	natio,onis; gens,gentis *f* ;		old age	senectus,senectutis *f*
	patria,ae		old man	senex,senis *m*
nature	natura,ae		old, aged	vetus (veteris)
near	prope (A)		older	senior (senioris)
necessary	necessarius,a,um; to be ~		omen	omen,ominis *n*
	necesse est, opus est		on account of	ob, propter (A)
neighbour	vicinus,i		on behalf of	pro (Ab)
neighbouring	finitimus,a,um		only	solum (Adv), tantum (Adv)
neither (of two)	neuter, neutra, neutrum		only, alone	solus,a,um
neither...nor...	neque...neque...		open	aperire (-ui,ertum);
never	numquam			apertus,a,um
			opinion,	opinio,onis *f* ; sententia,ae

opportune	opportunus,a,um, commodus,a,um	play	ludere (lusi,lusum)
opportunity	facultas,tatis *f*	poet	poeta,ae *m* !
opposite	contrarius,a,um	poison	venenum,i
or	aut, vel	polite	comis,e (Adv: comiter)
oracle	oraculum,i	poor	pauper (pauperis)
order	iussus,us *m* ; imperare, iubere (iussi,iussum)	possession, take of	potiri (ior,potitus)
		possibility	potestas,tatis *f*
ought to	debere (-eo,ui,itum)	poverty	paupertas,paupertatis *f*
our	noster,nostra,nostrum	power	auctoritas,auctoritatis *f*
out of	ex (e) (Ab)	powerful	potens,potentis
outer	exterior,ius	powerless	impotens,impotentis
outermost	extremus,a,um	praise	benedicere, laudare; laus,laudis N
outside of	extra (A)	pray	precari, orare
owe	debere (-eo,ui,itum)	prefer	malle (malo,malui)
own	habere (-eo,ui,habitum) ; proprius,a,um	prepare	parare
		present, gift	donum,i
		pretend	simulare
		pretty	bellus,a,um

P

pain, sorrow	dolor,doloris	prevent	abstinere (eo,ui), prohibere (eo,ui,itum), impedire (io,ivi,itum), arcere (eo,ui)
palace	regia,ae		
parents	parentes,um *m* Pl		
part	pars,partis *f*	price	pretium,i
participating	particeps (participis)	priest (bridge maker)	pontifex,potificis *m*
pass by	praeterire; praetermittere (misi,missum)	priest(ess)	sacerdos,sacerdotis *m/f*
		prison	carcer,carceris *m*
pay	pendere (pependi,pensum)	prisoner	captivus,i
peace	pax,pacis *f*	proceed	procedere (cessi,cessum)
people	populus,i; natio,nationis *f*	produce	producere (duxi,ductum)
perceive	percipere (-io,cepi,ptum)	prohibit	prohibere (-eo,prohibui,-itum)
perform	efferre (extuli, elatum)	promise	polliceri,(-eor,itus), promittere (misi,missum)
perhaps	fortasse (Adv)		
perish	perire, interire (eo,ii,itum)	prove	demonstrare
permit	sinere (sivi,situm); pati (-ior,passus), permittere (permisi,permissum)	prove oneself	se praestare
		provide	providere (-eo,vidi,visum)
		province	provincia,ae
persuade	persuadere (-eo,suasi,suasum)	publish	edere (edidi,editum)
pertain	pertinere (pertenui,-tentum)	pull	trahere (traxi,tractum)
phoenix	phoenix,phoenicis *m*	punish	multare; punire (ivi,itum)
pick	carpere (carpsi,carptum)	punishment	poena,ae
picture	imago,imaginis *f*	pure, clean	purus,a,um
pity	misericordia,ae; N misereri (-eor,miseritus)	put, place	ponere (posui,positum)
		put together	componere (-posui,-positum)
place	locus,i	put in charge	praeficere (-io,-feci,-fectum)
plan	intendere (intendi,intentum)		
plan, advice	consilium,i		

Q

queen	regina,ae
question	quaestio,quaestionis *f*
quick	velox (velocis);
	fast celer,celeris,celere
quiet	tranquillus,a,um

R

race	cursus,us *m*
race-course	circus,i
raise, remove	tollere (sustuli,sublatum)
rank	ordo,dinis *m*
rank, place,	locus,i
raven	corvus,i
reach	nancisci (nactus/nanctus);
	pervenire (io,veni)
read	legere (legi,lectum)
realm	imperium,i
reason	causa,ae
receive	accipere
recent	recens,recentis
recognize	cognoscere (cognovi)
red	ruber, rubra, rubrum
region	loca,orum Pl; regio,regionis *f*
rejoice	gaudere (gavisus), laetari
relate	referre (rettuli,relatum),
	narrare, dicere (dixi,dictum)
religion,	religio,onis *f*
remain	manere (mansi,mansurus);
	superesse (superfui)
remember	meminisse, recordari
remove	removere (movi,motum)
report	(de)ferre (fero,tuli,latum),
	nuntiare; fama,ae; nuntius,i
reported, it is	fertur, feruntur
reproach	vituperare
reputation	fama,ae
resist	resistere (restiti)
rest	otium,i, quietus,us *m*;
	quiescere (quievi,quietum)
result,	eventus,us *m*
retreat	recedere (cessi,cessum),
	se recipere (cepi,ceptum)
return	redire (-eo,redii,itum), reverti
	(-or,reverti); reditus,us

revenge	ulcisci (ultus)
reward	praemium,i
rich	dives (divitis)
riches	opes,opum *f*, divitiae,arum Pl
right (left)	dexter,dextra,dextrum
right, law	ius,iuris *n*
rise	surgere (surrexi)
river	flumen,fluminis *n*, fluvius,i
river bank	ripa,ae
rob	diripere (io,ui,raptum)
robber	latro,latronis *m* !
robbery	furtum,i
Rome	urbs,urbis *f*; Roma
roof	tectum,i
rooster	gallus,i
route	iter,itineris *n*
rule	regnare; regnum,i
rumor	rumor,oris *m*
run	currere (cucurri,cursum)

S

sacred	sanctus,a,um,
	sacer,sacra,sacrum
sacrifice	immolare; sacrificium,i
sacrificial animal	victima,ae
sad	tristis,e
safe	integer,gra,grum; salvus,a,um,
	tutus,a,um
sail	solvere (solvi,solutum),
	navigare
sailor	nauta,ae *m*
salt	sal,salis
same, the	idem,eadem,idem
sand	arena,ae
sane	sanus,a,um
save	servare
say	dicere, loqui; aio, inquam
say that not	negare
he/she/it says, said	ait, inquit
saying	sententia,ae
scales	libra,ae
scatter	fundere (fudi,fusum)
school	ludus,i
science	scientia,ae
second	secundus,a,um

see	videre (-eo,vidi,visum), conspicere (-spexi,-spectum)	size	magnitudo,dinis *f*
seem	apparere (-ui,-itum), videri (-eor, visus sum)	slave, servant	servus,i; serva,ae
		sleep	somnus,i
			dormire (dormio,dormivi)
seldom	raro (Adv)	slow	lentus,a,um; piger,pigra,pigrum
select	deligere (delegi,delectum)	small	parvus,a,um,
sell	vendere (vendidi,venditum)		*little* exiguus,a,um
senate	senatus,us *m*	small camp	castellum,i
senator	senator,oris *m*	smaller	minor,us
send	mittere (misi,missum)	smallest	minimus,a,um
send back	remittere (misi,missum)	smile	ridere (-eo,risi,risum)
serious	gravis,e	snatch	eripere (-io,eripui,ereptum)
serve	servire (servivi,servitum)	snow	nix,nivis *f*
set forth	exponere (posui,positum)	snow-white	niveus,a,um
set out	proficisci (profectus)	so	ita (w/verbs or Adj./Adv.),
settler	colonus,i		sic (with verbs),
several	complures,a		tam (with Adj.and Adv.)
severe	severus,a,um	so much, so far	adeo (Adv)
shadow, shade	umbra,ae	so great	tantus,a,um
shame	ignominia,ae	so many	tot
share	pars,partis *f* ; communicare	so often	totiens
sharp	acer,acris,acre	society	societas,societatis *f*
sheep	pecus,pecudis *f* , ovis,is	soldier	miles,militis *m*
	'wool-bearer' laniger, *lamb* agnus	some	nonnulli,ae,a
shepherd	pastor,pastoris *m*	someone, anyone	aliquis,aliquid;
shield	scutum,i		qisquam,quicquam
ship	navis,is *f*	son	filius,i
short	brevis,breve	song, poem	carmen,carminis *n*
shout	clamare	soul	anima,ae
show	(de)monstrare, ostendere (tendi,tentum)	sound	sonare
		spare	parcere (peperci,parsum)
show (off)	ostentare	speak	loqui (locutus sum), orare
shut	claudere (clausi,clausum)	speaker	orator,oratoris *m*
sight, appearance	aspectus,us *m*	speech	oratio,onis *f*
sign	signum,i	speed	celeritas,celeritatis *f*
silence	silentium,i	spirit, mind	animus,i; mens,mentis *f*
silent	tacitus,a,um; to be ~ tacere (eo,ui)		spiritus,us *m*
silver, money	argentum,i	stable, barn	stabulum,i
similar	similis,e	stand	stare (steti,statum),
since	ab (a) (Ab), cum (Conj. + Subj), ex (e) (Ab)		*stop* consistere (constiti)
		star	stella,ae
sing	cantare; canere (cecini)	state	civitas,tatis *f* ; res publica *f*
single	singuli,ae,a	stay	remanere (mansi,mansum)
sister	soror,oris *f*	step	passus,us *m*
sit	sedere (-eo,sedi,sessum)	stick	haerere (haesi,haesum)
sit down	considere (eo,consedi)	stone	lapis,lapidis *m*
situation	res,rei *f*		

stop	desinere (desii,desitum), desistere (stiti,stitum)	task	munus,eris
store	taberna,ae	tax	stipendium,i
story	fabula,ae	teach	docere (-eo,ui,doctum)
strange	alienus,a,um	teacher	magister,tri
strength,	vis (vim, vi) *f*; robur,roboris *n*	teaching	disciplina,ae
strengthen	confirmare	tear (cry)	lacrima,ae
stretch	vergere (versi); tendere	tell	narrare
strive	contendere (-tendi,-tentum), niti (-or,nisus/nixus), petere (-tivi,-titum) (ab+Abl)	tell a lie	mentiri (mentitus)
		temple	templum,i
		terrible	terribilis,e
		terror	terror,oris *m*
strong	validus,a,um; fortis,e	test	probare
struggle	contendere (-tendi,-tentum)	than	quam (comparison)
student	discipulus,i	thankful	gratus,a,um
stupid	stupidus,a,um; stultus,a,um	thanks	gratia,ae
subject	subicere (subieci,subiectum), subigere (subegi,subactum)	that one there	iste,ista,istud
		that, this	ille,illa,illud
succeed	contingere (contigi)	that, so that	ut (+ Subj.)
sudden	subitus,a,um; subito (Adv)	the other (of two)	alter,a,um(Gen. alterius)
suffer, toil	laborare, sustinere, pati (patior,passus)	the rest	ceteri,ae,a (Pl)
		the same	idem,eadem,idem
suit, fit	convenire (-venio,-veni,-ventum)	the bottom of	infimus,a,um; imus,a,um
		the closest	proximus,a,um
suitable	aptus,a,um; idoneus,a,um	the first	primus,a,um
summer	aestas,tatis *f*	the last	postremus,a,um
sun	sol,solis *m*	the top of, the highest	summus,a,um
supply	copia,ae	the underworld	inferi,orum Pl
surely, truly	sane (Adv)	he foot of (at))	sub (Ab), (to) sub (A)
suspicion	suspicio,suspicionis *f*	theater	theatrum,i
swamp	palus,paludis *f*	their	eorum,earum; refl. suus,a,um
sweet, lovely	dulcis,e	there	ibi; *to there* eo
swim	natare	thief	fur,furis *m*
sword	gladius,i	thing	res,rei *f*
		think	arbitrari, putare, existimare, cogitare, censere (-eo,censui)

T

table	mensa,ae	thirst	sitis,is *f*
take	capere (-io,cepi,captum), captare, sumere (sumpsi,sumptum)	this	hic,haec,hoc
		this place, to	huc
		thought	mens,mentis *f*
take away	adimere (-emi,-emptum) demere (dempsi,demptum)	throw	iacere (io,ieci,iactum),iactare
		throw away	abicere (io,ieci,iectum)
take care	curare	time (interval)	spatium,i
take part	interesse (intersum,interfui)	time	tempus,oris *n*
take possession of	potiri (potitus) (+Ab)	timid	timidus,a,um
take trouble with s.th.	operam dare	tire	fatigare
talk	loqui, colloqui (locutus)	tired	fessus,a,um
talkative	loquax (loquacis)	to, towards	ad (A)

toga,	toga,ae
toga with a scarlet hem	toga praetexta
tolerate	tolerare; pati (-ior,passus)
tongue	lingua ,ae
too much, too	nimis (Adv)
too little	parum (Adv)
too late	serius (Adv.)
tool	instrumentum,i
tooth	dens,dentis *m*
torment,	vexare
torture	torquere (-eo,torsi,tortum)
touch	tangere (tetigi,tactum)
towards home	domum
tower	turris,turris *f*
town	oppidum,i; municipium,i
train (Verb)	exercere (-eo,exercui)
transport	transportare
treat	tractare
treaty	foedus,foederis *n*
tree	arbor,oris *f*
tribute, tax	tributum,i
triumph	triumphare; triumphus,i
troops	copiae,arum Pl
true	verus,a,um
trumpet,tuba	tuba,ae
trust	confidere (-fido,-fisus sum), credere (-didi,-ditum)
truth	veritas,veritatis *f*
try	conari (conatus), experiri (expertus)
turn	vertere, verti (verti,versum)
type	genus,eris *n*
tyrant	tyrannus,i

U

ugly	foedus,a,um; turpis,e
uncertain	incertus,a,um
unclear	obscurus,a,um
uncover	detegere (texi,tectum), patefacere (Pass: patefieri)
under	infra (A)
understand	intellegere (-le<u>x</u>i,-lectum)
undertake	suscipere (-io,-cepi,-ceptum), subire (subeo,-ii,-itum)
undone	infectus,a,um
unique	unicus,a,um

universal	universus,a,um
unjust	iniustus,a,um
unknowing	nescius,a,um
unknown	ignotus,a,um
until	ad (A)
unwilling	invitus,a,um
up to	usque ad (A)
upright	rectus,a,um
use	uti (usus)(+ Ab); usus,us *m* N
use up	consumere (-sumpsi,-sumptum)
useful	utilis,e
useless	inutilis,e

V

valid	validus,a,um
valley	vallis,is *f*
vase	vas,vasis
vast	vastus,a,um
vehement	vehemens,vehementis
venerate	colere (colui,cultum), venerari
veneration	cultus,us *m* ; cultura,ae
verse	versus,us *m*
very much	valde (Adv)
vice	vitium,i
victory	victoria,ae
village	vicus,i
violent	vehemens (entis)
visible	conspicuus,a,um
visit	visitare, convenire (-venio,-veni,-ventum)
voice, sound	vox,vocis *f*
voluntary	sua sponte, voluntarius,a,um
vow	vovere (vovi,votum)
vulture	vultur,vulturis *m*

W

wait for	exspectare
wake up	excitare e somno
walk	ambulare; ire
wall	murus,i
wall (of house)	paries,parietis *m*
wander	errare
want	velle (volo,volui); cupere (-io,-ivi,-itum)
war	bellum,i

warlike	bellicosus,a,um
warm	calidus,a,um
warn	admonere (-eo,-ui)
wash	lavare (lavi,lautum)
watch	vigilare; praesidium,i
water	aqua,ae
wave, water	unda,ae
way	iter,itineris *n*
way, road	via,ae
we	nos
weak	infirmus,a,um
wealth	divitiae,arum Pl
weight	pondus,ponderis *n*
well-known	nobilis,e
west	occidens,occidentis *m*
what	quid
when	cum (Ind.)
where, when(ever)	ubi
where; how	qua
whereto	quo
which (of two)	uter,utra,utrum
while	cum (Subj)
white	albus,a,um; candidus,a,um
who ?	quis ?
who, which, that	qui,quae,quod
whole	totus,a,um
wide	latus,a,um; amplus,a,um
width	latitudo,latitudinis *f* amplitudo,amplitudinis *f*
wife	coniunx,coniugis *f* ; uxor,oris *f* ; matrona,ae
wild	ferus,a,um; ferox (ferocis); saevus,a,um
will, wish	voluntas,tatis *f*
wind	ventus,i
window	fenestra,ae
wine	vinum,i
wisdom	sapientia,ae
wise	sapiens,(sapientis)
wish	optare; cupere (-io,-ivi,-itum); desiderare
wish that	utinam
with, together w.	cum, una cum (Ab)
within	intra (A)
without	sine (Ab)
wolf	lupus,i / lupa,ae
woman	femina,ae; mulier,mulieris *f*

wonder	mirari
wondrous	mirus,a,um
wood	lignum,i
word	verbum,i
work	opus,operis *n*, labor,laboris *m*
work, trouble	opera,ae
world	mundus,i
worse	peior,ius
worst	pessimus,a,um
worthy	dignus,a,um
wound	vulnerare
wound, injury	vulnus,vulneris *n*
write	scribere (scripsi,scriptum)

Y

year	annus,i
yellow	flavus,a,um
yield, give in	concedere (-cessi,-cessum)
yoke	iugum,i
you (Sg.)	tu; *you* (Pl.) vos
young man	adulescens,centis *m* , iuvenis,iuvenis *m*
young woman	virgo,virginis *f*
younger	iunior
your (Sg.)	tuus,a,um
your (Pl.)	vester,vestra,vestrum
youth	iuventus,iuventutis *f*
zeal	studium

ILLUSTRATION CREDITS

Cover Pages:
Ch 1: Threshold of Goethe's house in Weimar: Salve.
Ch 2: Pompeiian fresco (detail).
Ch 3: Copy of a sign in Pompeii: Beware of the dog!
Ch 4: Children's game board made of stone, from Augst Switzerland.
Ch 5: Model of Rome, aerial view. (Rome, civic museum, photograph: K. Bennert).
Ch 6: Fresco in a garden room (detail). (photograph: M. Fleisser).
Ch 7: Etruscan Warrior (photograph: G. Biaggi).
Ch 8: Inside the colosseum (after a drawing by A. C. Carpiecci).
Ch 9: Water jar from Pompeii (Photograph: K. Bennert).
Ch 10: Detail from Trajan's Column in Rome.
Ch 11: At the butcher's shop. From a sarcophagus.
Ch 12: Water pump with buckets. Drawing after Orbis Pictus.
Ch 13: Women performing a dance of mourning. Fresco, detail
    (Photograph K. Bennert).
Ch 14: Chair from Pompeii.
Ch 15: Men drinking at a banquet, drawing after a fresco (Drawing: G, Candioli).

Illustrations in the text:
P. Aultzky: 79, 330, 341; K. Bennert: 156; H. Fries: 206;
W. Heuschneider: 91, 350; J. Hoiß: 240; U. Zedow: 261.

All other, and non-attributed photographs and drawings, are by the author.

The objects can be found in the following locations:
Captoline Museum, Rome: 211, 371. Etruscan Museum Volterra: 156.
Glyptothek, Munich: 85, 256, 265, 326, 333.
J.P. Getty Villa, Malibu: 29, 44, 68, 171, 355. Metropolitan Museum, New York: 156.
Pergamonmuseum, Berlin: 279. Pompeiianum Aschaffenburg: 279, 330, 341.
Römermuseum Augsburg: 388. Rheinisches Landesmuseum Trier: 278, 354, 356.
Saalburg, Bad Homburg: 245, 351.

INDEX